The Passionate Intellect

Rutgers University Studies in Classical Humanities

Series Editor: William W. Fortenbaugh

Advisory Board: Dimitri Gutas
Pamula M. Huby
Eckart Schütrumpf
Robert W. Sharples

On Stoic and Peripatetic Ethics: The Work of Arius Didymus, volume I

Theophrastus of Eresus: On His Life and Work, volume II

Theophrastean Studies: On Natural Science, Physics and Metaphysics, Ethics, Religion and Rhetoric, volume III

Cicero's Knowledge of the Peripatos, volume IV

Theophrastus: His Psychological, Doxographical, and Scientific Writings, volume V

Peripatetic Rhetoric After Aristotle, volume VI

The Passionate Intellect: Essays on the Transformation of Classical Traditions presented to Professor I.G. Kidd, volume VII

Edited by Lewis Ayres

THE PASSIONATE INTELLECT

ESSAYS ON THE
TRANSFORMATION OF
CLASSICAL TRADITIONS

Presented to Professor I. G. Kidd

RUTGERS UNIVERSITY STUDIES IN CLASSICAL HUMANITIES
VOLUME VII

LONDON AND NEW YORK

First published 1995 by Transaction Publishers

Published 2019 by Routledge
2 Park Square, Milton Park, Abingdon, Oxon OX14 4RN
52 Vanderbilt Avenue, New York, NY 10017

Routledge is an imprint of the Taylor & Francis Group, an informa business

Copyright © 1995 Taylor & Francis

All rights reserved. No part of this book may be reprinted or reproduced or utilised in any form or by any electronic, mechanical, or other means, now known or hereafter invented, including photocopying and recording, or in any information storage or retrieval system, without permission in writing from the publishers.

Notice:
Product or corporate names may be trademarks or registered trademarks, and are used only for identification and explanation without intent to infringe.

Library of Congress Catalog Number: 95-9847

Library of Congress Cataloging-in Publication Data

The passionate intellect: essays on the transformation of classical traditions presented to professor I.G. Kidd / edited by Lewis Ayres
      p.   cm. — (Rutgers University studies in classical humanities ; v. 7)
   Includes bibliographical references and index.
   ISBN 1-56000-210-7
   1. Civilization, Classical. 2. Classical literature—History and criticism. I. Ayres, Lewis. II. Series.
DE59.P373   1995
938—dc20   95-9847
                                                                                     CIP

ISSN: 0732-9814
ISBN 13: 978-1-56000-210-9 (hbk)
ISBN 13: 978-1-138-51660-1 (pbk)

Contents

Introduction	vii
Abbreviations	ix
Bibliography of I.G. Kidd	xi
Contributors	xv
The Greeks and the Passionate Intellect *Ian Kidd*	1–10

I. Plato — 11

1. Poetic Rhythms in the Myth of the Soul — 13–22
   Kenneth J. Dover
2. Plato, Imagination and Romanticism — 23–37
   S. Halliwell
3. Tradition and Innovation in the Transformation of Socrates' Divine Sign — 39–56
   Mark Joyal
4. Κρόνος, Κρόνους and Κρουνός in Plato's *Cratylus* — 57–66
   David B. Robinson
5. Counting Plato's Principles — 67–82
   R.W. Sharples

II. History, Poetry, Drama — 83

6. Pindar and the Victory Ode — 85–103
   Chris Carey
7. Euripides: *Ion* and *Phoenissae* — 105–115
   Elizabeth M. Craik
8. The Roman Mind and the Power of Fiction — 117–130
   J.S. Richardson
9. Did Thucydides Write for Readers or Hearers? — 131–142
   Shigetake Yaginuma

III. Philosophy and Science from Plato to Seneca   143

10. Aenesidemus versus Pyrrho: Il fuoco scalda "per natura"
    (Sextus *M.* VIII 215 e XI 69)   145–159
    Fernanda Decleva Caizzi
11. Theophrastus, no. 84 FHS&G: There's Nothing New Here!   161–176
    William W. Fortenbaugh
12. Alexandria, Syene, Meroe: Symmetry in Eratosthenes'
    Measurement of the World   177–202
    A.S. Gratwick
13. Seneca's *Natural Questions* — Changing Readerships   203–211
    Harry M. Hine
14. Crates of Mallos, Dionysius Thrax and the Tradition of Stoic
    Grammatical Theory   213–233
    Richard Janko
15. Aenesidemus and the Academics   235–248
    Jaap Mansfeld
16. The Pathology of Ps.-Hippocrates, *On Ancient Medicine*   249–258
    Robin Waterfield

IV. The Classical and the Christian   259

17. The Discipline of Self-knowledge in Augustine's
    De trinitate Book X   261–296
    Lewis Ayres
18. Melanchthon's First Manual on Rhetorical Categories in
    Criticism of the Bible   297–322
    C.J. Classen
19. "A Kind of Warmth": Some Reflections on the Concept of
    "Grace" in the Neoplatonic Tradition   323–332
    John Dillon
20. Ausonius at Prayer   333–343
    R.P.H. Green
21. The Philosophy of the Codification of Law in Fifth Century
    Constantinople and Victorian Edinburgh   345–361
    Jill Harries

Index of Ancient, Medieval and Renaissance Sources   363

Introduction

Professor Ian G. Kidd of the University of St. Andrews has the highest of reputations for scholarship, for friendship, and for service to his institution. His reputation in these areas makes the necessity of a *Festschrift* obvious. However, as well as offering tribute to Ian this volume has also been designed as an important contribution to the wider world of Classical scholarship.

Following education at St. Andrews University and The Queen's College Oxford, and service during the Second World War with the Argyll and Sutherland Highlanders, Ian became Lecturer in Greek at St. Andrews in 1949. He was promoted first to Senior Lecturer in 1965, and then in 1973 to a personal chair in Ancient Philosophy. In 1976 he succeeded Kenneth Dover as Professor of Greek at St. Andrews — after a little delay delivering the inaugural lecture printed in this volume. He retired from the chair in 1987. We wish him a long, happy and productive retirement.

Outside St. Andrews Ian was Visiting Professor of Ancient Philosophy at the University of Texas at Austin during 1965-6, visiting Fellow of the Institute of Advanced Study at Princeton in 1971-2 and 1979-80, and since 1989 he has been an Honorary Fellow of the Institute of Classical Philosophy and Science at Princeton. Ian has served his local community in East Fife and Scotland with equal distinction. Since 1993 he has been a Fellow of the British Academy.

The bulk of the volume concentrates around the title of Ian's inaugural lecture "The Greeks and The Passionate Intellect," offering a series of papers which attempt to assess the contribution of various authors, texts and movements to the formation and transformation of various Classical traditions. A majority of the papers concern philosophical topics, covering the whole Classical period, from Plato to Augustine — with a key section of papers covering the Hellenistic period — and this reflects something of Ian's own interests. At the same time there are important papers offered in the areas of literature and history which contribute to the perspective presented by the volume. Overall the volume helps to indicate the need to look at particular situations and particular texts if any generalisations about the transformation of Classical traditions are to be offered.

References to secondary literature in the volume follow the style of previous RUSCH volumes. In some cases — notably that of incunabula and early printed books — it has not always been possible or appropriate to provide details of publishers. While clarity and consistency within articles has been enforced — or at least encouraged — the style of reference to primary sources has been left to individual authors.

A number of people have offered help and wise advice in the planning and production of this volume. Prof. Chris Carey and Dr. Adrian Gratwick both encouraged me to take on organising and editing the project, and offered advice along the way. Prof. Bill Fortenbaugh quickly became essential to the project, providing publisher, advice and help of many sorts. The volume was typeset by Diane Smith, and I would like to thank her for her prompt, accurate and scholarly work; an accolade which should also be accorded Transaction Press who have patiently tolerated my attempts to meet deadlines. Bill and Diane have proved a joy to work with. I would also like to thank Brenda, Philippa and Natasha of the Central Secretariat at Christ Church College for their help with various sections of the book, including the index. Tamsin Simmill provided essential multi-lingual help with the proofs.

The University of St. Andrews, initially in the person of its vice-chancellor Prof. Struther Arnott, made a significant contribution to the financing of the project, and numerous other individuals have followed suit.

Lewis Ayres

Abbreviations

Where possible abbreviations are those of *L'Année philologique*.

AJPh	American Journal of Philology
ANRW	Aufstieg und Niedergang der römischen Welt
ASNP	Annali della Scuola Normale Superiore di Pisa
BICS	Bulletin of the Institute of Classical Studies
CJ	Classical Journal
CM	Clio Medica: Acta Academiae internationalis historiae medicinae
CronErc	Cronache Ercolanesi
CPh	Classical Philology
CQ	Classical Quarterly
CR	Classical Review
FHS&G	W.W. Fortenbaugh, P. Huby, R. Sharles & D. Gutas (eds.), *Theophrastus of Eresus: Sources for his Life, Writings, Thought and Influence*, 2 vols. (Leiden: Brill 1993)
G&R	Greece and Rome
GRBS	Greek, Roman and Byzantine Studies
GCS	Die griechischen christlichen Schriftstellen
HSPh	Harvard Studies in Classical Philology
JHPh	Journal of the History of Philosophy
JThS	Journal of Theological Studies
JRS	Journal of Roman Studies
Maia	Maia. Rivista di letterature classiche, Bologna
RAAN	Rendiconti dell'Academia di Archaeologia
PCPhS	Proceedings of the Cambridge Philological Society
REG	Revue des Etudes Grecques
RPh	Revue de Philologie
SIFC	Studi italiani di filologia classica
SP	Studia Patristica
TAPA	Transactions of the American Philological Society
VC	Vigilae Christianae
ZKG	Zeitschrift für Kirchengeschichte
ZPE	Zeitschrift für Papyrologie und Epigraphik

Professor Ian G. Kidd

Bibliography of Ian G. Kidd

1995

"Posidonius," S. Hornblower and A. Spawforth (eds.), *Oxford Classical Dictionary* (Oxford: Oxford University Press 1995³).

"Poseidonios," F. Ricken (ed.), forthcoming, *Philosophen der Antike* (Stuttgart: Kolhammer 1995).

"Some Philosophical Demons," forthcoming, *BICS*.

1992

I. G. Kidd (ed. & intro) and R. Waterfield (tr.), *Plutarch: Essays*, Penguin Classics (London: Penguin, 1992).

"Socratic Questions," B.S. Gower and M.C. Stokes (eds.), *Socratic Questions* (London: Routledge 1992) 82–92.

"Theophrastus' *Meterology*, Aristotle and Posidonius," W.W. Fortenbaugh and D. Gutas (eds.), *Theophrastsus, His Psychological, Doxographical and Scientific Writings*, RUSCH V (New Brunswick NJ: Transaction 1992) 294–306.

1991

"Posidonius," H. Burkhardt and B. Smith (eds.), *Handbook of Metaphysics and Ontology* (Munich: Philosophia 1991).

1990

"The Case of Homicide in Plato's *Euthyphro*," E.M. Craik (ed.), *'Owls to Athens'. Essays on Classical Subjects Presented to Sir Kenneth Dover* (Oxford: Clarendon Press 1990) 213–21.

1989

Ed. with L. Edelstein, *Posidonius I: The Fragments* (Cambridge: Cambridge University Press, 1989²).

"*Orthos Logos* as a Criterion of Truth in the Stoa," P. Huby and N. Gordon (eds.), *The Criterion of Truth: Essays Written in Honour of George Kerferd* (Liverpool: Liverpool University Press 1989) 137–50.

"Posidonius as Philosopher-Historian," M. Griffin and J. Barnes (eds.), *Philosophia Togata* (Oxford: Clarendon Press 1989) 38–50.

1988

Posidonius II: I. Testimonia and Fragments 1–149 (Cambridge: Cambridge University Press 1988).

Posidonius II: II. Fragments 150–293 (Cambridge: Cambridge University Press 1988)

1986

"Poseidonian Methodology and the Self-Sufficiency of Virtue," H. Flascher and O. Gignon (eds.), *Aspects de la philosophie hellenistique*, Entr. Hardt 33 (Vandoeuvres & Genève: Fondation Hardt 1986) 1–28.

1983

"Euemptosia - Proneness to Disease," W.W. Fortenbaugh (ed.), *On Stoic and Peripatetic Ethics*, RUSCH I (New Brunswick NJ: Transaction 1983) 107–13 [with a response by P.H. DeLacy, 114–17].

1982

Review of K. Schmidt, *Kosmologische Aspekte im Geschichtswerk des Poseidonios*, Hypomnemata 63 (Göttingen: Vandenhock & Ruprecht 1980), *Gnomon* 54 (1982) 184–7.

1979

"Plutarch against the Stoics," review of M. Baldassari, *Plutarco, Gli opuscoli contro gli Stoici*, 2 vols. (Trent: Pubblicazioni di Verifiche 1976), *CR* n.s. 29 (1979) 254–5.

1978

"Moral Actions and Rules in Stoic Ethics," J. Rist (ed.), *The Stoics*, Major Thinkers Series I (Berkeley CA: University of California Press 1978) 247–58.

"Philosophy and Science in Posidonius," *Antike und Abendland* 24 (1978) 7–15.
"Posidonius and Logic," J. Brunschwig (ed.), *Les Stoiciens et leurs logique. Actes du Colloque de Chantilly 18-22 Sept. 1976* (Paris: Vrin, 1978) 273–83.

1976

Review of A.A. Long, *Hellenistic Philosophy* (London: Duckworth 1974), *Phil.Quart.* 26 (1976) 169–71.

1972

Ed. with L. Edlestein, *Posidonius I: The Fragments* (Cambridge: Cambridge University Press 1972).
"The Impact of Philosophy on Graeco-Roman Literature," D. Daiches and B. Smith (eds.), *Literature and Western Civilisation*, vol. 1 (London: Aldus Books, 1972) 397–415.

1971

"Posidonius on Emotions," A.A. Long (ed.), *Problems in Stoicism* (London: Athlone, 1971) 200–15.
"The relation of Stoic Intermediates to the summum bonum, with reference to change in the Stoa," A.A. Long (ed.), *Problems in Stoicism* (London: Athlone, 1971) 150–72. [reprint of 1951 *CQ* article]

1970

Review of R.S. Brumbaugh and R. Wells, *The Plato Manuscripts* (New Haven CT: Yale University Press 1968), *CR* n.s. 20 (1970) 158–9.
Review of C. Moreschini, *Platonis Parmenides, Phaedrus* (Rome: Edizioni dell'Ateneo 1966), *CR* n.s. 20 (1970), 312–3.

1967

The following contributions to P. Edwards (ed.), *The Encyclopedia of Philosophy* (New York & London: Macmillan 1967): Antisthenes; Aristippus of Cyrene; Cynics; Cyrenaics; Diogenes of Sinope; Greek Academy; Socrates.
Review of L. Edelstein, *The Meaning of Stoicism* (Cambridge MA: Harvard University Press 1966), *Philosophical Books* 8 (1967) 9–10.

Review of H.B. Gottschalk, *Strato of Lampsacus* (Leeds: Philosophic and Literary Society 1965), *CR* n.s. 17 (1967) 153–5.

1964

Review of M. van Straaten, *Panaetii Rhodii Fragmenta,* Philosophia antiqua 5 (Leiden: Brill 1962), *Gnomon* 36 (1964) 346–9.

1962

Review of P. Wheelwright, *Heraclitus* (Princeton NJ: Princeton University Press 1960), *Phil.Quart.* 12 (1962) 365–6.

1961

"On Plato's Gorgias," *Phil.Quart* 11 (1961) 79–86.
Review of S. Sambursky, *Physics of the Stoics* (London: Routledge 1959), *Phil.Quart.* 11 (1961) 374–5.

1960

The following contributions to J.O. Urmson (ed.), *The Concise Encyclopedia of Western Philosophy and Philosophers* (London: Hutchinson 1960): Antisthenes, Aristippus, Chrysippus, Cicero, Cynics, Cyrenaics, Diogenes, Epictetus, M. Aurelius, Sceptics, Seneca, Stoicism, Zeno of Citium.

1958

"*Choephori* 1–2," *CR* 8 (1958) 103–5.
Review of J. van Camp and P. Canart, *Le sens du mot* ΘΕΙΟΣ *chez Platon* (Louvain: Nauwelaerts 1956), *Phil.Quart.* 8 (1958) 377–8.

1955

"The relation of Stoic Intermediates to the summum bonum, with reference to change in the Stoa," *CQ* 49 (1955) 181–94.

Contributors

Dr. Lewis Ayres, Dept. of Hebrew, Biblical and Theological Studies, University of Dublin, Trinity College, Dublin 2, Eire.
Prof. C. Carey, Dept. of Classics, Royal Holloway, University of London, Egham, Surrey, TW20 0EX, UK.
Prof. Dr. C.J. Classen, Seminar für Klassiche Philologie der Georg-August-Universität, Humboltdtallee 19, Göttingen D-37073, Germany.
E. Craik, School of Greek, Latin and Ancient History, University of St. Andrews, St. Salvator's College, St. Andrews, Fife, KY16 9AL, UK.
Prof. Dr. F. Decleva Caizzi, Dip. di Filosofia, Universita degli Studi di Milano, Via Festa del Perodino 7, 20122 Milano, Italy.
Prof. J.M. Dillon, School of Classics, University of Dublin, Trinity College, Dublin 2, Eire.
Prof. Sir K. J. Dover, 49 Hepburn Gardens, St. Andrews, Fife, KY16 9LS, UK.
Prof. W.W. Fortenbaugh, Dept. of Classics, Rutgers: The State University of New York, P.O. Box 270, New Brunswick, New Jersey 08903-0270, USA.
Dr. A.S. Gratwick, School of Greek, Latin and Ancient History, University of St. Andrews, St. Salvator's College, St. Andrews, Fife, KY16 9AL, UK.
R.P.H. Green, School of Greek, Latin and Ancient History, University of St. Andrews, St. Salvator's College, St. Andrews, Fife, KY16 9AL, UK.
Prof. S. Halliwell, School of Greek, Latin and Ancient History, University of St. Andrews, St. Salvator's College, St. Andrews, Fife, KY16 9AL, UK.
Dr. J. Harries, School of Greek, Latin and Ancient History, University of St. Andrews, St. Salvator's College, St. Andrews, Fife, KY16 9AL, UK.
Prof. H.M. Hine, School of Greek, Latin and Ancient History, University of St. Andrews, St. Salvator's College, St. Andrews, Fife, KY16 9AL, UK.

Prof. R. Janko, Dept. of Greek and Latin, University College London, Gower Street, London, WC1E 6BT.
Prof. M. Joyal, Dept. of Classics, Memorial University of Newfoundland, St. John's, Newfoundland, Canada, A1C 5S7.
Prof. Dr. J. Mansfeld, Faculteit der Wijsbegeerte, Rijksuniversiteit te Utrecht, Heidelberglaan 2, 3508 TC Utrecht, The Netherlands.
Prof. J.S. Richardson, Dept. of Classics, University of Edinburgh, David Hume Tower, George Square, Edinburgh, EH8 9JX, UK.
Dr. D. Robinson, Dept. of Classics, University of Edinburgh, David Hume Tower, George Square, Edinburgh, EH8 9JX, UK.
Prof. R. Sharples, Dept. of Greek and Latin, University College London, Gower Street, London, WC1E 6BT.
R. Waterfield, 97 Victor Road, Teddington, Middlesex, TW11 8SS, UK.
Prof. S. Yaginuma (Otsuma Women's University), 2-15-1-307 Fujigaoka, Fujsawa-Shi, 251 Japan

The Greeks and the Passionate Intellect

An Inaugural Lecture for the Chair of Greek at St. Andrews University

Delivered on 10 May 1978

Ian Kidd

Principal, colleagues and friends (and I nervously hope that I may use that phrase as a hendiadys), ladies and gentlemen:

I find myself standing here with some astonishment, for two reasons. The first is technical. I had argued, and to my mind with some force, that it was quite unnecessary for me to deliver an Inaugural Lecture at all (hence the lateness), since I was already hardly unknown to my colleagues, and it seemed frivolous to inflict pain on friends who would rather be enjoying themselves elsewhere, probably at committee meetings. I received no counter arguments to this at all, but simply repeated demands. But on reflection perhaps after the legal ceremony there should follow consummation of the union. And it ill becomes a professor of Greek in Scotland to be speechless. If you look up the *Scottish National Dictionary* under Greek, you will find the phrase "to become short of the Greek," meaning "to fail for words, become silent"; so much more civilised than the English gibberish —"it's all Greek to me." My second reason is deeper and more serious. You see, for the greater part of my life I had regarded the Chair of Greek at St. Andrews as a Mecca of my subject, a pot of gold at the end of the rainbow. I had soon made up my mind that I wanted to live and work and teach here and nowhere else; but while rainbows are not unknown at St. Andrews, a pot of gold seemed inconceivable — and still does.

I had good reason of course to admire this Chair (in fact one of the few things that I can say on my own behalf, is that I have better reason than anyone else to do so) because I had the unparalleled fortune to know intimately and work closely with three of the previous occupants. I hope that you will allow me to pay my personal debts by saying briefly and simply that it was from them more than any that that I learned the tools and caught something of the inspiration of my trade. And of course, I had one tremendous stoke of luck: not only were Rose, Lorimer and Dover of the very highest quality in their subject, but it is difficult to think of three more different men, and not only as men but also as scholars; so that the advantage of my apprenticeship was cubed as it were. To oversimplify grossly: it was Rose, with his immense range of reading, fixed and reproduced at call by his *almost* infallible and certainly phenomenal memory, who first opened my eyes and fostered, with ever to be remembered kindness, my interest in the enormous range and influence of Greek studies, far beyond the canonised authors of conventional courses. On the other hand Lorimer, from whom I learned much including irony, Lorimer who once lectured exhaustively and indefatigably for a whole year on a single play, leaving no particle unturned in the process, pointing out and substantiating that the most difficult words in the language are "the" "and" and "is", it was Lorimer who showed me the importance of the meticulous scholarship of detail in the synthesis of the whole. And from Dover what shall I pick out from what you all know? After all, Sir Kenneth is the complete Grecian of his generation. I think perhaps in scholarship that painfully ruthless and completely irreverent discipline of self-criticism. It is true that I had met this in someone I admire even more than Sir Kenneth; but he died in Athens in 399 B.C., and I had Dover at my elbow.

But there is one other St. Andrews Greek professor whom I can't leave out in a personal account, because he influenced me quite as much as these three, although at one step removed, and that is John Burnet. You see, in that famous radio programme (Desert Island Discs) that won't lie down, which seems to be infested by sea-birds I associate more with the Isle of May than with the south sea island of our imaginings, I admit that I have spent agonising nights trying to reduce my record collection to eight pieces of music and never succeeded; but I have never had any doubts over an answer to the inevitable ultimate question. If I had to take one book with the curious collection that is always on offer, I wouldn't hesitate. I would take Plato. And I first came to and remained with Plato through the works of Burnet. It is perhaps an odd thing to say, and I hope not presumptuous, but I have a very real personal sense of involvement, however humble, in the continuity of the Chair of Greek in this University for over a hundred years. Curiously this doesn't make me feel any older, but I suppose it must have some bearing on my passionate attachment to Greek in the context of this place, where Greek studies have been, and I hope will remain endemic.

But to my subject, Greek. Each new incumbent faces different problems, and one of the most pressing which did not tax my predecessors arises form the now rather precarious existence of Greek in the schools in our so-called restructured educational system. On this I would say no more today than to emphasise that in addition to helping schools by example and encouragement in any way we can, for I believe that there can be and will be a revival, I consider it of prime importance that we at University should teach beginners and persuade students that they will lose little and gain much by starting Greek studies at University; and I mean Greek studies in the widest sense.

But also each new generation reacts to the Classics after its own fashion. I don't mean simply that there is thus continual reinterpretation of the great writers and masterpieces; that after all is characteristic of all great works of art, whether we are talking of Shakespeare, Velasquez, Mozart, Homer or Plato. I mean that the whole sphere of Greek studies can be seen with fresh and contemporary eyes. There was a time, not so long ago, when the study of Greek in this country emphasised almost exclusively, and in rather a confined manner, language and literature, and that too in rather a restricted period (5/4th c. B.C.). Now of course, the last thing I want to do is to belittle that, with its concentration on the subtleties of language and translation. This very morning I had a PC from a German friend, who edits a learned journal and was trying to extract an article from me. His understanding of English is excellent, but he begins: "Dear Professor Kidd, please don't think that I am going to molest you ..." Such work is a continued and necessary base; but there was undeniable restriction and distortion. Of course the excesses of this, the days when a great play like "King Oedipus" could be regarded as a mine for the Greek subjunctive, or a much loved Professor of Greek at Oxford was described as a capacious memory for the textual misdeeds of his lesser colleagues, these days are long over (perhaps), but they have been a long time in passing. And I have sometimes wondered whether they were partly shaped by the dominance of Classics in the schools, where the traditional exhaustive linguistic commentary on a Greek text was of course a necessary interpretation, but at the ultimate and important level an insufficient one. The picture has been changing very much, I think, today; Athena has become (always was, really) a liberated woman. Greek scholars are bursting out in a most vivacious way in all directions; not only are they emerging boldly from their erstwhile rather inward-looking tight little empire, and so rightly taking advantage at last of comparative studies and disciplines, where light can come from unexpected directions. Parry found Homeric illumination from the Yugoslav guslars, and Kirk from Levi-Strauss; although for myself, I found still more last summer from rereading James Thurber; but in their own Classical field the horizon widens with much more emphasis on investigations into society, history, philosophy, religion, archaeology, the sciences, the visual arts — the whole spectrum of intellectual and aesthetic activity which was the Greeks. I welcome this development (in which under Sir Kenneth this Department took a positive role, and of which Dover himself is a prime example); but I welcome it not because the emphasis is new, which is insufficient grounds of virtue, nor because the Greeks engaged at a high level in all these activities, which they did, but because I believe that the close interrelation and interaction between them all is a peculiar and rewarding feature of the Greek intellectual world; in other words that there is a synoptic characteristic in Greek studies.

I should like to illustrate and argue this a little from work on which I have been, and am engaged. Not, I hasten to add, to speak of myself, but of my subject. A Chair in this University is not for the sake or benefit of the incumbent, but the holder is the servant of his subject for the University. I had been much interested in the philosophy of Stoicism, which had emerged quite recently from comparative obscurity, neglect and ignorance from under the giant shadows of Plato and Aristotle, to be revealed as a major intellectual and spiritual influence over some nine centuries in the Graeco-Roman world, and indeed in the history of ideas in general; something very different indeed from its trivial entry in the English language. Now in the middle of the history of Stoicism, there looms a gigantic but enigmatic figure, who, it was clear, had to be investigated *ab initio* because, if I may be paradoxical, too much seemed to be known of him.

Let me give you a sketched framework. Somewhere about 135 B.C. (and this, I may say, is a most unfashionable date in Greek studies), in the equally unfashionable place of Apameia on the Orontes in Syria, a boy with the good Greek name of Posidonius was born. He was bright and ambitious, went to Athens as a centre of advanced studies, was fired, no, that is ambiguous, inspired by the leading Stoic Panaetius, migrated to Rhodes, one of the chief scientific centres of the time, and proceeded to dominate from there the whole Mediterranean intellectual world of the 1st c. B.C. One of the most extraordinary things about him was his range of interests, which seemed all-embracing. Not only did he write on all categories of philosophy (which included theology and language), but on pure mathematics, astronomy, geography, tides and hydrology, seismology, mineralogy, botanical and zoological detail, a large authoritative history, and goodness knows what else. But he was no armchair theorist, he undertook long voyages of exploration over the whole Mediterranean area, along the north African coast to Cadiz, observing an ape here or a tide there, and then up to Gaul where the manners and customs were more spectacular (what would have happened if he had reached Scotland, I hesitate to think) and then back through Italy, the north east, and home; grand tours to observe phenomena and test theories. He did not evade public life, for Rhodes appointed him as an ambassador to Rome. His reputation and influence were very high; not only philosophers, scientists and writers, but the big bully boys of the political world called to see him at Rhodes. And my goodness, he could write. Cicero, who had claims to possessing one of the most powerful egos of the age yet did not allow it cloud his literary judgement, tried to persuade Posidonius to writ a monograph on his treasured political triumphs, and was politely refused. What a savant! What a Gelehrter!

But — and here's the rub — although there is much quotation and reporting of Posidonius for centuries later, by a cruel quirk of careless fortune, still later generations foolishly mislaid his works, and no complete book of Posidonius survives. And so, while the great shadow continued to fascinate scholars, the quicksands of the evidence overexcited the more susceptible of academic imaginations to the point of seeing Posidonius everywhere, a fictional Panposidonius I call him, of whom

Housman growled with dry irony and witty Latin, that it was now agreed that the Romans read nothing but Posidonius. There was nothing for it but to put the evidence on a more exact and scientific footing and collect and edit the attested fragments. Now I only mention this because I may have given the mistaken impression that in Greek studies I have been moving away from all the traditional techniques and skills involved in textual editing. Nothing is further from the truth. I have faced no more exacting, exciting or completely absorbing task of academic detection than the whole subsequent normal process from the initial inspection of manuscripts of the more obscure authors to the final gauging in detail of the more than sixty wildly different authors and reporters involved. This was absolutely necessary to establish the evidence, but of course it is only a preliminary. The real task is to assess it, and this is the problem of synthesis.

Now at first it is only too easy to be distracted by the fascinating details of the astonishing range of Posidonius' investigations, or rather indeed by the diversity of them. For example, and I am picking almost at random, there is a complete lunar theory of the periodicity of tides, which rightly held sway until Newton; where he verified by inspection at Cadiz the diurnal cycle, and there also completed the monthly, and from reported evidence inferred the annual cycle. And in all this he sharply distinguished autopsy and inference and secondary evidence, so that we can even now see the source of his one mistake in the annual cycle, for it derives from reported evidence of tidal action in the Red Sea.

Or again, quite different, we find an intriguing psychiatric theory of practical ethics, related to a concept of the human psyche as a kind of single personality with polar aspects of emotion and rationality. This is an original twist of a very Greek phenomenon, their fascination with and recognition in themselves of the two major pulls of passion and reason, which in turn dominated Greek moral thinking, and to which I shall return.

What again about the beautiful formal elegance of Posidonius' mathematical theory and construction of how to measure the circumference of the earth, which yet resulted in an eminently practical method of establishing geographical bands of latitudes; on which incidentally I have been engaged in quite heated controversy with a formidable lady from the Government Defence Mapping Agency in Washington, who worries me by sending me inflammatory arguments in envelopes marked Official Business, Penalty for Private Use, $300? Or, on a quite different tack, there emerges clear traces of an original logical analysis of the relational syllogism; and as far as I can find out, Posidonius was the first in the history of logic to examine its structure and the assumptions that lie behind it. Or, once more, in the quite distinct field of the philosophy of mathematics, we find a passionate defence of Euclidean axiomatic methodology on logical grounds, including puzzles which remind one of Lewis Carroll, against the claims of an empirical mathematics, an account which is of considerable interest in itself. Or, to move once more, there is a theory with illustrations of the influence of environment on human physiology and behaviour and personality. Or again, there is the biting pugnacity and caustic wit of even the little that remains of his historical prose style. I could go on even in the tantalising fragmentary evidence, but enough has been said to show how in one Greek thinker and writer there is a fantastic diversity of intellectual activity. If this were all, it would be remarkable (although hard it is true on his rueful editor and commentator), but one could simply nod respectfully in his direction as a remarkable polymath. But it is not all, and here lies my point. When we look closer, we see something else, and explicitly stated. We see, for example, that Posidonius was not interested in logic merely for its own sake, even less for the relational syllogism, fascinating intellectual tool and game though it be. No; he characterises logic, in a very carefully worded analogy, as the bones and sinews of philosophy, an organic aspect of philosophy's structure and movement. Or, consider ethics; ethics for him is a form of psychology, but in turn for him psychology is incomprehensible apart from his philosophy of nature. The sciences he regarded not merely to draw latitudes or predict tides or the like, but as a necessary tool to assist philosophical explanation, although he seems to have restricted their function to descriptive analysis. They help to map the cosmic canvas on which the rational organisation of phenomena may be traced. In similar fashion, history is not a separate study, but the display of human behaviour in its environment, which is the descriptive science complementary to ethics. It is not in fact the diversity of investigation that is the point; the diversity is not in any way episodic, it is a necessary feature of the synoptic mind, "seeing together" the whole in the relations of its diverse parts. What is at stake is an audacious aetiological attempt to survey and explain the whole field of the human intellect and the universe in which it finds itself. Questions such as: "Was Posidonius a scientist, or was he a philosopher, or was he a historian?" are probably the wrong questions to ask. And it is no answer either to say that he was all of them. The point is that he thought that they were all in some way related, that they were all organic aspects of human intellectual aspirations and operations. Knowledge is ultimately, not in its subdivisions, but ultimately, indivisible. Not of course, that everyone should embark on all disciplines, but that fundamentally it could be dangerous to consider any one purely in isolation on its own.

Now I want to suggest that this synoptic tendency, although displayed in extreme form in Posidonius, was characteristic of the Greeks. Not, naturally, that there were not pure mathematicians, or pure lyric poets; but not either that the phenomenon was confined to intellectuals in a restricted sense, although it is obvious in them. And I am not by any means suggesting either that it was a wholly beneficial characteristic; it brought danger as well as its rewards. The intertwined and inextricable histories of Greek philosophy and medicine, for example, created confusion as well as illumination. But the whole of Greek literature and thought seems to me to be permeated with a *blended* awareness and expression of the multiple facets of human curiosity and wonder, combining the feel, shape, structure and power of words, philosophy, theology, the sciences, society and law, historiography and the visual arts, in a blend which surprises the modern mind.

One result is that in Greek studies, demarcations to which we have become accustomed, are not only blurred, but would distort our understanding not only of the diverse unity of the sweep of Greek literature and thought, but also of certain characteristics of the Greek mind. This can be seen at a number of different levels. The great Athenian plays of the 5th c. B.C. were not merely dramatic masterpieces of theatre for the cognoscenti, they formed part of annual religious festivals in which a whole community, cheek by jowl, participated. They cannot be easily or entirely understood apart from their effect within such an occasion which in turn affected their form and contents, the myth-structure which has been called the inherited conglomerate of that whole society. The theatre itself is tied to the visual arts, and in turn they — architecture, vase-painting and sculpture, although clearly they must be studied through proper aesthetic criteria, are not expressions of pure form but instruments in function and content of the *literature,* religion and society of their time. The Greeks, I believe, did not tend to hide things away separately in art galleries; they used their beautiful things, or everyone walked amongst them, and everyone was exposed to them; they were one facet of a society's expression. Such things are also evidence for the historian, but Greek historiography, as the very name *historia* reveals, is only one common part of a whole group of *historiae* or enquiries which progressed uniformly and intertwined from the 6th c. B.C. on. Not only the *content* of History overlapped with, and was often hard to distinguish from that of other *historiae* like geography, but the very *form* of historiography is inextricably bound up with the development of Greek prose literature, to the extent that Greek historians are quite properly studied nowadays both by Departments of Ancient History and Greek, but neither can really do without the other, and I suspect that a Greek would have been surprised by the disjunction. And indeed I have heard modern ancient historians refer to Herodotus and Thucydides as the Mozart and Beethoven of the ancient world, which is itself indicative of my meaning.

Of the other *historiae*, I have already indicated how philosophy and science, although of course distinguished, were viewed together as complementary, so that Galen, the great doctor of the Ancient World, could declare himself a philosopher. One must remember too that philosophy, besides embracing the specialised activities of the modern philosopher, claimed, certainly after Socrates, and again driven by this synoptic tendency, to be the whole art of living and education; and as such naturally it reached out into art and literature. And this raised one of the seeming antinomies of the Greek spirit. Because the Greeks were also entranced by, captivated, sensitive in the extreme to language and the emotive power of words, and despised glib and slipshod expression as much as they despised slipshod thinking. So that the study of language and literature as such, which they called rhetoric, was also raised to a supreme educative art, to claim precisely the same comprehensive sphere that philosophy did. Both claims on their own, were wrong of course. But the seeming clash of synoptic claims reflects rather the fused poles of the Greek mind, the rational, and the imaginative and emotional. Hercaclitus of Ephesus, prince of paradox, once wrote: diversity is agreement, things at variance are in tune. So the demarcations between literature and philosophy will not hold either. Indeed they have *common* words in Greek for saying and thinking. In fact, Greek literature, like no other literature I know, is inbued with philosophy. The interpretation is Greek philosophy, like no other philosophy I know, is precarious without an ear tuned to its verbal and literary form and traditions. Plato is the proof of this to the highest degree, and makes him to me the most precious and perfect writer of all the Greeks. I don't simply mean the miraculous harmony of thought and expression that one finds in Plato, but the imaginative rationality, the philosophic insight of imagination into the university of the human search; again the blend of the rational and the imaginative, where the purely rational in Plato had its own inbuilt drive of passion. If I had to sum up the Greek genius in a single phrase (which of course is impossible), I think it would be: the passionate intellect. Plato with explosive economy transposed it into one single pregnant word, often so sadly and vulgarly aborted as Platonic love, *eros*; and typically embodied it in one human mind and form, Socrates.

The Greeks it is true, had a natural capacity which is well known and always rightly stressed, not least by me, certainly, for analysis and classification. But the background I have been sketching, shows something perhaps as valuable: a final hostility to confined, isolated, narrow departmentalisation, compartmentalisation as an end in itself, but rather the determination to see things as part of wholes, where the perfection (*telos*) of the whole gives meaning to the parts, unity to plurality. This is dangerous doctrine indeed, but a precious and imaginative one, and as the details of knowledge silt up, it should not be forgotten. Certainly Greek scholars can not forget it.

One view which I *will* counter with all the energy and resources that I possess, is that Greek studies are a kind of museum piece, that one occasionally takes out of the cabinet, dusts off respectfully, only to replace them once more in their case. It is a sorry mistake to see Greece as a far-off initial impulse to western civilisation. The Greeks were a people of quite extraordinary intellectual and aesthetic vitality; to study them now is to study the whole of our own human potentiality. Fortunate the man who is granted an opportunity to research more deeply into this hellenic cosmos; happiest of all he who can do so from the Chair of Greek in this University.

I. Plato

1

Poetic Rhythms in the Myth of the Soul

Kenneth J. Dover

In *Phaedrus* 257A, on concluding the great Myth of the Soul, Socrates describes the vocabulary in which he has expressed it as "somewhat poetic:" τοῖς ὀνόμασιν ... ποιητικοῖς τισιν ... εἰρῆσθαι. We are in a strong position to decide how much is covered by that τισιν, because from about 430 BC we can observe—for the first time—the lexical differences between prose and poetry composed in the same region during the same period; and we have enough citations from fourth-century Attic tragedy to assure us that the linguistic relation between Attic prose and Attic poetry at the time of *Phaedrus* was much the same as it had been two generations earlier.

What that relation is, ἐγὼ ἐν ἄλλῳ λόγῳ δηλώσω; my present concern is with rhythms, not words. Where the language is touched with poetry, we may reasonably expect Plato to have imparted a murmur of poetry to the rhythm also. He does just that in a famous passage of *Symposium*, the peroration of Agathon's speech in praise of Eros. After extemporizing a couple of hexameters (193C3–6), Agathon then (D1) embarks on a series of laudatory phrases which lasts until E5. These phrases largely present themselves to our ears as poetic cola, sometimes of familiar type, e.g.,

14 The Passionate Intellect

197D1	ἀλλοτριότητος μὲν κενοῖ,	–⏑⏑– ––⏑–	(iambic dimeter)
	οἰκειότητος δὲ πληροῖ	––⏑– –⏑––	(iambic, trochaic),[1]
D4	πρᾳότητα μὲν πορίζων,	–⏑–⏑ –⏑––	(trochaic dimeter)
	ἀγριότητα δ' ἐξορίζων	⏑⏑⏑–⏑ –⏑––	(trochaic dimeter),
D5	θεατὸς σοφοῖς,	⏑––⏑–	(dochmiac)
	ἀγαστὸς θεοῖς	⏑––⏑–	(dochmiac),

sometimes less familiar but invested with poetic character by repetition, e.g.,

E1	παραστάτης τε καὶ σωτὴρ ἄριστος	⏑–⏑–⏑–– –⏑––
E4	πάντων θεῶν τε κἀνθρώπων[2] νόημα	––⏑–⏑–– –⏑–⏑

In 198C1–5 Socrates' words make it plain that Agathon's speech is a parody of Gorgias, and we could have drawn that inference for ourselves from Agathon's obtrusive references in 194E4, 195A1–3, 196B4, D4 to the organisation of his own speech (cf. Gorgias B11.2, 6, 15, 21). The peroration may remind us of the long chain of phrases in Gorgias B6, but its incidence of hiatus is far lower and its recurrent lyric rhythms more conspicuous. Since Agathon was a tragic poet, it is appropriate that his peroration should be charged with poetic language and rhythm, and it is not necessary to invoke the influence of Gorgias in explanation of that phenomenon.

The Myth of the Soul in *Phaedrus* has more in common with the evangelical fervour of Diotima's peroration in *Smp.* 210E–212A than with Agathon's effusion, but once we have entertained the expectation of catching poetic rhythms in it examples leap to the ear, whether in the iambic trimeters of dramatic dialogue, e.g.,

255D3 οὔθ' ὅτι πέπονθεν οἶδεν οὐδ' ἔχει φράσαι
or 253C7f. καθάπερ ἐν ἀρχῇ τοῦδε τοῦ μύθου τριχῇ
διείλομεν ψυχὴν ἑκάστην, ἱππομορ(-φω κτλ.)

or in sequences which seem compellingly to dispose themselves in lyric cola, e.g.,

---

[1] On this rhythm see M.L. West, *Greek Metre* (Oxford: Clarendon Press 1982) 68, 103.

[2] καὶ ἀν- in the transmitted text.

248C6f.	καί τινι συντυχίᾳ χρησαμένη	–∪–∪∪– –∪∪–
	λήθης τε καὶ κακίας	––∪ –∪∪–³
	πλησθεῖσα βαρυνθῇ	––∪∪––
or 254A3f.	οὔτε μάστιγος ἔτ(ι) ἐντρέπεται,	–∪– –∪∪–∪∪–
	σκιρτῶν δὲ βίᾳ φέρεται	––∪∪–∪–

But may not this be accidental? Notoriously, in Attic oratory verses appear in circumstances in which we cannot conceive any reason for versification, e.g. *Dem.* xviii.71 καὶ καθιστὰς κτλ. (trochaic tetrameter acatalectic). This is not surprising. A succession of eight Greek syllables may constitute any one of 256 patterns of long and short, of which 34 are familiar in poetry, i.e. more than one in eight. Add the sequences of six, seven, nine or ten syllables which are equally familiar, and it becomes obvious that it cannot be easy to write Greek prose from which all poetic associations are excluded.

When we find what we expect to find in a given text, we are apt to conclude that it is characteristic of that text, even though we have not looked for it in comparable texts and do not know what we would find if we did. In all matters of form and style comparison is crucial to the quantification of such imprecise statistical terms as 'characteristic', 'distinctive', and the like. We therefore need some way of assessing how far any given rhythmical sequences in the *Phaedrus* myth occur in proportions differing from what could be expected as the product of chance.

In a volume designed to honour a scholar whose philological exactitude in the study of a text is only the starting-point for interpretation of its content, a mere compilation of data on patterns of long and short may seem almost insulting. But Socrates in claiming the authority not of an austere schoolmaster expounding the basics of psychology or theology (like Diogenes of Apollonia on the vascular system), but of an inspired poet, as his colourful and elaborate prooemium (243E–245C) makes plain, and consideration of the way in which he imparts the poetic charge is of some importance to our understanding of Plato's technique of persuasion. We might

---

[3] On this and other kinds of "choriambic heptasyllable" see A.M. Dale, *The Lyric Metres of Greek Drama* (Cambridge: Cambridge University Press 1968²) 138f. and K. Itsumi, "The 'Choriambic Dimeter' of Euripides," *CQ* N.S. 22 (1982) 62f., 73.

compare the Myth with Platonic texts of comparable scale in which we cannot imagine that he would have had any reason to compose poetically. However, the accessibility of Plato's motives to modern interpretation has its limits, and a better approach is offered by an experiment which may be performed on any Greek text of any author. Suppose we transpose the first two mobile tokens[4] of each clause, and the last two, scan the result, and compare that with the scansion of the original text—comparing, e.g.,

Phdr. 245C5–7 ψυχὴ πᾶσα ἀθάνατος. τὸ γὰρ ἀεικίνητον ἀθάνατον· τὸ δ' ἄλλο κινοῦν καὶ ὑπ' ἄλλου κινούμενον, παῦλαν ἔχον κινήσεως, παῦλαν ἔχει ζωῆς

with   *ἀθάνατος πᾶσα ψυχή. ἀθάνατον γὰρ τὸ ἀεικίνητον· τὸ δὲ κινοῦν ἄλλο καὶ κινούμενον ὑπ' ἄλλου, κινήσεως ἔχων παῦλαν, ζωῆς ἔχει παῦλαν.

Whatever poetic rhythmical sequences occur in the manipulated text are demonstrably the product of chance, *not* intended by the author, and the relative frequency of a given set of sequences in the original and in the transposition will give us an idea of how far those sequences were sought in the original.

In quoting 245C5–7 above I have reproduced Burnet's punctuation, hiatus (πᾶσα ἀ- , καὶ ὑπ') and elision (τὸ δ', ὑπ' ἄλλου). The transposition follows the same punctuation—it is quite important, in this experiment, that the punctuation should have been done by someone other that the experimenter—retains one elision (ὑπ'), and introduces new hiatus (τὸ ἀει-) while eliminating two (πᾶσα ἀ-, καὶ ὑπ-). Where a whole clause totals fewer than six syllables, I ignore it. Where the first two or last two mobile tokens of a clause are fewer, I bring in a third; and if that takes us to the end of a clause I perform a double transposition, as in *ἀθάνατος πᾶσα ψυχή and *κινήσεως κτλ. above.

---

[4] "Word" being ambiguous, it is customary to use "type" in the sense "lexeme," and "token" to mean "instance of a lexeme"; thus the Shakespearean line "Never never never never never" contains five tokens but only one type. By "mobile" I mean a Greek lexeme which may occur both immediately after and immediately before pause. What is not mobile is "appositive."

It is (to me, anyway) unthinkable that any transmitted text of Plato should be trusted as a guide to his own realisation of potential hiatus, elision, correption and synecphonesis; nor do I consider that I know how he spoke prosodically ambiguous syllables (e.g. ποιεῖν, τοιοῦτος) or what use he made of ephelcystic nu. Such uncertainties may be thought likely to frustrate our enterprise from the start, but escape is simple: in the first instance, isolate all sequences, in original and transposition alike, which allow any room for doubt. Thus in the original text of *Phdr.* 245C5–7 I disregard ψυχὴ πᾶσα ἀθάνατος and τὸ δ' ἄλλο ... κινούμενον, while in the transposition I disregard τὸ ἀεικίνητον ... κινοῦν.

Nevertheless, there is a reasonable probability that in speaking the text Plato adopted, all or most of the time, all or most of the elisions and synecphoneses which are the norm in dramatic dialogue. In the following table, therefore, I have divided the data into four categories:

(A) Sequences in the original which contain no prosodic ambiguity.
(B) Sequences in the original in which such ambiguities can be resolved in the manner of dramatic dialogue.
(C) Transpositions, excluding ambiguities as rigorously as in (A).
(D Transpositions in which the ambiguities are resolved as in (B).

The sign "|" indicates punctuation in Burnet's edition, the sign ":" "word-end," i.e. the boundary between mobile tokens, each with its appositives. In scanning, the last syllable before pause is treated as long; the last syllable at word-end, only if it would be so treated in verse. The last syllable of a rhythmical sequence is treated as anceps if it is preceded by ⌣–.

Group I
Anapaestic dimeter (⌣⌣–⌣⌣–⌣⌣–⌣⌣–)
  (A) :249D1|
  (B) |253A4:
Paroemiac (⌣⌣–⌣⌣–⌣⌣–x)
  (A) |246C3|; :252D3|; |256E6|
  (B) |245C7|; :248B7|; :248C1|; |252B3|; |252C5:; :256B1|; :253D6|; :256E4|
  (C) :256C6| *πράττοντες τῇ διανοίᾳ

Anapaestic metron (⌣⌣–⌣⌣–)
  (A) |249A6|; |256D1⁝
  (C) |249A6| *ἔτυχον κρίσεως

×–⌣⌣–⌣⌣–
  (A) ⁝246B2|; |254A4|
  (B) ⁝246A7|; |250E3|
  (C) |248A8⁝ *πρὸ τῆς ἑτέρας ἑτέρα; |249C8⁝ *ἀεὶ τελέους τελετάς
  (D) |247D1⁝ *ἅτ' οὖν διάνοια θεοῦ; |253A2⁝ *καὶ αὐτοῦ ἐφαπτόμενοι

–⌣⌣–⌣⌣–×
  (A) |254D1⁝; ⁝254E9|
  (B) ⁝253D7|
  (C) |253E1| *συμπεφορημένος εἰκῇ

Hemiepes (–⌣⌣–⌣⌣–)
  (A) ⁝246B7|; |248C6⁝
  (B) |246E6⁝; ⁝248A3|; ⁝248E6
  (C) |246B7⁝ *οὖσα μὲν οὖν τελέα
  (D) ⁝252A7| *τοῦ πόθου ἐγγυτάτω

Ionic dimeter (⌣⌣– –⌣⌣– –)
  (B) ⁝256A4|

⌣⌣– –⌣⌣–
  (A) ⁝249D6|; ⁝255A5|

⌣⌣–⌣⌣–×
  (A) ⁝251C2|
  (B) |248C5|; |250E5⁝; |254C7⁝

⌣⌣– –⌣⌣– –⌣⌣–
  (B) |249D5|

⌣⌣– –⌣⌣–⌣⌣–
  (C) |256E6⁝ *ὑπὸ πλήθους ἀνελευθερίαν

Anacreontic (⌣⌣–×–⌣–×)
  (A) |246B1|; ⁝246D3|; |247C8⁝; ⁝248C3|; ⁝251E2|
  (B) |254D6|

Group II
Alcaic dodecasyllable (×–⌣–×–⌣⌣–⌣–× (Alc. fr. 384))
  (A) |256D6⁝
Sapphic hendecasyllable (–⌣–×–⌣⌣–⌣–×)
  (A) ⁝250A5|; ⁝256D5|

Alcaic hendacasyllable (×–∪–×–∪∪–∪–)
(B) ⋮248D2|
"Enoplian" (×–∪∪–∪∪–∪–×)
(B) ⋮255C7|; ⋮256C2|
Phalaecean (∘∘–∪∪–∪–∪–×)
(B) |252E4|; |254D4|
Alcaic decasyllable (–∪∪–∪∪–∪–×)
(A) |251B7|
(B) |256C5⋮
Acephalous phalaecean (×–∪∪–∪–∪–×)
(A) ⋮255A5|
Ibycean (–∪∪–∪∪–∪–)
(A) |245E2⋮; ⋮249D8|
Third verse of Attic skolia (∪∪–∪– –∪∪–)
(A) ⋮246C4|; ⋮249D4|
Hipponactean (∘∘–∪∪–∪–×)
(A) ⋮254E5|; ⋮256D7|
(B) |245D3|; |246C7⋮; |247B6|; ⋮254E7|
(C) |256D6⋮ *εἰς γὰρ τὴν ὑπὸ γῆς πορείαν
(D) ⋮253E3| *ἑταῖρος καὶ ἀλαζονείας
Hagesichorean (×–∪∪–∪–×)
(A) |247D7|; ⋮254D2|; ⋮255D6|
(B) ⋮254C2|
Iambo-choriambic A (–∪∪– ×–∪–)
(A) |245C6|
(C) ⋮246B2| *ἡνιοχεῖ συνωρίδος
(D) |250A3⋮ *ὥσθ' ὑφ' ὁμιλιῶν τινων
Iambo-choriambic B (×–∪– –∪∪–)
(B) |250C7⋮; ⋮250D6|
(C) |255D8| *ἔρωτος εἴδωλον ἔχων
(D) |245E2| *πεφασμένου δ' ἀθανάτου; |247D7| *οὐχ ᾗ πρόσεστιν γένεσις; ⋮254C2| *ἄμφω τὼ ἵππω καθίσαι
Wilamowitzian (∘∘–×–∪∪–)
(A) ⋮245D8|; |247D6|; |248A8|; ⋮249C7|
(B) ⋮252C2|; ⋮253C6|; |256A5|
(C) |246B4⋮ *δύσκολος δὴ καὶ χαλεπή; |251B1⋮ *τοῦ κάλλους γὰρ δεξάμενος; |256D3⋮ *ἃς οὐ λύσαντας θεμιτόν
(D) |248A5⋮ *τῶν δ' ἵππων βιαζομένων

Glyconic (oo–⏑⏑–⏑–)
- (A) ⁞245E2⁞; l246E4l; l253E1l
- (B) l254C3⁞
- (C) ⁞253B8l *πρὸς τὰ παιδικὰ χρώμενοι
- (D) ⁞252A2l *ποιεῖται περὶ πλείονος

Choriambic heptasyllable (×–×–⏑⏑–)
- (A) l247B6⁞; ⁞248D1l; l251C8⁞; ⁞253C3l
- (B) l245C5l; l246D7⁞; ⁞250E3l; l250E4⁞; l251B3⁞; l251C1⁞
- (C) ⁞249C7l *τελούμενος τελετάς; l249D7⁞ *δίκην ὄρνιθος ἄνω
- (D) l248B1⁞ *ἅμιλλ' οὖν καὶ θόρυβος; l251C1⁞ ἐν οὖν τούτῳ ζεῖ ὅλη

Telesillean (×–⏑⏑–⏑–)
- (A) l247B2⁞; l247B3⁞; ⁞248E4l; l249B1⁞; l255B7⁞; ⁞256B2l
- (B) ⁞247A7l
- (D) l251E4⁞ λαβοῦσα δ' ἀναπ'νοήν

Pherecratean (oo–⏑⏑– –)
- (A) l245D1⁞; ⁞247A3l
- (B) ⁞255E6l
- (C) ⁞246A3l *αὐτῆς λεκτέον ὧδε; ⁞246D2l *συμπεφυκότα πάντα; l248D2⁞ *ἀλλὰ τὴν μὲν ἰδοῦσαν; l249C5⁞ *ἀεὶ γὰρ πρὸς ἐκείνοις; ⁞251E2l *τὸν τὸ κάλλος ἔχοντα
- (D) ⁞247A3l *ἣν ἐτάχθη ἕκαστος; ⁞254C6l *καὶ τοῦ πτώματος ἔσχεν; ⁞255D2l *ἐνέπ'λησεν ἔρωτος; l255E2⁞ *ἐκείνῳ δ' ἐπιθυμεῖ

Aristophanean (–⏑⏑–⏑– –)
- (B) l246D5l; l254B5⁞; l255A6⁞; ⁞256A6l
- (C) l251C8⁞ *τῆς ὀδύνης τε λωφᾷ; l253A5⁞ καὶ τὸν ἐρώμενον δή; ⁞255D7l *τῆς ὀδύνης ἐκείνῳ
- (D) ⁞254C7l *ὀργῇ ἐλοιδόρησεν

Reizianum (×–⏑⏑– –)
- (A) ⁞246B5l; ⁞248C7l; ⁞250E2l; l250E3⁞; l251A2⁞; ⁞251D2l; l256B1⁞
- (B) l245D1l; l247B3; ⁞250A2l; ⁞250B6l; ⁞250D4l; l250D6l; ⁞254A1l
- (C) l246D8l *καλὸν δὲ τὸ θεῖον; l248E1⁞ *ποιητικὸς ἕκτῃ;

|249A3| *ἐὰν τρὶς ἕλωνται; |249C3| *ἃ νῦν φαμεν εἶναι;
|251D1| *ὅταν δὲ γένηται
(D) |246E3| *κακῷ δὲ καὶ αἰσχρῷ; |250A7| *γίγνονται ⟨ἐν⟩ αὐτῶν; |256D3| *ἐλθεῖν ποτ' ἐς ἔχθραν

Group III

Alcaic enneasyllable (x−∪−x−∪−x)
(A) |246C1|; |253C7|; |256D2|
Trochaic dimeter (−∪−x −∪−x)
(A) |246C3|; |246E4|; |247B5|; |250D4|
(B) |248D2|; |254E8|
(C) |252D1| *οὗ χορευτὴς ἦν ἕκαστος
(D) |255C7| *ᾗ 'πὶ τὴν ψυχὴν πέφυκεν
Iambic dimeter (x−∪− x−∪−)
(A) |245E3|; |246A6|; |246E3|; |247C7|; |252C7|
(B) |245E6|; |246E3|; |248C2|; |252D6|; |254C1|; |254E5|
(C) |246D3| *διόλλυταί τε καὶ φθίνει |252C4| *ἄχθος τὸ τοῦ πτερωνύμου; |254E3| *γλῶτταν τε τὴν κακηγόρον
(D) |250D7| *ὥστ' εἶναι ἐκφανέστατον
Iambic + trochaic (x−∪− −∪−x)
(A) |251D1|
(C) |250A2|; |253E6| *πόθου τε καὶ γαργαλισμοῦ
(D) |249C6| *ἀνὴρ δὲ δὴ τοῖς τοιούτοις
Lekythion (−∪−x−∪−)
(A) |246D2|; |247A1|; |247B1|; |248C1|; |248C3|; |251A6|; |255B6|; |265A5|
(B) |254C6|; |257A2|
(C) |246E6| *δαιμόνων τε καὶ θεῶν; |250A1| *οὐχ ἁπάσῃ ῥᾴδιον; |254D7| *τὸν χαλινὸν ἐνδακών; |255B6| *πρὸς φίλον τὸν ἔνθεον; |256A6| *ἀντιτείνει τοῦ λόγου
Cretic dimeter (−∪− −∪−)
(A) |248B2|; |250D6|; |252B1|
(B) |249A7|; |249B3|; |249D4|; |251B4|
(C) |247A1| *Ἑστία γὰρ μένει; |251D5| *ὥστε κεντουμένη; |254E3| *τὸν χαλινὸν σπάσας
Iambic + bacchiac (x−∪− ∪−−)
(D) |251C2| *ὅταν φύωσιν ἄρτι

Ithyphallic (—∪—∪——)
- (A) |246D2|; |249B1|; |251A1|; |251C7|; |251D6|; |255E3|
- (B) |246A6|; |251D8|; |253B2|
- (C) |248E2| *ἁρμόσει τις ἄλλος; |250E2| *πρὸς τὸ κάλλος αὐτό
- (D) |253B2| *ταὐτὰ δρῶσι πάντα

Bacchiac dimeter (∪—— ∪——)
- (A) |249A7|; |249E4|
- (B) |250A6|
- (C) |252B1| *πόνων τῶν μεγίστων
- (D) |246C5| *ἐυλήθη τὸ σύμπαν; |250C4| *ἀσήμαντοι ὄντες

Totals: (A + B): 168 out of 606 = 28%
(C + D): 74 out of 673 = 11%

The figure for (C + D) reminds us that we must expect a given sequence of longs and shorts sometimes to be produced by chance, and for that reason we may go badly wrong if we insist on seeking an aesthetic reason for every instance. But the case is different when a passage as substantial as the Myth of the Soul exceeds the chance rate[5] by a factor of $2^{1}/_{2}$, and especially when it contains no less than eleven instances of 10-, 11- or 12-syllable sequences, whereas among the products of transposition only one instance (256E6, ionic rhythm) exceeds nine syllables. The association of these long sequences with Sappho and Alkaios is well known; at nine-syllable level, Ibykos and again Alkaios come to mind, and at eight-syllable level Anakreon. They were the poets of Eros, and in an exposition which honours Eros to the utmost of Socrates' ability (257A3f.) it is right that we should be reminded of the poets who honoured him in earlier generations. In rhythm and language alike Plato makes it plain to us that he is taking us for a ride in the chariot of the Muses.

---

[5] A "contingency table" for the data given, whether the three rhythmic Groups are kept separate or added together, shows that the probability that (A + B) and (C + D) could be two samples taken from the same "population" is very low indeed, far below $^{1}/_{1000}$. For the calculation of χ^2 and its relation to probability see Anthony Kenny, *The Computation of Literary Style* (Oxford: Pergamon Press 1982) 112–19.

2

Plato, Imagination and Romanticism

S. Halliwell

> "I am he attesting sympathy,...
> I am not the poet of goodness only, I do not decline to be the poet of wickedness also.
> What blurt is this about virtue and vice?"
>
> (Walt Whitman, "Song of Myself" §22)

In one of the aphoristic sections of his book *Morgenröte*, Friedrich Nietzsche numbers Plato among a group of figures (with Spinoza, Pascal, Rousseau, Goethe) whose thought constitutes the "passionate history of a soul" and embodies the product of a life which "burns with the passion of thinking."[1] Part of the abiding vitality of Plato's writing stems from the many ways in which it offers a supreme exemplification of what Ian Kidd, in the resonant phrase which gives the present volume its title, called "the passionate intellect." But the passions of the Platonic intellect involve many paradoxes, not least the fact that a writer whose own dialogues and myths frequently seem to blur the distinction between philosophy and literature, himself voices grave reservations

---

[1] *Morgenröte* (1881) §481; R.J. Hollingdale (tr.), *Friedrich Nietzsche: Daybreak* (Cambridge: Cambridge University Press 1981) 198.

about the imaginative power of the greatest Greek poetry. One form of passion which is central to Plato's explorations of human motivation is the desire for beauty, and it is precisely this which is said, at *Republic* 3.403c, to be the proper goal of "music," i.e. of poetry and the other arts of the muses. Yet that remark occurs at the end of a long discussion of poetry and music which has become notorious for its guiding thesis that the Homeric epics themselves need to be censored on account of the ethically and psychologically dangerous sentiments which they contain: the beauty and the danger of Homer are, it seems, inextricable (cf. 3.387b). The paradox of Plato's ambivalent relationship to poetry, and to art more generally, was often mentioned by Nietzsche himself, who once called Plato "the greatest enemy of art Europe has yet produced."[2] But in framing this description, Nietzsche was, in his own peculiarly trenchant way, paying a formidable compliment. The "greatness" of Plato's enmity to art denoted no mere extreme of antipathy, but was meant as a measure of what Nietzsche rightly saw as Plato's instinctive knowledge of art's vital significance – the knowledge possessed by a passionate intellect *par excellence*.

Nietzsche's compliment was no passing gesture. Much of his own aesthetics, with its defiantly celebratory invocation of illusion, intoxication and "lies," can be read as an implicit (sometimes explicit) response to the very terms in which Platonic mistrust of art had been expressed.[3] In fact, Nietzsche grasped, to a degree which very few others have done, the magnitude of the challenge posed to art and its "lovers" (*Rep.* 10.607d–e) by the Platonic insistence on the sovereignty of truth and morality even in the realm of what, since Romanticism, we have come familiarly to speak of as "the aesthetic." Nietzsche was compelled to feel a kind of sardonic respect for the fact that Plato had experienced and acknowledged art as something *worth* his earnest antagonism, something whose potentially formative power called for intensely serious scrutiny: "what right has our age," he bitterly exclaims in *Menschliches, Allzumenschliches*, "to offer an answer at all to Plato's great question about the moral influence of art? Even if we possessed art — what influence *of any kind* does art exercise among us?"[4] Plato's

---

[2] *Zur Genealogie der Moral* (1887) III 25; W. Kaufmann (tr.), *Basic Writings of Nietzsche* (New York: The Modern Library 1968) 590.
[3] For some Nietzschean endorsement of Platonic aesthetics cf. J. Barish, *The Antitheatrical Prejudice* (Berkeley CA: University of California Press 1981) 404–13.
[4] *Menschliches, Allzumenschliches* (1878) §212; (with one small change) R.J.

"great question" is a sign of the greatness, in every sense, of what Nietzsche reads as his enmity to art.

Whether or not one entirely shares Nietzsche's despair about the status of art in modern culture, his perception of Plato as a special point of reference and provocation for aesthetics is one which I believe can and should still be endorsed. But there are many ways of reading and reactivating Plato, whether in relation to aesthetics or other areas of philosophy. One of these ways is to treat certain Platonic arguments as "paradigmatic," not in the sense of supplying models for direct emulation (though that is one aspect of the influence they have in fact exercised), but as articulating in a valuably searching style some of the foundations of permanently available intellectual and cultural positions. In defining the idea of a paradigm in such terms there is a danger of suggesting what may sound like a highly static mode of importance. But that is not at all the point. Indeed, one powerful reason for reading certain texts in this spirit is that, partly on account of the long tradition of interpretation which they have already accumulated, they have a richness which is particularly responsive to constant reorientation in regard to the shifting bearings of intellectual history. In keeping with this approach, I propose in this essay to reconsider the status of certain Platonic arguments which bear on the functioning of imagination and emotion in the experience of representational (mimetic) art. I shall not here be concerned with the fine details of these arguments but with some of their broader conceptual implications and with the possibility of placing them in relation to some views adopted in more recent phases of Western aesthetics.[5]

The still standard account of what might aptly be called Plato's antiaestheticism is that of an ideological severity which translates itself, through the principles of state censorship outlined in books 2–3 (and reaffirmed in book 10) of the *Republic*, into one aspect of politico-cultural totalitarianism. But this is an excessively narrow way of reading

---

Hollingdale (tr.), *Human, All Too Human* (Cambridge: Cambridge University Press 1986) 98.

[5] I am here, and throughout, implicitly contending for a perspective which goes beyond the allegedly self-contained realm of "the aesthetic" and insists on dialogue between post- and pre-Enlightenment conceptions of art. From this perspective, "the aesthetic," narrowly conceived, is part of, but not foundational for, the history of aesthetics. See my essay, "The Importance of Plato and Aristotle for Aesthetics," J.J. Cleary (ed.), *Proceedings of the Boston Area Colloquium in Ancient Philosophy* 5 (Lanham MD: University Press of America 1991) 321–48.

both the passages in question and their larger implications within the *Republic* as a whole. I have argued myself elsewhere that the voice raised against the greatest Greek poetry in the *Republic* is better, if paradoxically, construed as that of a Romantic puritan or puritanical Romantic.[6] It is no coincidence that, alongside some obvious and radical differences, Plato has multiple connections — of both affinity and influence — with the Romantic movement itself, not least in his sense of the world as a unified field of value, his idealistic interest in transcendence, and his use of imaginative myth and symbolic imagery at the service of spiritual aspirations. But what I mean by calling him a Romantic puritan in this context is above all that his suspicion of great poetry stems, as I have suggested that Nietzsche recognised, from a deep sensitivity to its transformative power, its capacity to make us think differently and ultimately to become different selves. Both of the *Republic*'s major critiques of poetry and mimesis make richer sense when placed in the perspective of the work's central theme of the integrity of the individual soul. Such integrity is threatened by a psychic openness and diversity, fostered by imaginative art, which Plato describes as "becoming one person instead of many" (4.443e1). But Plato's fear of the imagination is that of a thinker and writer who does not simply stigmatise certain kinds of art as dangerous or corrupting, but claims to *appreciate*, to know *from the inside*, just how seductive are the transforming experiences which such art can provide. This is the Socratic voice of Plato's argument which talks, for example, in terms of the "love and respect, acquired in my childhood, which inhibits me from speaking [sc. critically] about Homer," (*Rep*. 10.595b9–10), or which intimates confessionally that "even the best of us" are unable to resist the sympathy-inducing force of both Homer and Attic tragedy (*Rep*. 10.605c 10–d5).[7]

I have ascribed to Plato a deep awareness of the transformative power of poetry; the point could be extended to music, and perhaps to other art too.[8] One elaboration of this idea which I would like to present here is that this awareness is tantamount to a realisation of some of the work-

---

[6] See "Plato on the Psychology of Drama," *Drama* 1 (1992) 55–73, esp. 69–71.

[7] Barish (above, n.3) 5 calls this last passage a "haunting acknowledgement" of theatrical potency.

[8] The power of music is discussed at *Rep*. 3.398b ff.; note 401d (music "sinks into the interior of the soul"). Extrapolation to other arts is indicated at 401a–c.

ings of imagination. But this formulation at once brings us up against the viability of the approach to the history of aesthetics which I am advocating, since there are *prima facie* grounds for questioning whether Plato had a concept of imagination at all in the relevant sense. While I do not underestimate the seriousness of that objection, I believe that it is far from decisive. We need to grasp that the criterion of terminology is of especially limited usefulness in this connection: for what it is worth, Plato does employ, both inside and outside his discussions of poetry and visual art, members of the Greek word-group which includes *phantasia* and for which the Latin *imaginatio* (etc.) became the standard equivalent from at least Augustine onwards.[9] But if we accept that imagination is an exceptionally multi-faceted concept, or family of concepts, with relevance to several areas of philosophical psychology, we need to seek understanding of its varieties, and of the strands of thought which bear on their elucidation, well beyond the range of any one class of vocabulary. This is especially true in cases where, as in those with which I am concerned, imagination is best taken to entail not a distinct mental faculty, but the operation of belief, emotion and judgement in connection with hypothetical events.

Leaving aside, then, any aspiration to arrive at a unitary, essentialist account of imagination,[10] I would like to develop the claim that wherever there exists a recognition of artistic representation — and I take Greek notions of mimesis to embody such recognition — attitudes to the *experience* (as well, of course, as the creation) of such art will necessarily touch upon imaginative processes. Imagination, in this context, can be roughly circumscribed as the mental tracing of fictional patterns of life signified by works of art. This minimal formulation is meant to separate, though not isolate, the relevant realm of experience from many other experiences which may involve different kinds of imaginative factor — experiences which include the vivid use of memory, engagement in fantasies or hypothetical deliberations about one's own life, historical reconstruction of others' lives, or even therapeutic psychodrama.[11] I use

---

[9] On Platonic and other ancient concepts of *phantasia*, see G. Watson, *Phantasia in Classical Thought* (Galway: Galway University Press 1988).

[10] A recent book which, though valuable, suffers from partly succumbing to the essentialist temptation, is J.M. Cocking, *Imagination* (London: Routledge 1991).

[11] I do not deny that some of these things can enter the experience of art, but they cannot be definitional of it. Nor do I claim that mental tracing of fictional patterns of life is *exclusive* to experience of art.

the term "tracing" to capture a broadly narrative dimension of the experience, to be distinguished from, for instance, explicit reflection on general or universal propositions.[12] This narrative factor will in turn allow for further discriminations, of the kind which interested Plato and other ancient theorists, and continue to interest modern critics, between various modes of representation, as well as the expressive points-of-view which they can project and the types of response which they can correspondingly elicit: I shall return to this point before long. Finally, it is important to emphasise, as Plato himself does in connection with drama at *Rep.* 10.606b1, that what is at issue here is the imaginative tracing of the lives *of others*: the point of this is not to exclude implicitly self-regarding factors, but to mark the scope for feelings and judgements which either draw the mind close to, or distance it from, the characters represented in art.

What these considerations might help to clarify is the mutual implication between ideas of artistic representation (mimesis) and certain functions of imagination. On this view, the contents of representational works of art exhibit patterns of life, produced by the imaginative activity of the artist, which their audiences are obliged in turn to imagine in so far as they follow and comprehend them. One important feature of this line of argument is that it allows us to identify a type of imagination which is not the exercise of a specific mental faculty. Rather, what is in question here is the focussing of generally identifiable kinds of mental response, including elements of both cognition and emotion, upon patterns of fictional(ised) human action and experience. This observation underlines the danger of tethering the history of concepts of imagination to explicit and narrow areas of terminology. To draw out the implication in its widest form, we can say that when ancient critics discuss responses to poetic and artistic mimesis, their thought tells us how they construe a certain kind of imagination even though they may not specify the point in their own vocabulary. In Plato's case, interest in the psychology of audiences is glimpsed as early as the *Ion*, where the description of the rhapsode's state of mind (which "thinks itself present at the very events," 535c1–2) picks out an imaginative factor that is in turn emotionally transmitted to the audience which shares in the performer's putative inspiration (535e). There is a sense in which the *Ion* can be

---

[12] Again, I do not imply that such reflection cannot be part of the experience of some art.

read as probing the source and authority of poetic imagination, but principally in relation to the poet himself and the performer. In the *Republic*, however, the social and political framework of the discussion brings the imaginative experience of poetic audiences to the forefront, and it is to these passages that my argument principally refers.

Since Plato's extended critiques of poetry concentrate on the strongly emotional kinds of experience which poetry can induce, it might be thought that I am inevitably committing him to a view of imagination as, in his terms, wholly irrational. But the position is not so simple. Firstly, Plato does not apply a consistent model of the soul to the analysis of poetry in the *Republic*: in books 2–3 the tripartite soul has not yet been mentioned; in 10, that model of the soul is not adhered to, even though a sharp distinction between reason and the "lower" soul is certainly employed. But there is, in any case, a deeper level at which Plato's arguments acknowledge that emotional responses to mimetic representation are not arbitrary or senseless: as reactions to projected images of life, they follow or entail — particularly where those images are *normatively* construed — implicit judgements of value. Both the treatments of poetry in the *Republic* make it clear that it is precisely because of the capacity to elicit assent to certain underlying beliefs and values that artistic works can make a difference to their audience's lives. Take, as a typical example, Socrates' question near the start of book 3: "do you think that someone who *believes* that Hades exists and that it is a horrifying place will be without fear of death...?" (386b) The question presupposes that the absorbed experience of certain passages of poetry *per se* involves the activation of certain beliefs and attitudes. The emotions aroused through imaginative experience of mimetic objects are ethically evaluative movements of the soul, even if Plato's case frames them as "irrational" in the sense of being opposed to the judgements of pure reason (which is itself profoundly evaluative).

Although it is an important premise of Plato's argument at *Rep.* 10.606a–b that an audience may yield, in watching tragedy, to impulses which it would try to inhibit in life, this is very far from granting to the experience of art a special aestheticist quality which sets it apart. On the contrary, this point is part of a fundamental anti-aestheticism which posits reciprocal interaction, and what might be called a circle of reinforcement, between experience of life and experience of art. Tragedy, for example, can only draw out an instinct for sympathy because a "natural" propensity to grief (606a5) is there to be tapped within the psyche and has been kept alive by the formation of deeply valued attachments to other people. In turn, so Plato's argument claims, the experience of sympathetic emotion in the theatre can influence life itself: "having nourished the capacity for pity on those [sc. fictional characters], it is not easy to repress it in one's own sufferings" (606b7-8).

If we put together the various strands of argument in both *Rep.* 2–3 and 10, it is possible to construct an implicitly tripartite scheme of what one might call modes of imagination:[13] that is, of the primary ways in which imagination can respond to fictional patterns of life. The elements of this scheme, which are all clearly invoked in Plato though never systematised into a single model, can be classified as: first, "identification," for which Plato sometimes uses the language of "self-likening" (e.g. *Rep.* 3.396a–b); secondly, "sympathy," which *Rep.* 10 glosses (for tragedy) as a condition of "surrender" or "yielding" to emotional power; thirdly, critical understanding and judgement,[14] which can recognise the ethical nature of life-patterns in fiction but refuses to be emotionally allured by them unless they are deemed to be unambiguously good. These three modes might be further described as enacting the mentalities or points-of-view of the quasi-participant (identification), the engaged witness (sympathy), and the detached observer (critical judgement). I do not contend that such a scheme is conceptually sufficient for all purposes, but it does provide a coherent and adaptable framework which can be profitably used as the starting-point for more detailed psychological analysis. In an area where modern views, from eighteenth-century discussions of sympathy to current controversies over the influence of cinematic and television violence, reveal a prevailing lack of even rudimentary consensus, the tripartite scheme I have sketched represents a sufficiently tight structure to draw attention to some highly urgent issues about attitudes to art, while at the same time not precluding the possibility of additional qualifications and refine-

---

[13] I have stated this interpretation more fully in my "Psychology" (above, n.6) 58–63. I. Lada, " 'Empathic Understanding': Emotion and Cognition in Classical Dramatic Audience-Response," *PCPhS* 39 (1993) 94–140, argues that general Greek attitudes were hospitable to the *fusion* of emotion and judgement.

[14] "Understanding," in this context, means a capacity to make correct moral judgements (cf. n.21 below); it is thus immune to the anxiety voiced by, e.g., Primo Levi, when he maintains, *à propos* Nazi anti-semitism: " 'understanding'...human behaviour means to "contain" it, contain its author, put oneself in his place, identify with him..." (*If This Is A Man*, Eng. tr. (London: Sphere Books 1987) 395).

ments. To carry this point a little further, I shall look briefly at a pair of contrasting positions, the first of which largely collapses the sort of distinctions with which Plato works, and the second of which elaborates, without any direct reference to Plato, a larger range of categories along the psychological spectrum.

In his *Theory of Moral Sentiments* (1759), a work which addresses much more than responses to art but is nonetheless pertinent here, Adam Smith explains "sympathy" (*alias* "altruism" or "fellow feeling") in terms of imagination, but gives an account of the sympathetic imagination that seems suspended between self-regarding and other-regarding considerations. Smith tells us that we need imagination, when reacting to the experiences of others in social life as well as in fiction, to conceive "what we ourselves should feel in the like situation," but also that "by imagination...we enter as it were into his [another person's] body, and become in some measure the same person with him..."[15] As this latter quotation indicates, Smith's "sympathy" is hard to distinguish from identification, where the latter is defined, as I have already defined it for Plato, in terms of a participant or strongly vicarious point-of-view. The synonymy of sympathy and identification reflects a wider eighteenth-century use of these two terms as largely interchangeable, and that has in turn left its mark on general modern usage, with the exception of certain technical applications (especially in psychoanalysis).[16] In addition, however, Smith argues that sympathy in its strongest forms, at least, depends on understanding and judgement of a situation, so that it is not at all purely instinctual but manifests cognitive interpretation. In effect, therefore, Smith presents a compound notion of imagination which, however serviceable it may be for an enquiry into the basis of moral feelings, elides distinctions of the kind I have extracted from Plato's thinking, and leaves us with the difficulty of how to separate different degrees of psychological closeness or emotional affinity in responses to the experiences of others (whether in life or in art).

---

[15] *The Theory of Moral Sentiments*, 6th rev. ed. (London 1790), D.D. Raphael and A.L. Macfie (eds.) (Oxford: Clarendon Press 1976) part I, sect. i, ch. 1. On the problematic importance of the fictional (esp. theatrical) model for Smith's thinking, see D. Marshall, *The Figure of Theater* (New York: Columbia University Press 1986) 167–92, with his *The Surprising Effects of Sympathy* (Chicago IL: Chicago University Press 1988) for the broader eighteenth-century context of ideas.

[16] R. Wollheim, "Imagination and Identification," *On Art and the Mind* (London: Allen Lane 1973) 54–83, esp. 73–9, discusses Freudian "identification" in relation to other imaginative processes.

In particular, Smith's position might make us wonder how becoming "in some measure the same person as another," which implies a psychological loss of self, can be reconciled with the stance of the attentive, judicious spectator from which, as Smith himself argues, ethical judgements need to be made.[17] It may be that Smith's theory can be saved by regarding the element of identification not as a discrete state of mind but a tacit *hypothesis* which takes place whenever sympathy occurs. But even if that is so, the effect of Smith's argument is to blur the distinction between two possible psychological relationships: those, say, of the person who feels grief along with a sufferer, and of the person who feels pity.[18] This distinction, which corresponds to two processes of imagination, is the difference between the enactive, self-likening mimesis of Plato *Rep.* 3.393c ff., and the sympathetic response of the audience of tragedy at 10.605c–6b.

In contrast to the way in which Adam Smith tends to condense the concept of sympathy, the contemporary literary theorist Hans Robert Jauss has constructed, from the historical perspective of his theory of "reception aesthetics," a scale of five major types of what he generically calls "identification."[19] Jauss's range runs from "cultic participation" to the relative detachment of "aesthetic reflection," though he also argues for the possibility of combining emotional engagement and aesthetic distance within a single response. Although Jauss does not link his psychological categories to those of Plato, and makes more use of Aristotelian concepts, his scheme could be shown to cover a comparable range to Plato's and to embrace the fundamental distinctions drawn by Plato. Thus, at one pole, Jauss's "associative identification," which involves the active assumption of a role, corresponds to Plato's conception of enactive, self-likening mimesis which I have already mentioned.[20] Similarly, Jauss's "admiring identification" closely matches the concern with emulation of heroic role-models which is conveyed by Plato in such passages as *Rep.* 3.387d–8b. Where Jauss principally differs from

---

[17] The point applies in reverse if we remember that Smith suggests we can judge *ourselves* only by trying to adopt a spectator's point-of-view towards our lives.

[18] Aristotle applies this distinction at e.g. *Rhet.* 2.8, 1386a17–23.

[19] H.R. Jauss, "Levels of Identification of Hero and Audience," *New Literary History* 5 (1974) 283–317.

[20] At the other pole, however, Jauss's (misleadingly labeled) "ironic identification" involves an aestheticist withholding of engagement which is very different from Plato's goal: see my next paragraph.

Plato is in his willingness to multiply categories along the psychological spectrum of responses, and to take account of a very large number of artistic forms. These differences are chiefly a reflection of the depth of cultural perspective adopted by Jauss.

The most fundamental observation that can be made about Plato's model of imaginative responses to art is that it is not only the oldest but perhaps the most resolute Western paradigm of a rejection of aestheticism, where the latter is characterised above all by a principle of "disinterested contemplation" or the like. It would be a grave mistake to equate the function of rational, emotionally detached judgement within Plato's scheme with the disinterestedness which has become a defining feature of so much modern aesthetic theory. Plato's view is not that we should cultivate a detached, contemplative attitude towards works of art, on the grounds that this is the most appropriate and sophisticated stance we can adopt towards them. On the contrary, his arguments repeatedly ascribe to art the capacity to exercise a spell-like control over the mind, and to make any kind of detachment hard or even, for most people, impossible: we need only remember *Rep.* 10.605c-d, cited earlier, where it is admitted that "even the best of us" yield to emotionally powerful art. The possibility of critical detachment from emotion is not, therefore, a realistically desirable and "aesthetic" goal for audiences in general, but an ideal of the necessary resistance to art that would be shown by a mind of complete discipline and philosophical rationality.[21]

There is, however, a crucial question which Plato's treatments of this subject never directly face, and which is rarely faced in more recent work on the psychology of artistic experience. How far is it possible and necessary to allow not only for variations between the responses to which different types of work lend themselves (something made much of by Jauss, for example), but also the possible coexistence of various operations of imagination — sympathy, identification, critical detachment — *within* a single response to a particular work? The criticism of literature and art provides copious if unsystematic evidence for such mixed responses, but theorists of aesthetic psychology, including Plato himself, seem much more reluctant to admit variability in this respect. Yet such variability would not be a surprising phenomenon on any view

---

[21] Cf. the conclusion of the discussion of poetry and music at *Rep.* 3.402c, where the capacity to "recognise/judge" (*gnōrizein*) virtues and vices, in both life and art, belongs to the ideally cultured (*mousikos*) person.

of art which, like that of Plato, sees a continuity, and even what I earlier called a circle of reinforcement, between responses to art and experiences of life outside art, since most people's dealings with the world are marked by subtle shifts and shadings of attitude towards the lives of others. But if that is true, it suggests that no monolithic theory of aesthetic responsiveness can accommodate the likely complexity and untidiness, both particular and general, of how people react to works of art. That inference does not, however, invalidate the basic psychological categories which can be seen at work in Plato's discussions of poetry. It means, rather, that the application of such categories to concrete cases will not often produce unequivocal results, and that Plato's own use of these categories may delineate essential lines of possibility rather than detailed adjustments to observed actuality.

The complexity of issues in this domain can be further glimpsed by brief consideration of a recent and major work of criticism, Wayne Booth's *The Company We Keep: An Ethics of Fiction*.[22] This book, which constructs an approach to the ethics of literature on the basis of a moral psychology of reading, deserves to be counted, however paradoxically, as a liberal adaptation of the Platonic paradigm which I have been discussing. Booth is happy to invoke Plato explicitly at certain points, and he uses language that has close affinities with some of Plato's terms: thus, "The essential first step [in reading fiction]...can only be that primary act of *assent* that occurs when we *surrender* to a story and follow it through to its conclusion."[23] Booth differs from Plato in two principal respects: first, he works with a much more extensive and carefully refined range of terms and criteria, and takes explicit account, as Plato rarely does, of potential divergence between an authorially internalised control (the "sense of life" associated with the "implied author") and the properties of individual characters; secondly, he argues for an ethics of reading that entails, as he puts it, "both surrender and refusal" (136), an openness to sympathy tempered by critical control.

Yet Booth also sometimes moves, I would say, towards a more uncompromisingly Platonic position, partly because he tends to assume

---

[22] Wayne C. Booth, *The Company We Keep: An Ethics of Fiction* (Berkeley CA: University of California Press 1988).

[23] Booth (above, n.22) 32 (only "assent" is italicised by Booth himself); Booth uses "surrender" repeatedly elsewhere: compare the sympathetic "surrender" of *Rep.* 10.605c–d. For explicit affiliation to the Platonic paradigm see esp. Booth 41.

that individual works project unitary sets of values. At one point, for instance, he writes: "...insofar as the fiction has *worked* for us, we have lived with its values for the duration: we have been *that kind of person* for at least as long as we remained in the presence of the work."[24] Two things are particularly striking here: one, the unqualified phrase "its values"; two, the overtones of "lived with," which of course echoes the title of Booth's book and gives a further Platonic dimension to the enterprise, for the comparison between works of art and personal "company" is found as a metaphorical motif in Plato too.[25] It is interesting that here, and not only here, Booth skirts perilously close to an implicit notion of what, in the terms of my earlier argument, amounts to "identification," even though he also shows some caution about such a concept.[26] In the final analysis I think that the reason for this is that, despite the critical detail and evaluative finesse of many of his individual readings, Booth's psychology of reading rests on a theoretical foundation that is actually narrower than Plato's. Although Booth advocates, as I mentioned, a type of reading that can *combine* "surrender and refusal," it is also true that he tends to see these two categories as fully defining the basic attitudinal dynamics available to a reader, and supposes *all* reading to require at least a stage of surrender or succumbing.[27] Booth's general psychological schema can be faulted for not providing a sufficiently supple model of the stances which a reader can adopt and explore towards a fictional text.

Having juxtaposed some aspects of Plato's analysis of aesthetic experience with a small selection of more recent approaches, it may be prudent to conclude that this remains a realm in which we understand ourselves very imperfectly. In part this is because of the difficulty of observing ourselves instructively in the midst of aesthetic experience, particularly in the case of works whose very power to grip the imagination is at the heart of the issue. There are also substantial obstacles, some of them probably insurmountable, to testing general propositions about the

---

[24] Booth (above, n.22) 41, his italics.
[25] See esp. *Rep.* 10.603b1, 605b1: in the former the imagery evokes a sexually dangerous woman (see my *Plato: Republic 10* (Warminster: Aris and Phillips 1988) 135).
[26] See esp. Booth (above, n.22) 138–42, where he appears to question the concept of identification as "misleading" and "excessive," but continues to use the term and to describe reading as "a kind of submersion in other minds."
[27] See esp. Booth (above, n.22) 140.

causal influence of art on life. If interpretation of behavioural consequences can prove so fraught even in the case of pornography, where controlled data and reasonably specific parameters are feasible,[28] it is inevitably difficult to trace the more diffuse and subtle influences of, say, tragic drama. But such difficulty should not be invoked, as it sometimes is, as though it amounted to negative evidence, since comparable difficulty would be encountered in the attempt to prove the concrete influence of most sufficiently rich areas of human experience. Though such uncertainties, therefore, might send us back with due caution about the apparent over-confidence of some Platonic contentions on this subject, they ought equally to encourage doubts about the still prevalent and essentially Romantic faith in the intrinsic wholesomeness of the free play of imagination. Since, as I initially suggested, Plato can himself be regarded as a suppressed Romantic, a Romantic puritan, not least in view of his displacement of the (trans)formative power of imagination from poetry to his own philosophy,[29] there may be an especially pointed challenge to the dangers of Romanticism to be located within his critique of certain kinds of aesthetic experience.

The nature of that challenge might be summarily posed as follows. If, as some currents of Romanticism suggest, imagination is an autonomous faculty, and therefore independent of both reason and emotion, it is difficult to see where it derives the power to take such a compelling purchase on the mind. But if, as Plato's arguments about poetry insist, imagination can draw upon forces which are rooted in, and grow out into, our larger mental lives, then imagination cannot possess a freedom which outruns other sources of value, and its potential to change us must be recognised as a possible source of corruption as well as enrichment. While one of the most damaging objections to Plato's own ostensible position is that it inhibits the plasticity of imaginative thought and feeling in the name of an absolutism that transcends the human, it is an equally urgent reservation about an unfettered Romanticism that it is prepared to proclaim its freedom without calculation of the psychological cost that may attach to imaginative acts of internalisation and as-

[28] B. Williams (ed.), *Obscenity and Film Censorship* (Cambridge: Cambridge University Press 1981) 61–95, cautiously surveys some studies in this field; C.A. MacKinnon, *Feminism Unmodified* (Cambridge MA: Harvard University Press 1987), esp. ch. 13, offers a more trenchant, feminist perspective.

[29] That, however ironically, is indeed a major reason for his actual influence on the idealism of some Romantics.

similation. Given that contrast, it may be impossible for most of us to become Platonists: we are likely, indeed, to want to invert Plato's reasoning, and to concur with George Eliot that "if Art does not enlarge men's sympathies, it does nothing morally."[30] But far from meaning that we must turn our backs on the Platonic paradigm, such a commitment is actually congruent with Plato's master idea that it is precisely the imagination's power to shape the life of the soul which requires it to be ethically accountable for the uses to which it is put. To that extent, at least, we can legitimately continue to feel, with Nietzsche, that any aesthetics worth having will be one which can face up to the questions still posed by "the greatest enemy of art".*

---

[30] Letter to Charles Bray, 5 July 1859: see G.S. Haight (ed.), *Selections from George Eliot's Letters* (New Haven CT: Yale University Press 1985) 217.
  * A version of this paper was drafted for a seminar at the Center for Ideas and Society, University of California at Riverside, in February 1993, during my period as Visiting Faculty Fellow. I am indebted to Martha Nussbaum for organising the seminar, and to my colleagues at the Center for their constructive contributions.

3

Tradition and Innovation in the Transformation of Socrates' Divine Sign

Mark Joyal

I. δαίμων and τὸ δαιμόνιον

In his prolix examination of the lemma *Alcibiades* I 103a4–6 τούτου...πεύσῃ, Proclus (*in Alcibiadem* 60–85 Segonds) makes two assumptions about Socrates' divine sign (τὸ δαιμόνιον) which may be considered typical of exegesis in the later Platonic tradition. First, Socrates' sign is identified as a δαίμων, usually implicitly (e.g. 60.13–18, 62.6–10, 62.14–24, 73.7–18, 83.14–17), but also explicitly (e.g. 78.10–19). This equation Proclus does not bother to argue out, doubtless because there was nothing novel in it. For the identification of τὸ δαιμόνιον as a δαίμων (quite rigorously eschewed by Plato and Xenophon, see below) we have the evidence of several of Proclus' predecessors, contemporaries, and successors: Plutarch, *Mor.* 588e (*de genio Socratis*); Apuleius, *de deo Socratis* 24.20–25.18, 30.17, 33.1, 3, 6 Moreschini; Maximus of Tyre 8.8 (68.190–69.206 Trapp); Hermeias, *in Platonis Phaedrum* 65.31–69.31 Couvreur; Olympiodorus, *in Platonis Alcibiadem* 21.1–14 Westerink.[1] Secondly, the δαίμων

---

[1] Cf. Iust. *Apol.* II.7.3; Tert. *Apol.* 22.1; Min. Fel. *Oct.* 26.9 (38.5 *fallacissimus*

equated with τὸ δαιμόνιον is — notwithstanding Proclus' elaborate classification of δαίμονες in general (71.1–73.6 S.) — an example of the personal, tutelary δαίμων which is allotted to each of us (71.1–78.6, 80.23–81.3 S.). The belief that Socrates' sign was an allotted guardian spirit — at once a synthesis with certain Platonic views about δαίμονες and a reflex of popular belief (see nn.11, 12) — is also amply attested: Plu. *Mor.* 580c; Max. Tyr. 8.8 (69.205–6 T.); Apul. *Soc.* 24.20–25.18 M.; Herm. *in Phdr.* 93–4 (esp. 66.1–67.12 C.); Olymp. *in Alc.* 21.1 W.[2]

Such a variety of sources demonstrates that in regard to these characterizations of Socrates' sign we are dealing with what had become a widespread orthodoxy.[3] That a certain degree of homogeneity should

---

daemon may refer to Apollo, so J.H. Waszink, *Tertulliani De Anima* (Amsterdam: Meulenhoff 1947) 92–3, but cf. Origen *c. Cels.* 6.8 τὸ Σωκράτους δαιμόνιον ὡς πλάσμα χλευάσουσιν; Procl. *in Alc.* 86.6–9 S., esp. 8–9 κενὸν ἀνάπλασμα τὴν δαιμονίαν ταύτην εἶναι νομίζοντες ἐπίνοιαν; Plu. *Mor.* 580c; Joseph. *Ap.* II.263; also K. Kleve, "Scurra Atticus: The Epicurean View of Socrates," G.P. Carratelli (ed.), *Suzetesis. studi sull' epicureismo greco e romano offerti a Marcello Gigante*, I (Naples 1983) 243 and n.93); Cyprian. *Quod idola* 6; Lactant. *Div. Inst.* II.14.9, *Instit. Epit.* 23.2; Calcid. *in Ti.* 199.1–4 Waszink; Aug. *Civ.* VIII.14 (on Apuleius' *Soc.*); Eust. *ad Il.* I.198 (I.129.9–11 van der Valk); *scholia vetera* and *scholia Arethae* on *Alc.* I 103a5–6 (see Greene's note on the former for probable sources). Cf. also [Plu.] *Mor.* 574b–c (*de fato*), with brief discussion of this passage in (vi) below. For the possibility that Tiberianus (saec. iv) wrote a work *de deo Socratis* see F. Lenz, *RE* 6, 772–3.

[2] Cf. Tert. *de Anima* I.5 (*suus socius*); Min. Fel. *Oct.* 26.9 (*adsidentis sibi daemonis*); Amm. Marc. XXI.14.3–5 (*familiaris genius*); Aug. *Civ.* VIII.14 (*[numen] adiunctum et amicitia quadam conciliatum*); Lactant. *Div. Inst.* II.14.9 (*adsiduus daemon*), *Instit. Epit.* 23.2 (*a prima pueritia custodem rectoremque vitae suae daemonem*); Calcid. *in Ti.* 199.2 Wsz. (*comes daemon*; cf. 263.20–264.2 Wsz.); Clem. Al. *Strom.* V.14.91.3–4 (cf. VI.6.53.2–3, quoted in (iv) below); Ael. *VH* 8.1 (φωνὴν...ἐγκεκληρωμένην αὐτῷ); *sch. in Aristid.* 286.18 (III.715–16 Dind.: ἴδιος δαίμων); Eust. *ad Il.* I.198 (I.129.11 van der Valk: οἰκεῖος δαίμων). Tertullian's description of τὸ δαιμόνιον as *pessimus paedagogus* (*de Anima* I.4) reflects a very similar conception (cf. *adhaesisse* in *Apol.* 22.1; Waszink on *de Anima* I.5 *adflatui*); cf. δαίμων as *paedagogus* in Sen. *Ep.* 110.1, Lib. *Decl.* 45.2.6 (VII.533.1–3 F.), Chrys. *hom. in Ac.* 41.314, *hom. in Col.* 3.347; the opposite equation in Pl. *Lys.* 223a2–3; see further (v) below.

[3] This orthodoxy seems to have extended to the exegetical techniques and commonplaces employed within the tradition of commentary on τὸ δαιμόνιον. For instance, the comparison between the personal ties "Socrates~τὸ δαιμόνιον" and the Homeric "Odysseus/Achilles~Athena" apparently became standard fare in the tradition: Plu. *Mor.* 580c; Max. Tyr. 8.5 (64.77–65.104 T.); Apul. *Soc.* 33.3–5 M.; Jul. *Or.* IV.6 (201.28–32 Bidez: Achilles~Hera, but the latter unnamed); Eust. *ad Il.* I.198 (I.129.9–11 van der Valk); *sch. in Il.* I.198[3] (*Gen. gr.* 44); cf. also the pairing of Socrates and Odysseus as religious *exempla* in Epict. I.12.1–3; antecedents already in Pl. *Ap.* 28b9–d5, also *Cri.* 44a10–b2. See further L. Bieler, ΘΕΙΟΣ ΑΝΗΡ, I (Vienna: Höfels 1935) 87–8, with n.42; A.D. Nock, "The Emperor's Divine *Comes*," *JRS* 37 (1947)

have emerged in beliefs about τὸ δαιμόνιον is no cause for wonder. After the Academy's shift from scepticism to dogmatism in the first century B.C. one of the features of the Socratic personality which continued to inspire comment was Socrates' divine sign;[4] this interest was in turn fuelled by the considerable attention paid to demonological systems in Middle Platonism and Neoplatonism, into which there was a strong desire to integrate Socrates' sign.[5] But are the ingredients which we have identified both in Proclus' account and in the surveys and remarks of others restricted to literature dating from the first century B.C. and on? Numerous scholars, some highly influential, have answered this question in the affirmative.[6] I believe that certain early evidence (mostly from the Platonic and Xenophontean Corpora[7]) indicates otherwise and deserves a closer look than it has been given.

110–11 (= *Essays on Religion and the Ancient World*, II (Oxford: Clarendon Press 1972) 666–7); J. Beaujeu, *Apulée: Opuscules Philosophiques et Fragments*, Budé (Paris: Les Belles Lettres 1973) 243. The parallelism was a natural consequence of the wider comparison, popular in later Platonism, between Homer and Plato (see H. Dörrie-M. Baltes, *Der Platonismus in der Antike*, III (Stuttgart/Bad Cannstatt: Frommann-Holzboog 1993) 64, 250–5): as Achilles and Odysseus were to Homer, so Socrates was to Plato.

[4] "For Socrates the aporeticist Platonism, after its return to dogmatism, had little use" (P. Merlan in A.H. Armstrong (ed.), *The Cambridge History of Later Greek and Early Medieval Philosophy* (Cambridge: Cambridge University Press 1967) 34 n.2); see also Dörrie-Baltes (above, n.3) 315–16; R.F. Hathaway, "The Neoplatonist Interpretation of Plato: Remarks on its Decisive Characteristics," *JHPh* 7 (1969) 19–26.

[5] In particular, his sign came to be viewed as the example *par excellence* of the guardian δαίμων, one of three kinds of δαίμονες accepted in the Platonism of the Empire; see J. Dillon, *The Middle Platonists* (London: Duckworth 1977) 219–21, 317–20. For the interest of early Christian writers see A. Willing, *De Socratis daemonio quae antiquis temporibus fuerint opiniones* (Diss. Jena 1909) 164–6; R. Heinze, "Tertullians *Apologeticum*," Sitz. Ber., Phil.-Hist. Klass. 62 (1910) 407–9, 471–2.

[6] E.g. E. Zeller, *Die Philosophie der Griechen in ihrer geschichtlichen Entwicklung*, II.1[5] (repr. Berlin: Olms 1963) 75 n.2; H. Maier, *Sokrates, sein Werk und seine geschichtliche Stellung* (Tübingen: Mohr 1913) 453–4; E.R. Dodds, "Supernormal Phenomena in Classical Antiquity," *The Ancient Concept of Progress* (Oxford: Clarendon Press 1973) 192–3; P. Friedländer, *Plato*, I[2] (Princeton: Princeton University Press 1969) 36–7, 41.

[7] The Platonic Corpus: *Ap.* 31c7–d6, 40a4–c3, *Euthphr.* 3b5–6, *Euthd.* 272e3–273a1, *Phdr.* 242b8–c3, *R.* 496c3–5, *Tht.* 151a2–5, *Alc.* I 103a1–b2, 105e2–106a1, 124c2–d3, *Thg.* 128d2–131a10; the Xenophontean Corpus: *Ap.* 4–5, 8, 12–14, *Mem.* I.1.2–5, IV.3.12, 8.1, 5–6, *Smp.* 8.5–6. Like most commentators I do not think that the Platonic *Alc.* I and *Thg.* (which figure quite prominently in the following discussions) were written by Plato, though I accept that they are early compositions (perhaps 350–325 B.C.). For general orientation on the treatment of τὸ δαιμόνιον in these two dialogues see Willing (above, n.5) 139–48.

An important preliminary point must however be made here: neither Plato nor Xenophon, nor indeed the authors of *Alc.* I and *Thg.*, ever designated Socrates' sign with the word δαίμων.[8] In fact, the wide variety of terminologies that are employed by these writers[9] promotes the impression that this failure was really a studied attempt to avoid the term δαίμων altogether in connection with the phenomenon. Since we need not doubt that Socrates did lay claim to a "divine sign," it seems reasonable to suppose that the terminologies were those of Socrates himself and were taken over from him by Plato and Xenophon. This inference presents us with a Socrates who, because he knows only that his sign is *not* a δαίμων but does not know what it actually *is*, relies unswervingly upon a set of vague phrases and circumlocutions—a pattern of linguistic behaviour appropriate for the sceptical Socrates whom we recognize from numerous Platonic dialogues and from other early sources as well.[10] It is moreover hard to see how the Platonic Socrates could sustain the assertion that his sign found virtually no parallel among all who had gone before him (*R.* 496c4–5) if he had called the phenomenon a δαίμων, a word which would have conjured up a fairly specific body of inherited belief, in particular the belief that individual δαίμονες accompanied or were allotted to *everybody*.[11] So there were

---

[8] For contrary evidence it is particularly fruitless to cite Pl. *Ap.* 26b2–28a1, which says nothing about Socrates' sign, much less that it is a δαίμων, or the product or offspring of a δαίμων or of Apollo (so C.D.C. Reeve, *Socrates in the Apology* (Indianapolis/Cambridge: Hackett 1989) 68–9, 26 n.27; cf. M.L. McPherran, "Socratic Reason and Socratic Revelation," *JHPh* 29 (1991) 353–4, with n.22).

[9] τὸ δαιμόνιον: Pl. *Ap.* 40a4, *Euthph.* 3b5, *Euthd.* 272e4, *Phdr.* 242b8–9; X. *Mem.* I.1.2, 4, *Ap.* 4, 13 etc.; τὸ γιγνόμενον μοι δαιμόνιον: *Tht.* 151a4; τὸ δαιμόνιον σημεῖον: *R.* 496c4; θεῖόν τι καὶ δαιμόνιον: Pl. *Ap.* 31c8–d1; τὸ εἰωθὸς σημεῖον: Pl. *Ap.* 40c2–3, *Euthd.* 272e3–4, *Phdr.* 242b9; τὸ τοῦ θεοῦ σημεῖον: Pl. *Ap.* 40b1; ἡ...εἰωθυῖά μοι μαντική: Pl. *Ap.* 40a4; φωνή τις: Pl. *Ap.* 31d3, *Phdr.* 242c1–2; X. *Ap.* 12 (φωνή *simpliciter*); certain of these phrases are sometimes conjoined (e.g. Pl. *Ap.* 40a4, *Euthd.* 272e3–4, *Phdr.* 242b8–9).

[10] See Zeller (above, n.6) 77 and n.2; H. Gundert, "Platon und das Daimonion des Sokrates," *Gymnasium* 61 (1954) 513–31; M. Nussbaum, "Commentary on Edmunds," J.J. Cleary (ed.), *Proceedings of the Boston Area Colloquium in Ancient Philosophy*, I (Lanham MD: University Press of America 1986) 233–5 ("an ironic way of alluding to the supreme authority of dissuasive reason and elenctic argument" [234] — surely an extreme view); also Gigon on X. *Mem.* I.1.3–4. Socrates' efforts not to pin his sign down to precise terms were enhanced by the fact that the phrase τὸ δαιμόνιον was current as a designation for undifferentiated divinity or divine activity; cf., e.g., Pl. *R.* 382e6; X. *Mem.* I.4.2, 10; Hdt. 2.120; E. *Ba.* 894; D. 19.239, 21.126; Hyp. *Epit.* 43; Arist. *Rh.* 1398ª15; Hipp. [?] *Morb. Sacr.* 3.

[11] Reflected both in Plato's demonology (cf. *R.* 620d8ff., *Phd.* 107d6–7, *Ti.* 90a2ff.)

specific reasons why the term δαίμων was avoided in early presentations of Socrates' sign. But as we have seen, a great many later writers were not inclined to be so scrupulous.

Yet despite fundamental differences in approach and treatment over a thousand years and more, a line of development in the transformation of Socrates' sign into a fully fledged δαίμων, clearer than has been thought to exist, can be discerned. The following notes (on ten of the passages cited in n.7) attempt simply to identify a few points on this line and are intended to be suggestive rather than exhaustive; a complete synthesis of all the evidence remains to be done.

II. Elements in the Transformation

(i) Pl. *Ap.* 31d1-2 and [Pl.] *Thg.* 128d3: In both these passages τὸ δαιμόνιον is described as ἐκ παιδὸς ἀρξάμενον (for text see n.15). This calls to mind a detail reminiscent of popular beliefs about δαίμονες, namely, that a δαίμων attaches itself to a person from birth.[12] The phrase ἐκ παιδὸς is itself ambiguous, since it can mean "from childhood," i.e. "in early years" (e.g. *Lys.* 211d7, *R.* 374c7), or "from earliest childhood," i.e. "from birth" (e.g. *R.* 608c6, *Lg.* 854e5-6), and it cannot be said with certainty what the precise reference in *Ap.* 31d1-2 was meant to be. Hence ἐκ παιδὸς ἀρξάμενον was suggestive enough to prove fertile in the minds of subsequent writers: for the nexus of associations in *Thg.* see (ii) and (iv) below; in Plutarch (*Mor.* 580c) the words gave rise to προποδηγὸν ἐξ ἀρχῆς τινα (a phraseology probably inspired by *Thg.* rather than *Ap.*[13]); Calcidius' translation of *Thg.* 128d3

---

and in popular religious belief; cf. Heraclit. DK 22 B 119 ἦθος ἀνθρώπῳ δαίμων, perhaps already a reaction against the notion of external influence from an allotted δαίμων. See Wilamowitz-Moellendorff, *Der Glaube der Hellenen*, I³ (Basel: Schwabe 1959) 362; E.R. Dodds, *The Greeks and the Irrational* (Berkeley: University of California Press 1951) 42-3; J.M. Rist, "Plotinus and the *Daimonion* of Socrates," *Phoenix* 17 (1963) 15-16; S. Darcus "*Daimon* as a Force Shaping *Ethos* in Heraclitus," *Phoenix* 28 (1974) 394-407 (with extensive survey of early evidence).

[12] Cf. the oft-cited Men. fr. 714 S.: ἅπαντι δαίμων ἀνδρὶ συμπαρίσταται εὐθὺς γενομένῳ μυσταγωγὸς τοῦ βίου; also Pi. *Ol.* 13.105 (δαίμων γενέθλιος), 9.28-9; Emped. DK 31 B 122; the belief underlies *Phd.* 107d6-7 ὁ ἑκάστου δαίμων, ὅσπερ ζῶντα εἰλήχει κτλ. (Plato however reacts against this traditional way of thinking in *R.* 617e1); see H. Usener, *Götternamen. Versuch einer Lehre von der Religiösen Begriffsbildung*² (Bonn: Cohen 1929) 295-7; P. Boyancé, "Les deux démons personnels dans l'antiquité grecque et latine," *RPh* 61 (1935) 189-202; and n.11 above.

[13] See my "A Lost Plutarchean Philosophical Work," *Philologus* 137 (1993) 94-5.

(263.20–1 Wsz.) produced *ab ineunte aetate*; while Lactantius' *a prima pueritia custodem* (see n.2 above) is perhaps less unequivocal about the time of life to which it refers.[14]

(ii) *Thg.* 128d2: Here, in part of a passage which runs closely parallel with Pl. *Ap.* 31c8–d4 (the *locus classicus* for the sign), we are told that τὸ δαιμόνιον attends Socrates θείᾳ μοίρᾳ (a detail absent from the *Ap.* passage).[15] The collocation of θείᾳ μοίρᾳ[16] and τὸ δαιμόνιον is unique and its presence here worth considering. Possibly θείᾳ μοίρᾳ simply underlines the extraordinary favour Socrates was shown by the attachment to him of τὸ δαιμόνιον (cf. X. *Ap.* 13–14, *Mem.* IV.3.12). But frequently in classical and earlier Greek literature a δαίμων is closely connected in one way or another with (θεία) μοῖρα.[17] The association

For the force of Plutarch's τινα see n.15 below.

[14] ἐκ παιδὸς ἀρξάμενον was influential in other ways too: to it may ultimately be traced both Tertullian's metaphor of *paedagogus* in *de Anima* I.4 (see Waszink *ad loc.* and n.2 above) and Plutarch's hagiographical story (*Mor.* 589e–f) of the oracle about Socrates' "guide" given to his father when Socrates was a boy.

[15] *Ap.* 31c8–d4: μοι θεῖόν τι καὶ δαιμόνιον γίγνεται [φωνή]...ἐμοὶ δὲ τοῦτ' ἔστιν ἐκ παιδὸς ἀρξάμενον, φωνή τις γιγνομένη, ἣ ὅταν γένηται, ἀεὶ ἀποτρέπει με τοῦτο ὃ ἂν μέλλω πράττειν, προτρέπει δὲ οὔποτε. *Thg.* 128d2–5: ἔστι γάρ τι θείᾳ μοίρᾳ παρεπόμενον ἐμοὶ ἐκ παιδὸς ἀρξάμενον δαιμόνιον. ἔστι δὲ τοῦτο φωνή, ἣ ὅταν γένηται ἀεί μοι σημαίνει, ὃ ἂν μέλλω πράττειν, τούτου ἀποτροπήν, προτρέπει δὲ οὐδέποτε. On Forster's seclusion of φωνή from *Ap.* 31d1 Burnet writes (*ad loc.*) that the word "could only mean here 'as a voice' (pred.), and that seems very harsh." I would add that elsewhere Plato does not call Socrates' sign φωνή, but rather φωνή τις, "a kind of voice," "a voice, as it were," which is certainly more diffident (*Ap.* 31d3, *Phdr.* 242c1–2 [even less assertive: τινα φωνὴν ἔδοξα αὐτόθεν ἀκοῦσαι]). Apuleius makes a very similar point (*Soc.* 32.8–11 M.): *at enim Socrates non vocem sibi sed vocem quampiam dixit oblatam, quo additamento profecto intellegas non usitatam vocem nec humanam significari* (cf. 31.10–12 M.); and he could hardly have generalized in this way if his text of Pl. *Ap.* had carried the errant φωνή (cf. Plu. *Mor.* 588d: τὸ δαιμόνιον is φωνῆς τινος αἴσθησις). For the "softening" τις cf. *Men.* 72a7, *Phd.* 62b3–4, and see J. Riddell, *A Digest of Platonic Idioms* (repr. Amsterdam: Hakkert 1967) 28.

[16] On the expression see, e.g., W.C. Greene, *Moira: Fate, Good, and Evil in Greek Thought* (Cambridge MA: Harvard University Press 1944); E.G. Berry, *The History and Development of the Concept of ΘΕΙΑ ΜΟΙΡΑ and ΘΕΙΑ ΤΥΧΗ down to and including Plato* (Diss. Chicago 1940); B.C. Dietrich, *Death, Fate, and the Gods* (London: Athlone 1965) 59–90, 194–231.

[17] E.g. δαίμων and (θεία) μοῖρα coupled or virtually equated: Emped. DK 31 B 122, S. *Ph.* 1466–8, *OT* 802–3, E. *IA* 1136, *Hel.* 211–12; δαίμων proceeding from (θεία) μοῖρα· Ar. *Thesm.* 1047, Pl. *Crat.* 398b10–c1; (θεία) μοῖρα allotted by (or to) a δαίμων: E. *Andr.* 1007–8, *Lys.* 2.78 (cf. Bacchyl. *Epin.* 14.1 Irigoin εὖ εἱμάρθαι παρὰ δαίμονος, Herm. *in Phdr.* 136.14–5 C. τοὺς μοιρηγέτας δαίμονας). For the relationship see Wilamowitz-Moellendorff (above, n.11) 356–63; Dodds (above, n.11)

was quite a natural one since the words were probably thought to be semantically related: a popular etymology of δαίμων gave it the meaning of "apportioner" (deriving it from δαίω),[18] while μοῖρα (from μείρομαι) always conveyed the meaning of "lot" or "share."[19]

I think it likely that (genuine) Plato had no inclination to link θεία μοῖρα with τὸ δαιμόνιον because such a connection would have strongly marked out Socrates' sign as an apportioned or allotted guardian spirit, that is, as a δαίμων.[20] But the author of *Thg.* obviously felt less compunction; and the same was no doubt true of later writers who articulated similar conceptions; cf. Max. Tyr. 8.6 (66.135–6 T.): οὐκ ἄξιον ἡγεῖ τὸν Σωκράτην μοίρας δαιμονίου κτλ. (also 8.8 [69.205–6

---

[23] n.65, 58 n.79; R.B. Onians, *The Origins of European Thought* (Cambridge: Cambridge University Press 1953²) 403–8; K.J. Dover, *Greek Popular Morality* (Oxford: Blackwell 1974) 138–41.

[18] See W. Burkert (tr. J. Raffan), *Greek Religion* (Cambridge, MA: Harvard University Press 1985) 420 n.1; Dietrich (above, n.16) 14, with n.1; West on Hes. *Op.* 122.

[19] See Berry (above, n.16) 1–3; Greene (above, n.16) 401–2; Dietrich (above, n.16) 11–13. With the pair δαίμων-μοῖρα cf. the frequent connection of δαίμων and λαγχάνω, e.g. Pi. *N.* 9.45, A. *Su.* 693, S. *OC* 1337, E. *Hel.* 211–12, Pl. *Phd.* 107d6–7, *R.* 617e1, Lys. 2.78, Theoc. 4.40 (see Gow *ad loc.*); and for the pair μοῖρα-λαγχάνω see J. Diggle, *Studies on the Text of Euripides* (Oxford: Clarendon Press 1981) 11.

[20] It is true that, according to Socrates (*Ap.* 33c4–7), θεία μοῖρα conveyed the signs which indicated that he must take up his mission of elenchus. But these signs are to be distinguished from the "messages" he received from τὸ δαιμόνιον (so Burnet *ad loc., pace,* e.g., J. Souilhé, *La notion platonicienne d'intermédiaire* (Paris: Alcan 1919) 201–2, esp. n.498; G. Vlastos, *Socrates, Ironist and Moral Philosopher* (Ithaca, NY: Cornell University Press 1991) 167, 170, 172, 284); for the commands given to him by god through oracles and dreams (ἐκ μαντείων καὶ ἐξ ἐνυπνίων c5) provided positive instructions (πράττειν c5), while τὸ δαιμόνιον was, in Plato, purely inhibitory. Moreover, Socrates' mission was enjoined on him in adulthood, whereas τὸ δαιμόνιον had attended him since he was a child (see (i) above). Here Plato's attitude may be contrasted with Xenophon's: whereas Xenophon sought to classify τὸ δαιμόνιον as a species of conventional μαντική (*Mem.* I.1.2–9) and thus to mitigate the opprobrium attaching to Socrates from popular stories about his divine sign, Plato clearly wanted to distinguish the two phenomena (see Zeller [above, n.6] 79 n.1; Willing (above, n.5) 130–5; Maier (above, n.6) 450–2; Gigon on *Mem.* I.1.2ff.; A. Dihle, *Studien zur griechischen Biographie* (Göttingen: Vandenhoeck & Ruprecht 1970²) 30–1; cf. Apul. *Socr.* 31.10–32.14 M.). Yet what *is* certainly conceivable is that *Ap.* 33c4–7 — misunderstood, as it has been by some modern scholars — exerted a direct influence on *Thg.* (as *Ap.* 31c8–d2 had done, see n.15 above), where Socrates' prophetic abilities endow him with the character of "wise adviser" (for μαντική as the product of θεία μοῖρα cf. also *Phdr.* 244a7–8, c3). Cicero's apparent confusion of τὸ δαιμόνιον with Apollo (*Div.* I.122) could have resulted from precisely this misinterpretation of *Ap.* 33c4-7 (for similar instances of exegesis through recourse to other Platonic passages see (vii) below and n.47).

T.] εἴληχεν); Procl. *in Alc.* 82.30 S.: τὸ Σωκρατικὸν δαιμόνιον, τοιαύτην ἰδιότητα λαχόν κτλ.; Ael. *VH* 8.1: φωνὴν…θείᾳ πομπῇ[21] *ἐγκεκληρωμένην* αὐτῷ (in a loose paraphrase of *Thg.* 128d2–129a1); also Calcid. 199.1 Wsz.: *id quod* sortiti sumus *singuli numen* (immediately before a paraphrase of *Thg.* 128d2–5, see Waszink's *app. font.*).[22]

(iii) Pl. *Ap.* 40a8–c3: Non-intervention from his sign is taken by Socrates as a guarantee that a contemplated course of action — his appearance in court the day of his trial — is the right one. But if Plato thought of τὸ δαιμόνιον quite generally as a guide at every moment in Socrates' life, whose non-intervention indicated its tacit encouragement, and believed that the sign was thus infallible as Socrates' guardian, he failed to say so anywhere else. That it is in the least implied here produces a remarkable inconsistency: it turns out that the inactivity of the sign was not quite enough to prevent Socrates in his final words (*Ap.* 42a2–5; cf. 29a4–b6, 37b5–7) from expressing his agnosticism about whether death is a good thing![23]

Apparently Plato was not very committed to this aspect of the efficacy of τὸ δαιμόνιον. Nor was Xenophon; but he may at least have been more inclined towards this view of Socrates' sign, since he assumes (*Mem.* IV.8.1–6, *Ap.* 5–6) that if death were not the better course for Socrates, an occurrence of τὸ δαιμόνιον would have indicated this to

---

[21] ὁσίᾳ πομπῇ Dilts (ὁσίαν πομπῆς mss., *corr.* Faber). The emendation (Davisius) is convincing, both as a reminiscence of θείᾳ μοίρᾳ and as the product of an easy majuscule confusion ΘΕΙΑΙ-ΟΣΙΑΙ (cf. Pl. *Grg.* 492b2 ὅσοις F, θεοῖς BTP). θεία πομπή is common: Hdt. 1.62.4, 3.77.1, 4.152.2, Ael. *NA* 3.47, Plu. *Mor.* 323e, *Rom.* 9.7, Aristid. I.36, 37 L-B, Joseph. *AJ* 11.335; whereas ὁσίᾳ πομπῇ would be, as far as I can tell, otherwise unexampled.

[22] See also n.47 below. I wonder too if Procl. *in Alc.* 165.22–4 S. is a reflex of *Thg.*: καὶ γὰρ τὸν ἀγαθὸν δαίμονα σύμπορον ἡμῶν εἰώθασι λέγειν καὶ ἕπεσθαί φασιν ἡμῖν αὐτὸν ἐκ θείας ὁρμῆς; n.b. in particular the conjunction of ἕπεσθαι (cf. παρεπόμενον in *Thg.* 128d2, see (iv) below) and θείας ὁρμῆς (cf. *Phdr.* 279a9, *Prm.* 135d2–3).

[23] Much is made of this inconsistency in T.C. Brickhouse and N.D. Smith, *Socrates on Trial* (Princeton NJ: Princeton University Press 1988) 237–57, where this eccentric, *ad hoc* account of the passivity of τὸ δαιμόνιον is turned into a basis for wide-ranging conclusions about the nature of Socrates' sign which go far beyond our (scanty) textual evidence. The authors' conviction that Socrates' remarks in *Ap.* must all cohere with one another is predicated upon the assumption that *Ap.* is essentially an historical document (see also McPherran (above, n.8) 345–73). Only in the educational sphere does Socrates explicitly hold the sign's inactivity to be positive grounds for continuing on a course of action (*Tht.* 151a2–5, see further below; also P. Friedländer, *Der Grosse Alcibiades*, II (Bonn: Cohen 1923) 23–4).

him. Xenophon therefore felt bound to explain the sign's silence: Socrates was already old, and death saved him from the inevitable collapse of his intellectual powers (*Mem.* IV.8.1); yet, Xenophon adds, τὸ δαιμόνιον *did* occur to Socrates after all — when he was contemplating his defence (IV.8.5). Possibly we are looking here at Plato's and Xenophon's responses to an uncomfortable problem with which early Socratics had to wrestle in the years following 399: Why did Socrates' sign, which occurred to him even "on quite trivial occasions" (Pl. *Ap.* 40a5–6), not steer him away from certain death?[24]

However that may be, what was at most merely implicit in Plato and Xenophon is brought more clearly to the fore in *Alc.* I: Socrates is at liberty to associate with Alcibiades since τὸ δαιμόνιον no longer prevents him from doing so (103a1–b2; cf. *Tht.* 151a2–5; X. *Smp.* 8.5); later this approval which Socrates has inferred from the inactivity of τὸ δαιμόνιον is made active and explicit: νῦν δ' ἐφῆκεν (106a1; contrast ἐᾷ in *Tht.* 151a5). Buttressed by this dialogue Olympiodorus could take it for granted centuries later that the non-opposition of τὸ δαιμόνιον was the equivalent of a protreptic force: ἀεὶ αὐτὸν ἀπέτρεπεν [sc. τὸ δαιμόνιον], καὶ σύμβολον ἦν προτροπῆς τὸ ποτὲ μὴ ἀποτρέπειν (*in Alc.* 21.2–3 W., cf. 59.6–8 W.; Clem. Al. *Strom.* I.17.83.4). The temptation to subscribe to this view is displayed in modern scholarship too: "In the silence of the demonic, Socrates might also have felt and recognized an element of positive co-operation."[25]

(iv) *Thg.* 128d2: From childhood the sign has "attended" Socrates (παρεπόμενον). This is the only place in the Platonic Corpus where ἕπομαι or a compound is used in association with the activity of τὸ δαιμόνιον. Yet the word is frequently applied to the behaviour of δαίμονες, both in Plato and elsewhere.[26] The reason why Plato (and Xenophon) did not predicate this word of τὸ δαιμόνιον is simply this:

---

[24] See O. Gigon, "Xenophons Apologie des Sokrates," *MH* 3 (1946) 233–9. Cf. the issue of Socrates' μεγαληγορία at his trial, which Xenophon considered it necessary to address in response to others who had written on the topic (cf. *Ap.* 1); see A.-H. Chroust, *Socrates: Man and Myth* (Notre Dame, IN: University of Notre Dame Press 1957) 17–22.

[25] Friedländer (above, n.6) 34 (= *Platon*, I³ (Berlin: de Gruyter 1964) 36); also Vlastos (above, n.20) 161.

[26] E.g. Pi. *P.* 3.108; Pl. *Phdr.* 246e6, *Lg.* 730a1–2, 848d2 (of τις...τῶν κρειττόνων in *Sph.* 216b4); Posidon. F 187.6–7 E-K; Plot. III.5.4; Procl. *in Alc.* 165.22–4 (quoted in n.22 above).

παρεπόμενον implies the omnipresence of the sign (the παρ- prefix reinforces this[27]) and its consequent status as a tutelary deity carefully watching over and protecting a person at all times.[28] But while such omnipresence is never stressed as a characteristic of τὸ δαιμόνιον in extant fourth-century Socratic literature,[29] it is not difficult to see it as a development from passages discussed in (iii) above.

Some later writers, possibly taking their cue from *Thg.*, or perhaps simply drawing upon traditional demonological language, also apply παρέπομαι *vel sim.* to Socrates' sign: Max. Tyr. 8.1 (61.2–3 T.): θαυμάζεις εἰ Σωκράτει συνῆν δαιμόνιον...ἀεὶ παρεπόμενον (ἀεὶ is a telling qualification, cf. Pi. *P.* 3.108–9 τὸν δ' ἀμφέποντ' αἰεὶ ...δαίμον'; contrast ἑκάστοτε γίγνεσθαι *Euthphr.* 3b3); Isidore *ap.* Clem. Al. *Strom.* VI.6.53.2–3 (fr. 6 Volker): φασὶ δὲ οἱ 'Αττικοὶ μεμηνῦσθαί τινα Σωκράτει παρεπομένου δαίμονος αὐτῷ (παρ' ἐπομένου ci. H. Jackson, *JPhil* 28 (1903) 131); Jul. *Or.* IV.6 (201.26–8 Bidez): εἵπετό [n.b. impf.] τοι καὶ Σωκράτει δαιμονία φωνὴ κωλύουσα πράττειν ὅσα μὴ χρεὼν ἦν; cf. Procl. *in Alc.* 83.17–18 S.: ἀνάλογον ὁ μὲν δαίμων ἐστὶ τῷ 'Απόλλωνι, ὀπαδὸς ὢν αὐτοῦ (cf. Procl. *in Ti.* III.262.16–17 Diehl; Philo *Conf.* 174); Aristid. II.79–80 L–B: οὐ γάρ ἐστιν ὅστις οὐ λέγει περὶ Σωκράτους ὅτι φάσκοι τὸ δαιμόνιον αὐτῷ σημαίνειν. οὐκοῦν μηδὲν μὲν ἐπίστασθαι τῶν δεόντων ἀμήχανον ᾧ γε *παρηκολούθει* [n.b. impf.] τὸ δαιμόνιον;[30] Suda IV.404 Adler (*s.v.* Σωκράτης): δαιμόνιον δ' αὐτῷ *προσομιλεῖν* ἔλεγεν (cf. Eust. *ad Il.* VII.53 [II.395.12–14 van der Valk] ὁμιλεῖν).[31]

---

[27] Cf. ὁ παρὼν δαίμων in A. *Pers.* 825, S. *El.* 1306, fr. 653 R., E. *Alc.* 561, *Andr.* 974.

[28] The role which a δαίμων plays as guardian or attendant in Greek belief is clearly very old, cf. Hes. *Op.* 121–3, and see Beaujeu (above, n.3) 187–8; Darcus (above, n.11).

[29] Hence Plato regularly uses the instantaneous γίγνεσθαι for occurrences of the sign (*Ap.* 31d1, 3, *Euthphr.* 3b6 [presented as a quotation of Socrates, n.b. φῄς], *Euthd.* 272e3, *Phdr.* 242b9, *Tht.* 151a4); see also Willing (above, n.5) 131–2; Burnet on *Euthphr.* 3b5. The view that Socrates' sign was something that "just happens" takes an extreme form in the belief expressed in Plu. *Mor.* 581a–c that the sign was a sneeze, both Socrates' and another's (cf. also *scholia Arethae* on *Ap.* 31c8–d1).

[30] See J. Puiggali, "ΔΑΙΜΩΝ et les mots de la même famille chez Aelius Aristide," *CM* 36 (1985) 123–4.

[31] The substitution παραπεμπόμενον *pro* παρεπόμενον in *Frag. Comm. in Arist. Rh.* 325.6 Rabe (in a loose quotation of *Thg.* 128d2–7) suggests that its author took for granted the demonological character of the *Thg.* passage, since πέμπω and related forms are not infrequently applied to δαίμονες (F. Pfister, *RE* suppl. 7, 106; see n.21

Some of the Latin vocabulary cited in n.2 above is analogous, especially *adsidens* (Min. Fel.), *adsiduus* (Lactant.), *comes* (Calcid. [actually translating παρεπόμενον of *Thg.* in 263.21 Wsz.] and Apul.), *paedagogus* (Tert.). A special influence on the use of *adsidens* and *adsiduus* in this context — and so, perhaps, on notions about Socrates' sign — seems to have been the concept of the δαίμων πάρεδρος, which appears with great frequency in the magical papyri and is, of course, linguistically parallel with the Latin terms.[32]

Before concluding this brief analysis we must also take note of Plato's remarks in *Smp.* 203c2 about the μέγας δαίμων: τῆς 'Αφροδίτης ἀκόλουθος καὶ θεράπων γέγονεν ὁ ῎Ερως. Given that this description of ῎Ερως occurs within antiquity's most influential discussion about δαίμονες, it seems reasonable to suggest that *Smp.* 203c2 conditioned the conception of τὸ δαιμόνιον evidenced by the wording of *Thg.* 128d2; see (v), (vi), (vii) below for further possible dependence on Diotima's speech in *Smp.*

(v) *Alc.* I 124c5–10: ὁ θεός, which in this dialogue is identified with τὸ δαιμόνιον (cf. 103a5–6 τι δαιμόνιον ἐναντίωμα, 105d5–6 τὸν θεὸν οὐκ ἐᾶν, e7 οὐκ εἴα ὁ θεός, and 124c8–9 οὐκ εἴα [sc. ὁ θεός]), is called by Socrates ὁ ἐπίτροπος ὁ ἐμὸς (c5). For θεός as ἐπίτροπος cf. Pi. *Ol.* 1.106 (Zeus; see Gerber *ad loc.*); and for ἐπίτροπος of a tutelary δαίμων cf. Epict. I.14.12, Them. *Or.* XIII 180a10; also Iamb. *Myst.* 6.7, Hld. *Aeth.* I.26.4. Within the same semantic field as ἐπίτροπος is φύλαξ, which appears very often in connection with δαίμονες (see (vi) below; cf. *custos* of τὸ δαιμόνιον in Lactant. [n.2 above], of δαίμων in Sen. *Ep.* 41.2).

But since ἐπίτροπος can be used of an older guardian (e.g. *Alc.* I 104b5, *Chrm.* 176c1, *Lg.* 766c5–d2), we are likely to be reminded also of the various applications of *paedagogus* to δαίμων and (Tertullian's) to τὸ δαιμόνιον, and of the reverse simile (παιδαγωγός as δαίμων) in *Lys.* 223a2, all cited in n.2 above (cf. *Alc.* I 124c2 παιδευθῆναι, d2 ἐπιμελείας). In fact the application of an educational metaphor to τὸ δαιμόνιον can be found in several authors: Plu. *Mor.* 589e–f:

---

above, and cf. Pl. *R.* 620d8). But παραπεμπόμενον may be a genuine and respectably ancient variant; see further my note "Aelian, *Varia Historia* 8.1" (forthcoming).

[32] See K. Preisendanz, *RE* 18.4, 1428–53; Waszink (above, n.1) 93, 362–3, and *id.*, *Timaeus a Calcidio Translatus Commentarioque Instructus* (London: Warburg Institute 1962) 199.

κρείττονα...ἐν αὐτῷ μυρίων διδασκάλων καὶ παιδαγωγῶν ἡγεμόνα πρὸς τὸν βίον; ps.-Socr. *Ep.* 1.10: διδάσκοντος τοῦ θεοῦ [i.e. τοῦ δαιμονίου]; Philostr. *VA* 313.30–1 Kayser: τί οὖν ἐνταῦθα ἐρεῖ Σωκράτης ὑπὲρ ὧν ἔφασκε τοῦ δαιμονίου μανθάνειν; Calcid. 199.2 Wsz. (Socrates' sign as *praeceptor*); Suda IV.404 Adler (see (iv) above: the context is the intellectual influences on Socrates and his influence on others; for προσομιλεῖν in this sense see LSJ *s.v.* I.3, Lampe *s.v.* 7); *sch. in Aristid.* 286.18 (III.715–16 Dind.): εἰσάγει Πλάτων τὸν Σωκράτην παρὰ τοῦ ἰδίου δαίμονος ἅπαντα διδασκόμενον. For a precedent for pedagogical τὸ δαιμόνιον (where others, not Socrates, are the beneficiaries) we may look beyond *Alc.* I to *Thg.* 129e1–130e4, a passage which illustrates ἡ δύναμις τοῦ δαιμονίου (129e1–2; see also (vi), (vii), (viii) below) through Socrates' account of the experiences of the young Aristides. Aristides claimed that he improved (ἐπεδίδουν 130d5) in proportion to his physical proximity to Socrates, and asserted (130d4) that "I never learned anything from *you*[33] (sc. Socrates)." This left it open for readers to infer that it was, instead, τὸ δαιμόνιον from whom Aristides' "learned"; his story, after all, was intended to exemplify its influence. And the account in *Thg.* is in its own right an aberration, since it represents a distortion of the role played by τὸ δαιμόνιον in the famous μαιευτική passage in *Tht.* (150d2–151a5).[34]

Yet the pedagogical interpretation of τὸ δαιμόνιον was promoted not only by distortion of *Tht.* but also by assimilation of τὸ δαιμόνιον to Platonic, educative Ἔρως. Aristides asserts in *Thg.* that he made his greatest progress when he sat right beside Socrates and touched him (130e1–3; cf. *Smp.* 175d3–7[35]). This effect illustrates the remarkable influence of τὸ δαιμόνιον as it operates through Socrates (now ἔνθεος, as it were);[36] another name for it is τὰ ἐρωτικά, precisely the one μάθημα to which Socrates had earlier in the dialogue laid claim (128b2–4). Now the words he uses there are strongly reminiscent of

[33] Reading παρὰ σοῦ with all editors (and BTW) except Burnet and Souilhé (παρά σου).
[34] See my *op. cit.* (above, n.13) 96 n.20; and for the pedagogical interpretation of τὸ δαιμόνιον, Gundert (above, n.10) 530 n.16.
[35] A parallel often noticed, e.g. D. Tarrant, "The Touch of Socrates," *CQ* 52 (1958) 95.
[36] Cf. the characterization of Socrates in Pl. *Smp.* as δαιμόνιος ἀνήρ and as the personification of Ἔρως (see (vi) below, and P. Hadot, "La Figure de Socrate," *Eranos-Jahrbuch* 43 (1974) 69–82); also Max. Tyr. 8.1 (61.3–4 T.): τὸ δαιμόνιον was μόνον οὐ τῇ γνώμῃ αὐτοῦ ἀνακεκραμένον; also 8.3 (63.46 T.) συγγίγνεσθαι τῷ δαιμονίῳ, (63.62 T.) τῇ πρὸς τὸ δαιμόνιον συνουσίᾳ.

those in *Smp.* 177d6–7 (οὐδέν φημι ἄλλο ἐπίστασθαι ἢ τὰ ἐρωτικά) which prefigure both his account of the mysteries of Ἔρως and Alcibiades' encomium of Socrates. Since in *Thg.* the miraculous educational effect of physical closeness to Socrates reflects the influence (ἡ δύναμις) of τὸ δαιμόνιον, and this effect may be identified as τὰ ἐρωτικά, it is very tempting to believe that τὸ δαιμόνιον has been implicitly conceived here as none other than Ἔρως, the μέγας δαίμων. Plato of course never identifies the two;[37] yet the identification in *Thg.* was possibly encouraged by *Phdr.* 242b8–c3, where τὸ δαιμόνιον prevents Socrates from crossing the Ilissos to return to Athens, thus affording him the opportunity to atone for the wrong he has committed against Ἔρως.[38]

The identification seems implicit also in *Alc.* I: Socrates is Alcibiades' ἐραστής (e.g. 103a2, 104c5, e4–6, 135e1–3); ὁ θεός (i.e. τὸ δαιμόνιον) has played an active role in drawing Socrates and Alcibiades together (106a1 ἐφῆκεν); so it is hard to resist the conclusion that ὁ θεός/τὸ δαιμόνιον here represents the erotic impulse. Proclus certainly thought it did (*in Alc.* 60ff. S., esp. 62.16ff., 63.13ff.). But the connection between τὸ δαιμόνιον and Ἔρως was apparently not commonly made (but cf. Plotinus' reflections [III.5.4] on Ἔρως as ὁ ἑκάστου δαίμων).

(vi) *Thg.* 129e7–8: οἷς δ' ἂν συλλάβηται τῆς συνουσίας ἡ τοῦ δαιμονίου δύναμις κτλ. The verb συλλαμβάνω, used here to denote the "assistance" provided by τὸ δαιμόνιον (or rather, by ἡ τοῦ δαιμονίου δύναμις), also occurs frequently to describe the activities of vague divine co-operation or intervention: cf. *Phdr.* 237a7–9, S. fr. 927 R., E. fr. 432 N., Ar. *Vesp.* 733–4.[39] As used in *Thg.* the word is redolent of conventional beliefs about divine behaviour.[40]

This fact seems not to have been lost on at least one later interpreter who quoted *Thg.* 129e7–9 to explicate the participatory role of δαίμονες. The author of [Plu.] *de fato* comments (*Mor.* 574b–c):

---

[37] Pace L. Strauss, *Studies in Platonic Political Philosophy* (Chicago IL: University of Chicago Press 1983) 46–7; T. Pangle, "Socrates on the Problem of Political Science Education," *Political Theory* 13 (1985) 132–3.

[38] See also D. Clay, "Socrates' Prayer to Pan," G.W. Bowersock, W. Burkert and M.C.J. Putnam (eds.), *Arktouros: Hellenic Studies presented to Bernard M.W. Knox* (Berlin: de Gruyter 1979) 349–50.

[39] Further passages in Fraenkel on A. *Ag.* 811.

[40] This point is overlooked and the force of συλλάβηται seriously fudged by W.S. Cobb, "Plato's *Theages*," *AncPhil* 12 (1992) 275–7.

οὐκοῦν ἐν τούτῳ τὸ μὲν συλλαμβάνειν τισὶ τὸ δαιμόνιον κατὰ τὴν τρίτην πρόνοιαν θετέον; this τρίτη πρόνοια is πρόνοιά τε καὶ προμήθεια τῶν ὅσοι περὶ γῆν *δαίμονες τεταγμένοι τῶν ἀνθρωπίνων πράξεων φύλακές τε καὶ ἐπισκοποί εἰσι* (573a; for δαίμονες as φύλακες cf. Hes. *Op.* 123, Pl. *R.* 620d8, Epict. I.14.12, Procl. *in Alc.* 79.16 S., and often). Possibly Proclus also had *Thg.* in mind when he remarks near the end of his comment on the lemma *Alc.* I 103a6 νῦν...b2 αὐτό (93.13–15 S.): οὐκοῦν ὅσῳ μᾶλλον ὁ νεανίσκος ἐπιδίδωσιν [cf. ἐπιδιδόασιν, ἐπιδιδόντων *Thg.* 129e9, ἐπιδιδόασιν 130a3] ἐκ τῶν ἐν φιλοσοφίᾳ λόγων, τοσούτῳ πλέον ὑπελάμβανε [sc. Socrates] καὶ τὸν δαίμονα *συλλήψεσθαι αὐτῷ πρὸς τὸν ἔρωτα*.

The cognate noun συλλήπτωρ is similarly used of a supernatural accomplice: cf. A. *Ag.* 1507, E. *Or.* 1230. The word is so employed in Max. Tyr. 8.7 (68.177–9 T.) with apparently general reference, though Maximus is in fact attempting to determine the nature of Socrates' sign as δαίμων: ἔνθα δὴ αὐτῇ [sc. ἀρετῇ] θεοῦ δεῖ συλλήπτορος καὶ συναγωνιστοῦ καὶ παραστάτου (cf. also 8.7 τούτοις καὶ τὸ θεῖον ἐθέλει ξυνίστασθαί τε καὶ *συνεπιλαμβάνειν* τοῦ βίου κτλ.). Likewise the verbal noun σύλληψις can be used to describe the activity of a god or gods.[41]

If we extend our range of linguistic items to embrace those which in general indicate divine complicity (mostly words with prefix συν- or μετα-), the number of relevant parallels to the kind of activity described in *Thg.* 129e7–8 naturally increases significantly.[42] I restrict myself to one case in particular, Pl. *Smp.* 212b3 (the μέγας δαίμων as συνεργός): τούτου τοῦ κτήματος τῇ ἀνθρωπείᾳ φύσει συνεργὸν ἀμείνω Ἔρωτος οὐκ ἄν τις ῥᾳδίως λάβοι; later (218d2–3) Alcibiades says of Socrates, the δαιμόνιος ἀνήρ (n.b. 219c1–2) and embodiment of Ἔρως:[43] τούτου δὲ οἶμαί μοι *συλλήπτορα* οὐδένα κυριώτερον εἶναι σοῦ — a deliberate echo (cf. Bury *ad* 218d). Cf. also *Alc.* I 105e5 μετὰ τοῦ θεοῦ and 106a1 ἐφῆκεν, both suggesting divine activity far transcending ἀεὶ ἀποτρέπει of *Ap.* 31d3–4; also (iii) above.[44]

---

[41] See R.B. Rutherford, *The Meditations of Marcus Aurelius: A Study* (Oxford: Clarendon Press 1989) 193 (on M.Aur. I.17.6).

[42] See Fraenkel (above, n.39) *ibid*; A.-J. Festugière, *Personal Religion among the Greeks* (Berkeley CA: University of California Press 1954) 144 n.10.

[43] See Hadot (above, n.36) 69–82.

[44] Cf. X. *Mem.* IV.3.12 (Socrates): αὐτοὺς (sc. τοὺς θεούς) ἡμῖν *συνεργεῖν*, διὰ

(vii) *Alc.* I 103a4–6: τούτου δὲ τὸ αἴτιον γέγονεν οὐκ ἀνθρώπειον, ἀλλά τι δαιμόνιον ἐναντίωμα, οὗ σὺ τὴν δύναμιν καὶ ὕστερον πεύσῃ. *Thg.* 129e1–3: ἡ δύναμις αὕτη τοῦ δαιμονίου τούτου καὶ εἰς τὰς συνουσίας τῶν μετ' ἐμοῦ συνδιατριβόντων τὸ ἅπαν δύναται. Within the Platonic Corpus, only in these two places (and *Thg.* 129e7–8, see (vi) above) is δύναμις applied to Socrates' sign (never in Xenophon). It is not hard to account for the infrequency: since it is impossible to say what τὸ δαιμόνιον actually *is* or *does*, it is excessively assertive to speak of its "power," "influence," or "function."[45] The word does however belong better in a context in which claims are made about the efficacy of a deity, δαίμων or θεός, as is done in *Alc.* I and *Thg.* where τὸ δαιμόνιον is presented more clearly as an agent (see (vi) above). Indeed in *Thg.* the actual area of influence of τὸ δαιμόνιον is clearly delimited — εἰς τὰς συνουσίας τῶν μετ' ἐμοῦ συνδιατριβόντων 129e2–3 —, and this suggests the attribution to it of a certain degree of personality (see also (viii) below).[46]

I suspect that *Alc.* I and *Thg.* drew their inspiration ultimately from one — very famous — Platonic passage. In *Smp.* 202d13ff. Socrates, recounting his discussion with Diotima, relates how she told him that Ἔρως is a "great δαίμων." She continues: καὶ γὰρ πᾶν τὸ δαιμόνιον μεταξύ ἐστι θεοῦ τε καὶ θνητοῦ. To this Socrates responds with the question (202e2): τίνα...δύναμιν ἔχον; (for the δύναμις of Ἔρως cf. 188d4–5, 212b8). In this exchange τὸ δαιμόνιον denotes the quality that makes a δαίμων what it is; there is certainly no intention on Plato's part to confuse it with Socrates' sign. But that is not to say that the

μαντικῆς τοῖς πυνθανομένοις φράζοντας τὰ ἀποβησόμενα καὶ διδάσκοντας ᾗ ἂν ἄριστα γίγνοιτο (there follows a clear reference to τὸ δαιμόνιον); E. *Med.* 844–5: ἔρως as συνεργός; also X. *Smp.* 8.24: ὁ ἀεὶ σύνοικος ἐμοὶ (sc. Socrates) ἔρως.

[45] Cf. G. Kruger, *Der Dialog Theages* (Diss. Greifswald 1935) 21; Gundert (above, n.10) 530 n.16.

[46] Schleiermacher recommended the excision of the last three words in *Ap.* 40a4 ἡ γὰρ εἰωθυῖά μοι μαντικὴ ἡ τοῦ δαιμονίου because he thought they overpersonalized τὸ δαιμόνιον. His intuition that Plato sought to avoid such a representation of Socrates' sign was certainly correct, though ἡ τοῦ δαιμονίου is not as offensive as he thought. But ἡ φωνὴ ἡ τοῦ δαιμονίου in *Thg.* 128e5 is, I think, another matter. For Socrates' sign as the voice of τὸ δαιμόνιον cf. [Plu.] *de Hom.* II.212.5; Olymp. *in Alc.* 21.9–14 W.; and for τὸ δαιμόνιον as itself the voice of a δαίμων cf. Apul. *Soc.* 32.19–33.7 M.; Herm. *in Phdr.* 68.4–69.18 C. The impetus for the latter interpretation may have come from X. *Ap.* 12 θεοῦ...φωνή; further, *Ap.* 13–14 make it plain that Xenophon viewed Socrates' "voice" or "sign" quite simply as the work of a δαίμων, since its occurrence proved how highly he was honoured by δαίμονες (ἐμὲ τετιμῆσθαι ὑπὸ δαιμόνων).

passage could not be taken up gratefully in Platonic exegesis on this topic: Procl. *in Alc.* 46.1–13 S. shows that it was (cf. esp. 46.5–6 [loose quotation of *Smp.* 202d13–e1: τὸ δαιμόνιον (n.b. omission of πᾶν) ἐκεῖ πού φησι μέσον εἶναι θεῶν καὶ ἀνθρώπων] and 46.9–13); and so does Herm. *in Phdr.* 66.1–3 C. (*Smp.* 202d13–e1 quoted immediately after the question τί ἦν τὸ δαιμόνιον Σωκράτους).[47] One result of the appropriation of the *Smp.* passage would have been for τὸ δαιμόνιον to be invested with the kinds of mediumistic δύναμις attributed to δαίμονες in *Smp.* 202e3–203a4: so in *Alc.* I Socrates' sign had prevented Socrates from speaking with Alcibiades, now it impels him to do so and acts as intermediary in their association; in *Thg.* τὸ δαιμόνιον endows Socrates with skill in μαντική (128d8–129d8) and becomes the potential object of "prayers and sacrifices and whatever else the μάντεις prescribe" (131a6–7, cf. *Smp.* 202e7–203a1; Apul. *Soc.* 157 [28.15–16 M.]: *hunc deum* [i.e. τὸ δαιμόνιον] *suum cognovit et coluit*). If our authors did indeed have their eyes fixed on *Smp.* 202d7–203a8 they were by no means the first: others quickly developed (with the aid of other Platonic texts on δαίμονες) the demonology they found there, or misunderstood it altogether.[48]

For δύναμις in connection with τὸ δαιμόνιον in later sources cf. Plu. *Mor.* 580f: τὸ Σωκράτους δαιμόνιον ἰδίαν καὶ περιττὴν ἐσχηκέναι δύναμιν; Procl. *in Alc.* 83.21–85.16 S. (on δύναμις in *Alc.* I 103a6), esp. 84.13–14: ἡ δύναμις οἰκειοτάτη τοῖς δαίμοσίν ἐστι; also Apul. *Soc.* 30.17–18 M.: *vi daemonis praesag[i]a regebat<ur>* [sc. Socrates]; more generally in treatises which subsume τὸ δαιμόνιον into the class of δαίμονες: Max. Tyr. 8.6 (66.129 T.) τινας δαιμονίους δυνάμεις; Apul. *Soc.* 15.10–14 M.: *sunt quaedam divinae mediae potestates...hos Graeci nomine* δαίμονας *nuncupant* (cf. 27.5 M.);

---

[47] In very similar fashion Clement (*Strom.* V.14.91.4) suggests, after quoting *R.* 620d6–e1 (on demonological sortition): τάχα δὲ καὶ τῷ Σωκράτει τὸ δαιμόνιον τοιοῦτό τι ἠνίσσετο (so also Eus. *PE* 13.13.6.12).

[48] See J.-A. Hild, *Étude sur les Demons dans la littérature et la religion des Grecs* (Paris: L. Hachette 1881) 286–337 (a wide-ranging but frequently speculative discussion). Xenocrates naturally looms large in our understanding of this development: R. Heinze, *Xenocrates* (Leipzig: Teubner 1892) 91–6; Beaujeu (above, n.3) 189–92; C. Zintzen, "Geister (Dämonen)," *RAC* 9 (1976) 640–1; Dillon (above, n.5) 31–2; O. Gigon, *Sokrates: sein Bild in Dichtung und Geschichte*[2] (Bern/Munich: Francke 1979) 164. For the development and modification of Plato's demonology in the Platonic *Epinomis* see L. Tarán, *Academica: Plato, Philip of Opus, and the Pseudo-Platonic Epinomis* (Philadelphia PA: American Philosophical Society 1975) 42–7, 283.

Calcid. 34.13–14 Wsz.: *at vero invisibilium divinarum potestatum quae daemones nuncupantur.*[49]

(viii) *Thg.* 129e1–3 (quoted (vii) above): The power (ἡ δύναμις) of τὸ δαιμόνιον exercises "absolute control," τὸ ἅπαν δύναται, in Socrates' associations with others; *Thg.* 130a4–e4 and *Alc.* I 103a1–106a1 (n.b. 105e5 μετὰ τοῦ θεοῦ) provide concrete examples of this (on *Alc.* I 103a4–6 Proclus remarks [*in Alc.* 77.19–78.1 S.]: μόνος δὲ ὁ δαίμων πάντα κινεῖ, πάντα κυβερνᾷ, πάντα διακοσμεῖ τὰ ἡμέτερα; cf. Herm. *in Phdr.* 66.3–15 C.). In its vague expression of divine omnipotence τὸ ἅπαν δύναται represents traditional phraseology (it occurs as early as Homer, cf. *Od.* 4.237, 10.306, 14.445);[50] for the general sense cf. also παγκρατής, πανδαμάτωρ *et sim.* We should however reckon with the possibility that a specific description of a δαίμων lay at the source: *Smp.* 188d4–5 πᾶσαν δύναμιν ἔχει...ὁ πᾶς Ἔρως.

As a deity's omnipotence frequently promotes capricious behaviour, so in *Thg.* no explanation is ever given of why τὸ δαιμόνιον should assist some of Socrates' companions but not others (129e3–130a4); and the question of why τὸ δαιμόνιον encouraged (ἐφῆκεν 106a1) Socrates' association with Alcibiades, fruitless though it was destined to be, represented a puzzle in the exegesis of *Alc.* I (Procl. *in Alc.* 85.19–92.3 S.; see Segonds *ad loc.*). Again it could be argued that Socrates' sign is endowed with a kind of personality and is made to resemble some familiar conceptions of Greek divinity.

III. Conclusions

To repeat: our earliest evidence for Socrates' divine sign makes no reference to it as a δαίμων. Various details in the way in which it is described make it clear, however, that it is exactly as a personal, tutelary, allotted, and active δαίμων that it was conceived at an early date. I would suggest that the impetus to represent it in this way, and to draw upon important demonological *loci* in the process, was provided by the Academy's interest in δαίμονες, fostered through Xenocrates'

---

[49] J. den Boeft suggests (*Calcidius on Demons* (Leiden: Brill 1977) 54–7), though without reference to these last three passages, that Maximus, Apuleius and Calcidius all drew upon the same Middle Platonic work on demonology.

[50] See W. Kiefner, *Der religiöse Allbegriff des Aischylos* (Hildesheim: Olms 1965) 25–6, 108–15; cf. X. *Smp.* 4.48, *Cyr.* 8.7.22; for mostly later evidence, E. Norden, *Agnostos Theos* (Stuttgart: Teubner 1956⁴; photomech. repr. of 1913 edition) 164 n.2, 240–50.

headship.[51] Admittedly this is speculation. But we can be firmer about the following general conclusions:

1) Two doubtfully Platonic dialogues, *Alc.* I and *Thg.*, were instrumental in the transformation of Socrates' divine sign. The role which *Alc.* I played in the process is rather easier to determine since it was the object of intense exegesis in later Platonism. In cases where *Thg.* is named, quoted, or paraphrased, it is not difficult to detect the nature and extent of its influence (cf. (i), (ii), (vi)); but at other times, especially where verbal reminiscences or conceptual similarities may be involved, we can reckon only with the possibility or likelihood of influence (cf. (ii), (iv), (v), (vi), (vii)).

2) In the instances where it is uncertain that *Alc.* I or *Thg.* was the model for a later source, similarities in wording or conception make it clear that some important features in the later accounts were at least substantially anticipated at an early date (cf. (iv), (v), (vi), (viii)).

3) Often it can be argued that a misunderstanding or distortion in the interpretation of a Platonic passage had a decisive influence on the way in which τὸ δαιμόνιον was presented in *Alc.* I or *Thg.* (cf. (iii), (v), (vii), n.20). This technique of interpreting Socrates' sign through reference to Platonic demonological discussions continued to be practised by later writers (cf. (vii) and nn.20 (Cicero) and 47 (Clement and Eusebius)).

4) Novelties introduced in *Alc.* I or *Thg.* are themselves frequently the product of assimilation of τὸ δαιμόνιον, or at any rate represent the first stages in the process of its assimilation, to the status of a conventional tutelary, allotted δαίμων; this becomes especially apparent from a detailed study of language. Sometimes the assimilation evidenced in these two dialogues was effected by the utilization of celebrated discussions about δαίμονες, in particular those about Ἔρως in Pl. *Smp.* (cf. (iv), (v), (vi), (vii), perhaps (viii)); sometimes inferences about τὸ δαιμόνιον were drawn from other Platonic and Xenophontean passages, and these inferences led to elaboration (cf. (i), (ii), (iii), (iv), (v)).

5) In a few cases τὸ δαιμόνιον was portrayed not so much along specifically demonological lines as in ways more typical of Greek notions of divinity in general (cf. (vi), (vii), (viii)). Xenophon had first shown a strong proclivity towards this kind of treatment (cf. nn.20, 46).

---

[51] Cf. Gigon (above, n.48) 164: "Dass aber Schöpfer der antiken theologischen Dämonologie, der Platonschüler Xenocrates, auch das sokratische Daimonion in sein System einbezogen hat, ist mir von vornherein wahrscheinlich."

4

Κρόνος, Κορόνους and Κρουνός in Plato's *Cratylus*

David B. Robinson

Ian Kidd will recognise this paper for what it is; it betrays only a rather modest interest in the real or fictitious etymology of Κρόνος; behind that lies an editor's enthusiasm to get a new lexical item into the text of Plato. Ian has given long time encouragement to the editing of a new OCT (Vol. 1) of Plato, and it is a pleasure to offer this paper to him in token acknowledgement of very welcome support from a staunch friend in a neighbouring university.

Etymological speculation on the meaning of the name Κρόνος began earlier than Plato's *Cratylus* and continued later. Certain elements known from later discussions can perhaps be used to elucidate the text of the *Cratylus,* and these will be adduced here. Other elements both of earlier and later speculation are probably irrelevant to the *Cratylus*. The aim here is not a complete account of all speculation on the etymology of Κρόνος, merely the identification of what is or is not probably helpful to readers of Plato. The rest must be left, so far as possible, to experts in Orphic and Neoplatonic allegory.[1]

---

[1] Abundant references to etymologies of Κρόνος can be found in: M. Pohlenz, s.v.

I

Cratylus 396b3–6

τοῦτον δὲ Κρόνου ὑὸν εἶναι ὑβριστικὸν μὲν ἄν τις δόξειεν εἶναι ἀκούσαντι ἐξαίφνης, εὔλογον δὲ μεγάλης τινὸς διανοίας ἔκγονον εἶναι τὸν Δία· "κόρον" γὰρ σημαίνει οὐ παῖδα, ἀλλὰ τὸ καθαρὸν αὐτοῦ καὶ ἀκήρατον τοῦ νοῦ. (I give here for the moment an unamended text.)

"One might think at first hearing that it was insulting, disrespectful, irreverent, outrageous, if one were told that Zeus was the son of Kronos." Why? Plato must intend a paradox; for Zeus had been conventionally the son of Kronos throughout Greek poetry. What had been insulting in that? It might, of course, seem possible that Kronos was mythologically such a notorious villain, having castrated his father and eaten his children, that Plato need have had nothing more than the mythology in mind; the reformed god Zeus, cause of all life, can have had no such father as that. But at b7 Plato seems to be presenting an equally reformed Kronos, *without* having offered any defence against the conventional mythology. So the horror of Kronos' mythological activities had better be left out of view in this particular context (though Plato of course might well have appealed to all sorts of notions in the general context of the *Cratylus* as a whole, were they germane to his frequently flippant arguments.)

Jowett, following Schleiermacher, added an explanatory phrase to his translation here. "There is an irreverence, at first sight, in calling him the son of Cronos (who is a proverb for stupidity)." LSJ under Κρόνος might seem to support this. But all their supposed examples of this sense of Κρόνος (e.g. Ar. *Clouds* 929, *Wasps* 1480) in fact support the more specific meaning "old-fashioned." It may be stupid to be old-fashioned,

---

Kronos, P.-W. 11, 1922, coll. 1986–7; A.S. Pease, *Cicero de Natura Deorum*, vol. 2 (Harvard: Harvard University Press 1958) 709–12. But these lists should be approached with the cautions suggested below (and also those suggested by Atkinson (see below)). For the "Derveni papyrus" I rely on *ZPE* 47 (1982), appendix and on W. Burkert, *Les Etudes Philosophiques* 25 (1970) 443–57. See also M.L. West, *The Orphic Poems* (Oxford: Clarendon Press 1983). Neoplatonic interpretations of Κορόνους are discussed by M. Atkinson, *Plotinus, Ennead*, V 1 (Oxford: Clarendon Press 1983) 78–9. Plato's etymologising predecessors are discussed by T.M.S. Baxter, *The Cratylus* (Leiden: Brill 1992).

I must acknowledge my debt to my co-editors, Drs. E.A. Duke and W.S.M. Nicoll, with whom I have enjoyed many discussions of the *Cratylus*, and also to Mr. F.G. Herrmann and Mr. R.M. Pinkerton for valuable back-up and long-stop services.

but "old-fashioned" does not precisely mean "stupid." Agreed, it was still doubtless an insult to call people "old-fashioned" by the use of the sobriquet Κρόνος; but something insulting in a way closer to the specific description of ὑβριστικόν can probably be found.

One should probably in fact suspect that in this context, in his preoccupation with etymologies, what Plato is concerned with is not mythology or proverbs, but a "first-sight" etymology of Κρόνος which he could subsequently refute. One must next observe that at b6 Socrates proceeds abruptly to discuss the various (or some of the various) possible meanings of the words κόρον and κορόν, — in the neuter and/or accusative, be it noted. But how do κόρον and κορόν come into the picture? Jowett added a further explanatory supplement "Κρόνος quasi Κόρος," echoed by Fowler as "κόρος (for Κρόνος)." But how can Jowett support this claim? Why should Plato's readers find the meanings of κόρον/κορόν relevant to the meaning of Κρόνος?

One must suspect that Jowett was misled, either (a) by the Latin etymologising of "Saturnus" from "satur" (cf. Cic. *N.D.* II 64), or (b) by a Neoplatonic belief that Κρόνος had κόρος; but that belief probably derives from just this passage of the *Cratylus*. Or conceivably (c) Jowett thought that Κρόνος was asociated with κόρος since he controlled the "abundance" of the Golden Age. But (i) this would not altogether license assuming that the name Κρόνος simply *was* the word κόρος; (ii) if such an etymology was well known, it would also be well known not to be insulting; (iii) κόρος in LSJ is in fact never cited as signifying "desirable abundance," but always as "undesirable surfeit," or of course "greed." The usual epithet of the Golden Age is (perhaps significantly) ἄφθονος. "Saturnus" looks much closer to "satur" than Κρόνος does to κόρος, and we have to discover how Plato first made this unobvious connection.

The probable solution can be found in LSJ, several pages earlier than Κρόνος and illustrated with perhaps less than a quarter of its available support. Late writers knew an etymology of Κρόνος which spelt the name as Κορόνους. LSJ cite only one place in Damascius, but he has it twice, and Proclus, Olympiodorus and almost certainly Theodoretus add support for the word. Proclus in his commentary on the *Cratylus* as we have it (see Pasquali's edition) fails to cite Κορόνους in that form at 56.24, where it would be most help to us, but he slips the form in at 59.5, where admittedly it might merely be a conceit of his own. Damascius, Proclus elsewhere and Theodoretus however (as I shall argue below) are probably to be taken to assert that Plato used this form in the *Cratylus*. Now even if they do assert this, they might still be wrong; so while I shall return to discuss these later writers, I shall first argue that it would make very good sense to restore Κορόνου in *Cratylus* 396.

If Plato *did* use the spelling Κορόνου to start his own discussion at 396b3, that would clearly solve most of our problems in this passage. (1) First of all we should instantly identify κόρον/κορόν as possible elements of Kronos' fully spelt out fanciful name, and that would be a great improvement to the clarity of our text.

(2) Secondly if we start in b3 from the name Κορόνου, the sense of 3–4 can fairly easily be established. *At first sight* to call a god Κορόνους might seem ὑβριστικόν for two reasons, one of them involving a pun. (a) If Κορόνους meant "having a mind focussed on greed", it would clearly be insulting and irreverent to attribute such villainy to one of a modern refined and reformed group of gods. But also (b) punningly, such an attribution would be ὑβριστικόν precisely because it would be concerned with κόρος, which is a near-synonym of ὕβρις; i.e. ὑβριστικόν would virtually mean "ascribing ὕβρις". This is part of what Proclus seems to be getting at by way of explaining this passage in his commentary at 54.12–21, cf. 55.16–17 (though as we shall see some elements of his discussion must be ruled irrelevant.)

(3) Thirdly, if we start with Κορόνου ὑόν in Plato's text at b3, we gain an easy lead into the sense of the remark εὔλογον δὲ μεγάλης τινὸς διανοίας ἔκγονον εἶναι τὸν Δία (b4–5). For, this time round, the element of -νους in Κορόνους explains why it is reasonable to assert that Zeus must be the son of διάνοια. That is to say, not only ought the form Δία have led us to think of διάνοια (this must doubtless be *one* part of Plato's meaning), but of course διάνοια = νοῦς, and if Κρόνος is Κορόνους, clearly he has some association with νοῦς.

(4) The fourth step to note here is of course that granted a spelling Κορόνους, discussion of the various possible senses of κόρος/κορός is exactly what can help Plato to find a "non-hybristic" sense of Κορόνους. He asserts, — or would have if he had read LSJ — that we are not concerned here with κόρος (A) in its sense of "greed", nor with κόρος (B) = παῖς, but with κορός (B) — note the accent — which is an adjective evidently synonymous with καθαρός and presumably associated with κόρος (C) = a "broom" and with κορέω "to sweep, clean". So Plato can assert that κορόνους is equivalent to κορὸς νοῦς, a "pure

mind", and Kronos is so called διὰ τὸ καθαρὸν (= κορὸν) αὐτοῦ καὶ ἀκήρατον τοῦ νοῦ. (No support is cited for the adjective κορόν other than what are doubtless echoes of this passage of the *Cratylus*, but these echoes are in writers who seem to believe in the adjective without quibble, and there seems to be no philological reason to doubt it. — One might perhaps wonder (this is pure speculation) whether κορός may perhaps have served as a colloquial and purely "domestic" term, for which καθαρός was always the formal or written word. This might make Plato's etymology even more typically flippant.)

So I think that the reading Κορόνου is clearly desirable in b3, so that even if it had been pure conjecture it should be accepted. But let us return to assess the evidence for this word.

(i) Damascius, *Dubitationes et Solutiones ... in Platonis Parmenidem* (ed. Ruelle, Paris 1889) uses κορόνους as the etymology of Κρόνος twice, at 267 = 304 R. and at 292 = 325 R. At the latter point his remark Κρόνος ... ἅτε κορόνους ὢν κατ' οὐσίαν, καὶ "νοῦς καθαρός", ὥς φησιν ὁ ἐν Κρατύλῳ (Σωκράτης) not quite certainly, but surely quite probably, implies that κορόνους stood in the *Cratylus*.

(ii) Proclus, *Theologia Platonica* V p.35 (ed. Saffrey-Westerink, Paris 1987) can hardly not be ascribing Κορόνους to Plato; διὸ δὴ καὶ κορόνους ἐστίν (sc. ὁ Κρόνος), ὡς ὁ Σωκράτης φησί, νοῦς γάρ ἐστιν κτλ. The editors note "Proclus ... a forgé la locution ...," but that flies in the face of Proclus' own statement here and of the cumulative evidence.

(iii) Theodoretus at *Graec. Aff. Curatio* III 43 should I think be read as follows

τούτων δὲ τῶν λόγων ὁ Κρατύλος ἀναπλέως· ἐν ἐκείνῳ γὰρ δὴ τῷ διαλόγῳ τὸν μὲν Κρόνον ποτὲ μὲν Κορόνουν ὡς τοῦ νοῦ κόρον ὠνόμασε, ποτὲ δὲ Χρόνον, καὶ ῥοώδη φύσιν τὴν 'Ρέαν καὶ ἀέρα τὴν "Ηραν.

Only one manuscript (according to Raeder (Leipzig 1904) followed by Canivet (Paris 1958)) reads κόρονον; that is S, Escorialensis 372 of the eleventh century. The other mss. read κόρον, and Canivet argues that κόρον must be kept to agree with Plato at *Crat*. 396b. But this seems a probable instance of *difficilior lectio potior*; S has κόρονον here because it is a trace of the true reading. We should in fact reverse Canivet's argument;

very probably Theodoretus had κορόνουν, because very probably Plato had κορόνουν.

Subsequently in Theodoretus to read with Canivet ποτὲ μὲν κόρον ὡς τοῦ νοῦ λόγον ὠνόμασε makes no sense; what is τοῦ νοῦ λόγον? and what has it etymologically to do with κόρον? Whereas κορόνουν ὡς τοῦ νοῦ κόρον is perfectly clear. I shall argue below that Theodoretus was probably wrong to find Χρόνον = Κρόνον in the *Cratylus;* on the other hand his report of ῥοώδη φύσιν τὴν 'Ρέαν καὶ ἀέρα τὴν ῞Ηραν is correct, though the paraphrase immediately following is presumably an expansion and not to be projected back into the text of Plato.

(iv) Proclus in his commentary on the *Cratylus* at 56.24 (Pasquali) remarked:

> ῞Οτι τὸ Κρόνος ὄνομα τριχῶς ἀναλύεται νῦν· ὧν ἡ μὲν πρώτη λέγουσα αὐτὸν εἶναι πλήρωμα τῶν νοερῶν ἀγαθῶν καὶ κόρον εἶναι τοῦ θείου νοῦ, τῷ ἔμφασιν ἔχειν τὸν ὑπὸ τῶν πολλῶν κακιζόμενον κόρον καὶ πλησμονήν, ὡς ὑβριστικὴ ἐκβάλλεται· ἡ δὲ δευτέρα, τὸν ἀτελῆ καὶ παιδαριώδη ἐμφαίνουσα, ὡσαύτως ἐκβάλλεται· ἡ δὲ τρίτη, καθαρότητος μεστὸν καὶ ἀχράντου νοήσεως καὶ ἀμειλίκτου ζωῆς προστάτην ἀνυμνοῦσα, εὐδοκιμεῖ. νοῦς γὰρ ἐστιν ὁ βασιλεὺς Κρόνος ...

Much of this bears out our reading of *Cratylus* 396b3–7; one or two details are perhaps helpful to us.

1. All three "analyses" of Κρόνος presuppose its origin from κόρος (A),/κόρος (B) or κορός (B) and νοῦς; so it would not be unsuitable to print τὸ Κορόνους ὄνομα at the beginning of the passage (though not mandatory. There is a similar problem at 54.12 and 17.) If anyone argued that we ought to take the appearance of Κρόνος in Proclus' mss. there as support for the mss. reading Κρόνου in the *Cratylus*, it remains perfectly possible to suppose Proclus' mss. of Plato were already corrupt in this respect. (He knew the form κορόνους and uses it at 59.5, but on this assumption he did not realise it was actually Plato's own form at 396b3. This would contradict his own words at *Theol. Plat.* V 35 (see above), but Proclus' consistency is not impeccable.)
2. Proclus implies that κόρος (A) τοῦ νοῦ would be a satisfactory etymology of κορόνους if it were not that it seemed

"hybristic" by suggesting τὸν ὑπὸ τῶν πολλῶν κακιζόμενον κόρον καὶ πλησμονήν. Now Plato, on the present view, does *not* in fact hint at any satisfactory reading of κόρος (A) τοῦ νοῦ; this is embroidery by other authors, who were perhaps like Jowett influenced by Saturnus/satur. But Proclus' argument that Plato indicates that κόρος here must not suggest "kakemphatic" πλησμονή recurs in his commentary on the *Republic* at II 269.28–270.1, τὸ γὰρ κορὸν τοιοῦτον εἶναι καὶ αὐτὸς ἡμᾶς ἐν τῷ Κρατύλῳ παρὰ τοῖς θεοῖς ἐδίδαξεν, οὐχὶ πλησμονὴν ἀλλὰ καθαρότητα σημαῖνον. This led my colleague Dr. W.S.M. Nicoll and myself to feel certain that *Crat.* 396 b 5–6 should read κορὸν γὰρ σημαίνει, οὐ παῖδα ⟨οὐδὲ πλησμονήν⟩ ἀλλὰ τὸ καθαρὸν αὐτοῦ καὶ ἀκήρατον τοῦ νοῦ. (Or one could alternatively write οὐ ⟨πλησμονὴν οὐδὲ⟩ παῖδα. In either case the confusion of ΟΥΠΑ and ΟΥΠΛ will have induced the omission.)

3. Proclus' assumption that Κορόνους might contain κόρος (B) and imply childishness in Cronos need be no more than embroidery on Plato's οὐ παῖδα in b6. Otherwise one might have to suppose a further lacuna in the Plato mss. But the bare οὐ παῖδα in b6 is no doubt thrown in rather casually by Plato as virtuoso sophistication; "κορός of course, not κόρος (A) nor κόρος (B)."

(v) Olympiodorus in his commentary *in Phaedonem* 61c = p.45 Westerink has καθαρτικῶς ζῇ ... διὸ καὶ Κρόνος εἴρηται, οἷον κορόνους τις ὤν ... This much of his note is probably an echo of the *Cratylus,* though what follows shows Neoplatonism reverting to a refined understanding of Κορόνους as involving a eulogistic sense of κόρος (A), which we shall observe later (and have seen hints of in Proclus.)

II

Cratylus 402b1–4
Τί οὖν; δοκεῖ σοι ἀλλοιότερον Ἡρακλείτου νοεῖν ὁ τιθέμενος τοῖς τῶν ἄλλων θεῶν προγόνοις " Ῥέαν" τε καὶ "Κρουνόν"; ἆρα οἴει ἀπὸ τοῦ αὐτομάτου αὐτὸν ἀμφοτέροις ῥευμάτων ὀνόματα θέσθαι;

I have printed "Κρουνόν" here against the Κρόνον of all the manuscripts. This is probably the point at which Theodoretus thought Plato was referring to the etymology of Kronos as Chronos. Critias (assuming DK88 B 18 is his and not by Euripides) had written

ἀκάμας τε χρόνος περί τ' ἀενάῳ
ῥεύματι πλήρης φοιτᾷ τίκτων
αὐτὸς ἑαυτόν.

So the association of χρόνος and ῥεῦμα was not unknown in Plato's time. Nevertheless Buttmann's interpretation taking Κρόνος to equal Κρουνός here seems more convincing. (i) " 'Ρέα" καὶ "Κρουνός" make a directly matching pair. (ii) To equate Κρόνος with χρόνος would surely have stimulated Plato to something much more pointed by way of comment or innuendo. (iii) The ἀέναον ῥεῦμα of Critias' view of χρόνος is perhaps not the kind of unstable Heracleitean "flux" Plato is fond of attacking here and elsewhere in this dialogue. For Critias evidently in these lines, as for Plato himself in the *Timaeus,* time is notable for its regularity rather than for its instability.

Heindorf held that while Buttmann's interpretation is correct, nevertheless in b3 we should retain the spelling Κρόνος "propter minimam inter o et ου apud antiquos differentiam." But this is a confusion. In Attic inscriptions earlier than 403 B.C. βουλή (exempli gratia) was indeed usually (officially and perhaps archaistically) spelt βολή, and Plato is certainly relying here on a suggestion that the familiar Κρόνος was an "old spelling" which may perhaps really have represented the word generally spelt as κρουνός. But the Ionic spelling used officially *after* 403 of course was capable of making this differentiation clear, and it is surely likely that for his readers' benefit Plato will have moved from the spelling Κρόνου at a5 to the supposedly more correct spelling Κρουνόν at b3. It is of course true that we can know practically nothing of Plato's personal taste in spelling from our manuscripts written twelve or more centuries later, and also true that Plato was not bound to follow the spelling habits of Attic inscriptions; but where a clarifying spelling was certainly available to him, perhaps we may presume him to have made use of it where appropriate. Certainly we find Plato elsewhere capable of explicit discussion of "old" and "new" spelling, e.g. at *Crat.* 426c6.[2]

---

[2] *Corrigendum*: L. Threatte, in *The Grammar of Attic Inscriptions* I (Berlin 1980)

III. Summary and Cautionary Corollary

To sum up. Probably at 396b3 Plato spelt the name in question as Κορόνου, very likely as a fancy of his own invention, and first (i) rejected any association with κόρος (A) = ὕβρις, then (ii) stressed an association with νοῦς, then (iii) suggested an etymology as κορὸς (B) νοῦς = "pure mind". Later at 402b3 Plato indulged a different fantasy and spelt the name as Κρουνόν, to associate even Cronos with instability and flux-theory.

If this is what best makes sense of the text of the *Cratylus*, a cautionary corollary to these remarks must run as follows:

Plato did *not* in the *Cratylus* employ the following etymologies of Κρόνος sometimes found elsewhere:

(i)* from κραίνω, which has been suspected at *Il.* II 419, (where Κρονίων is the god named), Soph. *Trach.* 124 (Κρονίδας).
(ii)* from χρόνος see above; many later examples (e.g. again Cic. *N.D.* II 64), and doubtless it may have an early origin, cf. Pherecydes DK 7 A 9, but this testimony is late, and deification or personification of Χρόνος, e.g. Pindar's Χρόνος ὁ πάντων πατήρ, *Ol.* II 17, does not necessarily identify Χρόνος with Κρόνος. The Homeric πατήρ is Zeus, not Kronos. So far as I can gather from M.L. West's book, in "Orphic" poems interest in Χρόνος was not universally (and not in earlier poems?) accompanied by identification with Κρόνος.
(iii)* from κόρος (A) "quod saturaretur annis" Cic. *N.D.* II 64, III 62 (which is an attempt to fuse Saturnus with Χρόνος.)

More to the point, perhaps, Plato did *not* interpret κορόνους as

(iv)* κόρος (A) τοῦ νοῦ = "abundance" of mind, which enters into certain Neoplatonic texts, e.g. Plot. V 1.4, and perhaps into Procl. in *Crat.* where a purely eulogistic sense of κόρος (A) is said to be defeated by the "kakemphatic" overtone of the same κόρος (A) =

238, denies that the ο to ου spelling change is closely associated with the adoption of the Ionic alphabet. But the change, though still only sporadic circa 400 B.C., was complete by 350 (Threatte, p. 241); so both the spelling Κρουνός and some recollection of the spelling βολή were certainly available to Plato.

"greed." If someone ever took 396b5–6 *out of context*, εὔλογον ... μεγάλης τινὸς διανοίας ἔκγονον εἶναι τὸν Δία, then μεγάλη διάνοια might have seemed to hint at κόρος (A) τοῦ νοῦ = "abundance of mind." But *in context* Plato is surely excluding all senses of κόρος (A) to focus on κορός (B).

Nor does Plato himself interpret Κορόνους as

(v)* κόρος (B) τοῦ νοῦ or κόρος (B) τὸν νοῦν, i.e. "child of mind" or "childish in mind." Again, we have seen Proclus detecting the presence of "childish in mind," though assuming of course that Plato was rejecting it. "Child of ..." may possibly enter into Plotinus' play on Κόρος Κόρου i.e. "child of abundance" at *Enn.* V.1.7.
(vi)* Finally, the commentator in the "Derveni papyrus," which preserves a commentary on an "Orphic" theogony, seems to discuss a derivation of Κρόνος from κρούω as νοῦς κρούων τὰ ὄντα (col. x–xi). Plato may doubtless have got the idea of Κορόνους from an existing fantasy-form Κρουόνους, but there is no sign that he himself wanted to employ or endorse this particular etymology from this commentator. (Burkert plausibly dates this commentator between Anaxagoras and the *Cratylus*).

The truth is probably that Plato invented Κορόνους = Κρόνος just as freely as for example elsewhere in the *Cratylus* he invented σελαενονεοάεια (if Heindorf is right) as an etymology of σελήνη (409b–c). Κορόνους gave him several identifications of κόρος/κορός to play upon. He will have needed no earlier doctrine to give him a lead, and equally he need not have intended to start all the etymological hares chased by later writers who gained flashes of inspiration from κορόνους.

5

Counting Plato's Principles

R.W. Sharples

I. The Evidence of Simplicius

The classification of physical theories by the number of principles involved goes back to Aristotle, *Physics* 1.2; in a less formal way to Plato, *Sophist* 242cd; and perhaps even further to the period of the Sophists.[1] It is still echoed in modern text-books on the Presocratics. What is perhaps less familiar is that, naturally enough, this approach was not in antiquity confined to the Presocratics. The present paper is concerned with ancient attempts to apply such an analysis to one notable successor of the Presocratics, namely Plato. It is greatly indebted to the work of scholars expert in the field, notably John Dillon and Harold Tarrant; but I hope that it may present familiar material in a new perspective, and, even if its main conclusion is highly speculative, stimulate further thought and debate on a period of the history of phi-

---

[1] J. Mansfeld, "Aristotle, Plato, and the Preplatonic doxography and chronography," G. Cambiano (ed.), *Storiografia e dossografia nella filosofia antica* (Turin: Tirrenia 1986) 36ff., reprinted in J. Mansfeld, *Studies in the Historiography of Greek Philosophy* (Assen: Van Gorcum 1990) 22–83.

losophy which, with some notable exceptions, has been too little studied as yet in English-speaking countries at least.[2]

In his commentary on Aristotle *Physics* 1.2 Simplicius, dealing with those who postulated a limited plurality of principles, mentions those who asserted two (Parmenides in the *Way of Seeming*, and the Stoics), three (Aristotle himself, later in *Physics* 1), and four (Empedocles). He then deals with Plato; and concludes with the Pythagoreans, who he says recognised ten principles – the numbers of the decad, or the ten pairs in the Table of Opposites.[3]

Where Plato is concerned Simplicius first states his own view, that Plato postulated three causes[4] in the strict sense (*kuriôs*) and three auxiliary causes (*sunaitia*); the causes in the strict sense are "the maker, the paradigm, and the end", the three auxiliary causes "the matter, the form and the instrument".[5] (Here "form" must refer to the Aristotelian imma-

---

[2] The notable exceptions include Ian Kidd's work on Posidonius. It gives me great pleasure to contribute this paper to his *Festschrift;* to do so seems doubly appropriate, both because of the period with which it is concerned, and because it takes its start from a report concerning Theophrastus. Ian has been a constant supporter of the Theophrastus Project (none who were present will quickly forget his visual demonstration, at the Project's 1989 conference in Eresos, of the effects of different types of earthquakes), and has taught us much concerning the editing of fragments and testimonia. — Earlier versions of this paper were given to a seminar at the Institute of Classical Studies, University of London, and to a meeting of the Scottish Association for Classical Philosophy at Edinburgh. I am grateful to all who contributed to the discussions, and especially to Tad Brennan, Luc Brisson, Sarah Broadie, Neil Cooper, Gabriela Carone, Fred Rosen, Dory Scaltsas, Anne Sheppard, Lucas Siorvanes, Richard Sorabji and Michael Trapp.

[3] Simplicius, *in Phys.* 25.14–26.30 Diels = Theophrastus texts FHS&G 227A and 230.

[4] Simplicius' discussion as a whole is concerned, like Aristotle's, with principles (*archai*), but here he refers to *causes* (*aitia*); however, he goes on to cite Theophrastus as attributing two *principles* to Plato. The terms are clearly being treated as synonymous. Cf. Aristotle *Metaph.* Γ 2 1003b24, and Porphyry, cited by Simplicius *in Phys.* 11.3 against Eudemus and Alexander as linking *archê* particularly with the moving cause and *aition* with the final cause (*in Phys.* 10.9ff.); W. Theiler, *Die Vorbereitung des Neuplatonismus* (Berlin-Zürich: Weidmann 1964²) 18–20; M. Frede, "The Original Notion of Cause," M. Schofield, M. Burnyeat, J. Barnes (eds.), *Doubt and Dogmatism* (Oxford: Clarendon Press 1980) 215–49, esp. 218–20, 227–8.

[5] Cf. Porphyry ap. Simplic. *in Phys.* 11.2; Philoponus *in Phys.* 5.7ff., *de aet. mund.* 159.5ff. Theiler (above, n.4) 20–2; J. Pépin, *Théologie Cosmique et Théologie chrétienne* (Paris: Presses Universitaires de France 1964) 27 n.3; P.L. Donini, "Testi e commenti, manuali e insegnamento: la forma sistematica e i metodi della filosofia in età postellenistica," W. Haase (ed.), *ANRW* II.36.7 (Berlin: De Gruyter 1994) 5027–100, at 5069.

nent form as opposed to the transcendent Platonic paradigm.[6]) But Simplicius then goes on to cite two other views. Theophrastus, he says, assigned only two principles to Plato: matter, called "receptive of all things" — clearly the Receptacle of *Timaeus* 51A, generally equated with matter by later interpreters[7] — and the cause and source of movement, which Theophrastus says Plato "attaches to the power of god and of the good".[8] Alexander of Aphrodisias, however, attributed to Plato *three* principles, "the matter, the maker and the paradigm". This seems a reasonable interpretation of the *Timaeus*, the "maker" being the Demiurge.[9] For, if a principle is that which is primary, not preceded by anything else,[10] on a literal interpretation of the *Timaeus* the Demiurge, the Forms[11] which he uses as his model, and the Receptacle each seem to be ultimates, not derived from any further principle. Nothing is said in the *Timaeus* about the derivation of the Forms from the One or the Good; and the Receptacle does not derive from another principle in the

---

[6] This distinction is present in Seneca, *Letter* 65.7, which adds the Platonic transcendent form to the four Aristotelian causes. Cf. H. Tarrant, *Scepticism or Platonism: The Philosophy of the Fourth Academy* (Cambridge: Cambridge University Press 1985) 136 n.7.

[7] Cf. F.H. Sandbach, *Aristotle and the Stoics* (Cambridge: Cambridge Philological Society, suppl. vol. 10, 1985) 36.

[8] Cf. H.-J. Krämer, *Der Ursprung der Geistmetaphysik* (Amsterdam: B.R. Grüner 1964) 379 n.20a. On the arrangement of Theophrastus' original account as compared to Simplicius', and the position of Plato in each, see David Sedley, "Theophrastus and Epicurean Physics," forthcoming in *RUSCH* VIII, eds. J. van Ophuisjen, M. van Raalte and P. Stork (New Brunswick: Transaction). I am grateful to Dr. Sedley for letting me cite his paper in advance of publication.

[9] Even though Simplicius immediately goes on to criticise Alexander for omitting the final cause; see W. Dooley, *Alexander of Aphrodisias: On Aristotle Metaphysics 1* (London: Duckworth 1989) 91 n.192. At *in Phys.* 43.4–6 Simplicius again cites Alexander, but this time giving Alexander's own words, as adding the formal cause to "substrate and matter" on the one hand and "the cause (see above, n.4) and mover, which he calls God and mind and the good" on the other. Theiler (above, n.4) 20 suggests that this shows Alexander was Simplicius' source for Theophrastus' view in the earlier passage too. But since Simplicius there quotes Theophrastus' own words, and since mind is referred to in the later passage but not in the earlier one, we must suppose either that Alexander gave two different formulations of the two-principles view, or else that Simplicius consulted Theophrastus directly as well as through Alexander. The latter is certainly the case elsewhere in Simplicius' account of views on the principles (cf. P. Steinmetz, *Die Physik des Theophrast* (Bad Homburg: Max Gehlen 1964) 345–6).

[10] Cf. Aristotle *Metaphysics* N1 1087a33, Alexander, *de fato* 25 195.28; also Aristotle *Physics* 1.5 188a27, 1.6 189a30.

[11] Or the Form of Living Creature, containing the other Forms: *Timaeus* 30cd.

way Neoplatonist Matter derives from the One. Indeed Dörrie contrasts the "paratactic" nature of this three-principles interpretation, treating the principles as equal and co-ordinate, with the "hierarchic" views of Xenocrates, and sees the former as holding back the development of transcendence in Platonism.[12] Certain passages of the *Timaeus* suggest rather a two-principles interpretation, but here the principles would be the Receptacle and the *Forms,* rather than the Demiurge.[13]

II. Two Principles

A distinction should be drawn between the general interpretation of Plato in terms of an opposition between two principles, and the specific version we find attributed to Theophrastus. There is clearly warrant for the former in the generation of the Forms from the One and the Indefinite Dyad, and indeed Theophrastus' interpretation has been seen as a vulgarisation of this metaphysical doctrine.[14] Significant too is the contrast in the *Timaeus* between reason and necessity;[15] at a later date Plutarch, in contexts concerned with causation, emphasises the thor-

---

[12] H. Dörrie, "Die Frage nach den Transzendenten im Mittelplatonismus," *Les Sources de Plotin,* Entretiens Hardt 5 (Vandouevres-Genève: Fondation Hardt 1960) 193–223, at 205–6, deriving the three-principles interpretation from *Timaeus* 28ac. See below, nn. 61, 64. Pépin (above, n.5) 23–5 describes the three-principles interpretation as a misreading of Plato prompted by Aristotle's insistence that a third, moving cause is needed as well as Forms and matter (*De gen. et corr* 2.9 335b7-8); G. Invernizzi, *Il Didaskalikos di Albino e il medioplatonismo* (Rome: Abete 1976) 33–5 defends the three-principles doctrine *as an interpretation of the* Timaeus, while pointing out that 48c, where Timaeus explicitly *declines* an enquiry into the first principle or principles of all things, calls it into question as an interpretation of Plato's philosophy generally. See also Krämer (above, n.8) 116; John Dillon, *Alcinous, The Handbook of Platonism* (Oxford: Clarendon Press 1993) 93–4; Donini (above, n.5) 5061–2.

[13] *Timaeus* 50cd refers to a triad of form, matter and the compound of the two, likening *form* to a father, rather than the Demiurge as at 28c, as Gabriela Carone has pointed out to me. A triad of which two members jointly produce the third contains only two *principles,* however. Cf. also *Timaeus* 48e–49a, 52d; *Timaeus Locrus* 205.5–206.10 Thesleff-Marg; Diogenes Laertius (below, n.25) 3.77; Simplicius, *in Phys.* 223.20. Invernizzi (above, n.12) 173 n.14; G. Lachenaud, *Plutarch: Moralia,* Budé t.XII² (Paris: Les Belles Lettres 1993) 215 n.6; L. Brisson, "Diogène Laërce, View et doctrines des philosophes illustres, livre 3," W. Haase (ed.), *ANRW* II.36.5 (Berlin: De Gruyter 1992), 3619–760, at 3735. Aristotle presents Form and Matter as Plato's two principles at *Metaphysics* A6 988a7–15.

[14] Invernizzi (above, n.12) 36.

[15] With which Theophrastus' account of Plato is connected by A.-J. Festugière, "Le Compendium Timaei de Galien," *REG* 65 (1952) 97–116, at 111.

oughly Platonic *dyadic* contrasts between true causes and necessary conditions (*Phaedo* 99a, *Timaeus* 68e) and between body and soul (*Laws* 10 892c).[16] It would not be unreasonable to link divine agency with the former, matter with the latter.

The interpretation of the two principles as *efficient* cause and matter can be seen as a response to Aristotle's demand, in criticism of Plato, for a moving cause.[17] If the Forms were regarded as God's thoughts, as they apparently were for Xenocrates, they would naturally be included with God rather than treated as a third, independent principle;[18] indeed Aristotle's own description of the form in the mind of a craftsman as an efficient cause might have contributed to this.[19] Pépin notes that a late source describes Aristotle, like Pythagoras, as placing the Ideas in the efficient rather than in the paradeigmatic cause, and argues that it was Aristotle himself, at an early period of his career, who originated the two-principles interpretation of Plato – though one might ask whether, in a text from the sixth century A.D., this is more likely to be an accurate report of Aristotle's interpretation of Plato, or rather a Platonising report of Aristotle's own doctrine.[20] The striking feature of the view attributed to Theophrastus, however, is the omission of all reference to the Forms;

---

[16] See Donini (above, n.5) 5069–73, and especially Plutarch *Plat. Quaest.* 2 1001bc.

[17] Influenced not so much by *De gen. et corr.* 2.9 335b7–8 (above, n.12) which suggests *adding* a third cause, as by criticisms like that at *Metaph.* A 9 991b5, 992b7. Cf. A.N.M. Rich, "The Platonic Ideas as the Thoughts of God," *Mnemosyne* 4 ser. 7 (1954) 123–33, at 132.

[18] J. Mansfeld, "Gibt es Spuren von Theophrasts Phys. op. bei Cicero?," W.W. Fortenbaugh and P. Steinmetz (eds.), *Cicero's Knowledge of the Peripatos*, RUSCH IV (New Brunswick: Transaction 1989) 133–58, at 156 n.38, asserts categorically that "Theophrast muss also die Idee in den göttlichen Geist hineinversetzt haben"; M. Giusta, "Due capitoli sui dossografi di fisica," Cambiano (above, n.1) 149–201, at 183, says that the existence of the two-principles interpretation as early as Theophrastus is evidence for the Forms already being regarded as God's thoughts by that date.

[19] *Metaph.* Z 7 1032a23, b23; Rich (above, n.17) 130–2; Dillon (above, n.12) 95. Richard Sorabji points out to me that the thoughts of a *Stoic* god (see below) would be efficient, rather than — or as well as — formal causes.

[20] Pépin (above, n.5) 512; *Anonymous Prolegomena to Platonic Philosophy* 5.38, p.13 ed. L.G. Westerink (Amsterdam: North-Holland Publishing Co. 1962) cited by Giusta (above, n.18) 198 n.82, who compares also the attribution to Pythagoras in "Aëtius" 1.3.8 of two principles, one active and formal, the divine mind, the other passive and material, the visible world (above, n.18). Krämer, *Platonismus und hellenistische Philosophie* (Berlin: De Gruyter 1971) 119–21, connects Xenocrates both with the three-principle interpretation of Plato (see below, n.28) and with the active and passive principles of Stoicism, citing the "Aëtius" passage as Xenocratean in the latter connection.

and that is so even in a context where Theophrastus explicitly refers to Plato in the context of "the enquiry concerning nature" as opposed to metaphysics.[21] Perhaps it can be attributed to the summary nature of Theophrastus' account. But Theophrastus is not the only writer to give us an interpretation[22] of Plato's principles which omits the Forms.

The interpretation of Plato's principles as moving cause and matter is found also in the list of divergent opinions in the Academic[23] attack on dogmatism in Cicero, *Academica* 2.118, where Plato is represented as holding that the world is made by god out of matter, and there is no reference to the Ideas in the immediate context,[24] and in Diogenes Laertius' account of Plato.[25] At this date it might be thought to show Stoic influence; indeed Aristocles, in the second century A.D., explicitly compared the Stoic doctrine of the principles with Plato's:

---

[21] Mansfeld (above, n.18) at 144 and n.39.

[22] On which see the papers of A.A. Long and D.N. Sedley forthcoming in *RUSCH* VIII (above, n.8). I am grateful to them for letting me cite their papers in advance of publication. See also Sandbach (above, n.7) 74 n.78; D.T. Runia, *Philo of Alexandria and the Timaeus of Plato* (Leiden: Brill, 1986) 482 n.37; J.J. Duhot, *La conception stoïcienne de la causalité* (Paris: Vrin 1989) 76–7; D.N. Sedley, "Chrysippus on psychophysical causality," J. Brunschwig and M.C. Nussbaum (eds.), *Passions and Perceptions* (Cambridge: Cambridge University Press 1993) 313–31, at 325.

[23] Representing Philo of Larisa, according to Tarrant (above, n.6) 118. On the derivation of this report ultimately from Theophrastus, cf. H. Diels (ed.), *Doxographi Graeci* (Berlin 1897; henceforth *Dox.*) 121 and Mansfeld (above, n.18) 151.

[24] They are implied later, in the *epistemological* context of 2.142; see Tarrant loc. cit, and below n.38. I take it that Cicero's description at 2.118 of matter as receiving everything into itself, like Plato's *pandeches,* is to be understood as proleptic. The Receptacle or matter is neutral and allows any characteristic to appear in it when the occasion arises; it is not implied that the things (i.e. semblances of forms) that appear in the Receptacle exist independently prior to matter's receiving them. (I am grateful to Tad Brennan for raising this point.) A two-principles doctrine also appears in the account of the views of "the Peripatetics and the Old Academy" at Cicero *Academica* 1.24, linked with Antiochus by Tarrant (above, n.6) 116, but with a doxographic source by Giusta (above, n.18) 158 and n.16. Again, the Ideas appear later in the account, in an epistemological context, at 1.30.

[25] 3.69; Festugière (above, n.15) 111. The passage has been thought to derive from Posidonius; Tarrant (above, n.6) 116 and n.3. Cf. also 3.76, though the text here is corrupt; M.M. Peretti, "Su alcuni passi della Vita di Platone di Diogene Laerzio," *Riv. fil. class.* 3 ser. 93 (1965) 447–9; L. Brisson (above, n.13) at 3734; D.T. Runia, "Was Philo a middle Platonist? A difficult question revisited," *Studia Philonica Annual* 5 (1993) 112–40, at 135. But Diogenes certainly mentions the Forms at 3.64 (in passing) and at 3.77; Pépin (above, n.5) 32 n.2. Cf. also n.13. — A two-principles doctrine *may* also be presented as Platonic by Tertullian, *adversus Hermogenem* 1, PL 2 198a; cf. J.H. Waszink, "Tertullian's treatise against Hermogenes," *VC* 9 (1955) 129–47.

They[26] say that the element of the things that exist is fire, as does Heraclitus, and that its principles are matter and god, *as does Plato*. But (Zeno) says that both are bodies, both what acts and what is acted upon, while (Plato) says that the first agent is an incorporeal cause.[27]

But the parallel with Theophrastus shows that we should not too readily assume that every Stoic-sounding interpretation of Plato or Aristotle in the first century B.C. is simply to be put down to wholesale borrowing of Stoic materials by Antiochus.

III. Three (or Two-and-a-Half) Principles?

My present concern, however, is not so much with the history of the two-principles interpretation, as with that of the three-principles interpretation attributed by Simplicius to Alexander. This is the standard interpretation of Plato in the two centuries preceding Alexander, and in later sources which are influenced by Middle-Platonist and doxographical traditions rather than by Neoplatonism.[28] But there is a distinction that needs to be drawn immediately. Some texts simply present Matter, the Demiurge or God, and the Forms as three principles and leave it at that;[29] others combine this doctrine, either in the immedi-

---

[26] The Stoics; but mention has been made of Zeno in particular.
[27] Aristocles cited by Eusebius *Praep. Ev.* 15.14.1 Mras = *SVF* 1.98. Festugière (above, n.15), 111; Sandbach (above, n.7) 36.
[28] R.E. Witt, *Albinus and the History of Middle Platonism* (Cambridge: Cambridge University Press 1937) 74–5; Donini (above, n.5) 5061–2. H.-J. Krämer, "Grundfragen der aristotelischen Theologie," *Theologie und Philosophie* 44 (1969) 489ff., argues for Xenocrates as the source of the three-principles interpretation, but his specific arguments are effectively answered by Invernizzi (above, n.12) 173–4 nn.15–16. See also above, n.20.
[29] *Timaeus Locrus* 206.11 Thesleff-Marg (but see above, n.13); Plutarch, *Quaest. conv.* 8.2 720ab; Apuleius, *de Platone* 1.5, p.86.9 Helm; Calvenus Taurus ap. Philoponus *De aet. mund.* 6.8 147.19–20 Rabe; [Justin Martyr], *Cohort. ad Graecos* 6.29, *PG* 6 296b Migne (but at [Justin Martyr] *De resurrectione* 6, *PG* 6 1581ab, there are *two* principles, god and matter); Irenaeus, *adv. Haeres.* 2.14.3, *PG* 7 751c; Epiphanius, in Diels *Dox.*(above, n.23) 587.8; 591.17 (differently at 588.20ff.); Hermias in *Dox.* 653.27; Ambrose, *Exameron* 1.1, *PL* 14 133a; Calcidius *in Tim.* 307 p.308.14-309.1 Waszink (but cf. J.H. Waszink, *Plato Latinus IV, Timaeus: Calcidius* (Leiden: Brill 1962) ad loc.; there are signs of a two-principles interpretation here too); Carolingian commentaries on Boethius (P. Courcelle, *La Consolation de Philosophie dans la tradition littéraire* (Paris: Études Augustiniennes 1967) 276, 293). The majority of these texts place the Forms *third* in the sequence. Philoponus, *in Phys.* 23.31ff., produces

ate context[30] or elsewhere in the same text,[31] with the doctrine that the Forms are god's thoughts. The first gives us a doctrine of three principles; the second, if I may put it this way, one of $2^1/_2$, the Forms and God not being truly independent of one another. (It should be emphasised that on any view of the *Timaeus* the Forms clearly *are* God's, that is the Demiurge's, thoughts in the sense that he is aware of them; the issue is perhaps better stated as that of whether the Forms have an existence of their own as well as being thought of by God — of whether or not the Forms exist outside the divine Intellect,[32] or of whether or not they are ontologically subordinate to it.[33])

The simple three-principles doctrine is often regarded as a later development from the $2^1/_2$-principles one. Tarrant points out that the simple version seems particularly characteristic of the second century A.D.[34] This account fits, indeed, with the common view that the Forms got back into Platonism, after its sceptical period, via the divine mind. Even

---

Plato in the *Timaeus* as an example of the view that the principles are plural, limited in number and unmoved, the three unmoved principles being God, the Ideas, and Matter (Philoponus here as elsewhere following Alexander; Steinmetz (above, n.9) 345); Simplicius *in Phys.* 22.17, on the other hand, says that no-one had asserted that the principles were many but not in movement (cf. Mansfeld (above, n.18) 138 and n.22). Cf. also Arius Didymus *fr. phys.* 1 (below, at n.39), and for references included in, and additional to, this and the next two notes cf. Festugière (above, n.15) 106–9; Pépin (above, n.5) 27, 33–4; Krämer (above, n.8) 21 n.1; J. Beaujeu, *Apulée: opuscules philosophiques*, Budé (Paris: Les Belles Lettres 1973) 254f.; C. Moreschini, *Apuleio e il platonismo* (Florence: Olschki 1978) 69-70; Donini (above, n.5) 5061–2.

[30] Varro ap. St. Augustine, *civ. Dei* 7.28 = Varro *Ant. rer. div.* XV, fr. 206 Cardauns (below, at n.57); "Aëtius" 1.3.21 (below, at n.45); Alcinous, *Didascalicus* 9 163.11–14 (below, n.44); Hippolytus, *Refut.* 1.19, *Dox.* 567.7ff.

[31] Alcinous, *Didascalicus* 12 (see below, at n.44), and Atticus, fr.26 = Proclus *in Tim.* 1.391.4–12 (<matter> supplied by Festugière). But Atticus' view on the relation between Forms and intellect is controversial; cf. John Dillon, *The Middle Platonists* (London: Duckworth 1977) 254–6; E. des Places, *Atticus: Fragments*, Budé (Paris: Les Belles Lettres 1977) 86 n.5; M. Baltes, "Zu philosophie des Platonikers Attikos," *Festschrift H. Dörrie, Jahrb. f. Antike und Christentum*, Ergänzungsband 10 (1983) 38–57, at 41.

[32] Tarrant (above, n.6) 115 observes that the three-principles doctrine "ill accords with the view that Ideas must be understood *primarily* as thoughts of God"

[33] Runia (above, n.25) 136–7 suggests that we should distinguish this question and that of the location of the Forms in God.

[34] Tarrant (above, n.6) 116. Runia (above, n.25) 135, describes the three-principles interpretation as a development probably of the first century A.D., while mentioning as an antecedent the Varro text that will concern us later.

if the view that the Forms are God's thoughts goes back to the Old Academy,[35] there is general agreement that Antiochus of Ascalon, the Platonist who, "if he had changed a few points, would have been a most genuine Stoic" (Cicero, *Academica* 2.132), connected this doctrine with the Stoic idea of *spermatikoi logoi* or seminal reasons contained within Zeus.[36] Where there has been scholarly disagreement is rather on how much the connection with Stoicism can have to do with later Platonist developments, the Stoics being pantheists and Forms identified with the thoughts of *their* god therefore not transcendent.[37] But both those who have emphasised Antiochus' role, and those who have looked elsewhere for the sources of later dogmatic Platonism, have stressed the epistemological aspect of the revival of the Forms.[38]

However, the attribution of the three-principles doctrine to Plato may begin earlier than some have thought. There is, first of all, no hint of the Forms existing only in the divine intellect in the two passages, from Eusebius and from Alcinous' *Didascalicus* ch.12, which Diels printed as fragment 1 of the physical epitome of Arius Didymus, Augustus' court-philosopher.[39]

> Form is eternal substance, the cause and origin of each thing being such as it is itself. So, just as the particular (forms) precede sensible bodies as their archetypes, just so does that which includes them all in itself, being the fairest and most perfect, exist as the exemplar for this world; for it is

---

[35] The interpretation of the Forms as God's thoughts raises the question of just how its proponents read *Parmenides* 132bc (I am grateful to Professor Neil Cooper for raising this point). Proclus *in Parm.* 892.17ff. takes the point of that passage to be that Forms cannot have their existence primarily in *souls* (as opposed to Mind).

[36] J.H. Loenen, "Albinus' Metaphysics: an attempt at rehabilitation," part ii, *Mnemosyne* 4 ser. 10 (1957) 35–56, at 43–6; and see below, at n.61.

[37] Witt (above, n.28) 71–2. Tarrant (above, n.6) 5–6, 10–13, 122–6 argues that Antiochus' Stoicising epistemology and reliance on the senses was a dead end and that the revival of dogmatic Platonism should be connected rather with the fourth Academy of Philo of Larisa and *scepticism* about the senses. Cf. also Loenen (previous note) 44, and J.M. Rist, *Eros and Psyche, Phoenix Suppl.* 6 (Toronto: University of Toronto Press 1964) 65 (attributing the transference of the Forms from human minds to the divine mind to Posidonius); cf. also Rist's *Stoic Philosophy* (Cambridge: Cambridge University Press 1969) 204ff., and, more sceptically, I.G. Kidd, *Posidonius*, vol.II (Cambridge: Cambridge University Press 1988) 535–6.

[38] See also Rich (above, n.17); Tarrant (above, n.6) 116–26; and further below.

[39] On Alcinous' use of Arius here cf. Dillon (above, n.12) 115–16, who expressly notes the absence of any indication of the location of the Forms. See also Giusta (above, n.18) 190ff.

by being made like this that (the world) has been produced in accordance with god's providence from the whole of substance.[40]

It is also necessary that the fairest construction, the world, should have been crafted by god looking towards some idea of the world, which exists as an exemplar for the world which is as it were fashioned after its image; it is by being made like to this that (the world) has been produced by the craftsman who proceeded to craft the world in accordance with a most marvellous providence and administration, because he was good. — So he crafted it from the whole of matter; ...[41]

These passages do not indeed give lists of principles as such. Matter is mentioned at the end of the Alcinous passage, but the parallel text in Eusebius, which here preserves Arius more accurately,[42] refers to creation not from matter but from substance (*ousia*). And the absence of a reference here to the Forms being God's thoughts is probably not evidence that Arius himself rejected that identification;[43] the significant thing is that he could express his view, in this passage at least, in a way that does not presuppose it. Alcinous himself asserts that the Forms are god's thoughts at 9 163.30 and 10 164.30, though in the former passage he does refer to the three principles and then describes the Form, *inter alia*, as thinking in relation to God but substance or essence (*ousia*) in relation to itself.[44]

The author "Aëtius" reconstructed by Diels, too, starts off his account of Plato's principles with a clear statement of three principles, but then adds the identification of the Forms with God's thoughts:

---

[40] Arius Didymus fr. phys. 1a (*Dox.* 447a17–27) = Eusebius, *Praep. Ev.* 11.23.5.
[41] Arius Didymus fr. phys. 1b (*Dox.* 447b12–23) = Alcinous, *Didascalicus* 12.1.
[42] Dillon (above, n.12) 117. The third source for this passage of Arius, Stobaeus, lacks any reference to creation from matter or substance. Cf. also pseudo-Archytas fr. 4 = Stobaeus, *Ecl.* 1.279–80 Wachsmuth, in which form and substance (*ôsia, estô*) require a further cause, god, to bring them together.
[43] Dillon (above, n.12) xviii–xix and 115–16 stresses the dependence of Alcinous on Arius, while warning against supposing that any *given* passage in the former derives from the latter, except where we have independent evidence. Cf. also Giusta (above, n.18) 191. If Giusta is right about the link between Arius and the *Vetusta Placita* (below, n.54) or Lebedev about the dependence of the "Aëtius" passages in Stobaeus on Arius (below, n.51) the presence in Arius of both a three-principles doctrine and the identification of the forms as God's thoughts becomes virtually certain.
[44] On the relation of the former passage to "Aëtius" and to Arius cf. Giusta (above, n.18) at 183–4, and on the whole problem also Runia (above, n.25) 136. For Alcinous' lack of coherence on the question of two principles or three cf. Giusta 183 and 185.

Socrates son of Sophroniscus from Athens[45] and Plato son of Aristo from Athens (for they each held the same opinions about everything [!!]) (say that there are) three principles, God and matter and Idea. God is the mind [of the world], matter is the first thing underlying coming-to-be and passing-away, and Idea is an incorporeal substance in God's thoughts and imaginings. [God is the mind of the world].[46]

Plato son of Aristo (says that there are) three principles, God and matter and Idea; that by which, that from which, that according to which.[47] God is the mind of the world, matter is what underlies coming-to-be and passing-away, and Idea is an incorporeal substance in God's thoughts and imaginings.[48]

Lebedev may be right in challenging, not just—with others—the legitimacy of Diels' presentation of two parallel texts with a single system of chapters and section numbers, and the way in which he selected and arranged passages from Stobaeus to fit those from [Plutarch],[49] but also the very existence of "Aëtius". Lebedev argues[50] that this name, at-

---

[45] Diels in *Dox.* relegates "Socrates ... Athens and" and "(for they each ... everything)" to the apparatus as "an ancient interpolation ... stupidly (*pinguius*) expressed" and not in the parallel Stobaeus text. (Cf. also *Dox.* p.14). Clearly the remark *is* an addition; but Diels is giving his readers neither a *single* definitive text of Aëtius nor the actual text of [Plutarch] as transmitted. For the forms as God's thoughts see also "Aëtius" 1.10.3 ([Plutarch] only).
[46] "Aëtius" 1.3.21 (Diels *Dox.* 287a17–288a6) = [Plutarch] *Epit.* 1.3 878b1–7.
[47] This reference to the "metaphysic of prepositions" is absent from the parallel passage in [Plutarch] at this point, but occurs in *both* [Plutarch] and Stobaeus at "Aëtius" 1.11.2, on causes rather than principles. Cf. Festugière (above, n.15) 109; Krämer (above, n.8) 21 n.1; Dillon (above, n.31) 138–9. Dillon connects it with either Antiochus or Eudorus.
[48] "Aëtius" 1.3.21 (Diels *Dox.* 287b17–288b6) = Stobaeus *Ecl.* 1.10.16.
[49] For critical accounts of Diels' procedure cf. D.T. Runia, "Xenophanes on the Moon: a *Doxographicum* in Aëtius," *Phronesis* 34 (1989) 245–69, esp. 268; id., "Xenophanes or Theophrastus? An Aëtian *Doxographicum* on the Sun," W.W. Fortenbaugh and D. Gutas (eds.), *Theophrastus: His Psychological, Doxographical, and Scientific Writings, RUSCH* V (New Brunswick NJ: Transaction 1992) 112–40, at 114–15. See also — criticising here not so much Diels as the way in which subsequent scholarship has used his work — J. Mansfeld, "Doxography and Dialectic. The Sitz im Leben of the 'Placita'," W. Haase and H. Temporini (eds.), *ANRW* II.36.4 (Berlin: De Gruyter 1990) 3056–229, at 3064–5.
[50] A. Lebedev, "Did the doxographer Aëtius ever exist?," V. Cauchy (ed.), *Philosophie et culture, actes du XVIIe congrès mondial de philosophie* (Montréal: Montmorency 1988) vol.3 813–17; also id., "*Phusis talanteuousa:* neglected fragments of Democritus and Metrodorus of Chios," *Proceedings of the first international conference on Democritus, Xanthi 6-9 October 1983* (Xanthi: International Democritus Foundation, 1984) vol.2 13–26, at 14.

tested only in Theodoret, was a slip of the pen for "Areius", that is Arius Didymus, and that Arius was the source of Stobaeus,[51] Eudorus of Arius and of [Plutarch].[52] If Lebedev is right, the ultimate common source of [Plutarch] and Stobaeus is pushed back to the latter part of the first century B.C. One may question whether this common source would have started its account of Plato with the attribution of three principles to Plato if this was not already familiar. And even if Lebedev is *not* right and we accept Diels' reconstruction of the tradition, the same considerations will apply, provided we regard the two passages above — as did Diels[53] — as going back beyond Aëtius (placed by Diels at the end of the first century A.D.) to the *Vetusta Placita* (which he placed in the first half of the first century B.C.)[54]

Plutarch wrote a work, now lost, entitled *Where are the Forms?*[55] It may at least be significant that Plutarch was prompted to write on the topic, for this may suggest an already existing controversy. When Seneca in *Letter* 65 (above, n.6) says that "it makes no difference whether the craftsman has an external model to which he directs his gaze, or an internal one which he himself conceived and laid down", he is referring not to the Demiurge, but to the human sculptor referred to in the example of the statue used to illustrate the four Aristotelian causes just before; so the point is *apparently* just to introduce the notion of the Platonic Forms as intelligible by emphasising that a human craftsman's model can be mental rather than physical. Cicero does the same in *Orator* 8–10. It is striking, none the less, that Alcinous 9 163.21ff. makes a similar point immediately after first stating the three-principles doctrine and then saying that the Forms are God's thoughts;[56] perhaps there is more than meets the eye behind the Seneca and Cicero passages too.

---

[51] Which, as Lebedev points out, was the view of Meineke; Diels' arguments against this view (*Dox.* 69 ff.) are, he argues, unconvincing (Lebedev (above, n.50 (1988)) 815). Cf. however, Runia (above, n.49 (1989) 257).

[52] G. Lachenaud (above, n.13) 15–16 n.20 is therefore wrong to ascribe to Lebedev the view that Arius was the author of the ps.-Plutarch *Placita* as we have it.

[53] Diels *Dox.* (above, n.23) 178–81.

[54] Invernizzi (above, n.12) 38 and 176 n.28, too, links the origin of the three-principles interpretation with a source close to the *Vetusta Placita*, and notes in this regard the possible influence of Posidonius on that collection. Giusta (above, n.18) 169 tentatively identifies Arius as the author of the *Vetusta Placita*.

[55] *Pou eisin hai ideai;* no. 67 in Lamprias' catalogue. Cf. Dillon (above, n.31) 48.

[56] Above, nn.30, 44. The passages in Seneca, Cicero and Alcinous are linked by Giusta (above, n.18) 181. On the part played by analogies with human craftsmen in the

IV. The Evidence of Varro

Nor are these passages unique. Whether or not Antiochus was a sideline in the main development of Platonism, he is important for our present theme. And that is because it is generally supposed that he is in some sense the inspiration behind the earliest extant, as opposed to reconstructed, text in which *either* a $2^1/_2$-principles or a 3-principles interpretation is found; a passage on the mysteries in Samothrace from Varro cited by Augustine and datable to 47 B.C.

> (Varro says that) there he inferred from many signs that among the images one indicated the sky, another the earth, the third the models for things which Plato calls Forms — Jupiter the sky, Juno the earth, Minerva the Forms; the sky that by which something is brought about, the earth that from which, the model that according to which.[57]

Admittedly, some caution may be needed here; the fact that Varro was influenced by Antiochus hardly shows that everything concerned with Plato in his writings must have been inspired by Antiochus. That sort of mistake has been made too often in the history of *Quellenforschung*. And in the most recent account of Antiochus — by Jonathan Barnes in *Philosophia Togata* — no mention is made of our Varro passage at all.[58]

What we have in this passage, initially, is a three-principles doctrine. But Minerva or Athena, notoriously, was born from the head of Jupiter or Zeus;[59] the triad turns out to be a dyad with a junior partner. Augustine complains that this makes the Ideas inferior to the sky when they should be superior; he also complains that the sky should be created rather than creator. Pedantic though these objections may be, they bring out the fact that Varro's principles reflect Stoic immanence rather than Platonist transcendence; they also emphasise the implication that the ideas are inferior to, and dependent on, the divine intellect.[60]

---

development of the doctrine of the Forms as God's thoughts see Rich (above, n.12) 130–2.

[57] Varro ap. St. Augustine, *De civitate Dei* 7.28 = Varro *Ant. rer. div.* XV, fr. 206 in B. Cardauns, *M. Terentius Varro, Antiquitates Rerum Divinarum*, Akad. der Wissenschaften und der lit, Abhand. der Geistes und Soz. kl. Einz (Weisbaden: F. Steiner 1976). For the reference to the "metaphysic of prepositions" (above, n.47) cf. Dillon (above, n.31) 139; (above, n.12) 62.

[58] J. Barnes, "Antiochus of Ascalon," M. Griffin and J. Barnes (eds.), *Philosophia Togata* (Oxford: Clarendon Press 1989) 51–96.

[59] Pindar, *Olympian* 7.34ff.

[60] J. Pépin, *Mythe et allégoire* (Paris: Etudes augustiniennes, 1976²) 351; Tarrant

Discussion of Varro's comparison has centred upon Stoic sources for the treatment of Minerva or Athena. Passages have been located in which the Stoics connect Athena with the divine reason,[61] and Varro's comparison of the Forms to Minerva has been used as evidence for the connection of the Forms-as-god's-thoughts doctrine in Antiochus with the Stoic doctrine of the divine *Logos*. For the Stoics Hera was generally identified with air;[62] Chrysippus however scandalised the prudish by his account of the unorthodox sexual relations between Zeus and Hera, giving them a cosmological role,[63] and one late source, Origen, interprets Hera in this connection as "matter".[64] What seems *not* to have been emphasised in discussion of the Varro passage is that, on the face of it, the Capitoline triad offers an ideal way of compromising between a three-principles and a two-principles interpretation of Plato.[65] What

---

(above, n.6) 118. — That Cicero, *Orator* 8-10, uses, as an example of the craftsman looking to the Forms, Phidias making a statue of *Jupiter or Minerva* is probably just coincidence; the Zeus at Olympia and the Athene in the Parthenon were after all Phidias' two most famous statues, and the former was to be used as an example in a similar context by Plotinus (5.8, 1.38). The passage from Cicero's *Orator* has sometimes been connected with Antiochus; it probably owes more, as Sandys in his note on the passage points out (J.E. Sandys, (ed.), *M. Tulli Ciceronis ad M. Brutum Orator* (Cambridge: Cambridge University Press 1885) 11–12), to Cicero's own reading of Plato, including the *Timaeus* which he was to translate into Latin in the following year.

[61] Galen says that certain Stoics used Athena's birth from Zeus' head as evidence for the unorthodox (for Stoics) view that man's ruling principle is in the head (*SVF* 2.908). According to Philodemus (*Dox.* 548b14 = *SVF* Diogenes of Babylon 33; Cardauns (above, n.57) vol.2 221), Diogenes of Babylon used the story of Athena's birth and the location of the ruling principle in the head as an argument for identifying Athena with Zeus as located in the heavens; cf. Diogenes of Babylon ap. Cicero *ND* 1.41 = *SVF* Diogenes of Babylon 34. Diogenes Laertius 7.147 = *SVF* 2.1021 reports that the Stoics called god Athena because his ruling principle extends through the *aither*; this etymological account, avoiding the connection of reason with the human head, was perhaps the more orthodox Stoic one, but it still connects Athena with divine reason. Cornutus *Theol. Gk. Comp.* 20 35.7 Lang, has both versions. Cf. also Justin *Apol.* 1.64, *PG* 6, 425C = *SVF* 2.1096, and Athenagoras *Leg. Pro Christ.* 22, *PG* 6, 940A; Theiler (above, n.4) 19; W.M. Green (ed.), *Augustine: City of God*, Loeb 2 (London: Heinemann 1963) 478–9; Krämer (above, n.8) 265; Pépin (above, n.60) 349.

[62] *SVF* 1.169, 2.1021, 1066, 1075, Diogenes of Babylon 33.

[63] *SVF* 2.622, 2.1071-3.

[64] Origen, *contra Celsum* 4.48 = *SVF* 2.1074. Pépin (above, n.60) 349.

[65] Pépin (above, n.60) and Invernizzi (above, n.12) 176 n.27 do indeed stress the presence of three principles in Varro's allegory, but not the fact that one is subordinate to another. Cf. nn.12, 64. Krämer (above, n.8) 265 n.261 emphasises the combination in Varro's analogy of a three-principles doctrine with the production of the Forms by God, but he sees this aspect of Varro's account as reflecting a Platonist doctrine of

Varro gives us is a triad, but a triad which, because Minerva is born from Jupiter, suggests a $2^1/_2$-principles doctrine rather than a three-principles one; and this is so whether, with the majority of interpreters, we see Minerva's origin as indicating that the Forms are simply God's thoughts, or whether we press the allegory so far as to suggest that the Forms have a separate, but dependent and derivative, existence.[66] (Minerva did not, after all, *remain* in Jupiter's head.)

Whatever the exact implications of the allegory for the location of the Forms, does the suitability of Varro's comparison for presenting something less than a full-blooded three-principles interpretation as none the less *being* a three-principles interpretation reflect his, or his source's, already being aware of a three-principles interpretation and wanting to accommodate it? Or is the straightforward three-principles doctrine a later and unconnected development, an unfortunate simplification of an originally more complex and subtle doctrine?[67]

Well: is it not odd that if neither the ultimate source of [Plutarch] and Stobaeus, nor yet Varro, had any awareness of a three-principles interpretation, the former should start by listing three principles, and the latter identify the principles with three gods? We are not, it may be noted, dealing with a situation where three principles are really *one* in that they all proceed from a single origin, matter too being derivative. When Dörrie described our Varro text as the first extant occurrence of the paratactic three-principles doctrine,[68] Theiler objected that the birth of Minerva from Jupiter shows subordination, *hupotaxis,* rather than *parataxis.* But that does not account for Juno, who is not produced by

---

double transcendence (God being even further from the sensible world than the Forms are) — i.e., he interprets the analogy in "hypotactic" terms, to use Dörrie's expression (above, n.12) rather than, as suggested here, as an uneasy combination of the hypotactic and the paratactic.

[66] As Tarrant (above, n.6) 118 suggests, comparing God's production of the Forms in Plato, *Republic* 10 597c; and see Krämer (above, n.8). At least one later Platonist, Atticus, *may* have combined the posteriority of the Forms to God with the claim of their independent existence; but see n.31 above.

[67] There is indeed a third possibility, which is that the creation of the allegory, whether by Varro himself or by his source, itself marks the very point at which a two-principles interpretation was deliberately and consciously for the first time turned into a three-principles one. But this does not seem very likely.

[68] Dörrie (above, n.12); cf. Invernizzi (above, n.12.) 39–40. Theiler's objection is on p. 232 in discussion in *Les Sources de Plotin,* Entretiers Hardt 5 (Vandouevres & Genève: Fondalion Hardt 1960).

Jupiter and plays no part in the production of Minerva. The point of the present paper is, in effect, that Dörrie and Theiler were both right.

If Varro or his source *was* already aware of, and tried to accommodate, a doctrine which treated the Forms as a third principle, we may even be able to suggest something about its possible context. Tarrant stresses that the doctrine of recollection, of which Cicero was well aware,[69] implies that the Forms are not just God's thoughts but ours as well, especially when our souls are disembodied. He further suggests that it is hardly plausible to suppose that our souls see into God's mind, or that our individual souls were at this period thought of as being or becoming parts of the divine mind. Rather our apprehension of the Forms should be interpreted, as the *Timaeus* would itself indicate, in terms of our minds becoming *more like* the divine mind. Tarrant does not himself draw any implications from this about the ontological status of the Forms, stressing rather, for the first century B.C., their epistemological function and the fact that they "tend to be confined to the mind, whether God's or ours".[70] But is it not the logical implication of a doctrine of Forms, apprehended *either* by God's mind *or* by ours, that the Forms should be regarded as principles in themselves independent of both — especially when the epistemological doctrine is based on the *Timaeus*?

The Capitoline triad was distinctively Roman rather than Greek. Its introduction into the discussion must be due either to Varro himself, or to some Greek writer who wanted to align himself with the cultural institutions of his Roman masters. Perhaps indeed Varro or his Greek source, familiar with the idea of Athena as symbolising the thoughts of Zeus, did simply have the idea of making the association with the Capitoline triad, and did not trouble himself with the question of how this related to a two-principle interpretation of Plato on the one hand and a three-principle interpretation on the other. But I do not think we can rule out the possibility that a three-principles doctrine was already in the air, and that Varro might have been aware of it.

---

[69] Above, n.6, pp.118ff. E.g. *Tusculans* 1.57; Tarrant (above, n.6) 119, 124.
[70] Tarrant (above, n.6) 124.

II. History, Poetry, Drama

6

Pindar and the Victory Ode

Chris Carey

The scant and lacunose remains of Greek lyric poetry which have been preserved for us make attempts to highlight the contribution of any one exponent hazardous. In the case of the victory ode, although we have been able for a century (since the discovery of the Bakchylides papyrus) to compare Pindar with one of his major rivals, and to reconstruct at least in part the expectations, shared by poet, patron and audience, within which the epinician poet composed, we are hampered by the loss of the entire output of Simonides (and possibly Ibykos[1]) in this area, save for a few fragmentary scraps. In addition, we have none of the output of minor talents whose work did not achieve panhellenic status and with it the canonization which for the lyric poets was already in progress by the late fifth century,[2] but who must have contributed something at least to the generic context inherited by Pindar and Bakchylides.

---

[1] For the possibility that Ibykos composed victory odes see J.P. Barron, "Ibycus, Gorgias and Other Poems," *BICS* 31 (1984) 20–2.

[2] See *Ach.* 532ff., 850, *Eq.* 406, 730, 1264–6, 1329, *Nub.* 967, 1354ff., *Pax* 775ff., 796ff., *Av.* 250f., 917ff., 939ff., 1410f., *Thesm.* 161f., *Plout.* 1002, fr. 235 KA, Eupolis fr. 148 KA. The list of poets mentioned or parodied in these passages is larger than the Alexandrian canon. And I have ignored many Aristophanic passages which are lyric in register but whose source is unknown. But it is striking that eight of the Alexandrian nine lyricists are already classics for Aristophanes.

What follows does not purport to encapsulate the uniqueness of Pindar. It is merely an attempt to highlight a number of significant ways in which Pindar responded to the constraints and opportunities presented by a tradition which was already mature by the time he began to compose.

I. The Message

The victory ode is a complex artefact. It has been stated that there is no part of the victory ode which is not in its primary intention encomiastic.[3] Though this approach has proved an invaluable corrective to the historical-biographical conjectures which have run riot in Pindaric criticism since antiquity, it is too narrow. As the ethical generalizations in Pindar and Bakchylides make abundantly clear, the victor forms the focus of an approach which seeks to make sense of certain aspects of human experience through the medium of his achievement. Like much early Greek poetry, the victory ode is in part didactic. The encomiastic and didactic functions are in fact mutually supportive. The praise of the victor together with the mythic narrative provides the specific instantiation without which the poet's general reflections would lack focus, while the use of the immediate occasion to explore wider issues liberates the poem from the temporal and spatial constraints which attach to any simple narrative of achievement or list of qualities. As a result, the victor's praise is guaranteed both a reception beyond his socio-political group or his *polis*, and the subsequent performances (attested by Pindar, Bakchylides and Aristophanes)[4] which ensure the posthumous renown which the epinician poets promise to their patrons.

The content of the epinician was largely fixed by the traditions of choral lyric and the specific conventions of the genre. From Alkman onward celebratory choral lyric tended to include mythic narrative and gnomic moralizing alongside reference to the occasion of the song. Within the victory ode itself certain recurring themes of praise were

---

[3] E.L. Bundy, *Studia Pindarica*, Vol. I: *The Eleventh Olympian Ode* (Berkeley CA: University of California Press 1962) 3. For a useful discussion of the didactic dimension of the victory ode see P.W. Rose, "The Myth of Pindar's First Nemean: Sportsmen, Poetry, and Paideia," *HSPh* 78 (1974) 149ff.

[4] See Pind. *N*.4.14–16, Bakch. 3.96–8, Ar. *Eq.* 405, *Nub.* 1355f., *Av.* 941ff. The last passage is taken from a Pindaric *enkomion*, not a victory ode, but it nonetheless supports the view that songs composed for named individuals continued to form part of an international repertory of music.

inevitable, the victor, his family (including earlier successes), his city, the god at whose festival the victory was won. Praise of the poet had also been established in the choral tradition at least by the time of Alkman. With the extension of choral poetry from the service of the *polis* as a whole to the praise of individuals and the rise of the panhellenic lyric poet, this element achieves greater prominence; in Pindar and Bakchylides it becomes closely associated with the posthumous renown of the patron, a development which is already visible in Ibykos (frs. 151–282.47f.). The epinician as a genre also embraces certain assumptions and values, such as the inevitable envy attracted by success, which reflect the shared perspective of poet and audience.

For the classical poet such generic expectations are merely the raw material with which he works; as the epinicians of Pindar and Bakchylides demonstrate, there is room for strikingly divergent responses to the tradition, by manipulating the form in which shared ideas are expressed, by the selection of concepts and values for emphatic treatment, by elevating otherwise implicit values to the level of explicit themes. Perhaps the most striking aspect of Pindar's approach to the genre is the way he intensifies the element of convention to create a stylized epinician of his own within the established conventions. This he does both by taking generic elements (that is, elements whose status as generic *topoi* can be established with some plausibility from their presence both in Pindar and in Bakchylides) and returning to them repeatedly, and also by generating recurring motifs which appear to be peculiar to his own odes. I offer a few examples.

The importance of athletic success is amply attested by the tangible rewards offered by cities to victors in the games, by the political advantages which could be derived from such success, and by the readiness of members of the most powerful families throughout Greece to participate. It is not surprising therefore that athletic success could be viewed as compensation for earlier misfortune, and accordingly we find Pindar utilizing misfortune to highlight by contrast the victor's good fortune. That this was a natural Greek response is suggested by Bakchylides Ode 11, where Alexidamos' victory is presented as a compensation for an earlier defeat. However, Pindar both broadens the scope of the motif by utilizing victory to offset political and non-athletic personal disasters, as well as athletic failure, and returns repeatedly to this idea, which forms part of a tendency to insist on the element of vicissitude in human life. This model for human experience plays a significant role in no fewer than eight odes (almost 20% of the corpus), *O.2, O.12, P.5, N.11, I.1, I.4, I.7,* and *I.8*.

Pindar places great emphasis, both explicit and implied, on birth as a factor in achievement. This is not peculiar to Pindar. The significance of inherited qualities is accepted by Bakchylides, as can be seen for instance in his selection of Aiakid myth in Ode 13 for an Aiginetan athlete. Both poets are responding to the value system of the aristocratic groups which had time, energy and money to devote to athletics. The superiority of old, wealthy and distinguished families was a truism for the social group for which Pindar and Bakchylides composed; indeed, even in democratic Athens such ideas lingered long after the creation of what was by Greek standards a remarkably egalitarian system. What Pindar does is firstly to develop this idea as an explicit theme and secondly by returning to the principle of birth repeatedly to raise it to one of the dominant elements in his presentation of achievement, past and present.[5] Although he accepts the need for training, he is emphatic that no amount of learning can eradicate the difference between those who are born to excellence and those who are not. Not surprisingly, Pindar is dismissive of the democratic systems which were rising to rival and to threaten the aristocratic tradition (*P*.2.87). He thus takes a firm elitist stance on the superiority of the class which was able to devote itself to athletics.

Bakchylides and Pindar share an awareness of the need for effort if one is to achieve success in the major games. What is significant about Pindar is the emphasis placed on this aspect of athletics. He returns repeatedly to the theme of labour and success, and the concentration on this element is increased by the constant return to Herakles, the great toiler, in his mythic narratives. In contrast, Bakchylides refers to the labour (πόνος) of athletics only once (13.56). However, toil itself is regularly evaluated negatively by Pindar. Words like *ponos, mochthos, kamatos* which are used by Pindar to designate the effort of athletics regularly denote activities and experiences which are unpleasant in themselves.[6] The effect is to present athletics as self-sacrifice, specifi-

---

[5] Constraints of space preclude a full repertory of passages in which this idea is implicitly present; a list of passages where birth is a more or less explicit issue would include *O*.2.86ff., *O*.10.20, *O*.11.19f., *O*.13.13, *P*.5.17f., *P*.6.46, *P*.8.35ff., *P*.10.12f., *N*.1.25, *N*.2.16ff., *N*.3.14ff., 40ff. *N*.5.6ff., *N*.6.8ff., *N*.10.37ff., *N*.11.33ff., *I*.3.13f., *I*.8.63ff.

[6] On the negative value (in non-pindaric contexts) of the terms used by Pindar for athletic effort see F. Dornseiff, *Pindars Stil* (Berlin: Weidmann 1921) 59f.

cally for the good of the state. This colouration is enhanced further by Pindar's tendency to link athletics with war. In this way the individual's desire to excel is emphatically placed at the service of the *polis*. Pindar clearly has in mind the ethics of the Homeric hero (suitably modified, as is the depiction of the warrior ethic in the martial elegies of Tyrtaios, to take account of the importance of the *polis* in the archaic period) in his depiction of athletic activity. This is made explicit at *O*.1.81ff. and *P*.4.184ff., which are clearly influenced by the Iliadic view of the relationship between death and heroic activity, expressed most fully in Sarpedon's speech at *Il*. 12.310–28. But it is already implicit in the nexus effort/success/survival in song which is invoked throughout the corpus. Equestrian events, which generally (as the emphatic reference to personal participation by the victor at *I*.1.15 confirms) placed the victor at one remove from the physical process of competition, are also drawn into this nexus of ideas through the presentation of expenditure on athletics (again a principle shared with Bakchylides, who lays heavy emphasis on the need to spend in Ode 3) as a risk undertaken for the glory of self and *polis*.

As is clear from the passages from *O*.1 and *P*.4 cited above, Pindar emphatically finds the same values at work in the heroic past as in contemporary athletic competition. This is as true of his insistence on birth as of his evaluation of effort and his presentation of the motivation behind the ambition to excel. There is no reason to doubt that Bakchylides would have agreed with him. Where Pindar differs from Bakchylides is in explicitness and in emphasis. But the difference is significant, since the effect is to stress the continuity between the values of the heroes and those of the contemporary aristocrat.

It is most unlikely that in any one case the ethic expressed is peculiar to Pindar. But the frequency of the ideas does appear to be unusual, at least to judge from Bakchylides. The consistency with which Pindar insists on a limited range of concepts creates a set of values which for all its narrowness is remarkable for its coherence.[7] As well as enhancing the persuasiveness of each idea presented, this process of selection and repetition has the effect of expressing the athletic experience with compelling intensity. The impression of coherence is enhanced by Pindar's tendency to work with a limited but consistent range of images (song as

---

[7] H. Lloyd-Jones, "Pindar," *PBA* 68 (1982) 139, 162 rightly notes the "distinctive vision of the world" communicated by Pindar's odes.

weapon, song as vehicle or journey, song as nurturing water, the poet as athlete, the urge to achieve as sexual desire and achievement as sexual consummation)[8] which recur throughout the corpus. But as well as being internally consistent, the choice of themes for emphatic treatment makes Pindar's approach more ideological than that of Bakchylides. He not only deals with general moral issues. His explicit emphasis on the demands of athletics, the motives for participation and the qualities of those who participate makes the corpus a statement of the ideology of athletics. This ideology is explicitly aristocratic,[9] and the continuity of ethic and achievement with the heroic past is emphasized. Of course, each audience only heard one Pindaric ode at a time. But this should not be taken to indicate that each audience only knew one Pindaric ode. The victory odes probably circulated in some form during Pindar's lifetime. Pindar clearly envisages such circulation at the opening of the *Fifth Nemean*, while the Aristophanic references to the performance of songs of praise dedicated to individuals suggest that the importance of music both to education and to the symposion created an international audience eager for new compositions and guaranteed a public for each ode beyond the place of performance. There was a Pindaric corpus before the era of the book. I imagine that the process of dissemination ranged from performer's copies of complete odes which were copied by professional musicians and interested amateurs through to purple passages which were transmitted orally. The result however is that each ode probably took its place within and resonated with an expanding corpus. The

---

[8] For a recent treatment of Pindar's imagery see D. Steiner, *The Crown of Song: Metaphor in Pindar* (London: Duckworth 1986).

[9] For Pindar's odes as ideological documents see P.W. Rose (above, n.2) 151ff. The extent to which athletics activity was dominated by aristocrats is disputed. D.C. Young, *The Olympic Myth of Greek Amateur Athletics* (Chicago IL: Ares 1984) 98ff., 150ff. rightly rejects the idea that Greek athletics was *exclusively* the domain of the aristocrat. There was of course no property qualification for participation in the games. But although Young is rightly suspicious of attempts to explain away later accounts of the humble origins of some distinguished athletes, I see little reason to doubt that in the archaic and early classical period the overwhelming majority of contenders, in equestrian and non-equestrian events alike, came from "old" wealthy families or from *arrivistes* eager to present themselves as, and to display the values of, members of the aristocracy. For the intensive training and prolonged absence from home required for successful participation existing wealth was necessary. Athenian politics offers a useful parallel. Although political activity in democratic Athens was theoretically open to all and, like athletics, brought substantial material rewards, in practice the majority of active politicians had private wealth. Certainly wherever we can establish the social class of Pindar's clients they prove to be men of property.

coherent ideology is not therefore an accidental by-product of post-Alexandrian experience of the text but was part of the experience of the contemporary public.

Another effect of this stylization is an increased emphasis on the typical. Again the difference between Pindar and Bakchylides is one of degree, not one of kind. The presence of myth and *gnome* inevitably generalize the victor's achievement. But Pindar's emphasis on a narrow range of recurring ideas represents each victory emphatically as typical of victory, and of success in general. The didactic and normative dimension of the victory ode is thus thrust more forcefully to the fore.

The stylization of the Pindaric epinician is enhanced by a silence which has often been noted. For a poet whose praise is stimulated by a specific event, Pindar is remarkable for his reluctance to describe the victory which occasions the ode. The few descriptions he gives are generally both brief and generic. In contrast, Bakchylides is more ready (as, to judge from the meagre remains, was Simonides[10]) to give a detailed description of athletic success. The Pindaric ode is more austere in this respect. Pindar is equally sparing in his treatment of historical events touched on in the course of the ode. In order to understand this (at first sight) surprising silence, it is useful to observe what Aristotle has to say on the subject of the distinguishing features of poetry at *Po.* 1451a36–b7:

> "It is clear from what has been said that the poet's task is not to tell what happened but what might or could happen according to probability or necessity. For the difference between the historiographer and the poet is not the presence or absence of metre ...; it is this, that one tells what happened, the other what might happen. Accordingly poetry is both more philosophical and more serious than history; poetry deals more with the general, history with the particular."

Although Aristotle has drama and epic in mind, his observations are applicable to Pindaric lyric. By stripping the victory of adventitious detail, Pindar is able to concentrate on the factors necessary for and consequent upon success. This serves both the didactic/ideological and the encomiastic aims of the ode, the former by making the victory a para-

---

[10] See frr. 516 and 517 PMG (if these are rightly assigned to the *Epinikia*), both of which appear to come from vivid descriptions of chariots racing. Fr. 514 (indisputably from an epinician) likewise suggests that the Simonidean victory ode was less austere than the Pindaric (contrast Pind. *O*.9.97).

digm for human achievement in general, the latter by enhancing the relevance of the ode outside the victor's immediate circle and so ensuring a panhellenic audience for his praise. As a result the monumentality of the praise is increased.

II. Manner and Mannerism[11]

Pindar is unusual among choral lyric poets for the emphasis on the poet's personality.[12] It must be emphasized that by the poet's personality is meant not the real Pindar, for whom we have almost no information beyond the bare and incomplete facts of chronology, together with what we can deduce or conjecture about his popularity and possible movements from the date and provenance of his commissions, but the *persona* projected by the poems.[13]

The presence of the poet in the poem is of course by no means unique to Pindar but is common to almost all lyric poetry. In this respect both personal lyric, which draws its themes from the life and experiences of the poet, and public lyric, poetry composed for public celebration by the *polis* or a subdivision thereof, are differentiated from heroic *epos*, whose narrator remains an indistinct and anonymous figure.

When we turn to Pindar, we find a striking difference in the positioning of references to the poet. Although other lyric poets display self-confidence, they tend to marginalize the poetic *persona*, almost literally. The poet puts in a cursory appearance at beginning or end. This is true of Alkman and Ibykos. It is also true for the most part of Pindar's contemporary Bakchylides. It is not difficult to find Pindaric codas of a traditional sort. The *Fourth Pythian*, for instance closes with a brief reference to the poet and his city, as does the *Sixth Isthmian*. But In Pindar as distinct from other choral lyric poets references to the poet are distrib-

---

[11] The subtitle is borrowed from C.M. Bowra, *Pindar* (Oxford: Clarendon Press 1964) ch. 5.

[12] The most useful treatment of the poetic persona in Pindar is by M.R. Lefkowitz, *First Person Fictions* (Oxford: Clarendon Press 1991) 111–46, to which my discussion is indebted.

[13] I follow W.J. Slater, "Futures in Pindar," *CQ* n.s.19 (1969) 86–94, esp. 89, who suggests that the first person in Pindar "implies a vague combination of Pindar, chorus and choral leader." Since with rare exceptions the *persona* which emerges both within each poem and across the corpus is remarkably consistent, I do not believe that the distinction between poet and chorus will in most cases have been in the minds of the audience as the odes were performed.

uted throughout the poem. The poetic *persona* thus achieves a quite unusual degree of prominence.

The ways in which these personal references are presented are also distinctive. The Pindaric epinician is unusual in the kind of information which the poet provides about himself. References to the poet's excellence abound, sometimes (as with Bakchylides) in contrast with lesser lights.[14] Statements of the patron's need of the poet's intervention for the survival of his reputation are equally common.[15] However, in contrast to the bare information (name and/or origin, plus merits) supplied by other choral lyric poets, Pindar provides us with far more biographical detail. Pressure of other commitments (*I*.1.*init.*, *I*.2.*init.*), his tardiness in meeting the commission (*O*.10.*init.*, *N*.3.1ff., 80f.), his grief at the losses in the Persian Wars (*I*.8.5ff.), even (at least on the most plausible reading) his impassioned response to criticism arising from an earlier composition (*N*.7.102–4). Although all this information relates in one way or another to the task in hand, one effect is to increase the emphasis on the poet's personality, on the poet as a distinct identity.

The panhellenic poet is by definition a hireling. He composes not primarily from any personal commitment to patron or community but because a substantial fee has been paid. This is made explicit on occasion by Pindar (*P*.11.41f., *I*.2.*init.*). The mercenary nature of the relationship threatens to compromise the sincerity and therefore the credibility of the panegyrist's praise. The professional panegyrist's response is to place the emphasis on other aspects of the relationship with the patron, to suggest other personal links. Thus Bakchylides speaks of the tie of *xenia* which binds him to Hieron (5.11; cf. 13.224). When we turn from Bakchylides to Pindar, we find a dramatic difference in scale, manner and emphasis in the treatment of this element. Firstly, even when we take account of the enormous difference in scale between the epinician output of the two poets, one cannot but be struck by the greater frequency of Pindar's insistence on his personal bond with his patron in comparison with his contemporary. Pindar's ties with the victor are repeatedly mentioned. Equally striking is the variety of means used to connect poet closely with victor and Pindar's efforts to establish such links. Schadewaldt drew attention decades ago to the frequency of refer-

---

[14] Cf. Bakch. 5.16ff., Pind. *O*.2.83ff., *N*.3.80ff.
[15] See especially W. Schadewaldt, *Der Aufbau des pindarischen Epinikion* (repr. Tübingen 1966) 277 n.1.

ences to the *xenia* between poet and victor, as at *O*.1.11ff., *P*.3.69, *P*.10.64ff., *N*.1.19ff., *N*.7.61,[16] *I*.2.48. More generally, he may represent his relationship with the victor as one of *philia*, as *P*.1.92, *P*.4.1, *N*.3.76. Not infrequently he seeks to create a closer tie still, by presenting himself as racially related to the patron. This is easy enough in cases where the victor is a Theban, as at *I*.1.*init.* or *I*.7.37ff. (where poet and chorus alike are represented as sharing the grief for the loss of the victor's uncle). But Pindar also manufactures such links. A case in point is *O*.6.84ff. Although the connection defined here will have carried conviction in a society for which the rationalizing away of incidents in myth is not an established aspect of the response to the mythic past, the link is not an obvious one, and its introduction here is indicative of the weight Pindar attaches to the personalization of his relationship with the victor, as is the absence of such devices from Bakchylides. The same can be said of *I*.8.16ff., where the poet links himself to Aigina by referring to the relationship between the mythic figures of Thebe and Aigina. Again, he may emphasize his commitment to the mythic heroes of the victor's city, as *I*.5.20, *I*.6.19ff.

As well as the greater frequency of such effects, the amount of space devoted to the relationship is noteworthy, as is the tendency for such references to be charged with emotion. This tendency is already visible in Pindar's earliest dateable composition, *P*.10. In contrast with the brief and colourless reference to *xenia* in Bakch.5, the motif is expanded by mention of the efforts of Thorax on behalf of poet and victor. The lines describing the relationship (*P*.10.64ff.) are replete with loaded terminology, trust (πέποιθα), kindness (ἐμὰν ποιπνύων χάριν), zeal (προφρόνως), friendship (φιλέων φιλέοντ') and reciprocity (ἄγων ἄγοντα). At *N*.7.61ff. the reference to *xenia* is closely linked to the poet's determination to protect the patron from envious attack and to give truthful praise. Even a brief example such as *P*.4.299 has a poignancy absent from Bakchylides. The closing verses of *P*.4 allude to Pindar's relationship with Damophilos, the Cyrenaean exile who may have commissioned Pindar's magnificent ode in praise of Arkesilas.[17] But the verses follow Pindar's depiction of the exile's yearning for his

---

[16] Schadewaldt (above, n.15) 56ff. I take the word προξενία at *O*.9.83 and *N*.7.65 as referring to the political function of the *proxenos*, not (as the passages are sometimes interpreted) as a general reference to hospitality (ξενία).

[17] See C. Carey, "The Epilogue of Pindar's Fourth Pythian," *Maia* 32 (1980) 143f.

home, itself part of the poet's plea for the exile's return; the juxtaposition testifies to the poet's fulfilment of his responsibility to his *xenos*. Particularly important here is the use of the first person. In contrast to the more detached third person of Bakch. 5.11, such statements in Pindar frequently take the form of first person declarations. The first person carries with it a stronger sense of the poet's commitment to the relationship.

One effect of this emphasis on personal relationships is to create an illusion of intimacy, both between poet and audience and between poet and patron. It is highly probable that the occasions for which the odes were composed were for the most part grand celebrations. So one would conclude from the importance which the *polis* attached to victory in the panhellenic games. In some cases it seems that the victory celebration was shared by the whole city. This is probably the case with *O*.3, which the scholia link, plausibly enough, with a *theoxenia* involving the Dioskouroi and Helen, and *P*.5, which may well have been performed at the Cyrenaean Karneia.[18] These odes were composed respectively for a tyrant and a king. But celebrations on this scale may not have been confined to autocrats, to judge from *O*.7.93f. With the possible exception therefore of brief odes composed for performance at the place of victory, the context of celebration was probably formal, and the audience may have been very large in many cases. Though he is pains to emphasize that his praise is offered on behalf of the victor's society, Pindar shrinks the context of praise, substituting intimacy for formality and friendship for the coldness of the contractual relationship. This illusion of informality is also visible in the language Pindar uses of celebration. Terms like *komos* and *symposion* present the celebration as something immediate and spontaneous.

This approach to the composition of public poetry is, as far as the evidence allows us to judge, highly idiosyncratic. Its inspiration appears to come not from the traditions of choral lyric but from those of solo personal poetry. The quasi-intimacy suggests the symposion of Alkaios

---

[18] See in general C. Carey, *A Commentary on Five Odes of Pindar* (New York: Arno Press 1981) 19 n.70, E. Robbins, "Intimations of Immortality: Pindar, *Ol*. 3.34–35," D.E. Gerber (ed.), *Greek Poetry and Philosophy* (Chico CA: Scholars Press1984) 220, W.J. Verdenius, *Commentaries on Pindar I*, *Mnemosyne Suppl.* 97 (1987) 6, and more generally E. Krummen, *Pyrsos Hymnon* Untersuch. zur antiken Lit. & Gesch. 35 (Berlin: de Gruyter 1990), who links the performance of *O*.3, *P*.5 and *I*.4 with civic festivals.

or Anakreon, or the Sapphic group, rather than the broader context of civic celebration. The distinction between traditional modes of composition is thus collapsed. This more intimate approach is in a sense a natural response to the change in application of choral lyric, from its traditional use in the contexts of cult and civic celebration to the praise of a single individual or family. But it was by no means inevitable, and as far as we can tell it was not a typical feature of mature choral lyric.

The poet also enters the poem more forcefully in Pindar's work as a moral authority. Of course, moral judgement is an integral part of all archaic lyric poetry. The earliest choral poem of which we have substantial fragments, Alkman fr. 1, uses *gnomai* both within the narrative (vv. 15ff.) and at the conclusion to the narrative (vv. 37ff.) to make explicit the moral of the tale. As was noted above, Pindar's tendency to use his praise to make broad statements about human life is not significantly different in kind from the general trend in lyric poetry, personal or public. It is however distinctive in manner. There is a tendency to personalize the moral judgement with the use of first person statements or the equivalent. It is a marked feature of Pindar's poetry that ethical statements tend to be couched in the form of first person assertions of practice or desire. To take a simple example, the *Third Olympian* ends with a statement, in itself common in Pindar, that the victor has reached the limits of human achievement. Such statements can be expressed in third person terms, as at *P*.10.27ff., *N*.3.19ff., *N*.11.13ff., *I*.4.11ff. Here however Pindar moves from third to first person statement:

νῦν δὲ πρὸς ἐσχατιὰν Θήρων ἀρεταῖσιν ἱκάνων ἅπτεται
οἴκοθεν Ἡρακλέος σταλᾶν. τὸ πόρσω δ' ἐστὶ σοφοῖς ἄβατον
κἀσόφοις. οὔ νιν διώξω· κεινὸς εἴην.

Now Theron by his achievements reaches the furthest limit, touching the pillars of Herakles from home. What lies beyond wise cannot tread nor unwise. I shall not pursue it. Or count me a fool.

When expressing the importance of accepting one's lot in *P*.3, Pindar uses first person statement or equivalent interchangeably with third person *gnomai*, as at 105ff:

ὄλβος οὐκ ἐς μακρὸν ἀνδρῶν ἔρχεται
σάος, πολὺς εὖτ' ἂν ἐπιβρίσαις ἕπηται.
σμικρὸς ἐν σμικροῖς, μέγος ἐν μεγάλοις
ἔσσομαι.

Man's good fortune does not long continue
safe, when it follows with full weight.
Small in small circumstances, great in great
shall I be.

This tendency to personalize moral imperatives, which has been noted intermittently since the last century, has been termed by D.C. Young the "first person indefinite." [19] But although formulations of this sort effectively encapsulate the generalizing function of such utterances, they do not capture the full resonance of the choice of form. As Lefkowitz observes, one effect of the form in which the injunctions are cast is to present the poetic *persona* as a moral example.[20] In rhetorical terms, Pindar is seeking to create *ethos*, moral character. This establishes the speaker's authority and impacts on the persuasiveness of the odes both as ethical documents and as panegyric. The effect of the first person moralizing is enhanced further by the high density of *gnomai*, which reinforce the moral weight of the poetic *persona*, and by Pindar's lapidary style, which increases the air of certainty conveyed by his moral pronouncements, and therefore the tone of authority. Once more the inspiration for this practice does not come from the epinician, nor from choral lyric in general. The nearest parallel in fact for this combination of marked emphasis on the person of the speaker and weighty moralizing, with pronounced use of *gnomai*, is wisdom literature, especially the *Works and Days* of Hesiod. Generic distinctions are thus collapsed.[21]

This emphasis on the poet as a moral force is increased by Pindar's tendency to make explicit moral judgements about the myths he tells. Again, it is not the fact of moral judgement but the manner which is

---

[19] D.C. Young, *Three Odes of Pindar: A Literary Study of Pythian 11, Pythian 3, and Olympian 7, Mnemosyne Suppl.* 9 (Leiden: Brill 1968) 58.

[20] Lefkowitz (above, n.12) 114f. However, she overstates Pindar's "isolation" in the longer first person statements. As poet of praise *par excellence*, Pindar stands out from the common ruck of poets. But since his moralizing appeals to widely held values, he is a representative rather than an isolated figure in his moral pronouncements.

[21] This tendency to stretch the genre and to hybridize is very typical of Pindar. *O*.2 shows affinities with the *threnos*; *I*.7, as D.C. Young, *Pindar, Isthmian 7: Myth and Exempla, Mnemosyne Suppl.* 15 (Leiden: Brill 1971) 24 with Appendix, has shown, draws on the motifs of martial poetry; *N*.11 is epinician in appearance but in fact celebrates induction into a political office; and of course in *P*.4 Pindar stretches the epinician literally, with a narrative of unrivalled length and richness which creates the illusion of Stesichorean lyric epic, as well as using lyric to address a specific political issue in the manner of Alkaios.

distinctive. A striking feature of these judgements is the strength of the poet's emotional response. As an example we may cite his interruption of the myth of Herakles at *O*.9.35ff.:

> ἀπό μοι λόγον
> τοῦτον, στόμα, ῥῖψον·
> ἐπεὶ τό γε λοιδορῆσαι θεούς
> ἐχθρὰ σοφία, καὶ τὸ καυχᾶσθαι παρὰ καιρόν
> μανίαισιν ὑποκρέκει.
>
> This tale I bid you,
> mouth, throw it away.
> For to revile the gods
> is hateful skill, and bold utterance in excess
> chimes with madness.

The language here is highly charged. The poet does not merely cease to tell his story, he throws it away (ῥῖψον). The tale of Herakles' battle with the gods amounts to λοιδορία, vilification, of the gods. This is a hateful abuse of poetic skill (ἐχθρὰ σοφία), tantamount to madness (μανίαισιν). Similar emotional and (at least in syntactical form and tone) highly personal responses to myth are registered at *O*.1.52f., *P*.2.52ff., *N*.5.15ff., *N*.7.20ff., 102ff., *N*.8.35ff. This stance is in fact highly unusual in public lyric. It is not found in the remains of other choral lyric poets. And if we may judge Simonides' manner from fr.543, where emotional effects are achieved indirectly, in the manner of Bakchylides, it seems unlikely that Pindar has inherited this approach with the epinician genre. For the intensity of the speaker's response to the mythic narrative the antecedents again appear to be from personal, not from public, lyric, for instance in Alkaios' emphatic statement that the Greeks should have killed Lokrian Aias (fr. 298) or Sappho's presentation of the Helen myth in fr. 16 as an example of her own distinctive view of what is most beautiful. One effect of such passages is to emphasize further the moral character (*ethos*) of the speaker. It is striking that as a rule Pindar's passionate statements relate not simply to the content of myth but to the role of the poet in perpetuating certain kinds of story. Again the effect is in general to emphasize poetry as moral activity, as *prohairesis*. And the poet's ethical choices establish him as the ideal poet of praise, discerning in his search for a worthy theme, and contribute to the overall effect of the *persona* and therefore to the persuasiveness and the monumental quality of the poems.

Pindar is also unusual in the degree to which he makes the actual process of composition the subject of his song, so that the odes acquire a reflexive quality. Thirty years ago Sir Maurice Bowra began his book on Pindar with the words: "No Greek poet says so much as Pindar about his art."[22] Bowra was clearly right about the uniqueness of Pindar's extensive reflection on the activity in which he is engaged, but not in detecting in such reflections an insight into Pindar's art. In fact, what we are offered is illusion. When we press Pindar's poetic statements, they are frequently uninformative. We could have divined even without the aid of *O*.6.*init*. that Pindar habitually seeks an arresting opening, just as we could have determined without recourse to *P*.10.53f. and *P*.11.41ff. that the epinician contains different elements which must be balanced and combined successfully. Sometimes Pindar's statements about his art are positively misleading. When he speaks at *N*.4.33 of a *tethmos* governing his composition, it would be a mistake to extrapolate an objective rule from the text.

Most of Pindar's statements about his art are misleading in another sense, in that they present the poet as reflecting on the act of composition in a seemingly naive way. It is as though we were given access to the creative act itself. The model for this may be the Homeric bard, who sings to order on the spot.[23] Pindar provided his patrons with a complex artefact whose performance (if the traditional view is correct), combining instrumentation, multiple voice and synchronized dance, probably required (at least in the case of the longer odes) lengthy rehearsal. The first performance was the polished result of rigorous drilling. Yet Pindar is at pains to present a different impression, for he constantly creates a dramatic fiction that the audience is witnessing an act of creation, not an artefact being recited. The ode is presented as a process, not as the product of that process. It is an imperative, an intention, not a realized idea. It has been observed for over a century that Pindar tends to use the future or an equivalent expression where a present would be more appropriate. For a long time it was assumed that this was the product of Pindar's naive approach to his task, which unreflectingly imposed on the ode the

---

[22] Bowra (above, n.11) 1.

[23] *P*.9.103ff., *O*.1.17, Hom. *Od*. 8.487ff. For further discussion see Carey (above, n.18) 5; "The Victory Ode in Performance: The Case for the Chorus," *CPh* 86 (1991); A.M. Miller, "Pindaric Mimesis: The Associative Mode," *CJ* 89 (1993) 21–53 (though Miller bases his interpretation on a model of extempore speech rather than extempore composition, 21 n.1).

standpoint of the moment of composition rather than that of performance. However, following Bundy, W.J. Slater set this use of the future in the context of a whole range of future-related expressions and argued that it was conventional, not naive.[24] Discussion since Bundy has often been uncritical; scholars have persistently failed to distinguish between conventional and real futures. What emerges clearly however is Pindar's tendency to project his praise into the future, as something which is about to happen. This is in fact the simplest aspect of a broader tendency in the odes to represent the poet as creating the song as the audience hears it. Thus e.g. at the opening of *O*.10 the poet asks the Muses to jog his memory; he has forgotten to produce the song which is owed to the victor. At the opening of *N*.3 he bids the Muse go to Aigina, where the chorus is waiting for a song from Pindar. At *P*.9.103ff. he is about to finish when he receives a request for another theme, in the manner of the Homeric bard.

This technique is especially clear in Pindar's use of the formalized break-off. Pindar regularly terminates a unit of the ode with a passage rejecting or curtailing what precedes on ethical, poetic or practical grounds. The ode progresses as though the poet were composing orally and did not have the opportunity to alter or expunge, merely to redirect. What is most striking about these passages (apart from Pindar's remarkable variety in the redeployment of a very limited range of ideas) is that almost all represent the poet as facing danger. He may be led into impiety (*O*.9.35ff) or slander (*P*.2.53) or irrelevance (*N*.3.26ff.); he must strive to keep his song within the bounds of the correct proportion (*N*.4.33ff.) and he must beware of boring his audience (*N*.10.20). Such passages, which could be multiplied, present the ode as a struggle.

Clearly the audience did not believe that the ode was composed on the spot or that Pindar had difficulty controlling his song. All such passages are self-evidently fictive. This is clear for instance from the fact that Pindar's reflections on his activity fall so conveniently into the elaborate metrical configurations required by the strophic and triadic systems. It is equally clear from the positioning. There is nothing accidental about Pindar's references to the activity in which he is engaged. These reflections fall at the beginning or end or an ode, or at the transition between themes. At one level therefore such utterances have a structural function. But since Pindar had alternative, and more fluent,

---

[24] Slater (above, n.13).

means of creating transitions, the structural function cannot be the only one.

The effects achieved by these devices are in fact complex. One effect is to tease audience expectation by opening up boundless possibilities, by presenting the illusion of an open-ended composition. A second effect is to add further emphasis to the poet's praise. When Pindar struggles to curtail or terminate a theme of praise, he stresses the difficulty of containing the theme within the bounds of the ode; the excellence of the person praised is thus emphasized. A further effect of such passages is to stress the variety of themes incorporated within the epinician; indeed, one might go further and say that Pindar creates the impression of a centrifugal force at work within the ode. The skill with which the various demands are met by the poet is thereby emphasized. Another effect, already indicated above, is to stress the element of choice in the poetic process; since the break-offs usually concern the need to praise the right themes in the right proportion and in the right way, we are again reminded of the moral dimension to the poet's function and Pindar's success in fulfilling this aspect.

The dramatic quality[25] of such passages also enlivens the performance as experience by turning the audience into onlookers witnessing a developing and tense situation. This tension is increased by the poet's emphasis on the other forces ranged against him as he seeks to complete his task. Not only must he curb his natural enthusiasm for his subject and cope with the themes demanded by the genre, he must also engage in battle with the envious who would decry the merits of victor and poet alike (*N*.1.24, *N*.4.36ff., *N*.8.19ff.) or against the oblivion which threatens him (*N*.7.11ff.). As a result, a number of commonplace ideas gain in *enargeia*, vividness, and consequently in force. The modern reader is hampered by the experience of the Pindaric ode as *text*. It is important to bear in mind that for the original audience the ode was experienced as performance, and the dramatic fiction described is one of a number of ways in which Pindar exploits the fact of performance. In the case of the break-off in particular, a further effect is surprise. Although the audience would not take such passages literally, it is unlikely that any member of Pindar's audience was in a position to predict the occurrence or position of a break-off. This element of surprise is increased in those odes where a myth is begun and terminated to give way to another myth,

---

[25] So rightly Miller (above, n.23) 53.

as in *O*.1, *O*.9, *N*.3, *N*.4, *N*.5. In these cases it is difficult to believe that the audience would anticipate the sudden termination of a brief myth. It is more likely that they would anticipate a prolonged narrative. In this respect the use of terms such as 'conventional' to describe Pindar's formalized transitions can be misleading, since although it rightly emphasizes the element of stylization it can convey an erroneous impression of inevitability which distorts the experience of the individual ode for its original hearers. The importance of the element of surprise is especially clear if one bears in mind the simple fact of the antiquity of the tripartite structure of occasion-myth-occasion. The return from myth to actuality was (almost) inevitable, but the manner and the moment were not.[26]

One important result of the presentation of the ode as an extemporaneous creation is that the developed epinician regains contact with its origins. At the opening of *O*.9 Pindar describes the informal celebration at the site of the games which probably marked all successes for which no ode was commissioned. Pindar's most formal compositions thus mimic the most informal level of celebration. As with the emphasis on the poet's *persona* and relationships, noted above, the effect is to superimpose an illusion of informality on a celebratory context which was probably very formal.

Dramatic fictions which blur the processes or times of composition and performance are not of course unique to Pindar, nor were they a new phenomenon when Pindar began to compose. The projection of the performance into the future is a device found as early as Alkman 3.1ff., situated chronoligically at a point when the chorus has yet to reach the dancing place. Alkman's audience would no more take all this literally than Pindar's, since they could see the choir performing as it sang of its intention to prepare for performance. Likewise, Bakch.19 opens with the poet reflecting on the rich choice of themes available before bidding the Muse begin the chosen theme. The same motif is implicit in Bakchylides' address to the Muse at the opening of Ode 3. Likewise, the formalized break-off can be exemplified from Bakchylides (5.176ff.). It can be traced back at least as far as Hesiod (*Theog.* 35). Thus the presence of quasi-reflective statements from poet or chorus is not unique to

---

[26] It is not suggested that Pindar is alone either in his general (but insufficiently studied) exploitation of the fact of performance or in his use of surprise. My interest here is in the form of this exploitation. Bakchylides for instance exploits surprise no less frequently, specifically in his tendency to terminate a narrative immediately before the climactic point, as at 5.175, 16.31ff., 17.129, 18.60.

Pindar. However, the consistent presentation of the ode as an extemporizing process and the *systematic* deployment of rhetorical transitional devices appear to be peculiar to Pindar, to judge by what remains of archaic lyric. Just as Pindar creates a unique tone within the odes and a unique concentration on a relatively narrow range of themes, so he casts over the ode an illusion of spontaneity and unpredictability which in its range and complexity is all his own.

III

In evaluating Pindar's role in the evolution of lyric poetry, it is important to note his chronological position. By the time of Pindar's birth lyric poetry had been established for generations as a major art form and had attracted a substantial number of gifted exponents. Solo lyric had already passed its prime during his lifetime; the last monodists to achieve classic status (to judge by citations in Aristophanes) were Timokreon and Anakreon. The major choral forms were already fully developed. The victory ode in particular had certainly attracted one major exponent in Simonides, possibly a second in Ibykos, and without doubt a host of minor authors. Though Pindar could not know it, lyric poetry was about to undergo a revolutionary change. But there is no reason to doubt that he was aware of the weight of tradition and the need to create new effects. His blurring of the distinction between public and personal, his striving for a more intense expression of the nature of the athletic experience, his creation of a more overtly rhetorical epinician form, are all part of his response to this artistic inheritance and the challenge it presented. It is an alternative response to that of the next generation of lyric exponents. But in part at least it is to be interpreted in the same way.[27]

---

[27] I am grateful to Dr. S.T. Instone for reading and commenting on an earlier draft of this chapter.

7

Euripides: *Ion* and *Phoenissae*

Elizabeth M. Craik

Much criticism of Euripidean drama has centred on the poet's presentation of the gods: is he detached and intellectual in disbelief or active and passionate in religious engagement; does the head rule the heart? Or, in the chestnut formulation of the undergraduate essay topic: is Euripides rationalist or irrationalist?[1] And, as assessment of Euripides' attitude to religion cannot be wholly divorced from perception of his treatment of political and social issues or the general matter of his attitude to his age and the tragic art, there is an important related question: what is the place of Euripides in the tragic tradition? Is he essentially different from, or simply analogous to, Aeschylus and Sophocles?[2]

---

[1] This formulation was that of A.W. Verrall, *Euripides the Rationalist* (Cambridge: Cambridge University Press 1895) and of E.R. Dodds, "Euripides the Irrationalist," *CR* 43 (1929) 97–104.

[2] For general (very sensible and moderate) discussions of the gods in Euripides, see G.M.A. Grube, *The Drama of Euripides* (London: Methuen 1941) 41–62 and D.J. Conacher, *Euripidean Drama: Myth, Theme and Structure* (Toronto: University of Toronto Press 1967) 3–23; also B.M.W. Knox, in *Cambridge History of Classical Literature*, Vol.I Pt. 2 (Cambridge: Cambridge University Press 1989) 69–73. For a general (but slanted) treatment of Euripides' place in the tradition see A.N. Michelini, *Euripides and the Tragic Tradition* (Madison WI: University of Wisconsin Press 1987).

From Aristophanes, who presented his contemporary Euripides as debunking established religion, and from the biographical accounts of immediately succeeding centuries, which presented him in the same light, Euripides would seem to be an anti-traditional figure. This external evidence would seem to be corroborated by much internal evidence in the plays, suggestive of a sceptical and questioning intellect, taking up the challenging ideas of such philosophers as Xenophanes and interacting with the thought of the sophistic enlightenment. And so Euripides was perceived by Victorian scholars,[3] and so indeed generally perceived until recent decades, when the veracity of the ancient evidence and the validity of the corresponding interpretation of the plays have been seriously questioned.[4] It has long been argued — again on the dual basis of the nature of the ancient evidence and the content of the plays — that Euripides is iconoclastic in social attitudes and innovatory in breaching the conventions of the tragic genre.[5] Of course, radical treatment of social and political issues and artistic adventurousness need not preclude conventional treatment of religion; but one might reasonably feel these differing attitudes to sit uncomfortably together.

My aim in this paper is to defend the tradition of an anti-traditional Euripides — a paradox which might have appealed to the poet himself.

---

[3] Verrall (above, n.1); also *Essays on Four Plays of Euripides: Andromache, Helen, Heracles, Orestes* (Cambridge: Cambridge University Press 1905) and *The Ion of Euripides* (Cambridge: Cambridge University Press 1890) took an extreme view, which was followed by G. Norwood and, to some extent, G. Murray.

[4] See, on the biographical tradition, M. Lefkowitz, *The Lives of the Greek Poets* (Baltimore MD: Johns Hopkins Press 1981); "Was Euripides an Atheist?," *SIFC* 5. No.2 (1987) 149–66 and "Impiety and Atheism in Euripides' Dramas," *CQ* 39 (1989) 70–82; on the plays P.D. Kovacs, *The Heroic Muse* (Baltimore MD: Johns Hopkins Press 1987) and J.D. Mikalson, *Honor thy Gods: Popular Religion in Greek Tragedy* (Chapel Hill NC: University of North Carolina Press 1991). For a trenchant corrective to over-confidence in interpreting the external evidence of antiquity (without due regard to source) and the internal evidence of the plays (without due regard to context and speaker) see K.J. Dover, "The Freedom of the Intellectual in Greek Society," *The Greeks and their Legacy* (Oxford: Basil Blackwell 1988) 135–58.

[5] See P. Vellacott, *Ironic Drama: A Study of Euripides' Method and Meaning* (Cambridge: Cambridge University Press 1975) for a lively, though sometimes extreme, interpretation of the plays as social comment, with particular reference to the position of women; P.T. Stevens, "Colloquial Expressions in Euripides," *Hermes Einzelschr.* 38 (1976) for a solid analysis of diction; B. Seidensticker, *Palintonos Harmonia: Studien zu komischen Elementen in der griechischen Tragödie* (Göttingen: Vandenhoeck & Ruprecht 1982) and B.M.W. Knox, "Euripidean Comedy," *Word and Action: Essays on the Ancient Theatre* (Baltimore MD: Johns Hopkins Press 1979) 250-74, for elements of humour in the plays.

I argue mainly from *Ion*, adducing also *Phoenissae*.[6] These two late plays are rather different in character. *Ion* has often been seen as essentially non-tragic, as it has a "happy ending", whereas *Phoenissae* is a play of relentlessly unremitting pessimism. And whereas *Phoenissae* is unusual in that no god appears on stage, *Ion* is remarkable in that Hermes and Athena both appear, and Apollo's past presence is important to the dramatic situation. However, it will be argued, there are resemblances in their presentation of the supernatural with a sophisticated syncretism which is quite alien to traditional cult practice, and has more to do with virtuoso artistic effect.

Views of the gods in *Ion* are peculiarly polarised. It is an attack on Apollo or a vindication of Apollo.[7] Athens and the aetiology of the Arrephoria are central or Delphi and Apollo are more significant; or Eleusis is a vital link.[8] Certainly it has multifarious elements: characters both human and divine, divinities both Olympian and chthonic, separate locales in Athens and Delphi, magic allied with realism, coincidence and chance affecting plot while geographical precision governs setting. Views of the political content of *Ion* are similarly mixed: it is a play of patriotism or of political questioning, an exploration of national

---

[6] All quotations from *Ion* are from the *OCT* of J. Diggle (Oxford: Clarendon Press 1981); for *Phoenissae* see E.M. Craik, *Phoenician Women* (Warminster: Aris & Phillips 1988).

[7] Verrall (above, n.3) argues that the play attacks not only Apollo, but Olympian religion generally; contrast A.P. Burnett, *Catastrophe Survived. Euripides' Plays of Mixed Reversal* (Oxford: Clarendon Press 1971) 127: "Apollo's divinity is the essential point of the play."

[8] N. Loraux, "Autochthonous Kreousa: Euripides' *Ion*," *The Children of Athena* (Princeton NJ: Princeton University Press 1993), also "Kreousa the Autochthon: A Study of Euripides' *Ion*," J.J. Winkler & F.I. Zeitlin, (eds.), *Nothing to Do with Dionysus?* (Princeton NJ: Princeton University Press 1990) finds autochthony linked to Athenian representation of citizenship and images of division between the sexes. N. Robertson, "The riddle of the Arrhephoria at Athens," *HSPh* 87 (1983) 241–88 explores the play's aetiology. R. Parker, "Myths of Early Athens," Jan Bremmer, (ed.), *Interpretations of Greek Mythology* (London and Sydney: Croom Helm 1987) offers a thorough exploration of the myth, with particular reference to its origins at Athens. Burnett, however (above, n.7) 103 finds *Ion* "a Delphic play" and this view is shared by critics who attach significance to the Delphic locale, possibly an innovation for this drama: Th. Colardeau, "Ion à Delphes," *REG* 29 (1916) 430–4, following Dalmeyda, "Observations sur les Prologues D'*Ion* et des *Bacchantes*," *REG* 28 (1915); but for caution on this score see H. Grégoire, *Euripide*, Budé t.III (Paris: Les Belles Lettres 1923) and Conacher (above, n.2). F.I. Zeitlin, "Mysteries of Identity and Designs of the Self in Euripides' *Ion*," *PCPhS* 215 (1989) 144–97 finds Dionysos the transitional figure who links Athens and Delphi by way of Eleusis.

past or of imperial present, with a positive or a negative slant.⁹ Attempts have been made to reconcile some of these apparently disparate elements, in terms of a continuum of interaction between the two planes, human and divine; and the two settings, Athens and Delphi.¹⁰

Seeking a new approach to an old problem and hoping for a degree of objectivity, I intend to focus first on the names and titles given to the gods in *Ion* and then, with parallels from *Phoenissae*, on interconnections between different deities. In Greek parlance, divine titles are *eponymiai* or "eponyms". Herodotos (5.53.2–3) famously ascribes an important role in the formation of Greek religion to Homer and Hesiod. This includes assigning eponyms, a word variously interpreted as "patronymics ... local names etc." or "such epithets as γλαυκῶπις".¹¹ Pollux (1.1.23 περὶ ἐπωνυμίας θεῶν) gives some examples of eponyms given to Zeus and Poseidon, but quickly dismisses the topic: τοιαῦτα ὅμοια ... ποιηταῖς ἀνείσθω "Let such matters be left to poets". The examples given by Pollux for Zeus are *hyetios, kataibates, nephelegeretes* and, at Athens, *Phratrios*. The final instance is different in kind from the earlier ones, being specific to one locality and naturally capitalised. Dual usage is implicit also in Plato's paraphrase (*R*. 394a) of the Chryses episode in *Iliad* 1.37 sqq.: [Chryses] τῷ Ἀπόλλωνι ηὔχετο τὰς ... ἐπωνυμίας τοῦ θεοῦ ἀνακαλῶν, the names used in Homer being the vocatives ἀργυρότοξ᾽ and Σμινθεῦ.

The two types of eponyms featured in these ancient writers may be distinguished as descriptive (usually in lower case) and naming (usually capitalised) words; and may for convenience be designated epithet and, to use another Greek term, *epiklesis*. *Epiklesis* is regularly used of an additional name, often semantically chosen: for instance, Astyanax is *epiklesis* for Skamandrios (Hom. *Il.* 22.506) and Assesia is an *epiklesis* of Athena (Hdt. 1.19). The word *epiklesis*, peculiarly appropriate to divine titles, is often used of invocation. The *epiklesis* is crucially im-

---

⁹ For political interpretations see Grégoire (above, n.8); A.S. Owen, *Euripides Ion* edited with introduction and commentary (Oxford: Clarendon Press 1939); B. Goff "Euripides' *Ion* 1132–65: the Tent," *PCPhS* 34 (1988) 42–54.

¹⁰ C. Wolff, "The Design and the Myth in Euripides' *Ion*," *HSPh* 69(1965) 169–94 argues for the seriousness of the play and a Delphic setting for an Athenian story. M. Kuntz, "Narrative setting and Dramatic Poetry," *Mnemosyne Suppl.* 124 (1993) 38–58 finds a double narrative with continuity between the real and the mythic.

¹¹ W.W. How and J. Wells, *A Commentary on Herodotus* (Oxford: Clarendon Press 1912) ad loc.

portant in defining the character of a deity: different gods invoked with the same *epiklesis* (for instance, Soter or Polias) have affinities which transcend their apparent differences. With *epiklesis* we are in the world of cult practice, or real ritual, for which inscriptions are the main primary source; with epithet we are in the world of myth, as represented mainly in literature. The *epiklesis* is formal and fixed, typical of cult practice; whereas the epithet is informal and fluid, a matter of literary choice or convention. The distinction here drawn between two types of eponyms, epithet and *epiklesis*, is sometimes in theory a nice one; but in practice, most titles fall clearly into one category or the other.[12]

Apollo was a Protean deity with many titles, which varied from place to place. Of these the most prevalent in fifth century cult, on the evidence of inscriptions, was Delios, Delian. It is evident that the Athenians capitalised on religious sentiment in making Delos the nominal focus of their military alliance.[13] But in tragedy the epiklesis Delian occurs infrequently (S. *Aj.* 690, *OT* 154, E. *Rh.* 224). In cult, Apollo was closely associated with his son Asklepios, who took over the healing function originally that of Apollo Paian. But, although progressively more important in fifth century cult, Asklepios is mentioned only incidentally in tragedy (E. *Alc.* 4, as Apollo's son; *Hipp.* 1209, the rock of Asklepios, a landmark; S. *Ph.* 1423 and cf. 1317, to cure Philoktetes at Troy). Similarly, the common cult titles Pythios and Karneios are not literary appellations; the latter occurs in tragedy only of the month at Sparta (E. *Alc.*448). Conversely, the association between Apollo and the sun, so common in literature and implicit in the epithet Phoibos, "bright", is not an aspect of Apollo cult or ritual practice. Similarly the appellation Loxias, lit. "slanting one", is seen in literary, not epigraphical, sources.

Euripides demonstrates in *Ion* (as at the end of *Andromache*) a close familiarity with the terrain and topography of the Delphic site. But this

---

[12] In the case of the Homeric Smintheus/smintheus, there may be connections with the place Sminthe or, alternatively associations with *sminthos*, mouse. Similarly, Lykeios/lykeios may derive from the place Lykia, or from *lykos*, wolf. Greek names are peculiarly open to such different interpretations on the basis of semantics: cf. Prometheus, Pentheus, Oidipous.

[13] There may be an element of religious schism in the fact that Melos and Thera, which declined to join the alliance, are precisely the islands where the cult of Delian Apollo does not occur: cf. E.M. Craik, *The Dorian Aegean* (London: Routledge 1980) 178.

geographical realism is not matched by realism in allusion to the god. The adjective Pythios is, with one dubious exception, applied simply to the locality.[14] It is just like Delphos, with its feminine form Delphis, which is purely civic or local in reference.[15] The eponyms or cult titles applied to Apollo are literary or decorative rather than realistic or ritualistic in character, epithet not epiklesis. The dominant titles given to Apollo are Phoibos (46 instances — Ion 26, Kreousa 10, Hermes 4, Pythia 1, Chorus 3, servant 1, Athena 1; and in addition the chorus twice use Phoibeios)[16] and Loxias (23 instances — Kreousa 6, Hermes 4, Ion 3, Chorus 4, servant 2, old man 2, Pythia 1, Xouthos 1).[17] The simple name Apollo also occurs (10 times — Athena 3, old man 2, Hermes 1, Ion 2, Kreousa 1, Xouthos 1)[18] and the simple term "the god" (ὁ θεὸς or, once, ὁ δαίμων).[19] Apollo is twice, in refrain, Paian.[20] There are hints at an association with *helios*, the sun and at the title Aguieus.[21] Genealogy is indicated, Apollo being known as son of Leto or of Zeus and Leto; and the birth of the god on Delos features.[22]

It is evident from this simple breakdown that characters do not confine themselves to one method of naming the deity. Closer examination indicates that titles are chosen with regard, above all, to dramatic context. Initially, in Hermes' prologue, Phoibos predominates, then there is a move to Loxias. In the hymn of Ion, when the sun is twice mentioned, the title Phoibos, indicative of brightness, is much (12 times) repeated.[23]

---

[14] Pythios 458, 550, 1251 and, similarly Pythikos 1219; except possibly 285 τιμᾶι σφε Πύθιος ἀστραπαί τε Πύθιαι.

[15] Delphos, Delphoi 33, 54, 94, 416, 821, 1219; Delphis, Delphides 44, 92, 318, 551, 665, 1323, 1365.

[16] Phoibos 6, 10, 28, 50, 90, 94, 104, 111, 114, 129. 136, 140, 151, 164, 178, 182, 223, 227, 302, 306, 321, 334, 338, 339, 357, 371, 384, 410, 437, 467, 504, 534, 541, 941, 1227, 1284, 1322, 1368, 1384, 1482 bis, 1487, 1527, 1547, 1568, 1609; Phoibeios 461, 1089.

[17] Loxias 36, 67, 72, 78, 188, 243, 311, 425, 531, 728, 774, 781, 931, 974, 1197, 1218, 1287, 1347, 1455, 1531, 1540, 1548, 1608.

[18] 66, 93, 249, 424, 946, 952, 1275, 1556, 1560, 1595, and cf. 1619.

[19] "*Theos*" in the prologue 14, 42, 54, 56 and by Xouthos on first entry 401, 407, 413 and often by Ion; "*daimon*" by the Pythia 1353, probaly of Apollo, and by the old man 827; but elsewhere used in general terms, of fate 1065, 1269.

[20] Paian 125, 141.

[21] Helios 82 and throughout parodos, 1516; Aguieus 186 ἀγυιάτιδες θεραπεῖαι.

[22] Genealogy 188, 410, 465, 681, 885, 907, 922; Delos 919–22.

[23] Cf. Owen (above, n.9) on 90 and, on the tenor of the passage, S.A. Barlow, *The Imagery of Euripides* (London: Methuen 1971) 46–8.

In the first episode Phoibos is dominant, but Loxias is employed when Xouthos goes off to consult the oracle. It is noticeable that Athena, herself divine, tends to refer to Apollo simply as Apollo (3 times, as opposed to Phoibos once); Hermes however — divine, but lower in status — uses Loxias or Phoibos (4 each) rather than Apollo (once). In short, literary or dramatic effect, not realistic cult considerations, governs choice of title: epithet, not epiklesis, is found.

The treatment of Athena is similarly artistic in character. The mythical Athena of the play is distanced from the Athena of contemporary cult practice. Athena is here primarily a warrior goddess; not defending the contemporary city but battling against primeval giants and slaying monsters. The stress on the name Pallas, rather than Athena, itself indicates the activity of brandishing a weapon; and a punning usage reinforces this connection (210–1).[24] This is the goddess of combat, "killer of gorgons" (1478 Γοργοφόνα) and opponent of giants (parodos); a goddess "with a golden spear" (9) and a shield with the aegis emblem (210). Even as goddess of victory, given a topical title, she is invoked as victor with Zeus against Giants (1528–9).

Hermes, the prologue speaker, is not significant in state cult, being an informal deity invoked more by individuals than by communities. But as in the case of Apollo and Athena, the god of myth is presented: Hermes is the lackey of the gods, unceremoniously ordered about by Apollo. The otiose genealogical information with which he is introduced is decorative or antiquarian in character; and the allusive indirectness of the introduction enhances this distancing effect (1–4). That the play is introduced by a mere emissary epitomises the indirectness with which the divine order works; and that Hermes is god of deception foreshadows the deceptiveness with which Apollo in this play operates. Description and presentation are in accord. Other deities too are alluded to by conventional epithets: Zeus "the greatest" (4) and Poseidon "of

---

[24] Athens is said to be named after Pallas (8–9, repeated 1555–6); as in the case of Ion this is an allusive connection: cf. Owen (above, n.9) on 9 "The city is named not from Pallas but Athena; it is not called Pallene any more than Ion is called Antaeus" and on 802 "The derivation ... depends on the synonym." Euripides' preoccupation with names and semantics, often remarked, is to the fore in this play. Incidental details of nomenclature are paraded (1, Atlas; 1261, Kephisos); the idiom "be named", i.e. simply "be", is gratuitously employed (as twice, 13 and 937, of the *Makrai petrai* at Athens); the aegis is absurdly connected with the verb ἀίσσειν (996–7); the naming and identity — paternity, rather — of Ion is a recurrent business, fraught with confusion and ambiguity; and, of course, etymological naming pervades the end of the play.

the sea" (282); and such mythical exploits as their amorous adventures are recounted (444–51, with censure).

The three Olympians are siblings, in a close though unequal relationship (28, 29, 37 Hermes and Apollo brothers). Athena at the end acts as a stand-in for Apollo; Hermes is subordinate to both. Other gods too are aligned with them, in a tacit conjunction of Olympian forces. Dionysos is associated with Apollo at Delphi, as is conventional (550, 714–17, 1125–6). But other conjunctions are more problematical or paradoxical and ultimately Olympic and chthonic forces converge in a disturbing way. It is in the lyrics of the play that these associations are suggested. The lyrics of *Ion*, though less elaborate and highly wrought, present a sequence similar to the lyrics of *Phoenissae*. In *Phoenissae* there is a gradual rapprochement of apparently benign and evidently hostile forces: Apollo with Dionysos and Ares; Demeter with Gaia and Sphinx. Apparent opposites are impressionistically linked and there is a fluid interconnection between good and bad.[25]

Initially in *Ion* (parodos 184–236)[26] the forces of the upper world seem to be separate from and victorious against the forces of subterranean primeval powers. The chorus admire the artistic marvels they encounter at Delphi: a depiction of gods and heroes gloriously victorious against giants and monsters. Herakles, helped by Iolaos, defeats the Hydra of Lerna; Bellerophon defeats the Chimaira; Athena vanquishes the giant Enkelados, Zeus overwhelms Mimas and Dionysos an unnamed adversary. The creatures slain are collectively "children of Earth" (218 Γᾶς τέκνα). But the initial clearcut distinction between the combatants is not maintained.

In the first stasimon (452–508) the birth of Athena from the head of Zeus is described; and it is the Titan Prometheus — not, as regularly in the myth, the god Hephaistos — who assists at the birth (455): the enemy is midwife. Euripides is the first known source for this variation (cf. Apollod.1.3.6), which has puzzled commentators. Then, in prayers

---

[25] See *Phoenician Women* (above, n.6), notes on 109, 202–60, 638–89, 784–833, 1019–66; also Index under gods and imagery.

[26] The parodos has been subjected to varied analysis; see D.J. Mastronarde, "Iconography and Imagery in Euripides' *Ion*", *California Studies in Classical Antiquity* 8 (1975) 166 — pretty description, archaeological curiosity, irrelevancy, distancing effect, reinforcement of theme of violence. V.J. Rosivach, "Earthborns and Olympians: the Parodos of the *Ion*," *CQ* 71 (1977) 284–94 finds the ultimate triumph of Apollo prefigured in the parodos.

to Athena, the darkness of the nether world obtrudes on the upper world. Initially, the prayer to Athena as Nike (457), who has nothing to do with birth pangs (453) seems couched in conventional terms. But as the verse continues, Athena is linked with Artemis, "two goddesses, two virgins, august sisters of Phoibos" (465–7). The link with Artemis is in itself unusual. Artemis, though herself virginal, was commonly invoked by women in childbirth, and in this capacity was regularly equated with Eilythuia, from whom the birth of Athena has just been dissociated. And then the prayer to Athena and Artemis as κόραι (468) suggests the common equation of Artemis (but certainly not Athena) with Kora, Persephone, goddess of the underworld. Athena then is associated with Artemis as a chthonic power. The third stasimon (1048–105) begins with an invocation to Einodia, daughter of Demeter. Einodia, here Kore, is elsewhere identified with Hekate, a sinister magical power. The implication, via Kore, that such a figure is at one with Athena (and indeed with Phoibos the bright himself, Athena as "sister" of Artemis being his sister also) makes a bold syncretism of upper and lower worlds, divine and monstrous powers.

Ge/Gaia — Earth or earth, and sometimes it is hard to determine whether metonymy is intended (278, 1220) — plays a crucial part in the ambivalent values of the play. Earth gave birth to the giants and monsters of the parodos. In another Euripidean innovation, Earth gave birth also to the gorgon (989), killed by Athena. Earth was ousted by Apollo at Delphi. But at Delphi, the centre of the earth, gorgons were still to be seen in Apollo's shrine (224); and Athena maintained the emblem of the gorgon on her accoutrements. Earth gave birth to Erichthonios (20 "earthborn"), taken from earth by Athena (269), as well as to monsters; and the language is the same in these superficially different cases (1000). Kreousa is seen by Ion in monstrous guise (1261-3).[27] Caves and subterranean places are throughout juxtaposed with upper regions; the grotto of Pan is close to the shrine of Athena on the Acropolis (especially 492–8, 938) and Xouthos' consultation of Apollo's oracle is prefaced by a visit to the cavern of Trophonios (300–2, 393, 405 and 407–9). Earth is the nurturing source of life (147); but also the destination of the

---

[27] This crossing of imagery is similar to the technique employed in *Bacchae*, where Dionysos and Pentheus are alternately hunter and hunted; and animal, especially bull, imagery is pervasive. In *Hippolytus* too there is much interplay between Phaidra and Hippolytos, Aphrodite and Artemis, apparent opposites who are in some respects aligned.

body on death (1441). The two drops of gorgon's blood entrusted by Athena to Erichthonios have potential for healing or destruction (1002).

It has been argued above that the eponyms used to designate the gods in *Ion* — especially Apollo but to some degree also Athena and other deities — are epithet, not epiklesis. They do not replicate the titles of contemporary fifth century cult, but are literary, decorative and sometimes antiquarian in character. These titles are not casually chosen alternative ways of designating the gods — similar, perhaps to the designation of characters in the modern Russian novel — but are important indications of dramatic intent, with variation in different parts of the play. It has been argued also that Euripides presents an impressionistic and syncretistic amalgam of apparently disparate powers; and in particular suggests interconnections and fluidity between good and bad, upper and nether regions. Designation of the gods, through titles and descriptions, aims at general associative impact or contextual dramatic effect; and presentation of the gods is formulated to suggest fluid interconnections between them. Neither designation nor presentation has much to do with traditional views. This is not a simple accolade for old religious certainties; but a sophisticated expression of intellectual aporia amid new ambiguities. Aporia, however, is not atheism.

The history of scholarhip often indirectly illumines the historian and the historian's era as well as the subject and era studied. It has long been a commonplace that Aeschylus reflects the certainties of the old Marathon-men and Euripides the diffidence of the generation which suffered the Peloponnesian war. Perhaps the Victorian era and the late twentieth-century replicate such a divide. Perhaps in nineteenth-century England, when formal religious observance was strong and many scholars were ordained in the Church (as, for instance, was Lewis Campbell, a distinguished incumbent of the chair of Greek at St. Andrews), Euripides' attitudes were bound to seem fundamentally irreligious. Today, when even the heir to the throne sees himself as defender of faith rather than Defender of the Faith (BBC interview, June 1994) and when it took the assertion "There is nothing out there or, if there is, we can have no knowledge of it"[28] for a parish priest (Rev. Anthony Freeman, author of

---

[28] This has an uncanny resemblance to the celebrated introduction of Protagoras to his treatise *On the Gods* (DK 80 B 4): "On the gods, I am not in a position to know either that they exist or that they do not exist, or what they are like in appearance; for there are many things which prevent knowledge, the obscurity of the matter and the brevity of human life."

God with Us) to be sacked for his theological views, it may be easier to accommodate Euripides as a traditionalist. But as usual the truth surely lies between the extremes. It is not the purpose of poetry to present a clear crisp view of the world. Euripides was evidently fascinated by religion, and gave some extraordinarily vivid portraits of its effects as well as circumstantial accounts of its practices; but at the same time, as argued above, he presented the gods in his own idiosyncratic way. Ultimately the ambiguity which characterises so much of his art is evident here also.

8

The Roman Mind and the Power of Fiction

J.S. Richardson

In 1987, when Ian Kidd retired from the Chair of Greek at St Andrews, I also left that university to move fifty miles south to Edinburgh. Although we had been members of different departments, and he for far longer than I, I gained immensely from the time that I was a colleague of Ian's, and collegiality amongst classicists in St Andrews was and has continued to be a source of intellectual excitement and pleasure. I now offer to a friend and an inspiring senior colleague some thoughts on a subject I began to formulate when we were both members of the University of St Andrews, and which relate directly to the theme of this volume.

The title I have chosen, "The Roman mind and the power of fiction", requires some explanation. There has been for some years an understandable scepticism among British ancient historians of such generalised concepts as "the Roman mind", a reaction to a tendency in the late nineteenth and early twentieth centuries to romanticise the ancient world into an ideal that would serve for the education of young men destined to govern an empire. In response to this, a more pragmatic and empirical approach to the subject has developed, based on a thorough and careful examination of the surviving evidence, literary and archaeological. More recently, not least under the influence of the French group of historians known as the *Annales* school, with their emphasis on the need to examine the "*mentalités*" of particular societies in order to understand their histories, work has been undertaken to establish the patterns of thought and behaviour, the attitudes and beliefs, what might be called the "mind-set" of ancient societies. This approach is not a substitute for the precise examination of evidence, but is essential if we are to begin to make sense of the past, and in particular of a past so remote as that of Greco-Roman antiquity. It is one facet of the Roman way of looking at themselves and their own institutions that I want to explore in this paper.

Fiction is not a word normally associated with the Romans. As a literary genre, the telling of a story in prose, or a mixture of prose and verse, is a fairly late development, and not continuously employed even when it does appear. In the first half of the first century BC, L. Cornelius Sisenna, otherwise known as a writer of history, produced translations of the Milesian tales of Aristides, of which almost nothing survives, apart from their somewhat raffish reputation. The Parthian general, Surena, who defeated the Roman general, M. Crassus, at the battle of Carrhae in 53 BC, was scathing of the effeminacy of his vanquished foes, in whose baggage he discovered copies of these works.[1] There was always something rather "unRoman" about fictional stories of this sort, and even the later productions of more original Latin writers were either Greek in setting, or somewhat risqué, or both. As a French writer is reported to have said of Petronius' *Satyricon*, "On lit Petrone, on ne cite pas" — you read Petronius, you don't quote him. To many, this will scarcely seem odd. The Romans do not have a reputation for being an imaginative race, and it is not very surprising to discover that imaginative fiction was not one of their major achievements.

Such a view however seems to me itself to lack imagination. What the Romans did achieve was a control over the great majority of the land-space of modern Europe, of the Near East and of North Africa for half a millennium. A people who could manage that did not lack imagination, for, however great their political and military power in the terms of their own time, the sheer longevity and territorial extent represented by the mere existence of the Roman empire indicates a grasp of the way in which the human mind functions that certainly implies a form of

---

[1] Plut. *Crassus* 32.5–6.

imagination that is far from contemptible. When it is remembered that the entity which managed this feat was itself not a populous nation-state but in origin and in essence a relatively small city, the point becomes sharper still. It may be true that their imagination was not that which produced the fictional masterpieces of nineteenth and twentieth century Europe, but it was none the less formidable, in every sense of the word.

Fiction, as I have used it in the title of this paper, refers not (as you may have guessed by now) to the creation of literary works, though I would be the last to deny the quality of Latin literature; but to a usage in the construction of legal formulae in the court of the urban praetor in Rome, from the second century BC onwards. Briefly, an *actio ficticia* was the extension of one of the standard types of formulation of a case in civil law to be considered by a judge (the praetorian *formula*) to cover an instance for which such a formula might be appropriate, but could not otherwise be employed. One of the examples given by Gaius,[2] writing in the second century AD, is that of the normal action for theft (*actio furti nec manifesti*). The usual formula has been reconstructed as follows: IUDEX ESTO. SI PARET AULO AUGERIO A NUMERIO NEGIDIO OPEVE CONSILIO NUMERII NEGIDII FURTUM FACTUM ESSE PATERAE AUREAE QUAM OB REM NUMERIUM NEGIDIUM PRO FURE DAMNUM DECIDERE OPORTET, QUANTI EA RES FUIT, CUM FURTUM FACTUM EST, TANTAE PECUNIAE DUPLUM IUDEX NUMERIUM NEGIDIUM AULO AUGERIO CONDEMNATO. SI NON PARET, ABSOLVETO. ("Let the judge be appointed. If it appears that the theft of golden bowl has been committed by Numerius Negidius (the defendant) on Aulus Augerius (the plaintiff) or with the aid and counsel of Numerius Negidius, on account of which he ought to compound the loss as a thief, let the judge condemn Numerius Negidius to Aulus Augerius for double the value of the object at the time of the theft. If it does not so appear, let the judge absolve him.").[3] However, this action, being part of Roman civil law, could not, as such, be applied to a non-Roman. But, as Gaius explains, "If a non-Roman sues or is sued on a cause for which an action has been established by Roman statutes, there is a fiction that he is a Roman citizen, provided that it is equitable that the action should be extended to a non-Roman." If, for instance, a Greek steals from a Ro-

---

[2] Gaius 4.37.
[3] O. Lenel, *Das Edictum Perpetuum* (Leipzig: Tauchnitz 1927³) 324–30.

man, the formula would run: IUDEX ESTO. SI PARET LUCIO TITIO OPE CONSILIOVE DIONIS HERMAEI FILII FURTUM FACTUM ESSE PATERAE AUREAE, QUAM OB REM EUM, SI CIVIS ROMANUS ESSET, PRO FURE DAMNUM DECIDERE OPORTERET, et rel. ("Let the judge be appointed. If it appears that the theft of a golden bowl has been committed on Lucius Titius by Dion, son of Hermaeus, such that, if he were a Roman citizen, he would be bound to compound the loss as a thief ...")

Such a mechanism was clearly extremely useful. Moreover it seems to have been developed early in the use of formulae in the praetor's court. The exact date of the introduction of the formulary procedure is unknown, but it seems to belong to the second century BC. The process itself, which provided an alternative to the rigid verbal forms of the old *legis actio* procedure, gave a far greater amount of flexibility to the praetor as to which cases he would allow within the prescriptions of the law. The *fictio* extended this power still further. The earliest modification of the process, if its author is correctly identified, was the Rutilian formula, whereby a plaintiff, who based his claim on the right of a third party, could be given a formula which made that right the matter for investigation, in the "if it appears..." clause, but inserted the name of the real plaintiff in the final condemnatio. Thus if Smith purchased the estate of Jones, a bankrupt, he could sue Bloggs, who owed Jones money, under the formula, "If it appears that Bloggs ought to pay Jones 200 denarii, condemn Bloggs to pay Smith; if not, absolve." This is, as Gaius states, a form of fiction,[4] and was first used by one P. Rutilius, from whom it took its name, who was probably the consul of 105 BC, and would have been praetor in the last two decades of the second century.[5] In any case, we have evidence for the use of a *fictio* in the only extant example of a *formula* used in an actual dispute in the Republican period, the *Tabula Contrebiensis*, discovered by an illicit excavator, equipped with a metal detector, at Botorrita, near Zaragoza in northern Spain in 1978, which is dated to 87 BC.[6] By the end of the second

---

[4] Gaius 4.35.

[5] On Rutilius, see O. Lenel, *Palingenesia Iuris Civilis* 2 (Leipzig: Tauchnitz 1889) 186–7; R. Bauman, *Lawyers in Roman Republican Politics,* Münchener Beitr. z. Papyrusforsch. u. antiken Rechtsgesch. 75 (Munich: Beck 1983) 382.

[6] J.S. Richardson, "The *Tabula Contrebiensis*," *JRS* 73 (1983) 33–41; P. Birks, A. Rodger and J.S. Richardson, "Further Aspects of the *Tabula Contrebiensis*," *JRS* 74 (1984) 45–73.

century and beginning of the first century BC, then, this method of extending the application of Roman law was part of the praetor's repertoire.

It is important to notice at this point exactly what is fictional about these *fictiones*; important because however useful such a device might be, it was also clearly dangerous if not used with proper discipline. It would not help the litigants in the praetor's court if it were possible for the praetor, simply by employing a *fictio*, to change the facts of the case. Indeed it is precisely this difficulty that has given legal fictions such a bad reputation in English law, where, because of the way the fiction is formulated, they do have this effect.[7] The fictions of the Roman formulary procedure do not do this. In the example given, the praetor is not saying that the self-evidently Greek Dion, son of Hermaeus, is in fact a Roman (indeed the language of the formula makes it explicit that he is not), but rather that, for the purposes of the case in hand, he is to be treated as though he were a Roman. What is altered by the *fictio* is not the status of Dion but the consequences of that status.

The adaptabilty which the use of the *fictio* demonstrates is of course a well-known trait of the Romans. It can be seen in their literature, which is, almost in its entirety, taken over from the Greek, and adapted to serve a gamut of new and Roman purposes. The same is true in more mundane spheres. Roman mining techniques and Roman taxation, to name but two, were, in the varied areas of the Mediterranean world where they were practised, almost always variations on the methods employed in those areas before the Romans arrived. It is however in their legal and constitutional structures, where development and precision are equally essential, that their genius for a combination of *ad hoc* adaptation and intellectual discipline can be seen most clearly, both in its successful working and in its occasional lapses.

To illustrate what I mean, I want to look briefly at two instances that are of particular importance for Roman history. The first is the development of the position of the pro-magistrate.[8] Until the second half of the fourth century BC, the only men entitled to command the forces of the Roman people were those elected to annual magistracies by the people,

---

[7] P. Birks, "Fictions Ancient and Modern," N. MacCormick and P. Birks (eds.), *The Legal Mind* (Oxford: Clarendon Press 1986) 83–101.

[8] See in general, W.F. Jashemski, *The Origins and History of the Proconsular and Propraetorian Imperium* (Chicago IL: Chicago University Press 1950).

as consul or dictator or (occasionally) praetor. It was in virtue of their election that these magistrates were given the *imperium* appropriate to their office, the power of the Roman people, on whose behalf, almost indeed in whose stead, they were to act. Such a scheme, common among those cities of the ancient world which had constitutions, was well adapted to provide commanders for the wars which the republic fought against its neighbours in the first century and a half of its existence. By the later fourth century, however, the inflexibilty of the annual term was beginning to show, particularly when Roman armies were fighting further from home. Thus in 327 BC the consul Q. Publilius Philo was occupied in the seige of the Greek city of Naples when he was due to return to Rome to preside at the elections which would choose his successor. In order not to interrupt the campaign, the tribunes of the plebs proposed to the popular assembly that Philo should be allowed to continue the war until its completion pro consule, "as though a consul."[9] This device was to prove of immense value to the Romans as their field of military activity spread to cover not only Italy, but Sicily, Spain, Greece, North Africa and Asia Minor through the third and fourth centuries. It was, of course, as a comparison with the passage of Gaius examined above illustrates, a legal fiction. The proconsul and propraetors, as they were eventually to be called, were not magistrates, but were permitted, normally in later times by the senate, to behave as though they were. Their status was not changed, for they remained *privati* (private citizens), but the consequences of that status were. This is shown by an event in the early second century BC, when Rome was fighting in Greece and Asia Minor. In the year 187, the senate proposed to extend for a second time the *imperium* of the two consuls of 189, M. Fulvius Nobilior and Cn. Manlius Vulso, respectively in Greece and Asia Minor. At this point, according to the historian Livy,[10] one of the consuls of the year, M. Aemilius Lepidus, protested at being sent to his province in northern Italy, saying that, if the senate thought that there should be armies in Greece and Asia, they should be commanded by consuls, not by mere *privati*, who were by now almost substitute kings in place of the defeated Philip V of Macedonia and Antiochus III of Syria. The protest was, needless to say, self-interested, and ignored by the senate, who dis-

---

[9] Livy 8.23.12; cf. the entry in the *Fasti Triumphales*: "primus procos de Samnitibus" (*Inscr. It.* 13.1.70–1.)
[10] Livy 48.42.9–13.

patched both consuls to northern Italy; but the point that Lepidus was making was in fact true, and not denied. The commanders *pro consule* were indeed private citizens, and not magistrates of the republic.

It was these men, these fictive magistrates, who were responsible not only for the extension of Roman control through the Mediterranean basin, but also for its maintenance thereafter for as Roman control became the Roman empire, so the tasks alotted to proconsuls and propraetors by the senate, their provinciae, became the provinces of that empire. The fiction was not merely convenient; it was essential if the rigid system of annual magistrates was to be used to fight distant wars, and control great areas of territory. The use of the pro-magistrates imported the necessary flexibility into that system, without destroying its essential nature. Moreover as the republic moved, by fits and starts, towards the civil wars which brought about its end, the commanders of the great armies, whether fighting against the tribes of Gaul or the kings of Pontus or Syria, or against other Romans, were holders of *imperium pro consule*. Nor, surprisingly, was the difference between the "real" magistrate and his fictive counterpart ever quite lost sight of. In 43 BC, in the aftermath of the assassination of Julius Caesar, the orator Cicero complaining that *imperium* should not be given to someone who was a *privatus*, quoted the somewhat bitter joke of the distinguished consular, L. Philippus.[11] Of the appointment of the young Pompey in 77, who had previously held no magistracy at all, to the command of the war in Spain, following the refusal of both the consuls of that year, Philippus had said that he was being sent not *pro consule* but *pro consulibus*, not "as though he were a consul" but "as though he were the consuls." Even after prolonged and frequent usage, the distinction was still observed between the actual and the fictive, between status and its consequences.

Cicero's point in 43 was weakened by the fact that he had himself earlier in the same year sponsored the giving of *imperium pro consule* to Caesar's heir and adopted son, the young C. Julius Caesar. It was this same Caesar, who, under the name of Augustus, used the pattern of the *imperium pro consule* to provide the constitutional basis for that most unconstitutional position, that of emperor, or to be more precise, of *princeps*. When, in the year 23 BC, he gave up the annual office of consul, which he had then held eleven times, and nine in succession since 31 BC, he was voted a farrago of powers, mostly fictive in charac-

[11] Cic. *Phil.* 11.2.18.

ter, just as the *imperium pro consule* was fictive. Thus from this year, he held the power of a tribune of the plebs (*tribunicia potestas*) without being a tribune, and for the next five years in the first instance the *imperium pro consule*, without being consul. When, three years later, he undertook the work of censor, he did so not in virtue of holding the censorship, but through a grant of censorial power (*censoria potestas*). The position of emperor, as created by Augustus, was not that of a magistrate, though from time to time the *princeps* might hold magistracies, but of a *privatus*; and when he came to write the official account of his deeds for posterity, Augustus was able to state, with his customary disarming and misleading precision, that he had held no greater power than any of his colleagues in the several magistracies.[12] This was true. He had held his immense constitutional power as a private citizen. The skill and imagination which Augustus showed in giving formal expression to his position is characteristic of "that artful prince" (as Gibbon was to describe him); but if the fictions which he employed were new, the habit of mind to which they belonged had a long and illustrious history.

The second example of this use of "fiction" which I want to examine is that of adoption. The taking of the offspring of another family into one's own as a son or daughter is of course fictive in its very essence. In the Roman case, not surprisingly from what we have seen already, the fiction was quite explicit. The legal relationship of father to child in Roman law depended upon the *patria potestas*, the power of life and death that the *pater familias* had over not only his own children but over all other members of his *familia*. An adoption consisted in the acquisition by the adoptive father of such power over an individual who had not previously been subject to it. Thus in the process of *adrogatio*, the adoption of of a male who was at the time not under the *patria potestas* of another, that is one who was *sui iuris*, after preliminary enquiries had been made by the college of priests (necessary because such an adoption would extinguish the family of the person to be adopted), the intended adoptive son appeared before a specially constituted form of assembly of the people (the *comitia calata*). There he was asked the question, "Do you give your consent that P. Fonteius (or whoever was to be the adoptive father) should have the power of life and death over you, as over a son?"[13] The assembly was then asked, in the formula used for the

[12] *Res Gestae* 34.3.
[13] Cic. *de Domo* 77.

proposing of legislation in other assemblies, whether it wished and decreed that this person should be as though he had been born to the mother and father of the family, and under the father's power of life and death.[14] The fictive nature of the process is apparent, and in the same style as those we have seen already. The adopted son is not said to be the son of his adoptive father, but to be in the same position as such a son.

In the case of an adoption where the natural father was still alive (*adoptio*, properly so called) there was a further problem, that the father's *patria potestas* was in principle incapable of being broken. In the Twelve Tables, however, it was stated that if ever a son was emancipated three times, the son was free from his father's *potestas*.[15] This had been done to prevent a cruel father emancipating a son over and over again, and continually reclaiming him. Later this was used as the basis of the process of *adoptio*. The natural father emancipated the son by means of a ritual sale three times in a row, and the son was handed back twice. After the third emancipation, the adoptive father claimed before the praetor that the son was his, and, as the natural father made no objection, the claim ws upheld. This process, it must be admitted, is not so much fictive, in the sense I have been using that word, as fictional. Certainly it seems to be asserting that a state of affairs was true that clearly was not. *Adoptio* seems to be a later development than *adrogatio*, and to be designed to involve a less complicated series of transactions. It had, however, the same result as the older process, in that it transferred the son to the *patria potestas* of the adoptive father.

Adoption was of immense importance not only to the individuals involved, but also to their families; and because of its importance to the family, it was inevitably of significance for Roman political activity. The importance of the family, indicated by the power of the *pater familias* and its coverage of all offspring in the male line, whether or not they were children, was apparent in all areas of social life, not least in the maintenance and management of political support by the great families which dominated the magistracies and the senate of the Roman republic. For these families, adoption became one method of creating links between families, and, more importantly, of ensuring the continuity of a family when there were no sons born to a *pater familias*. Two of

---

[14] Aulus Gellius, *NA* 5.5.19.
[15] *XII Tab.* 4.2.; cf. Gaius 1.132ff.

the sons of L. Aemilius Paullus, the Roman commander who at the battle of Pydna in 168 BC finally destroyed the kingdom of Macedon, were given in adoption during his life-time to other great houses, one to the Fabii Maximi and the other to the Cornelii Scipiones, the adoptive fathers in both cases having apparently failed to beget surviving natural sons. The political importance of these adoptions seems to have led to a further development, indeed a further layer of fiction, which appeared in the last century of the republic. In 91 BC the orator, L. Licinius Crassus died, leaving two daughters, both already married, but no sons. In his will he adopted his grandson by one of his daughters, a Cornelius Scipio.[16] This is the first case of which we have evidence of the practice of testamentary adoption, of which there are several instances in the decades which followed. The form, in the one instance of such an adoption we have in detail, seems to follow that of *adrogatio*, and if, as is probable, the natural father in this case was already dead, that would be normal. What is odd about such a process is, of course, that the essential element in an adoption, and explicitly so for *adrogatio*, was the transfer of the adopted son into the *patria potestas* of the adoptive father. In a testamentary adoption, the adoptive father is, *ex hypothesi*, dead, and thus quite incapable of assuming *patria potestas*. Indeed some historians of Roman law have denied that such an adoption was possible, and have argued that all that was involved was a requirement in the will that the beneficiary should bear the name of the deceased, a provision known from legal sources of the second century AD.[17] Such a position seems perverse. There is no doubt that those adopted in this fashion were regarded as sons in the full sense of the word, and indeed for the political purposes for which testamentary adoption was employed, that was the object of the exercise. This is seen most clearly in the best-known case from the late republic, the adoption of the future Augustus under the provisions of the will of Julius Caesar in 44 BC. Not only was he known, as we have already seen, by the name C. Julius Caesar, but his whole political position in the chaotic months and years which followed the assassination of the Ides of March 44 depended upon his recognition, not simply as Caesar's heir, but as Caesar's son.

---

[16] Cic. *Brut.* 58.212.
[17] Cf. Gaius *D*.36.1.65(63).10; Maecianus *D*.36.1.7. Note the comments of R. Syme, "Clues to Testamentary Adoption," *Roman Papers* 4 (Oxford: Clarendon Press 1988) 159–73.

It was then on the basis of this doubly fictive form of testamentary adoption that the former C. Octavius could claim to be *divi Iulii filius*, the son of the deified Julius Caesar, and the avenging of his father's death (his adoptive father, of course) was a major part of the propaganda he employed on his way to undisputed control of the Roman world. Small wonder that Marcus Antonius could describe him bitterly as a boy who owed everything to his name.[18] It is perhaps less surprising that when Augustus himself, who had no male offspring, wished to designate his own successor, adoption was one of the chief mechanisms he used.

Of the two forms available from private law, that most frequently used by Augustus and his successors was the older (and incidentally, more fictive) form of *adrogatio*. The only case of *adoptio* that can be identified with certainty is the adoption by Augustus himself of his two grandsons, Gaius and Lucius Caesar, in 17 BC, during the life-time of their natural father, M. Agrippa. The biographer, Suetonius, describes the "sale" of the boys to their grandfather in terms which certainly suggest the formal emancipation that was part of the process of *adoptio*.[19] With this exception, the Julio-Claudian emperors, from Augustus to Claudius, adopted intended successors by means of *adrogatio*, or at least (for there is dispute about some cases) by a form which reflected the pattern of *adrogatio*, in its public and legislative aspects. Not all those adopted succeeded to the principate, nor were all those who became emperor men who had been adopted. The emperor Gaius, better known by his childhood nickname of Caligula, adopted his cousin and adoptive brother Tiberius Gemellus (the emperor Tiberius had adopted both of them) on his accession in 37; but (if our sources are to be trusted) he was driven to suicide by Gaius during the following winter.[20] The emperor's unadopted uncle, Claudius, was the man chosen by the praetorian guard to succeed in the turmoil which followed Caligula's murder.

The use of *adrogatio* is not of itself remarkable. In all the cases mentioned, the adopted son had already lost his father, and was *sui iuris*, so that *adoptio* was in any case inappropriate. It is more surprising that the notion of an imperial dynasty had taken root at all, let alone taken root

---

[18] Cic. *Phil.* 13.24.
[19] Suet. *Aug.* 64.1.
[20] Suet. *Gaius* 15.2, 23.3; Dio 59.8.1; Philo *leg.* 23–31.

so rapidly, so strongly and in so short a time. The tradition of the Roman republic did not encourage the idea that power within the state was passed from father to son, however important in political terms the great families of the republican period might have been. Yet, as a result of the example set by Augustus, the dynastic pattern was taken for granted by his successors, even though it could only be achieved by the means of the fictive creation of male offspring by *adrogatio*. Moreover the pattern was continued through to the late second century, interrupted only by the accident of assassination and usurpation, or the oddly rare instances of succession by a natural son of an emperor. Only the sons of the emperor Vespasian, Titus and Domitian, and the disastrous, if colourful, son of Marcus Aurelius, the emperor Commodus, come into this select group.

It was no doubt the expectation that adoption would be the means of indicating a successor that accounts for the almost total disappearance of another part of the Augustan heritage, the doubly fictive adoption by will. As the process of *adrogatio* became one of the chief means by which an emperor displayed his intention, it was normal for political reasons for matters not to be left until after his death. Occasionally, however, such forward planning became impossible. In the year 117, the emperor Trajan died suddenly at Selinus in Cilicia, in the course of his eastern campaigns. He is said, in circumstances which inevitably caused dispute later,[21] to have adopted on his death-bed his former ward, P. Aelius Hadrianus. If the account of Trajan's last hours is correct, Hadrian cannot have been formally adopted by *adrogatio*, since, as we have seen, this process required a formal declaration which could take place only in Rome. It may be, however, that Hadrian and his supporters, who included Trajan's widow, Plotina, presented Hadrian's adoption as testamentary. Although the intention of the deceased emperor was not recorded in any document that would be recognised by a Roman court, regulations, which had originated in the reign of Augustus, and had been further elaborated by Trajan himself, allowed a soldier, or anyone else in a military camp on active service, to count as a will any wish deliberately expressed before witnesses.[22] If this was the basis of

---

[21] Dio 69.1.
[22] M.-H. Prévost, *Les adoptions politiques à Rome* (Paris: Inst de Droit Romain 1949) 50–2, on Hadrian's adoption; Gaius 2.109–11, Ulpian *tit.* 20.10, Justinian *Inst.* 2.11.1 and 2.12.pr on military wills.

Hadrian's claim to adoption, his was the first since Augustus' own, and the fragility of his case emphasises the reason why. A publicly acknowledged form of adoption could scarcely be challenged as such; a clause in a will, let alone a death-bed wish, was far easier to forge, and there were those who insisted that in Hadrian's case, the crucial words had been uttered by a substitute, speaking in a tired voice in the presence of the corpse of the deceased emperor.[23] Both Hadrian and his successor, Antoninius Pius, though they had problems enough about the choice of men to follow them in the imperial office, were more circumspect. Testamentary adoption, let alone by use of *testamentum militare*, was not an ideal method of designation.

The power of the fiction of adoption had not yet, however, reached its high point, though it must be said that the later instances show what, from the viewpoint of a historian of law and institutions, can only be seen as a sad decline from the precision and discipline apparent in its earlier forms. In AD 197, after the defeat of his rival for the emperorship, Clodius Albinus, the usurper Septimius Severus styled himself, in addresses to the senate, as the son of the emperor Marcus Aurelius and the brother of Aurelius' natural son, the emperor Commodus.[24] Aurelius had been dead for seventeen years, and certainly had had no intention of adopting the then somewhat obscure senator from the province of Africa. At one level, Severus' assertion was simply absurd, and recognised as such at the time. A notorious wit of the period, Pollienus Auspex, is recorded as saying to the emperor, "I congratulate you, Caesar, on finding a father".[25] On another level, it is a sign of the continuing significance of a completely artificial conception of a family tie: artificial not only in that Severus was not the son of Marcus Aurelius, which is the fiction common to all adoptions; nor that he could not be transferred into the *patria potestas* of a dead man, which was the further fiction implicit in testamentary *adrogatio*, but that he could claim to be the son of a man who had not indicated in any way, either in the face of the *comitia curiata*, or in a will or even in his last words, uttered in a military camp, that he wished to make Severus his son. Although there is no evidence what form of procedure, if any, Severus employed in order to establish his claim, the matter is, in such a case, of no signifi-

---

[23] *SHA Hadr.* 4.10.
[24] Dio 75.7.4.
[25] Dio 76.9.4.

cance. The pattern of the civil law tradition, which Augustus and his successors had employed, and by which they had allowed themselves to be constrained, was now being distorted by the immediate political requirements of an emperor. It is fascinating to reflect that it is under Severus and his dynasty (whose members, whatever their various virtues and vices, were at least as cavalier in such matters as Severus himself) that Roman civil law reached its first great flowering, in the hands of such as Papinian and Ulpian; but it is also noteworthy that it was Ulpian who stated in its classic form the doctrine, known from the beginning of the principate, *princeps legibus solutus est*, the emperor is not bound by statutes.[26]

I have demonstrated, I trust, how powerful were these two instances of a "fictive" mentality; powerful both in the sense that they made possible the articulation of the military and political power of the Roman state and its emperors, and in the enduring influence that they had in shaping the ways in which such power was exercised and expressed. The power of such fictions represents one facet of the imagination of a fascinating people, an imagination that enabled the Romans to use and reuse the history and traditions of their ancestors to deal with the ever-changing circumstances of the world in which they lived, and which they so effectively controlled. It is a trick worth learning, even to-day. Not least in the turbulent complexities of the twentieth century, the exercise of an imaginative discipline in the simultaneous preservation and adaptation of our own civilisation is in the most literal sense essential for survival.

---

[26] Ulpian *D*.1.31.1; cf. *lex de imp. Vesp.* 22ff.

9

Did Thucydides Write for Readers or Hearers?

Shigetake Yaginuma

Athenaeus (ii 56e), quoting Eupolis, ῥαφανίδες ἄπλυτοι σηπίαι (*unwashed radishes and cuttle-fish:* fr. i 302 Kock), says that ἄπλυτοι (*unwashed*) should be taken (literally *heard*: ἀκούειν) with radishes (ἐπὶ τῶν ῥαφανίδων), not with cuttle-fish (οὐκ ἐπὶ τῶν σηπιῶν), for, he says, Antiphanes has a phrase ῥαφανῖδας ἀπλύτους (fr. ii 124 Kock). I do not know how this sole example could have encouraged Athenaeus to cook radishes, rather than cuttle-fish, unwashed. I am referring to this passage only because it shows a writer, as late as Athenaeus, still using the term ἀκούιεν in the sense "to read." This passage shows that one of the commonest ways of "reading" was, until the beginning of the third century, to hear someone reading, just as Pliny used to do (*Epistulae* iii 5);[1] whether or not the man was specifically called

---

[1] As far as I know, A.W. Gomme, *A Historical Commentary on Thucydides*, Vol. I (Oxford: Clarendon Press 1945) 139 and P. Chantraine, "Les verbes grecs signifiant <<lire>>" *Annuaire de l'Institut de Philologie et d'histoire orientales et slaves* X (1950): ΠΑΓΚΑΡΠΕΙΑ, *Mélanges Henri Grégoire* (Brussels, 1950) 115–26, esp. 118 were the

ἀναγνώστης. Together with the famous passage from Augustine's *Confessiones* (vi 3), this seems to indicate that silent reading was not usual in ancient times, and that those examples of silent reading which we do sporadically find (e.g. Claudius Ptolemaeus, in *De judicandi facultate* 5, strongly urges us to read in silence whatever would require us to concentrate the mind) should be regarded as representing exceptional cases. Bernard Knox, who believed, in 1968, that he had found not a few Greek and Latin passages where silent reading was meant or implied had to modify his opinion in 1985.[2] Now that all the materials and arguments have been set out in two important recent books (though written in a completely different context) it seems finally clear that silent reading cannot have been usual in ancient times[3] (whether in groups or alone), and that, until the end of the fifth century books were usually "published" by reading aloud to an audience.

II

One of the few possible obstacles to this conviction comes from the language and style of Thucydides.[4] Rosalind Thomas says[5] that his style was notorious for its denseness and difficulty even in antiquity, and that it is hard to believe it could be readily understood on a single hearing.

---

first to notice the use of ἀκούειν in this sense. Recently Dirk M. Schenkeveld gave very detailed discussions on an expression ἀκούειν Χ λέγοντος in "Prose Usage of AKOYEIN 'To Read'," *CQ* 92 (1992) 129–41. According to him this expression is a proper Greek idiom from the end of the Hellenistic period onward, while ἀναγιγνώσκειν was never used to express the notion of "I've read X saying that ...."

[2] See Bernard M.W. Knox, "Silent Reading in Antiquity," *GRBS* 9 (1968) 421–35 and his "Books and Readers in the Greek World," P.E. Easterling and B.M.W. Knox (eds.), *The Cambridge History of Classical Literature*, Vol. I (Cambridge: Cambridge University Press 1985) 1–41.

[3] Rosalind Thomas, *Literacy and Orality in Ancient Greece* (Cambridge: Cambridge University Press 1992) and M.B. Parkes, *Pause and Effect: An Introduction to the History of Punctuation in the West* (Aldershot: Scholar Press 1992).

[4] Another possible obstacle I am thinking of comes from a surprisingly great number of "misquotations" observable in ancient writers. These are usually attributed to their mis-memorisation. But if reading aloud was their usual way of reading, it would be inconceivable that they should have made such a huge amount of mis-memorisation.

[5] Rosalind Thomas (above n.3) 104. Julius Steup, in the "Einleitung" to his commentary (*Thukydides*, Vol. I (Berlin: Weidmann 1963; repr. of 1919 edition) lxxxiii), says that ancient critics overstate the difficulty of Thucydides' language, which I disagree with.

"But," she continues, "his complex antithetical style is closely akin to that of the contemporary Sophists, for example Antiphon and Gorgias, and they must certainly set great store by performance and recitations." The problem is that Thucydides' style seems to be something more than "very closely akin to that of the contemporary Sophists." When I say this, I am thinking, for instance, of the extraordinary size of his periods, his use of -*sis* nouns, and his very peculiar phrasing, sometimes called "economy of words."

Let us begin with the size of Thucydides' sentences. The average number of words per sentence is 25, while that of Antiphon is 19. This may not seem a noticeable difference, but it is. Certainly we could find no difference between a single sentence of 25 words and the one of 19 words. But this 25 is an average figure obtained from all the sentences which Thucydides wrote in his narrative passages (i.e. the whole text except speeches), and 19 is also an average obtained from all the sentences which Antiphon spoke before the Athenian audience. Incidentally the longest sentence Thucydides wrote contains 160 words (v 16.1), and his next longest one 141 words (viii 99), while Antiphon's longest sentence consists of 97 words, and his next longest 91 words, both in *De choreuta*. Again, 32.9% of the sentences Thucydides wrote have more than 31 words in them, while 12.0% of those by Antiphon do so. All these can safely be called differences. As for Antiphon's sentences themselves, there can also be found a very conspicuous difference: the average number of words per sentence in *De choreuta* amounts to 23, while that of those in all the other speeches remains less than 18; and in *De choreuta* 23.2% of the sentences contain more than 31 words, while in other speeches no more than 10%. Therefore, it is *De choreuta* that should be looked into in comparison with Thucydides.

Let us look at Antiphon's sentence of 97 words (*De chor.* 23). This is composed of four clauses, paratactically connected by καί; of these the first three are very small and simple (having 7, 6 and 8 words respectively), with the last clause consisting of 76 words. The structure can be represented by the following diagram:

a καὶ ἰέναι ἐκέλευον λαβόντα μάρτυρας
b ὁπόσους βούλοιτο ἐπὶ τοὺς παραγενεμένους,
c λέγβων αὐτῷ ὀνόματι ἕκαστον
d τούτους ἐρωτᾶν καὶ ἐλέγχειν,
e τοὺς μὲν ἐλευθέρους ὡς χρὴ τοὺς ἐλευθέρους,
f οἵ σφων τ' ἕνεκα καὶ τοῦ δικαίου ἔφραζον ἂν
τἀληθῆ καὶ τὰ γενόμενα,
g τοὺς δὲ δούλους,
h εἰ μὲν αὐτῷ ἐρωτῶντι τἀληθῆ δοκοῖεν λέγειν,
i εἰ δὲ μή,
j ἕτοιμος εἴην διδόναι βασανίζειν τούς τε ἐμαυτοῦ πάντας,
k καὶ εἴ τινας τῶν ἀλλοτρίων κελεύοι,
l ὡμολόγουν
m πείσας τὸν δεσπότην παραδώσειν αὐτῷ βασανίζειν
n τρόπῳ ὁποίῳ βούλοιτο.

(To put this into English as literally as possible) *And I ordered him to go and take as many men as he would like as witnesses against those who were present there, telling him all their names, and to ask and cross-examine them; (and I advised him) if they were free men, he should treat them in such a way as would be befitting free men, who would, for their own sake and for the sake of justice, tell the truth and facts; as for slaves, if they seem to be telling him the truth; if not, I should be ready for offering all my slaves to be tortured; if he should want slaves of others than mine, I agreed to persuade their master to let them be examined by whatever torture he liked.*

The whole clause is made up of rather short cola. The main clause (within this clause) comes first (**a**, thus making what Blass called an "absteigende Periode"[6]), a relative clause (**b**) and a participial construction (**c**) connected to it; τούτους in **d** is, of course, connected with ὁπόσους in **b**; two infinitives in **d**, ἐρωτᾶν and ἐλέγχειν together with ἰέναι in **a**, are connected to ἐκέλευον in **a**. Τούτους in **d** is further explained by τοὺς μὲν in **e** and τοὺς δὲ in **g**. **h–n** are added for the

---

[6] Friedrich Blass, *Die attische Beredsamkeit* I (Leipzig, 1887²) 224. According to him, only the other type of period, the "aufsteigende Periode," in which the subordinate clauses precede, with the main clause concluding the sentence, can properly be called "period," while the "absteigend" one is virtually the same as "parataxis." "Virtually" or not, I don't think they are the same, though it is true that they are very similar in that one can put as many cola as he likes after the main clause. Blass seems to regard the "aufsteigende Periode" as ideal style of prose, but they are not found so frequently as he seems to have expected: in my rough calculation, about 60% of Greek periods are written in the "absteigende Periode."

explanation of treatment of slaves suggested in **g**; interrelation of each colon of **h–n** is quite clear, while **h** is only loosely connected with the preceding cola, but the audience would not mind, finding no difficulty in following the speaker.

Now let us turn to a similar sized sentence from Thucydides, of which there are many instances. I quote here i 132.5 (104 words). This is one of the 13 sentences of i 130.1–133, where affairs concerning Pausanias, Spartan general, are recounted. (It is very interesting to notice how many words Thucydides gave to each of these 13 sentences: 72, 17, 11, 83, 18, 33, 97, 25, 23, 13,13,104 and 106).

```
a  ἀλλ' οὐδ' ἠξίωσαν νεώτερόν τι ποιεῖν ἐς αὐτόν,
    b  ὡς οὐδὲ τῶν Εἱλώτων μηνυταῖς τισι πιστεύσαντες
c  χρώμενοι τῷ τρόπῳ ᾧπερ εἰώθασιν ἐς σφᾶς αὐτούς,
d  μὴ ταχεῖς εἶναι περὶ ἀνδρὸς Σπαρτιάτου   βουλεῦσαί τι
                                                  ἀνηκέστατον,
    e  ἄνευ ἀναμφισβητήτων τεκμηρίων,
f  πρίν γε δὴ αὐτοῖς,  ὁ μέλλων τὰς τελευταίας βασιλεῖ ἐπιστολὰς
                        πρὸς Ἀρτάβαζον κομιεῖν,
    g  ὡς λέγεται,
h  ἀνὴρ Ἀργίλιος,  μηνυτὴς γίγνεται,
    i  παιδικά ποτε ὢν αὐτοῦ καὶ πιστότατος ἐκείνῳ,
j  δείσας κατὰ ἐνθύμησίν τινα
k  ὅτι οὐδείς πω τῶν πρὸ ἑαυτοῦ ἀγγέλων πάλιν ἀφίκετο,
l  καὶ παρασημηνάμενος,
  m  ἵνα   μὴ ἐπιγνῷ,
      n  ἢν ψευσθῇ τῆς δόξης,
      o  ἢ καὶ ἐκεῖνός τι μεταγράψαι αἰτήσῃ,
p  λύει τὰς ἐπιστολάς,
    q  ἐν αἷς ὑπονοήσας τι τοιοῦτον προσεπεστάλθαι
    r  καὶ αὐτὸν ηὗρεν ἐγγεγραμμένον κτείνειν.
```

But, as ephors didn't trust even then certain Helots who turned informers, they thought it best for them not to take any harsh means against Pausanias, having recourse to their customary measure, in order not to be hasty about a Spartan, without indisputable proof, in adopting irrevocable decision, until at last, it was rumoured, a man who was to take Pausanias' last letters to Artabazus, a man from Argilus, who had once been Pausanias' favourite and most faithful to him, turned informer; it was because he feared, after some consideration, that none of the mes-

sengers before him had ever come back, and so having made a false seal himself, in case either his fears should be groundless or Pausanias should ask some change in the letter, he opened the letter, in which he did find something which he had suspected he might find: it was written that he should be killed.

The whole sentence is divided into two huge parts, **a–e** (A: the main clause, 35 words) and **f–r** (B: the subordinate clause, 69 words; thus an 'absteigende Periode' again). Within A itself, **a** is the main clause, and the rest serves it as subordinate elements; as for B, **f**, **h** and **n** are main clauses. First of all, other writers would not write πρίν γε at **f**, but start a new independent sentence here. But that is just what Thucydides would not do, for he follows invariably what I called his "one-sentence-for-one-action-principle."[7] Thucydides observes the action of one person as a group of persons, and then tries to describe in *one* sentence a series of actions, motivations, expectations, results and so forth. In this one sentence every "minor" action is made to contribute to a main action (the main clause) as subordinate elements (by means of adverbial clauses, participial constructions, genitive absolute and what not). This principle of his naturally makes his sentence structure fairly rigid and complex, though, on the other hand, if we observe it carefully, we can trace exactly just as he saw an action or an event. But I presume this sort of sentence structure can only be grasped by observation over printed pages; when heard, Thucydides' sentence will only leave the impression that it is very hard to grasp. Compared with this, Antiphon's sentence is not complicated.[8]

Another of Thucydides' favourite styles of composition is also observable in the passage above: insertion of a colon or cola into another colon, as can be seen where **b** is inserted into **a**, **e** into **d**, **g** into **f**, **i** into **h**, and **n** and **o** into **m**. This can easily be notice, when we see them in the written text, but I am not sure whether it is ever as easily noticed when heard.

---

[7] See my paper, "On Thucydides' Long Sentences," *Studies in Language and Literature* 15 (Institute of Literature and Linguistics, University of Tsukuba 1988) 1–28, esp. 22–3 and also "Thucydides 6.100," E.M. Craik (ed.), *'Owls to Athens'; Essays on Classical Subjects Presented to Sir Kenneth Dover* (Oxford: Clarendon Press 1990) 281–5.

[8] The only similarity I can find between Antiphon and Thucydides is their favourite use of antithesis. Complexity is not characteristically Antiphon's; if it is, it is something other than Thucydides.

Let me quote another sentence, neither too long (58 words) nor too complicated, but typically Thucydidean: ii 53.4, part of the famous description of the plague.

a *No fears of gods or law of men had restrained (them),*
b *on the one hand* (μέν), *people forming a judgement,*
c *from seeing* (inf. τὸ ὁρᾶν) *all, pious* (inf. σέβειν) *or not,*
           dying in the same way,
d *on the other* (δέ), *for their misdeeds, no one expecting to live*
e *until* (μέχρι) *he is brought to trial and punished*
           (inf. with article in gen.)
f *(everybody believing) much severer sentence having already*
     passed (κατεψηφισμένην) *on him and was hanging over him*
           (ἐπικρεμασθῆναι),
g *before whose arrival, it was reasonable to get some pleasure*
           out of life (inf. phrase).

a is the main clause, and two participial constructions, **b** and **d**, introduced by μέν and δέ, are added to explain why it was so. **c** is connected to **b**, **e** to **d** both infinitive phrases. In **f** the participle phrase *having passed* is put into the accusative, thus making the sense subject of the infinitive (*was hanging over*). This infinitive is formally connected with *expecting* in **d**, but I supplemented *everybody believing* in parenthesis to avoid an impression of awkwardness. Other writers would turn this into three or four separate sentences, but Thucydides thinks that he is only writing concerning the one fact that the Athenian people came not to fear gods or law, and that the other items only explain why and how they did so. So he wrote **a**, connecting with it all the necessary explanations by participles and infinitives. Several sentences are forcedly made into an "absteigende Periode," and so would be rather hard to follow in hearing.

III

I am interested in *-sis* nouns only when they are used periphrastically, that is to say, when they are used in combination with verbs or prepositions, expressing what otherwise we need clauses to say.[9] This use of

[9] See my papers, "Use of *-sis* Nouns in Greek Poets" and "Use of *-sis* nouns in Prose," *Studies in Language and Literature* (above, n.7) 4 (1979) 91–114 and 5 (1980) 1–22. In these papers I was much indebted to R. Browning, "Greek Abstract Nouns in *-sis, -tis*," *Philologus* 102 (1938), and to A.A. Long, *Language and Thought in Sophocles: A Study of Abstract Nouns and Poetic Technique*, University of London Classical Studies 6 (London: Athlone 1968).

-*sis* nouns has a long history, mainly in poetry since Homer. In prose, although a vast number of -*sis* nouns were coined (especially by the Hippocratics and Plato as technical terms), periphrastic use was evidently decreasing, except in Thucydides and, to a much smaller extent, in Antiphon. With Thucydides, this should not be ascribed to his love of poetic figures or archaism; it rather shows his attempt to render his sentence as compact as possible. Just look at the list below (Works referred to: as for Homer, Herodotus, Thucydides and Antiphon, the whole texts of extant works; for Xenophon, *Anabasis* i and ii; for Lysias, Nos. 1, 2,12,13,16,19 and 33; for Andocides, *De mysteriis, De reditu suo* and *De pace*; for Isocrates, *Panegyricus* and *Evagoras*; for Demosthenes, *De corona*; for Aeschines, *In Ctesiphontem*).

	Occurences of -*sis* nouns	Percentage of Periphr. Use
Homer	132	21%
Aeschylus	94	22%
Sophocles	151	21%
Euripides	338	20%
Herodotus	388	13%
Thucydides	700	41%
Xenophon	564	6%
Antlphon	16	22%
Lysias	41	17%
Andocides	36	11%
Isocrates	83	4%
Demosthenes	89	12%
Aeschines	111	3%

Incidentally we find 4,039 occurences of -*sis* nouns in Plato's corpus, but 826 of them are of φύσις! We see how prose writers (especially orators) tended to use less and less periphrastic -*sis* nouns, and how peculiar Thucydides was in this respect. Look at another list, showing cases in which periphrastic -*sis* nouns are used.

	Nominative	Accusative	Dative
Homer & Tragedians	37%	61%	2%
Herodotus	38%	39%	23%
Thucydides	10%	51%	39%
Orators	24%	56%	20%

-*Sis* nouns in nominative are subjects of sentences, thus more or less personified, unless the verbs are εἶναι, γίγνεσθαι or ἔρχεσθαι. Almost all the datives are instrumental. Here again we recognize Thucydides' peculiarity: he uses-*sis* nouns much less in nominative, and much more in adverbial phrases in dative with or without prepositions.[10] For instance, consider iii 82.3–4.

    a *And so the cities began to revolt,*
    b *and the cities which were late [in revolting]* (part. τὰ ἐφυστερίζοντα)
                                         carried zeal of inventing new devices,
    c *by learning* (-*tis* noun in dat. πύστει) *what had been done*
                                          before them (part. in gen. τῶν προγενομένων),
    d *inventing extraordinary art* (-*sis* noun in dat. περιτεχνήσει)
                        of attacking (-*sis* noun in gen. ἐπιχειρήσεων)
    e *and by unheard-of-way of revenging.*
    f *And they changed the ordinarily accepted meaning* (-*sis* noun in
                                       acc. ἀξίωσιν) *of words*
    g *in reference to the actual according to what they thought fit*
                              (-*sis* noun in dat. δικαιώσει).

This is part of the description of Civil War at Cercyra, on which A.W. Gomme, op. cit., commented, "The importance of cc. 82 and 83 is so great, and Thucydides' language, clearly chosen with much care, is yet so difficult...." This is also the passage which Dionysius of Halicarnassus criticised sharply, saying that it is written in an involved manner, full of unnecessary periphrases, and the use of substantival constructions (οἱ τῶν ὀνομάτων σχηματισμῶν, meaning periphrastic use of -*sis* nouns) unpleasant to the ear. He is right here (although he is very often unreliable).[11] Indeed, "substantival construction" is just what Greek prose writers like to avoid, is it not?

IV

Dionysius (ibid.) complains that τὰ ἐφυστερίζοντα in **b** of the above passage is hard to make out, and suggests that Thucydides could have made the meaning clearer, if he had written αἱ ὑστεροῦσαι πόλεις. He is right, but Thucydides had to write in this strange way, because he had

---

[10] For more details see my papers mentioned in note 9 above.
[11] See his *De Thucydide c.* 29. On his unreliability see A.W. Gomme (above, n.1) ii, 181 (Thuc. ii 64.6); more fully my paper, "Dionysius' Criticism of Thucydides' Style," *Studies in Language and Literature* (above, n.7) 10 (1986) 1–22.

already written, in **a**, *the situation of the cities* (τὰ τῶν πόλεων) instead of simply saying *the cities* (αἱ πόλεις). Why, then, he wrote τὰ τῶν πόλεων is beyond our understanding. No one except Thucydides would have chosen such wording. Who can know: when one finds the same phrase τὰ τῶν πόλεων in vi 34.5, it means *the attitude of the cities*? Every hearer would have understood that the Syracusan generals began to man their ships *when they saw the Athenians too*, on hearing ἐπειδὴ καὶ τοὺς Ἀθηναίους ᾔσθοντο (vii 69.1), unless told by Thucydides himself that it should be understood to mean that the Syracusans began to man their ships *when they saw the Athenians do the same*. At iii 82.7, hearers would have asked Thucydides to explain the meaning of the phrase διὰ τὴν πίστιν *rather than openly*. They would not have thought they understood it fully, even after they heard that it meant *taking advantage of being trusted*. We know how to read παράδειγμα τόδε τοῦ λόγου οὐκ ἐλάχιστόν ἐστι (i 2.6), thanks to Klassen-Steup's kind note, but this word order — τόδε, the subject, intervenes in the middle of an otherwise syntactically inseparable unit παράδειγμα τοῦ λόγου — must have confused the audience on the first hearing.

This kind of peculiar wording is found far more in the speeches than in the narrative passages, which I believe is why speech is reputedly more difficult to read. One of these speeches, vi 18.6, extremely complex in structure, contains yet more examples of peculiarity: διάτασις τοῖς νέοις ἐς τοὺς πρεσβυτέρους (*putting young men at variance against the old*); no one knows why Thucydides put *young men* in the dative, instead of the usual genitive. In the μέν/δέ co-ordination in the last part of the same speech, different kinds of element are made to go with μέν and δέ: μέν in a conditional clause, and δέ with a participle. This speech is made by Alcibiades in order to stir up the Athenian citizens for the expedition to Sicily. They must have had great difficulty in grasping what he meant. Since he stood up after Nicias had made a lengthy speech against the expedition, they may have known what they were going to hear through his tone of voice and gesture.

V

Thucydides' audience, if he had one, must have been very keenly intelligent and very deeply appreciative, though perhaps small in number, for his language requires extreme concentration, refusing to be heard (or read) easily. Even so, if he had an audience, he must have been plied with questions about his peculiar wording, which was so much of his own that anyone else could not have fathomed what he meant by it. This is especially the case with such omissions as those seen above (e.g. *when the Syracusans saw the Athenians do the same*). Thucydides strained in every way possible to make his sentences compact: he tried to omit words wherever it seemed possible, and in so doing he sometimes overstepped the mark, and in other cases produced results which seem to ignore the contemporary idiomatic structures of his day. He must also have received complaints about the extraordinary complexity of his sentence structure, which must often have proved unbearable to follow even for the most patient hearers (or readers).

We do not know how Thucydides dealt with these questions and complaints. The only thing we can be sure of is that there is no trace of any attempt at simplification in our text. If he had listened to those who complained, his very peculiar wording would have had to have disappeared from the text. As for the complexity and huge size of his sentences, he may have insisted that he had to write in this manner, for, he would have said, he was only copying by words the structure of actions or facts; yet, among their complaints there must have been some which he himself had to admit right. If so, there ought to be less sentences of extreme complexity in our text. Since it is clear that our text of *History* is the result of revision,[12] we shall have to assume that these peculiarities were left untouched at the final revision.

This means one of two things: either that Thucydides neglected their questions and complaints, or that no one offered him questions nor made complaints, because he had no audience. If the former is the case, we shall have to blame him for arrogance, which is one of the most unlikely attributes of Thucydides. If the latter is the case, he had kept his huge volumes of manuscripts at his side all the time, revising one of another passage by himself and for himself, until he finally published.

Gomme, loc. cit. (see note 1 above), commenting on the possibility of ἡ ἀκρόασις including reading, says, "We have not therefore necessarily an express reference here to public recitiation, ... though ἀγώνισμα,

---

[12] Besides the well-known fact that Books v and viii are unfinished, I notice, in Book viii (not so in Book v), his language itself is unfinished. I mean that sentences are more often inexplicably long, with cola connected loosely with one another, and more *anakolutha* are found here than in other books. This means that in all the other books language is polished.

22.4, hints at them." But Thucydides says that his *History* was not composed in order to be heard (ἀκούειν) here and now, as *a material for declamation with which one contends* (ἀγτώνισμα); he mentions ἀκούειν only in association with ἀγώνισμα, which, he says, he has nothing to do with.[13] Therefore, though ἀγώνισμα may hint at public recitiations, it does not necessarily suggest the possibility of Thucydides' *History* being recited before an audience. Though we cannot be too confident, I presume that we are on the safer side when we assume that Thucydides wrote his *History* for the readers as a κτῆμά τε ἐς αἰεί.[14]

---

[13] In i 21.1, ἀκρόασις (*hearing*) is mentioned in association with λογόγραφοι (prose writers before him), and he emphasizes that he is not like them in that he is indifferent to attractiveness to ἀκρόασις. In these two places and at iii 38.4 and 8, ἀκρόασις is mentioned as something undesired for. But, except at i 21 and 22, neither ἀκούειν nor ἀκρόασις has a possible connotation of reading.

[14] His notorious indifference to rhythm and hiatus may also be due to his lack of interest in speaking to an audience.

III. Philosophy and Science from Plato to Seneca

10

Aenesidemus versus Pyrrho: Il fuoco scalda "per natura" (Sextus *M.* VIII 215 e XI 69)

Fernanda Decleva Caizzi

Malgrado la manualistica sullo scetticismo ci abbia abituati ad alcune apparenti certezze, non è facile dar conto in modo realmente soddisfacente del perché, ad esempio, possiamo sentirci autorizzati ad affermare che i dieci tropi, in cui confluisce materiale ben più antico e in qualche caso rintracciabile in autori famosi,[1] sono *di* Enesidemo e spiegare che cosa questo genitivo realmente significhi. Se, per quanto riguarda le personalità che la compongono, la storia della tradizione scettica è piena di problemi di questo tipo, non meglio vanno le cose allorché si passi ad analizzare le singole argomentazioni: solo eccezionalmente esse vengono attribuite ad un autore specifico; e anche allorché questo avviene, sorge il problema ulteriore di quale sia il grado di adesione che i contenuti di tali argomentazioni ricevono da parte di chi le utilizza contro gli avversari. Eppure, su tutto questo si fonda la possibilità di individuare i contributi originali all'interno di una tradizione come quella scettica, di ricostruirne le fasi e di comprendere

---

[1] Basti per tutti citare Plat. *Tht.* 154ab.

le relazioni intellettuali, all'interno o verso l'esterno, che, in positivo o in negativo, la alimentano e la identificano come tale.

Da questo punto di vista, Enesidemo è una figura forse non meno enigmatica di Pirrone. Uno dei temi su cui attualmente si concentra l'attenzione degli studiosi dello scetticismo antico riguarda il ruolo da lui svolto nel rilancio della tradizione pirroniana. Come è noto, due dati sono in proposito importanti: l'informazione di Aristocle (*ap*. Eus. *P.E.* XIV 18, 29), che egli avrebbe rianimato la corrente filosofica, ormai praticamente senza seguaci (o, forse meglio, senza seguaci famosi), i cui esponenti erano stati Pirrone e Timone, e l'ampio spazio che, all'interno del riassunto di Fozio (*Bibl*. 212) degli otto libri dei suoi *Discorsi pirroniani*, occupa la parte introduttiva del primo libro, dedicata al confronto polemico con gli Accademici. La successione di filosofi esposta in D.L. IX 115–16, qualunque ne sia l'origine e il valore dal punto di vista storico, non conferma lo iato tra pirroniani antichi e recenti, non reca nessuna traccia di rapporti con l'Accademia, e mostra piuttosto, in positivo, l'intreccio fra tradizione scettica e tradizione medica: l'importanza di Enesidemo è indicata comunque dal fatto che, a parte il caso di Sesto, solo di lui si cita il titolo di un'opera, la stessa riassunta da Fozio. Il problema del rapporto con l'Accademia è molto complesso e oggi assai studiato: altrove ho cercato di mostrare che il testo di Fozio non autorizza *da sé solo* a ritenere che Enesidemo si fosse formato all'interno dell'Accademia;[2] e non si deve trascurare completamente anche il fatto che lo spazio dedicato nella *Biblioteca* alla polemica antiaccademica potrebbe essere frutto del particolare interesse del patriarca per questa parte del libro, rischiando così di ingenerare nel lettore una visione deformata, o perlomeno ingigantita, del ruolo che lo scetticismo accademico avrebbe svolto nella formazione di Enesidemo.

Un problema non meno rilevante solleva il rapporto tra Enesidemo e Pirrone-Timone, ed il modo in cui un pensatore del I sec. a.C. ripresentava, in modo da renderla forte e ricca di possibilità di successo, una posizione filosofica sorta nella seconda metà del IV sec., e cioè prima del fiorire di quella a cui siamo soliti dare il nome di filosofia ellenistica. Il solo fatto di raccogliere autonomamente le testimonianze su Pirrone lo ha posto in primo piano, se non altro per il notevole risalto

---

[2] F. Decleva Caizzi, "Aenesidemus and the Academy," *CQ* XLII (1992) 176–89.

che inevitabilmente vengono ad assumere gli elementi dissonanti all'interno della tradizione pirroniana.[3]

Le questioni da affrontare prima di poter offrire un quadro coerente di questa figura sono dunque ancora molte e della più varia natura; in un campo così vasto, qualche indicazione utile può tuttavia provenire anche percorrendo sentieri apparentemente marginali. Nelle pagine che seguono intendo seguire uno di questi percorsi, concentrando l'attenzione su un'idea che funge da premessa in un'argomentazione tratta dal quarto libro dei *Discorsi pirroniani* (libro che, come ci informa Fozio, *Bibl*. 170b12–14, conteneva la critica al segno); la sua formulazione precisa ci è stata trasmessa da Sesto (*M.* VIII 215) il quale, con procedura non consueta, si sofferma ad analizzarla lungamente dal punto di vista logico, per tornare a citarla per esteso in VIII 234:

> "Aenesidemus, in the Fourth Book of his *Pyrrhonean Discourses*, propounds an argument on the same subject and to much the same effect in the following form: 'If apparent things appear alike to all those in a similar condition, and signs are apparent things, signs appear alike to those in a similar condition. But signs do not appear alike to those in a similar condition; and apparent things appear alike to all those in a similar condition; therefore signs are not apparent things'...".[4]

Su questo passo e su *M.* VIII 8, dove ai "seguaci di Enesidemo 'secondo Eraclito'" viene attribuita l'idea che vi è tra i fenomeni una certa differenza, perché alcuni appaiono in comune a tutti, altri privatamente ad un singolo individuo e che i primi sono veri, i secondi falsi, si fonda l'importante ricostruzione della figura di Enesidemo di Paul Natorp.[5] A prescindere dalle varie obiezioni che possono essere

---

[3] Che si tratti di un problema reale, basta da solo a mostrarlo ciò che leggiamo in Diogene Laerzio, IX 62 (= Pyrrho T. 6–8 Caizzi, con il relativo commento, nel quale ho cercato di mostrare perché la testimonianza di Antigono di Caristo non può essere sbrigativamente eliminata come pura invenzione).
[4] Transl. Bury (per tutti i passi citati).
[5] *Forschungen zur Geschichte des Erkenntnisproblems im Altertum. Protagoras, Demokrit, Epikur und die Skepsis* (Hildesheim: Olms 1965; repr. of 1884 edition). Non credo che il tentativo di Natorp di interpretare in modo unitario tutte le testimonianze su Enesidemo sia riuscito, ma ciò non ne diminuisce l'importanza. In direzione non molto lontana da quella di Natorp sembra muoversi anche la ricostruzione abbastanza recente di Charlotte Stough, *Greek Skepticism. A Study in Epistemology* (Berkeley and Los Angeles CA: University of California Press 1969) 95–7, che però aggira troppo disinvoltamente alcuni degli ostacoli più gravi. Per esempio, citando *M* VIII 8, taglia la frase iniziale contenente la menzione di οἱ δὲ περὶ τὸν Αἰνησίδημον

oggi sollevate contro il suo lavoro, che resta in ogni caso uno dei saggi più importanti che siano stati scritti su Enesidemo e la tradizione scettica, l'interpretazione dello studioso tedesco presuppone che Enesidemo aderisca — in qualche forma — al contenuto dei due passi; si presenta così subito il problema di carattere generale cui accennavo all'inizio, che richiede accurate verifiche specifiche per i singoli casi: se e quando sia lecito attribuire ad uno scettico (pirroniano o accademico che sia) l'adesione — in forma debole per quanto si voglia — a determinate proposizioni utilizzate nella polemica antidogmatica.

Prenderò dunque in esame, in questa prospettiva, la proposizione (d'ora in poi Π) che costituisce la premessa dell'argomento sopra citato: τὰ φαινόμενα πᾶσι τοῖς ὁμοίως διακειμένοις παραπλησίως φαίνεται, che compare molto spesso, in questa o forme affini, nella letteratura scettica. Non verrà invece neppure sfiorata la questione del suo rapporto con *M*. VIII 8, che implicherebbe la riconsiderazione di tutto l'insieme di testimonianze su Enesidemo "secondo Eraclito," o quella della sua portata per la ricostruzione generale della figura dello scettico.

Commentando il passo di Enesidemo, Sesto osserva subito che φαινόμενα deve essere interpretato come equivalente a αἰσθητά.[6] Per mostrare la verità delle premesse e che la conclusione è corretta, Sesto fa in effetti ricorso ad una serie di esempi di αἰσθητά (il bianco, il dolce), che per coloro che hanno gli organi di senso non impediti (ἀπαραποδίστους) si presentano in modo simile, senza differenze (ὁμοίως ... οὐ διαφόρως) e osserva che invece, nel caso di un sintomo patologico, che è pur esso sensibile, non vi è concordia, tra medici che si trovino nelle stesse condizioni (cioè, evidentemente, con i sensi non impediti: per esempio, si può presumere, in grado di percepire febbre, arrossamento, rantoli ecc.), su ciò di cui sia segno. Nulla induce a ritenere, leggendo il passo, che agli occhi di Sesto Π sia una premessa valida solo per i dogmatici. In 240–1 egli ribadisce: "For it is plain (συμφανές) at once that apparent things appear equally to all who have

---

καθ' Ἡράκλειτον e prescinde completamente dal contesto (una *diaphonia* tra filosofi "dogmatici" sulla natura del vero).

[6] Sesto spiega l'argomento di Enesidemo servendosi sempre di esempi tratti dall'ambito sensibile (miele, dolce/amaro, fuoco, neve, caldo/freddo), ma ciò non significa, naturalmente, che i *phainomena* comprendano soltanto gli *aistheta*. La precisazione in *M*. VIII 234 rivela anzi che non è così.

their senses unimpeded; for white does not appear differently to different people, nor sweet in distinct ways, but they affect (κινεῖ) all similarly."

Il ruolo importante che Π svolge nella polemica antidogmatica risulta dalla frequenza con cui ritorna, talora in forma variata, talora in forma abbreviata.[7] Al posto di φαινόμενα possiamo trovare, indifferentemente, αἰσθητά, θερμόν/ψυχρόν, γλυκύ/πικρόν, πῦρ/χιών, μέλι. In particolare, nel passo sul "segno" che precede la citazione di Enesidemo, dopo aver presentato in VIII 187 una variante di Π, Sesto introduce l'esempio del fuoco e della neve (189: ὥσπερ τὸ πῦρ αἰσθητὸν ὂν πάντας τοὺς καίεσθαι δυναμένους καίει καὶ ἡ χιὼν αἰσθητὴ καθεστηκυῖα πάντας τοὺς ψύχεσθαι δυναμένους ψύχει), a cui fa seguire il resoconto di una articolata discussione con i dogmatici centrata proprio su questo esempio (192 sgg.)

Il ricorso all'esempio del fuoco e della neve e della loro δύναμις richiama inevitabilmente un passo sul quale è necessario soffermarsi un po' più a lungo: *M*. XI 68–9.

Dopo aver mostrato, grazie a numerosi esempi, la discordanza delle prolessi umane su beni, mali e indifferenti, Sesto aggiunge:

> "It will be our next task to deal with the arguments of the Sceptics about the problem before us. If then, there exists anything good by nature or anything evil by nature, this thing ought to be common to all men and be good or evil for all. For just as fire which is warmth-giving by nature (φύσει ἀλεαντικὸν καθεστός) warms all men, and does not warm some but chill others, — and like as snow which chills <by nature> does not chill some and warm others, but chills all alike, — so what is good by nature ought to be good for all, and not good for some but not good for others".[8]

Lo stesso argomento compare, in forma più breve, in D.L. IX 101:

> "There is nothing good or bad by nature, for if there is anything good or bad by nature, it must be good or bad for all persons alike, just as snow is cold to all. But there is no good or bad which is such to all persons in common; therefore there is no such thing as good or bad by nature".[9]

---

[7] Per es. *M*. VIII 239, 242; VIII 184, a proposito di Democrito; VIII 280; *P.H*. III 254; III 266; I 14, I 27; M XI 229; XI 240.

[8] Cfr. anche *P.H*. III 179, *M* . I 147 ecc.

[9] Transl. Hicks. Per il confronto tra il passo di Sesto e quello di Diogene, cfr. K. Janácek in F. Stiebitz and R. Hosek (eds.) *Charisteria F. Novotny octogenario oblata* (Praha: Opera Univ. Purkynianae Brunensis 1962) 143–46, che pensa ad una fonte comune, che Diogene riporterebbe in modo più fedele.

Ad un primo sguardo, non sembrano esserci dubbi: benché l'esempio di fuoco e neve evochi il modo in cui Sesto altrove esemplifica Π, la premessa 'il fuoco scalda per natura' (d'ora in poi: Φ) si presenta come incompatibile con l'idea standard che non è possibile stabilire quale sia la natura del fuoco: che esso brucia, lo percepiamo, ma circa la sua natura caustica ci asteniamo: καὶ ὅτι τὸ πῦρ καίει αἰσθανόμεθα· εἰ δὲ φύσιν ἔχει καυστικὴν ἐπέχομεν.[10] Lo stesso risulta da D.L. IX 102–5, dove viene citata anche la frase di Timone: "che <il miele> sia dolce non lo affermo, ma che appare lo concedo." I tropi sono diretti proprio a mostrare che non siamo in grado di passare dalla nostra percezione all'oggetto in sé, alla sua natura intrinseca (cfr. ad es. *P.H.* I 78; 93, 123, 125; 134; 140) e che una delle cause di ciò è proprio l'impossibilità di scegliere tra percezioni differenti.[11]

Tutto ciò induce a pensare che parlare di "fuoco che per natura scalda" o di 'neve che per natura raffredda' sia incompatibile con lo sforzo compiuto dagli scettici per convincerci che noi non siamo in condizione di stabilire quale sia la natura del fuoco.

Se le cose stanno così, il riferimento che Sesto fa agli Scettici come autori del *logos* che si fonda su tale premessa (*M.* IX 68: τῶν παρὰ τοῖς σκεπτικοῖς εἰς τὸ προκείμενον λεγομένων) dovrebbe riguardare solo la sua utilizzazione nel contesto generale dell'argomentazione antidogmatica, in nessun modo invece l'adesione al suo contenuto.

Ad ulteriore conferma della tesi che ci troviamo davanti ad un uso dialettico di una premessa dogmatica viene naturale ricordare che un ragionamento di questo genere, che contrappone enti sui quali o sui cui effetti non sorge discussione a entità come bene-male, sui quali la discordia è dominante, viene attaccato esplicitamente già da Polistrato, *de contemptu*, XXI sgg.; che tale *logos* è presente nelle *Dialexeis*, II, 18 sgg., e che se ne serve anche Platone, *Phdr.* 263a e *Alc. I* 111bc. Il variare dell'oggetto che di volta in volta viene contrapposto, per le reazioni uguali che suscita, a bene/male o bello/brutto, non è importante: comune a tutti i testi citati è il riferimento a oggetti: oro, argento, ferro, legno o pietra, uomo o cavallo sono utilizzati come

---

[10] Cfr. anche *M.* VII 368.
[11] Si veda anche un passo come *M.* VII 365 sg., dove si argomenta che πάντα τὰ ἐκτὸς sono ἄδηλα, perché inferiamo la loro natura sulla base di un intermediario, il nostro πάθος· γλυκανθεὶς γὰρ μέλιτος προσαχθέντος στοχάζομαι ὅτι γλυκύ ἐστι τὸ ἐκτὸς ὑποκείμενον μέλι, καὶ ἀλεανθεὶς πυρὸς προσαχθέντος σημειοῦμαι ἐκ τῆς περὶ ἐμὲ διαθέσεως ὅτι τὸ ἐκτὸς ὑποκείμενον πῦρ ἀλεεινόν ἐστι.

esempi di cose intorno alle quali gli uomini non dissentono: sanno riconoscerle e distinguerle perché esse hanno una natura che viene colta da tutti ugualmente.

Se prescindiamo dalle *Dialexeis*, la cui data è incerta, Platone è l'autore per noi più antico nel quale troviamo attestati ragionamenti di questo tipo;[12] e proprio Platone è l'autore citato subito dopo da Sesto (*M*. XI 70):

> "Wherefore also Plato, in establishing that God is good by nature, argued on similar lines. For, he says, as it is the special property of heat to make hot and the property of cold to chill, so it is the special property of good to do good (τὸ ἀγαθοποιεῖν); but the Good is God; therefore it is the property of God to do good."

Notevole è tuttavia il fatto che il ragionamento attribuito a Platone, qui introdotto a conferma di ciò che gli scettici sostengono perché associa il tema degli effetti di caldo e freddo (cfr. gli esempi di fuoco e neve utilizzati subito sopra da Sesto) al bene, non trova nessun riscontro puntuale nei dialoghi ed è piuttosto il risultato dell'accostamento e dalla combinazione di passi diversi: in *Resp*. I 335d Socrate osserva che "non è opera del calore il raffreddare, ma del suo contrario;[13] né della siccità inumidire, ma del suo contrario; né del buono danneggiare ma del suo contrario" e utilizza il ragionamento in riferimento al principio sostenuto da Polemarco che è giusto far bene agli amici e male ai nemici; il tema della bontà di dio deriva invece dal *Timeo*, 29d sgg.;[14] un'ulteriore conferma che ci troviamo davanti ad una costruzione tardiva è data dalla presenza del verbo ἀγαθοποιεῖν.[15]

Se esaminiano i passi di altri autori antichi in cui si presenta, sia pur con piccole varianti, un ragionamento simile a questo, sembra delinearsi

---

[12] Il fatto che Socrate si riferisca al nome che esprime tali oggetti, e dunque al suo significato, non è importante ai fini del nostro discorso. Questo tipo di osservazione poteva naturalmente sorgere all'interno della sofistica e della discussione sui rapporti tra natura e convenzione: né l'autore delle *Dialexeis*, né Platone presentano come proprio questo modo di ragionare.

[13] In che modo gli Stoici utilizzassero, a scopi differenti, un ragionamento simile risulta da D.L. VII 103.

[14] Un passo che lo stesso Sesto cita in *M*. IX 105, in un contesto che avvicina la concezione stoica-zenoniana del divino a quella di Platone.

[15] Il verbo è usato da Sesto in analogia a θερμαίνειν/ψύχειν, e non ricorre, per quanto sappiamo, in autori anteriori all'età imperiale. L'aggettivo ἀγαθοποιός è frequente soprattutto, come è noto, in ambito astrologico.

un quadro in cui motivi stoici e motivi platonici convergono intorno all'esegesi del *Timeo*. Uno di questi, Clemente, *Strom.* I 17, 86, è stato incluso da H. von Arnim negli *SVF* (II, 1184), ma la ripresa dello stesso motivo in *Strom.* VI 17, 159, in Synes. *Ep.* 57, nonché in Procl. *In Prm.* 830, conferma il sospetto che si trattasse di una tematica fortemente platonizzante e che forse in questa forma essa non risaliva allo stoicismo crisippeo; non a caso il motivo torna, sia pure in forma condensata, in D.L. III 72: ...τῆς μὲν ὅλης γενέσεως αἴτιον εἶναι τὸν θεόν, ὅτι πέφυκεν ἀγαθοποιὸν εἶναι τὸ ἀγαθόν.

Che tuttavia il suo contenuto avesse a che fare anche con lo stoicismo è confermato dal parallelo più stretto con Sesto: un brano di Ierocle, conservato da Stob. II 9, 7, dove Platone viene invocato contro coloro che negano l'assoluta bontà di dio.[16]

Sembra dunque di dover ricondurre l'origine del riferimento a Platone che leggiamo in *M.* XI 70 ad un'esegesi di Platone, e in particolare del *Timeo*, o di alcune sue parti, di coloritura stoicheggiante: non intendo dare un nome preciso al suo autore, perché allo stato attuale delle mie conoscenze ciò significherebbe tradire la lezione di rigore scientifico che abbiamo appreso dallo studioso a cui questa mia ricerca è dedicata: mi sia solo concesso di evocare personalità come Antioco o Posidonio[17] e di segnalare il fatto che nel brano di Sesto che stiamo esaminando la *diaphonia* dei filosofi contiene l'unica menzione di Panezio presente nella sua opera. Tutto ciò rinvia in ogni caso, mi pare, ad una fonte scettica per l'insieme del brano (comune a Sesto e Diogene Laerzio) che lavora su materiale risalente al I sec. a.C.

Ma torniamo ora al problema da cui siamo partiti: poteva uno scettico far propria la proposizione "il fuoco scalda per natura"? Abbiamo visto finora i motivi che porterebbero a rispondere con sicurezza in modo

---

[16] ἐκ πολλῶν ⟨ἂν⟩ νοήσειέ τις, πρὸς δὲ τὸ παρὸν ἀποχρήσειεν ἂν ἴσως ὁ Πλάτωνος ἐκεῖνος λόγος. οὐ γὰρ θερμοῦ φησι τὸ ψύχειν ἀλλὰ τοὐναντίον, οὐδὲ ψυχροῦ τὸ θερμαίνειν ἀλλὰ τοὐναντίου· οὕτως οὖν οὐδὲ ἀγαθοποιοῦ τὸ κακοποιεῖν, ἀλλὰ τοὐναντίου. καὶ μὴν ἀγαθὸς ὁ θεός κτλ.

[17] Per chi ritiene dominante nei *placita* platonici riportati nel terzo libro di Diogene Laerzio l'impronta medioplatonica (come K. Praechter, cfr. ora B. Centrone, "Alcune osservazioni sui *placita* di Platone in Diogene Laerzio III 67–80," *Elenchos* 8 (1987) 105–18) il primo sarà certamente un candidato più probabile; la tesi di M. Untersteiner, *Posidonio nei Placita di Platone secondo Diogene Laerzio III* (Brescia: Paideia 1970), non sembra aver riscosso sostanziali consensi. Cfr. anche L. Brisson, "Diogène Laërce, Livre III," *ANRW* 36.6 (1992) 3722 sgg.

negativo. Ma, alla luce del quadro di insieme, questa risposta non appare più così scontata.

Abbiamo visto sopra che Sesto (*M.* VIII 189 sgg.) utilizza una forma di Π dove al posto di τὰ φαινόμενα compaiono il fuoco e la neve. In questo contesto egli non caratterizza la capacità del fuoco di scaldare servendosi del termine φύσει, come invece fa in *M.* XI e altrove; ma pare difficile negare che ci troviamo nello stesso ordine di pensiero. Uno dei passi forse più significativi a riprova del collegamento tra Π e Φ è *M.* I 147–8 dove si ribadisce che gli scettici, a proposito dei nomi, utilizzeranno il *logos* secondo il quale "what affects (κινεῖ) us 'naturally' affects all men alike, and not some in one way and others in the opposite way. Fire, for instance, 'naturally' warms barbarians and Greeks, unskilled and skilled, and does not warm Greeks but chills barbarians; and snow 'naturally' chills, and does not chill some but heats others. Thus, that which affects us 'naturally' affects in similar way those who have their senses unimpaired."

A questo punto, a mio parere, ci troviamo di fronte ad un'alternativa: (1) se Φ è sicuramente inaccettabile per uno scettico, anche Π deve esserlo e dunque lo scettico non aderisce in nessuna forma né a Π né a Φ; (2) se Π è accolto dallo scettico, e Φ si collega ad esso, si dovrebbe poter interpretare il riferimento alla φύσις in Φ in modo da renderlo compatibile con Π.

Ora, sostenere, sulla base dell'uso frequente che ne fa Sesto e di quanto sappiamo su Enesidemo, che Π è *solo* una premessa dogmatica utilizzata dialetticamente non mi pare così agevole e non fa di (1) una scelta automatica e ovvia. Cercherò, nella parte che segue, di suggerire un modo di interpretare Φ in modo da attenuare l'apparente contrasto con Π, rendendo così perlomeno plausibile l'opzione (2).

Torniamo alla discussione sul segno: commentando il ragionamento di Enesidemo (VIII 218) Sesto mostra la verità di Π in questo modo:

"For if all those who have unimpeded sight (ἀπαραποδίστους ἔχοντες τὰς ὄψεις) perceive white colour similarly and not differently; and if all whose taste is in a natural state (οἱ κατὰ φύσιν τὴν γεῦσιν ἔχοντες) apprehend what is sweet as sweet (γλυκαντικῶς) etc."

Per Sesto ἀπαραποδίστους equivale dunque a κατὰ φύσιν, né questo deve stupirci: la distinzione tra stato "contro natura" e stato "secondo natura" rientra infatti fra ciò che secondo lo scettico rende possibile la vita (cfr. *P.H.* I 23: ὑφήγησις φύσεως; *P.H.* I 236 τὰ φύσει ἀλλότρια).

E' evidente che la distinzione dei soggetti percipienti in due gruppi omogenei, quello di coloro che si trovano in condizioni secondo natura o normali, e quello di coloro che si trovano in condizioni contro natura o patologiche, è funzionale allo scopo di Π: mostrare che non si verifica, nel caso del segno (o del vero) una situazione di sostanziale uniformità percettiva a parità di condizioni che permetta di far rientrare segno e vero tra i sensibili.

L'uso di γλυκαντικῶς ci conferma che ciò che viene descritto è il πάθος in cui la sensazione consiste (cfr. *M.* VII 354 sg.; 367 sg.); è appena il caso di ricordare che lo scettico non respinge i πάθη, mentre mette in discussione che essi esprimano la natura dell'oggetto (*P.H.* I 12 sgg.; 19–20). In *P.H.* I 21–2, dopo aver indicato nel fenomeno il criterio dell'indirizzo scettico, Sesto aggiunge: περὶ μὲν τοῦ φαίνεσθαι τοῖον ἢ τοῖον τὸ ὑποκείμενον οὐδεὶς ἴσως ἀμφισβητεῖ, περὶ δὲ τοῦ εἰ τοιοῦτον ἔστιν ὁποῖον φαίνεται ζητεῖται. Una frase come questa, che presuppone che non sia fonte di disputa il modo in cui un oggetto si manifesta, mostra che, se considerata in una certa prospettiva, la proposizione Π non solo è compatibile con il pirronismo, ma anzi può esprimere bene la posizione degli scettici. La dolcezza del miele o il calore del fuoco o il gelo della neve sono *phainomena* che accompagnano la vita di tutti gli uomini (tranne riconoscibili eccezioni, che non fanno che confermare la regola) e come tali non vengono messi in discussione, anche se la presenza di effetti diversi in soggetti in condizioni diverse non permette di stabilire la vera natura dell'oggetto che li provoca. Lo scettico può dunque servirsi di questa comune esperienza conoscitiva (*P.H.* I 23: ὑφηγήσει μὲν φυσικῇ καθ' ἣν φυσικῶς αἰσθητικοὶ καὶ νοητικοί ἐσμεν) che rientra nella sua condizione naturale, cioè nel fatto di essere una persona umana, e di reagire a determinati stimoli. Nella stessa direzione vanno le osservazioni che Sesto utilizza per contestare ad Enesidemo il fatto che lo scetticismo sia una via verso l'eraclitismo (*P.H.* I 211): "...for certainly no one would venture to say that honey does not taste sweet to people in sound health or that it tastes bitter to those suffering from jaundice."

Si tratta, osserva Sesto, di una prolessi comune a tutti gli uomini, accolta da scettici e dogmatici ugualmente.

Ma, detto questo, si può ricondurre nell'ottica scettica un'espressione come πῦρ φύσει ἀλεαντικόν, che di per sé appare legata al modo di esprimersi tipico dei dogmatici, tante volte attaccato dagli scettici?

Per capire il significato di tale espressione nel suo contesto, è utile un passo di Sesto tratto dal capitolo *Sul vero* (*M.* VIII 37): "Again, the true is either an absolute and natural thing (τῶν κατὰ διαφορὰν καὶ φύσει) or a relative thing; but it is neither of these, as we shall establish; therefore the true does not exist. The true does not exist absolutely or by nature (κατὰ διαφορὰν...καὶ φύσει) inasmuch as what subsists absolutely and by nature moves those who are in a like condition in the same way - the hot, for instance, is not hot to one man and cold to another but hot to all who are in the same condition...."

Qui viene utilizzata una categorizzazione del reale di cui Sesto fa menzione in *M.* IX 161 come di uno strumento di cui gli Scettici si servono,[18] e che in X 263 attribuisce, in forma diversa, ai Pitagorici.[19]

Vi sono due generi di cose: quelle κατὰ διαφορὰν e quelle πρός τι. Nel primo gruppo rientrano per Sesto gli αἰσθητά (*M.* VIII 206); nel passo sopra citato (VIII 37) gli enti κατὰ διαφορὰν vengono anche detti φύσει, e contrapposti α τὰ πρός τι: e la caratteristica dei primi viene indicata proprio nel fatto del κινεῖν, cioè del suscitare un "movimento" analogo in tutti coloro che sono nella stessa disposizione: l'esempio del caldo e del freddo conferma che ci troviamo di fronte ad una forma di Φ. Abbiamo visto che, utilizzando Π, Sesto sostituisce a caldo/freddo, come esempi di enti che ὁμοίως πάντας κινεῖ, il fuoco o la neve (*M.* VIII 189; XI 69; I 149): considerati alla luce di *M.* VIII 37, essi rientrano tra gli enti κατὰ διαφορὰν καὶ φύσει e questo richiama gli esempi di enti κατὰ διαφορὰν della *diairesis* pitagorica in X 263.[20] Non è per fortuna necessario, ai fini dell'oggetto del presente studio, addentrarci nella selva di problemi esegetici che queste categorizzazioni del reale comportano: mi sembra che Sesto (e così pure la sua fonte scettica) utilizzi questa distinzione liberamente, senza curarsi delle sottili articolazioni dei dogmatici, stoici o accademici o pitagorici,[21] perché gli offre un utile strumento per classificare i

---

[18] Cfr. ad es. M VIII 206 e D.L. IX 96.

[19] Sui precedenti stoici (cfr. *In Ar. Cat.*, 167 sgg. = *SVF* II 403; 390) e accademici, e le complesse questioni che queste categorizzazioni implicano, mi limito a rinviare a M. Mignucci, *The Stoic Notion of Relatives*, J. Barnes and M. Mignucci (eds.), *Matter and Metaphysics* (Napoli: Bibliopolis 1988) 129–221; M. Isnardi Parente, *Senocrate-Ermodoro. Frammenti* (Napoli: Bibliopolis 1982) spec. 439 sgg.

[20] Vengono menzionati: uomo, cavallo, pianta, terra, acqua, aria, fuoco.

[21] La distinzione viene utilizzata anche nell'ottavo tropo (*P.H.* I 135 sgg., in un confuso ragionamento diretto a mostrare che anche τὰ κατὰ διαφορὰν rientrano tra τὰ πρός τι).

sensibili: essa indica, potremmo dire roughly, cose che vengono colte assolutamente, autonomamente (siano esse, intermini aristotelici, sostanze o qualità), e cose che non possono essere colte se non in relazione ad altro (per es., "miele," o "dolce" da una parte, "più dolce" dall'altra).

Se ora, tenendo presente *M*. VIII 37, torniamo a *M*. XI 69, ci rendiamo conto che φύσει nell'espressione πῦρ φύσει ἀλεαντικόν, è equivalente a κατὰ διαφοράν e indica, in altre parole, un'entità (il fuoco o il caldo; il miele o il dolce) distinta e autonoma rispetto ad un'altra entità, il che consente di usare per essa un certo nome, di non confonderla con un'altra e di farsi capire quando ne parliamo. Questo è proprio secondo Sesto, dei sensibili, in quanto φαινόμενα, e dei loro effetti, ed è anche ciò che spiega la costanza della percezione (in condizioni uniformi), in quanto l'incontro dell'oggetto con il soggetto in uguali condizioni suscita lo stesso tipo di *pathos* nello stesso individuo in tempi diversi, e in più individui contemporaneamente: su questa base si giustifica il contenuto delle κοιναὶ ἔννοιαι che insegnano agli uomini a non mettere la mano nel fuoco o a usare il miele come dolcificante.

Se le cose stanno così, parlare di πῦρ φύσει ἀλεαντικόν in questo contesto, qualunque fosse il significato che all'espressione attribuivano i dogmatici, non implica necessariamente per uno scettico esprimere un impossibile giudizio sulla natura del fuoco in sé, ma piuttosto sottolineare che il fuoco, in quanto sensibile, si manifesta all'uomo come un certo oggetto, capace di scaldare (cioè di suscitare un *pathos* "riscaldante," diverso dalla neve, che a sua volta è un certo oggetto, capace di raffreddare, e che questo si verifica costantemente in soggetti che si trovino in una normale disposizione (ἀπαραποδίστους...τὰς αἰσθήσεις, κατὰ φύσιν). Questo tipo di esperienza delle cose rientra precisamente in quella che gli Scettici chiamano la ὑφήγησις τῆς φύσεως (*P.H.* I 23): noi siamo esseri costituiti naturalmente per percepire e pensare (φυσικῶς αἰσθητικοὶ καὶ νοητικοί ἐσμεν) ed è questo che rende possibile la vita, il linguaggio, la tecnica. Lungi dal respingere ciò, lo scettico lo ribadisce per difendersi dagli attacchi dei dogmatici e lo utilizza, come abbiamo visto, contro di loro, come strumento argomentativo.

Se questo è corretto, ne deriverebbe che gli Scettici utilizzavano a livelli differenti la divisione categoriale in "assoluti" e "relativi:" a chi pensi, oltrepassando il "movimento" che esse suscitano in noi, di cogliere le cose come tali, non si può che mostrare che "tutto è relativo" (cfr. per es. Anon. *in Plat. Tht.* LXIII, 1 sgg.: οὐδὲν καθ' αὐτό ἐστιν, πάντα δὲ πρὸς ἄλλα θεωρεῖται (ll. 4–6); Aul. Gell. *N.A.* XI 5, 65; Sext. *P.H.* I 135, 175 ecc.); ma se consideriamo la realtà nel suo manifestarsi, la "differenza," che si suole anche chiamare "natura," torna ad imporsi: il mondo che noi percepiamo, nel quale viviamo, è costituito da una molteplicità di oggetti κατὰ διαφοράν.

Se il legame tra Π e Φ che ho cercato di mettere in luce ha qualche fondatezza, sorge spontanea la domanda se, come Π, anche Φ possa risalire a Enesidemo, che in tutto il libro *Contro i moralisti* viene però citato solo al § 42. Senza poter approfondire la questione, mi limiterò a segnalare alcuni indizi che, sparsi nel brano contenente Φ, vanno in questa direzione; li citerò brevemente, sottolineando naturalmente il carattere ipotetico di ciascuno di essi preso singolarmente:

—XI 44: la citazione di Omero, *Od.* XIV 228, ritorna nel secondo tropo, *P.H.* I 86; anche la successiva citazione di Archiloco (fr. 36 Bergk) appare abbastanza significativa se si considera che (a parte due menzioni del suo nome, in *M.* IX 110 e *M.* I 298) il poeta viene citato solo in *P.H.* III 216 a conferma della *diaphonia* su ciò che bello fare; che un altro frammento archilocheo (70 B.) compare nell'esposizione del pensiero di Eraclito in *M.* VII 128, un brano che viene da molti, a mio parere con ragione, messo in rapporto con Enesidemo; e, infine, che la citazione più completa dello stesso frammento 70 B. torna in D.L. IX 71 (ripreso in Suid., *s.v.* Πυρρώνειοι). Questo conferma che si trattava di versi utilizzati tradizionalmente in collegamento con lo scetticismo,[22] anche se non dimostra che la fonte fosse proprio Enesidemo.

—l'uso della divisione bicategoriale di origine accademica, presupposto da Φ, è indizio di una data in cui la categorizzazione aristotelica non si era ancora diffusa ed imposta: è plausibile pensare al I sec. a.C. (il che ovviamente non esclude un'epoca precedente)

—la citazione di Platone (*M.* XI 70 presuppone, come abbiamo visto, una fonte scettica che abbia familiarità con esegesi platonico-stoiche del I sec. a.C. (il che ovviamente non esclude un'epoca successiva)

---

[22] L'accostamento della citazione di Hom. *Od.* XIV 228 a Arch. fr. 36 torna, con l'aggiunta di Eurip. fr. 560 N., in Clem. *Str.* VI.2, 7, 3, p. 426 St. In Clemente questi versi vengono citati per dimostrare l'abitudine dei pagani al plagio, ma non escluderei che egli li trovasse accostati proprio in un contesto "scetticheggiante" e li utilizzasse ai propri scopi. In D.L. IX 71 ad Omero e Archiloco viene accostato Euripide, *Suppl.* 734–6.

—potrebbe risalire ad Enesidemo l'uso del verbo κινεῖν/κινεῖσθαι nel senso di "stimolare" "essere affetto," che riappare in varie occorrenze di Π e di Φ: si tratta di un verbo utilizzato nell'esposizione della teoria cirenaica (*M*. VII 192, 344, 355; 356), dove è esposta ampiamente la tesi radicale che neppure i φαινόμενα sono comuni, soltanto i nomi lo sono. Altrove, in questa particolare accezione, il verbo non è frequentissimo, ma ricorre, significativamente, in *P.H*. I 50 (primo tropo); I 87 (secondo tropo); I 130 (settimo tropo); I 193: τοῖς κινοῦσι ἡμᾶς παθητικῶς) e nell'esposizione del pirronismo in Anon. *in Plat. Tht*. LXIII 12–13, che dipende da Enesidemo.[23]

Enesidemo sembra avere accolto il modo di esprimersi dei Cirenaici (a meno che la teoria cirenaica non sia stata tradotta in linguaggio scettico, cosa anche possibile), ma averne in certo senso moderato le conclusioni riconoscendo cioè che gli uomini sono uniti tra loro da affezioni simili e comuni in analoghe condizioni, e non solo dall'uso di parole comuni per esprimere affezioni la cui identità o somiglianza è del tutto fantomatica: ciò non significa, come abbiamo visto, pensare di poter parlare delle cose in se stesse, quanto riconoscere che fa parte della natura umana l'essere "mossi" o "stimolati" dagli oggetti esterni, e in modo diverso da oggetti diversi, in modo simile da oggetti simili purché in condizioni simili. Ciò di cui Enesidemo sembra parlare in Π e in Φ — se ho visto giusto — è quel tipo di differenza tra le cose, e dunque di stabilità, che ci si manifesta e ci permette di parlarne[24] e di associarle con determinati *pathe* in determinate condizioni: l'estensione dell'idea dell'indeterminatezza e indistinguibilità alle cose percepite avrebbe avuto, agli occhi di Enesidemo, degli esiti assurdi: sarebbe stata incompatibile con uno scetticismo che si proponga di sottrarsi ad ogni estremismo dogmatico,[25] sarebbe andata "contro la vita," così come

---

[23] Si vedano le note di D. Sedley all'edizione (in collaborazione con G. Bastianini) di PBerol 9782, in *Corpus dei Papiri Filosofici* III 9 (Firenze 1995) 545 sgg.

[24] Cfr. ancora Anon. *in Plat. Tht*. LXIII, 11–14: οὐκ ἂν γὰρ τὰ αὐτά γε ὄντα διαφόρως ἐκίνει κατὰ τὰ διαστήματα κτλ., e la nota di Sedley, *ad l*.: "L'A. non pone sullo stesso piano 'essere lo stesso' e 'avere una ἰδιότης'": se quanto ho cercato di mostrare è fondato, questa distinzione, apparentemente strana, cerca di esprimere il pensiero di Enesidemo meglio di quanto potrebbe sembrare a prima vista.

[25] Per esempio, la teoria del flusso, attribuita a Protagora in Sesto *P.H*. I 217, serve a fondare il fatto che le cose non possiedono una caratteristica propria: ma i Pirroniani non invocano il flusso, che rientra tra gli ἄδηλα, bensì il variare della percezione, che è verificabile empiricamente proprio in quanto presuppone delle entità identificabili e distinguibili nei loro effetti: per es. il fatto che "lo stesso miele" in alcuni casi appare dolce, in altri amaro.

"contro la vita" poteva essere giudicata la negazione cirenaica della comunanza dei *pathe*. Tale negazione sarebbe stata del tutto incompatibile con il suggerimento di vivere seguendo i fenomeni, comportandosi come, secondo Enesidemo, già aveva fatto anche Pirrone,[26] a dispetto delle storie fantasiose che su di lui si raccontavano. Tra un precipizio, un carro che ti viene addosso ed un sicuro sentiero c'è una differenza che la 'natura' non solo ci permette, ma anche ci insegna a riconoscere.

[26] Cfr. Pyrrho, T 6 Caizzi. Anche Aristocle, *ap.* Eus *P.E.* XIV, 18, 20: ὁπόταν μέντοι φῶσι τὸ σοφὸν δὴ τοῦτο, διότι δέοι κατακολουθοῦντα τῇ φύσει ζῆν καὶ τοῖς ἔθεσι κτλ. conferma che Enesidemo faceva esplicito ricorso alla φύσις per indicare il criterio di vita.

11

Theophrastus, no. 84 FHS&G
There's Nothing New Here!

William W. Fortenbaugh

In 1844 Theodor Waitz published an impressive edition of the several works which make up the Aristotelian *Organon*. As an introduction to the Greek texts, he discussed over seventy manuscripts and printed a selection of scholia. Three of the scholia name Theophrastus, but one is of especial interest in that it appears to challenge Aristotelian doctrine and to portend a later advance in logic.[1] At least that is the way modern scholars interpret the scholion. My own view is different. As I see it, Theophrastus neither departed from the teaching of his master nor broke new ground. Scholars have been misled by the initial publication of the scholion and as a result misrepresented the logic of Theophrastus. What is needed is a sound philological investigation of the scholion. In what follows, I want to offer such an interpretation, recognizing that the dedicatee of this volume, Professor Ian Kidd, is himself a master of the method. If my essay approaches his standard, I shall be happy. If it proves interesting to him and provides enjoyment, even better.

---

[1] Two of the scholia are printed by Th. Waitz, *Aristotelis Organon Graece*, pars prior (Leipzig: S. Hirzel 1855) 40 (= FHS&G 82C and 84) and 41 (= FHS&G 87D). Our concern is with the second of the scholia found on p. 40.

I. The State of Current Scholarship

According to Waitz,[2] codex Ambrosianus L 93 sup., contains a scholion which names Theophrastus in a comment on *De interpretatione* 7 17b16. Here is what Waitz printed.

πρὸς τοῦτό φησιν ὁ Θεόφραστος ὅτι ἐπί τινων, ἐὰν μὴ ὁ προσδιορισμὸς ᾖ καὶ ἐπὶ τοῦ κατηγορουμένου, ἡ ἀντίφασις συναληθεύσει, οἶον, φησίν, ἐὰν λέγωμεν· Φαινίας ἔχει ἐπιστήμην, Φαινίας οὐκ ἔχει ἐπιστήμην, δύναται ἀμφότερα εἶναι ἀληθῆ.

Since Waitz provided no translation—it would have been in Latin, had he done so—I offer one of my own.

> In regard to this, Theophrastus says that in some cases, if the *prosdiorismos* is not applied to the predicate too, the contradictory will be true as well. For example, he says, if we say, "Phainias possesses science"—"Phainias does not possess science," both statements can be true.

This scholion was reprinted in 1862 by Friderick Wimmer in his edition of the fragments of Theophrastus.[3] He cited Waitz as his source and dropped the first two words, i.e., πρὸς τοῦτο. The rest of the text is identical with that of Waitz.

Thirty-five years later, in 1897, a fuller version of the scholion was published by Adolf Busse in the introduction to his edition of Ammonius' commentrary on the *De interpretatione*.[4] Busse referred the entire scholion—actually two scholia on different sides of folium 64—to *De interpretatione* 7 17b14. I shall print and discuss this fuller version below in Section II. Here I want to say only that the place of publication, i.e. an introduction to a commentary by Ammonius, had a negative effect on Theophrastean scholarship. Valuable evidence was

---

[2] Waitz (above, n.1) 44.
[3] The fragment is no. 57e in F. Wimmer, *Theophrasti Eresii opera quae supersunt omnia* 3 (Leipzig: Teubner 1862) 228. Wimmer republished the fragments together with a Latin translation (Paris: Didot 1866; photographic repr. Frankfurt am Main: Minerva 1964). The scholion in question is translated as follows: "Th. ait in nonnullis, nisi etiam in praedicato sit praemissa definitio, contrariam quoque enuntationem simul esse veram, ut si dicamus, Phaenias habet scientiam Phaenias non habet scientiam, utrumque esse potest verum" (p. 429).
[4] *CAG* vol. 4.5 p. xxxiii.

effectively "buried," so that the shorter text of Waitz has guided recent discussion.

The modern discussion[5] of the scholion may be traced back to Joseph Bocheński, who in 1947 published his influential work *La logique de Théophraste*. Bocheński adopted the Greek text printed by Waitz and repeated his reference to *De interpretatione* 17b16.[6] Furthermore, Bocheński construed προσδιορισμός as a logical quantifier and spoke of Theophrastus opposing Aristotle, who rejected quantification of the predicate. The Aristotelian passage in question is 17b12–16.[7]

ἐπὶ δὲ τοῦ κατηγορουμένου τὸ καθόλου κατηγορεῖν καθόλου οὐκ ἔστιν ἀληθές·[8] οὐδεμία γὰρ κατάφασις ἔσται, ἐν ᾗ τοῦ κατηγορουμένου καθόλου τὸ καθόλου κατηγορηθήσεται,[9] οἷον ἔστι πᾶς ἄνθρωπος πᾶν ζῷον.

In the case of the predicate, it cannot be true to predicate the universal universally, for there cannot be an affirmation in which the universal is predicated universally of the predicate, for example "every man is every animal."[10]

---

[5] I limit my survey of the scholarly literature to publications which post-date World War II. In doing so, I do not want to suggest that no earlier scholar commented on the scholion. Already in 1855, C. Prantl, *Geschichte der Logik im Abendlande* 1 (Leipzig: S. Hirzel 1855) 356–7 took notice of Waitz' (above, n.1) publication and anticipated current scholarship by offering an interpretation in terms of the logical quantifier.

[6] I.M. Bocheński, *La logique de Théophrast*, Collectanea Friburgensia 32 (Fribourg: Libraire de l'Université 1947; repr. New York: Garland 1987) 44 n.173.

[7] Bocheński (above, n.6) n.175.

[8] That is the text printed by L. Minio-Paluello, *Aristotelis Categoriae et liber De interpretatione* (Oxford: Clarendon Press 1949; repr. with corrections 1956). It is also the text found in codex Ambrosianus L 93 sup., fol. 64ʳ. Waitz' (above, n.1) text is different: ἐπὶ δὲ τοῦ κατηγορουμένου καθόλου κατηγορεῖν τὸ καθόλου οὐκ ἔστιν ἀληθές. The commentary of Stephanus has the following: ἐπὶ δὲ τοῦ κατηγορουμένου καθόλου τὸ καθόλου κατηγορεῖν καθόλου οὐκ ἔστιν ἀληθές (*CAG* vol. 18.3 p. 29 Hayduck).

[9] As with the preceding sentence, the text here is problematic. See the discussion of H. Weidemann, "Textkritische Bemerkungen zum siebten Kapitel der aristotelischen 'Hermeneutik': Int. 7, 17b 12–16/16–20," J. Wiesner (ed.), *Aristoteles, Werk und Wirkung* 1 (Berlin: de Gruyter 1985) 46–51, who suggests supplying καθόλου before κατηγορηθήσεται. I am not happy with this suggestion and think that we should pay attention to the glosses of Ammonius, τοῦτ' ἔστιν ἐν ᾗ συντάττεσθαι δυνατὸν τῷ καθόλου κατηγορουμένῳ τὸν καθόλου προσιδορισμόν (*CAG* vol. 4.5 p. 101.24–5), and the scholiast of cod. Ambrosianus L 93 sup., ἐν ᾗ τῷ κατηγορουμέμῳ ὅρῳ πρόσκειται ὁ προσδιορισμός (lines 3–4, below in section II).

[10] Except for the last few words (Aristotle's example), the Greek text is notoriously difficult to translate, not least because of doubts concerning the Greek text itself. A full discussion of the difficulties is not necessary for the purposes of this paper and therefore would be out of place. Here I want to say only that the beginning of the

Bocheński also said that the word κατηγορούμενον is used differently in the scholion and in the Aristotelian passage. In the latter, it refers to the predicate; in the former, to a part of the predicate, i.e., "science." Bocheński called that a confusion,[11] but he still claimed to see in the scholion an important advance in the history of logic. "Thanks to Theophrastus," he asserted, ancient logic "knew a beginning of a theory of two quantifiers."[12] The idea is that Theophrastus recognized the importance of statements like "Some man possesses some science" and pointed toward a term logic in which two parts of a subject ("Man" and "Knowledge") are quantified and placed in a relation ("Possession") to each other: $(\exists x)(Mx.(\exists y)(Ky.Pxy))$. And for that reason, Theophrastus should receive "a honorable mention in the history of logic."[13]

In 1961, Bocheński reaffirmed his interpretation, albeit succinctly,[14] and this interpretation has guided subsequent discussion. In 1962 William and Martha Kneale cited Waitz, referred the scholion to *De interpretatione* 7 17b16 and spoke of Theophrastus disagreeing with his master in regard to the quantification of the predicate.[15] Similarly in 1973, Andreas Graeser printed Waitz' text, though not without error, and repeated his reference to the *De interpretatione*.[16] The comments of

---

passage is transitional. Aristotle has been considering the quantification of the subject. With the phrase ἐπὶ δὲ τοῦ κατηγορουμένου (a12), he turns to the predicate. The preposition ἐπί is used in the sense of "in the case of" or "with regard to" (cf. 9 18a33 together with a28), and τὸ κατηγορούμενον, both here and in 17b14–15, refers to the predicate.

[11] Bocheński (above, n.6) 45.

[12] Bocheński (above, n.6) 46: "Quant à la logique ancienne, grace à Théophraste, elle connut un commencement d'une théorie de deux quantificateurs."

[13] Bocheński (above, n.6) 46: "Rien que pour cette découverte si importante, notre auteur méritait une mention honorable dans l'histoire de la logique."

[14] I.M. Bocheński, *A History of Formal Logic*, (tr.) I. Thomas (Notre Dame IN: University of Notre Dame Press 1961) 100: After giving the text of the scholion in translation, Bocheński commented: "This is not a matter, as Theophrastus mistakenly supposed, of quantification of the predicate, which Aristotle had rejected ... but of a quantification of both parts of a subject when there is a two-place functor .... This structure was only later treated in detail .... We have here the first beginnings of it."

[15] William and Martha Kneale, *The Development of Logic* (Oxford: Clarendon Press 1962) 111–12.

[16] A. Graeser, *Die logischen Fragmente des Theophrast*, Kleine Texte für Vorlesungen und Übungen 191 (Berlin: De Gruyter 1973) fr. 6, p. 7. Like Wimmer (above, n.3) Graeser omitted the first two words (πρὸς τοῦτο) of Waitz' (above, n.1) text. He erred in dropping ἐὰν μὴ and substituting ἄν in a mistaken position. He also

Graeser are in large measure a synthesis of those made by Bocheński and the Kneales.[17] Again in 1977, Luciana Repici reproduced the text of Waitz, along with one of Graeser's errors,[18] cited the same Aristotelian passage and drew heavily on the existing scholarship.[19]

In 1983, Mario Mignucci added something new to the discussion. He mentioned the fuller publication of the scholion by Busse[20] and suggested a connection with Ammonius' rejection of a quantified predicate. In particular, he called attention to Ammonius' discussion of the statement "Every man is capable of every science"[21] and compared this statement with the Theophrastean examples reported in the scholion. He argued that the discussion of Ammonius is directed against Theophrastus, who opposed Aristotle in regard to quantifying the predicate. Ammonius, we are told, was not wrong in saying that the quoted sentence involves only quantification within the predicate and not of the predicate; but this way of viewing the matter along with an obstinate hostility to the Aristotelian position, prevented Ammonius from adequately appreciating the position of Theophrastus and from making a leap forward in logical theory.[22]

To the best of my knowledge Mignucci is the last scholar to discuss the scholion. It was, however, printed again in the recent collection of Theophrastean sources as FHS&G 84. This time Busse's edition was cited as the source text and an additional sentence was printed. For as Busse's edition makes clear, the Theophrastean material continues beyond what Waitz printed. The subsequent comment by the scholiast was, however, omitted. The editors adopted Busse's reference to *De*

---

replaced ἀντίφασις with ἀπόφασις. See M. Mignucci, "La teoria della quantificazione del predicato nell' antichità classica," *Anuario Filosófico* 16 (1983) 39 n.35.

[17] Graeser (above, n.16) 65–6.

[18] L. Repici, *La logica di Teofrasto: Studio critico e raccolta dei frammenti e delle testimonianze*, Pubblicazioni del centro di Studio per la Storia della Storiografia Filosofica 2 (Bologna: Società Editrice il Mulino 1977) fr. 12 pp. 195–6. She does not replace ἀντίφασις with ἀπόφασις, but she does print ἂν instead of ἐὰν μὴ.

[19] Repici (above, n.18) 58–62.

[20] Mignucci (above, n.16) 39 n. 35 credits Pamela Huby with drawing his attention to the fuller publication.

[21] *CAG* vol. 4.5 p. 107.8: πᾶς ἄνθρωπος πάσης ἐπιστήμης ἐστὶ δεκτικός.

[22] Mignucci (above, n.16) 40: "Ammonio perde l'occasione di far fare alla logica quel salto di qualità a cui avrebbe condotto un'adeguata comprensione del punto di vista di Teofrasto."

interpretatione 7 17b14 and translated προσδιορισμός with "quantifier."[23]

From this survey of scholarly opinion, it may appear well established that Theophrastus opposed Aristotle in regard to quantifying the predicate of a statement making sentence. Perhaps that is correct, but I have my doubts. Here are three reasons for further study. First, on the view surveyed, Theophrastus was the first philosopher to use the term προσδιορισμός in the sense of logical quantifier. That is remarkable, not because Theophrastus was incapable of introducing a technical term, but because the term is not found again in this sense until much later.[24] Second, if we believe that Theophrastus opposed Aristotle's remarks on quantification in *De interpretatione* 7 17b12-16, then we seem committed to speaking of a confusion in the use of κατηγορούμενον. That is certainly possible, but I would prefer an interpretation which does not involve confused usage. Third, the Theophrastean examples reported in the scholion are statements with a particular individual as subject, "Phainias." In the Aristotelian passage we have a universal taken universally, "every man." That suggests to me that Theophrastus was not objecting to or even commenting on *De interpretatione* 17b12–16.

II. A Philological Approach

The scholion which concerns us occurs in the margin of a manuscript now deposited in the Biblioteca Ambrosiana, Milan, Italy. The manuscript, L 93 sup., contains a *vita* of Aristotle and the text of his *Categories*, *De interpretatione*—f. 60^v–79^v—and *Analytics*. There are scholia throughout the manuscript, largely but not exclusively written in the margins. In the case of the *De interpretatione*, the scholia found on f. 60^v–69^v lack the name of their author; a few on folia 70^v–79^v are expressly said to derive from Ammonius. Busse believes that most of the anonymous scholia should be attributed to the scholiast, though some

---

[23] In a footnote to their translation of the scholion, FHS&G (p. 145) suggest "extra qualification" as an alternative rendering of προσδιορισμός, but the note appears on a later page (p. 147) and is unlikely to occasion a serious reexamination of the scholion.
[24] See Bocheński (above, n.6) 401.12, 14; 44 n. 174 and Repici (above, n.18) 62. As far as I can determine, it is in Ammonius that we first find προσδιορισμός used as a technical term for the logical quantifier.

derive from an unidentified commentary.²⁵ In a footnote, Busse tells us that the scholion mentioning Theophrastus is exceptional in that someone might want to attribute it to Ammonius; but he says that its contents are so vacuous that it appears inappropriate to dull the splendor of Ammonius by making him the source.²⁶ I shall return to this judgment in Section III; here I want to give the full text of the scholion—or rather scholia—in question.

εἴωθεν ἀεὶ τὸ πᾶς καὶ τὸ οὐδεὶς καὶ ὅλως ὁ προσδιορισμὸς ἐπὶ τοῦ ὑποκειμένου τάττεσθαι ὅρου καὶ οὐκ ἐπὶ τοῦ κατηγορουμένου· τοῦτο οὖν καὶ αὐτὸς ἐνταῦθά φησι ὅτι ψευδὴς ἡ ἀπόφανσις γίνεται, ἐν ᾗ τῷ κατηγορουμένῳ ὅρῳ πρόσκειται ὁ προσδιορισμός. ἀλλ' ἴδωμεν τούτου
5 τὴν αἰτίαν ἡμεῖς· εἴωθεν ὁ κατηγορούμενος ὅρος ὅπου μὲν περιληπτικώτερος εἶναι τοῦ ὑποκειμένου καὶ ἐπὶ πλέον ἐκτείνεσθαι, τοὐλάχιστον δὲ ἐξισάζειν ἐπί τινος ὕλης· ὥσθ' ὅπου μὲν ψευδῆ ποιήσει τὴν πρότασιν, ἔνθα ὑπερπαίει ὁ κατηγορούμενος· ἐὰν γὰρ εἴπωμεν ὅτι πᾶς ἄνθρωπος πᾶν ζῷον, ψευδόμεθα· οὐ γὰρ δὴ καὶ ὁ ἵππος ἄνθρωπος.
10 ὅπου ⟨δὲ⟩ * * * (f. 64ʳ) πρὸς τοῦτό φησιν ὁ Θεόφραστος ὅτι ἐπί τινων ἐὰν μὴ ὁ προσδιορισμὸς ᾖ καὶ ἐπὶ τοῦ κατηγορουμένου, ἡ ἀντίφασις συναληθεύσει, οἷον, φησίν, ἐὰν λέγωμεν· Φαινίας ἔχει ἐπιστήμην— Φαινίας οὐκ ἔχει ἐπιστήμην, δύναται εἶναι ἀμφότερα ἀληθῆ· ἐγχωρεῖ γὰρ αὐτὸν εἰ τύχοι γραμματικὴν μὲν ἔχειν ἐπιστήμην, ἰατρικὴν δὲ μή·
15 καί φαμεν ὅτι παραλογίζεται ἡμᾶς ὁ τοῦτο λέγων ἄλλον μὲν ἐπὶ τῆς καταφάσεως τὸν κατηγορούμενον λαμβάνων ἄλλον δὲ ἐπὶ τῆς ἀποφάσεως τῇ ὁμωνυμίᾳ τῆς ἐπιστήμης εἰς τὴν ἀπάτην προσχρώμενος· ἔφη γὰρ αὐτὸς Ἀριστοτέλης ὅτι δεῖ τοὺς δύο ὅρους ἐν ἀμφοτέραις ταῖς ἀποφάνσεσι ταῖς ἀποτελούσαις ἀντίφασιν ⟨τοὺς⟩ αὐτοὺς εἶναι.

It is customary for "all" and "no one" and generally the quantifier to be assigned always to the subject term and not to the predicate. Therefore he (Aristotle) says here that the statement is false in which the quantifier is attached to the predicate term. But let us see the reason for this. It is customary for the predicate term in some case to be more inclusive than the subject and to have greater extension, and for certain subject-matter to have at least equal extension. As a result, in cases in which the predicate surpasses (the subject), it will make the premise false. For if we say that "every man is every animal," we make a false statement. For indeed the horse is not man. In other cases * * * In regard to this, Theophrastus says that in some cases, if the *prosdiorismos* is not applied to the predicate too, the contradictory will be true as well. For example, he says, if we say, "Phainias possesses science," and "Phainias does not possess science," both statements

---

²⁵ *CAG* vol. 4.5 p. xxxi: "anonyma scholia magna ex parte ex scholiastae ingenio profecta esse videntur, quaedam dubium non est quin ex nescio quo commentario fluxerint."
²⁶ *CAG* vol. 4.5 p. xxxi n.3: "unum (f. 64ʳ), in quo Theophrastus laudatur, Ammonio plus afferre putaveris. sed id, quod Theophrasto tribuitur, tam vanum ac futile est, ut inconveniens esse videatur hoc testimonio illius splendorem obscurare."

can be true. For it is possible for him to possess, say, grammatical science, but not medical science. We say that the person who says that misleads us by fallacious reasoning. He assumes one predicate in the affirmation and another in the denial, and uses the homonymy of "science" to deceive. For Aristotle himself said that the two terms in both statements producing contradiction must be the same.

I have inspected the codex by means of a microfilm copy obtained from the Ambrosian Collection of the Medieval Institute at Notre Dame University.[27] There appears to be nothing wrong with Busse's reporting of the text;[28] I differ only in adding δὲ in line 10. The shorter version of the Theophrastean scholion printed by Waitz and Wimmer is found in lines 10–13. The sentence added by FHS&G occurs in lines 13–14. If we look at the manuscript, we shall see that the shorter version begins at the top of folium 64^v. What precedes in Busse's text is taken from folium 64^r. Following Busse, I have marked a lacuna at the end of folium 64^r. The existence of a lacuna is undeniable; it would, however, be a mistake to think that the lacuna occurs in the middle of a single scholion. There are in fact two scholia, as the manuscript makes clear, and each is referred to a different line of the *De interpretatione*. The first (lines 1–10) is flagged to 17b12 and the second (lines 10–19) to 17b14.[29] It follows that only FHS&G have given the correct reference—or at least that which is found in the manuscript. Busse has 17b14, but he makes it the reference for either the first or both scholia. That may appear to be a quibble; but in an investigation ultimately concerned with the proper reference of the second scholion, exactitude at the outset is desirable.

Turning now to content, we can say that the first scholion begins in a straightforward manner. Its author tells us that normally a quantifier is not assigned to the predicate (lines 1–2) and then paraphrases Aristotle's statement at 17b12–14, saying that a statement in which a quantifier is attached to the predicate is false (lines 2–4). After that the scholiast urges consideration of the reason (αἰτία) for denying quantification of the predicate (lines 4–5), and toward this end he distinguishes between a predicate which is more inclusive (περιληπτικώτερος, πλέον ἐκτείν-

---

[27] I want to thank Dr. Louis Jordan and his staff at the Medieval Institute for providing the film with remarkable promptness. Also to be thanked is Elisabetta Matelli, Milan, who directed me to the Institute.
[28] *CAG* vol. 4.5 p. xxxiii.27–41.
[29] That means that ἐνταῦθα (line 3) and πρὸς τοῦτο (line 10) do not have the same reference.

εσθαι) than the subject and one which is equal (ἐξισάζειν) to it (lines 5–7). The first case is made clear by the example "every man is every animal." The second case is not developed in the scholion. We have only the beginning (ὅπου ⟨δὲ⟩ line 10) after which the text breaks off.

What the scholiast intended to write cannot be established with certainty. Nevertheless, a closely related passage in Ammonius' commentary is suggestive. I am thinking of the last page of the commentator's discussion of 17b12–16. Ammonius refers to what has already been said and declares it now obvious that the universal positive quantifier should not be attached to the predicate (108.7–11). He distinguishes between the predicate which is wider (κοινότερον) than its subject and one which is equal (ἐξισάζον) to the subject. The former case is illustrated by the same example we find in the scholiast, "every man is every animal." and the latter is illustrated by "every man is every risible" (108.7–10). My guess is that the scholiast would have introduced the same proposition or one very similar in order to illustrate his second case. If that conjecture seems too bold, let me point out that the connection between Ammonius and the scholiast is strengthened a few lines later when Ammonius asks what is the reason (τὸ αἴτιον) for the predicate's inability to tolerate the universal positive quantifier (108.18–19). In this context, he repeats the distinction between two kinds of predicate, using much the same vocabulary as the scholiast (περιλαμβάνειν, ἐξισάζον, ὑπερτεῖνον 108.21–2). Of course, none of this proves that the scholiast is drawing directly on Ammonius, but the similarities are so striking that I am inclined to think that he may be.[30] Alternatively the scholiast may be drawing on an unidentified but closely related commentary, or he may be influenced by several such sources. I leave the matter undecided.

The second scholion is our special concern and far more puzzling. Let me begin by saying again that the manuscript clearly refers the scholion to 17b14. An asterisk appears over the first word of the scholion and over the first word of the Aristotelian sentence: οὐδεμία γὰρ κατάφασις ἔσται, ἐν ᾗ τοῦ κατηγορουμένου καθόλου τὸ καθόλου κατηγορηθήσεται, οἷον ἔστι πᾶς ἄνθρωπος πᾶν ζῷον. That means the

---

[30] A. Busse, *Ammonius, In Aristotelis* De interpretatione *commentarius, CAG* 4.5 appears to reject the possibility, for he tells us that the anonymous scholia contain no traces of Ammonius: "neque Ammonii vestigia usquam apparent" (xxxi).

scholion is tied to a sentence in which the topic is quantification of the predicate. Given this tie it may seem foolish to question current scholarly opinion, but I think the codex itself provides reason to do so. Scholiasts are not perfect in marking references, and the scholiast of codex L 93 sup. is no exception. On folium 65ᵛ he offers comments on *De interpretatione* 8. Two-thirds of the way down the margin we find a scholion concerning Aristotle's example of ambiguous usage in 18a19–21. The scholion is correctly flagged to 18a19. At the bottom of the folium there is a scholion on 18a21–5. It is flagged in with less precision, but still correctly, at 18a24. What comes in the middle is truly startling. We have a scholion concerning chapter 9, apparently on 18a34–5. It is flagged into chapter 8 at 18a21, as if it were a note on 18a21–3. The scholion tells us that Aristotle wants to refute the *astrologoi*. These people are not mentioned in the *De interpretatione*, nor are they mentioned in the commentary of Ammonius. My guess is that the scholiast has drawn on a source which is now lost. For whatever reason his mind wandered, and he entered a note at the wrong place.

Something similar can, I think, be said about the scholion mentioning Theophrastus. It is out of place, and if one asks where it belongs, the answer is provided by the scholiast himself. I am referring to lines 15–19, which were omitted by Waitz and for that reason have not received the attention they deserve. The scholiast tells us that the man who says "Phainias possesses science"—"Phainias does not possess science" misleads us when he understands the two predicates in different ways. The scholiast speaks of homonymy in the use of "science" and then introduces Aristotle who is credited with observing that the terms in both parts of a contradiction must be the same. There are two places in *De interpretatione* 7 to which theses remarks may be referred. They are 17b39 and 18a3, where Aristotle is explicit that the same fact must be affirmed and denied if contradiction is to occur. One of those lines may be the proper reference, but there is, I think, an even more likely candidate. It is *De interpretatione* 6 17a33–7. Having said that every affirmation has an opposed denial and *vice versa* (17a32–3), Aristotle defines contradiction and tells us that contradiction involves affirming and denying the same thing of the same thing. Here is the text of 17a33–7.

καὶ ἔστω ἀντίφασις τοῦτο, κατάφασις καὶ ἀπόφασις αἱ ἀντικείμεναι· λέγω δὲ ἀντικεῖσθαι τὴν τοῦ αὐτοῦ κατὰ τοῦ αὐτοῦ,—μὴ ὁμωνύμως δέ, καί ὅσα ἄλλα τῶν τοιούτων προσδιοριζόμεθα πρὸς τὰς σοφιστικὰς ἐνοχλήσεις.

And let this be contradiction: opposed affirmation and denial. I speak of being opposed when statements affirm and deny the same thing of the same thing,—but not homonymously, and any other such specifications we add in order to meet the annoying objections of sophists.

A close relationship with the scholion is obvious. In both texts the subject is contradiction, and the need to affirm and to deny the same thing is clearly acknowledged (*De int.* 17a35, schol. lines 18–19). Homonymy is recognized as something to avoid (*De int.* 17a35, schol. line 17). Furthermore, προσδιορίζεσθαι in the Aristotelian text corresponds to προσδιορισμός in the scholion (*De int.* 17a36, schol. line 11). I shall return to the last point of correspondence later. Here let me mention one minor difference. The scholiast says that we are mislead when one predicate term is assumed in the affirmation and a different one in the denial (τὸν κατηγορούμενον ⟨ὅρον⟩ line 16); and he has Aristotle say that the two terms in both propositions must be the same (τοὺς δύο ὅρους ... ⟨τοὺς⟩ αὐτούς lines 18–19). The use here of "term" (ὅρος) is not found in the Aristotelian passage. It is the scholiast's language, though Aristotle would not have objected. For the idea conveyed is the same. Homonymous usage should be avoided in the predicate as well as in the subject.

It may be helpful to say something about three scholia which, in cod. L 93 sup., actually accompany *De interpretatione* 17a33–7. All are printed by Busse (on pages xxxii–iii).[31] Concerning the first two, I shall only mention relevant details. The first is flagged to 17a33. It begins by paraphrasing Aristotle's definition of contradiction (17a33–4), but it goes beyond the Aristotelian definition in that it includes a reference to content. The scholiast is anticipating what Aristotle says next: namely that a contradiction must affirm and deny the same fact (17a34–5). In what follows the scholiast makes the point negatively, saying that there is no contradiction when "Socrates loves wisdom" is opposed to "Plato does not engage in dialectic" (xxxii.48–51). For our purposes there are two matters of importance. First, when the scholiast reports what someone says (φησίν xxxii.48) he does so with some freedom. Second, the scholiast uses an example in which the subjects are not universals but

---

[31] In codex Ambrosiana L 93 sup., they occur on folium 63ᵛ. I have compared Busse's texts (*CAG* 4.5) with a microfilm of the folium (see n. 28); and aside from one typo (see the next note), I can find no mistaken readings. Busses's references to the *De interpretatione* correspond to the signs given by the scholiast on the folio.

individuals: Socrates and Plato (xxxii.50–1). That should remind us of the Theophrastean example, in which the subject, Phainias, is an individual.

The second scholion is flagged to 17a34; and like the first, it paraphrases what Aristotle says (φησί xxxiii.1). While Aristotle tells us how he uses the verb ἀντικεῖσθαι, the scholiast shifts to the noun ἀντίθεσις (xxxiii.1). That may tell us something about προσδιορισμός in the opening of the Theophrastean scholion. I return to that soon. Here I want to note that the scholiast explains the first occurrence of "the same" (τοῦ αὐτοῦ 17a35) as "the predicated term" (τὸν κατηγορούμενον ὅρον xxxiii.2). That is the language of the Theophrastean scholion (lines 11 and 15–16). The same is true of the phrase "in (propositions) producing contradiction" (ἐν ταῖς ... ἀποτελούσαις τὴν ἀντίφασιν xxxiii.3). It recalls the last sentence of the Theophrastean scholion (lines 18–19).

The third scholion concerns 17a35 and seems especially important for interpreting the Theophrastean scholion. I give it here in full.

> ἐπειδή πως ἔφη δεῖν ἐν ταῖς δύο προτάσεσι τὸν αὐτὸν ὅρον κατηγορεῖσθαι τοῦ αὐτοῦ ὑποκειμένου, φησὶν ὅτι ἀλλ᾽ ἵνα μὴ ὁμωνύμως μηδὲ συνωνύμως ἡ κατηγορία γίνοιτο· ὅρα γὰρ πῶς ἐν τοῖς ὁμωνύμοις σοφισμῷ περιπίπτομεν καὶ οὐ γίνεται ἀντίφασις, καίτοι δοκούντων τῶν αὐτῶν ὅρων ἐν
> 5 ἀμφοτέραις ταῖς προτάσεσι παραλαμβάνεσθαι. λέγω γὰρ ὅτι ὁ κύων τετράπουν ἐστὶ καὶ πάλιν οὐκ ἔστιν ὁ κύων τετράπουν, καὶ οὐ γίνεται ἀντίφασις· δύναται γὰρ τὰ δύο ἀληθῆ εἶναι, ἡ δὲ ἀντίφασις[32] διαιρεῖ τὸ ψεῦδος ἀεὶ καὶ τὸ ἀληθές. αἴτιον δὲ τούτου, ὅπερ ἔφην, ἡ ὁμωνυμία. καὶ ὁμοίως ἐπὶ τῶν συνωνύμων, οἷον ἐὰν λέγωμεν· πᾶς ἄνθρωπός τινα
> 10 ἀριθμὸν κατέχει—οὐ πᾶς ἄνθρωπος ἀριθμόν τινα κατέχει· ταῦτα γάρ, ὡς ὁρᾶς, οὐ ποιεῖ ἀντίφασιν· δύναται γὰρ συναληθεύειν.

Since he has said as it were that the same term must be predicated of the same subject in the two propositions, he (now) says: but where the predication occurs not homonymously and not synonymously. For consider how a sophism makes us stumble in cases of homonymy and a contradiction does not occur, even though the same terms seem to be employed in both propositions. For (if) I say that "The dog is fourfooted" and again "The dog is not fourfooted," no contradiction occurs. For both can be true, but contradiction always divides truth and falsity. Homonymy is, as he said, the cause of this. And likewise in cases of synonymy, for example if we say "Every man possesses some number"—"Not every man possesses some number." For these, as you see, do not produce contradiction. For they can be true together.

---

[32] ἀντίφασεις in Busse's text (*CAG* 4.5, p. xxxiii.19) seems to be a typographical error.

The scholiast begins by restating what has been discussed in the preceding scholion; again he speaks of "the predicated term." After that he turns to Aristotle's warning against homonymous usage; and drawing on a distinction made in *Categories* 1 1a1–12, he adds a second case: namely that of synonymous usage. He discusses the case of homonymy first, giving as an example the two statements "The dog is fourfooted" and "The dog is not fourfooted." Here the subjects are homonymous. In the first case "dog" refers to an animal; in the second it picks out a particular star. The scholiast observes correctly that the two statements can both be true.[33] Cases of synonymy are regarded as similar and treated in fewer words. We are given two statements "Every man possesses some number" and "Not every man possesses some number," and told that they can be true together. The use of the verb συναληθεύειν in line 11 should remind us of the Theophrastean scholion (ἡ ἀντίφασις συναληθεύσει lines 11–12), and the same is true of the opposed statements. For in both scholia contradiction fails to occur because the predicates are different. The words and their meaning are the same, but the specific cases covered by the predicate are different. "Possessing some number" covers "being five feet tall" and "being six foot tall." As a result it is true that every man has some number and that not every man has some number. Every man has a height, but not every man has this or that height.[34] Similary in the Theophrastean example, "possessing knowledge" has one meaning, but it also covers many different specific cases. The scholiast mentions possessing grammar and medicine (line 14). The list is open ended and easily exploited by a sophistic trickster.

The above considerations suggest to me that the Theophrastean scholion is misplaced. It never mentions quantification because it is not concerned with that topic. Its concern is contradiction. The noun ἀντίφασις occurs twice (lines 11 and 19), and the example of Phainias

---

[33] The example of the dog as animal and star is Aristotelian. See *SE* 4 166a16 and *Rhet.* 2.24 1401a15–16.

[34] The example of height is my own; it has been chosen for its familiarity. How the scholiast would have explained "possessing some number" is not clear. Robert Sharples has suggested to me *via* e-mail that ἀριθμός may be understood as a sum of money (LSJ I.5), or a social position (LSJ I.5) He has also conveyed a suggestion of Walter Cockle: namely, that ἀριθμός may be construed as the sum of numerical values of letters in a name (LSJ X). For the purposes of this paper, the matter may be left undecided.

is one of apparent contradiction. The occurrence of the noun προσδιορισμός also speaks for this interpretation. It corresponds to Aristotle's use of the verb προσδιορίζεσθαι at *De interpretatione* 6 17a36. It means "further specification" or "additional qualification." Theophrastus may have used the noun in this sense, but my suspicion is that we have another case of the scholiast offering a paraphrase. Just as he replaced the verb ἀντικεῖσθαι with ἀντίθεσις in the scholion on 17a34, so here he may have varied προσδιορίζεσθαι with προσδιορισμός.[35] Furthermore, we should understand ὅρου after ἐπὶ τοῦ κατηγορουμένου (line 11) and attribute the use of συναληθεύειν (line 12) to the scholiast.[36] If that is correct, then the only direct quotation from Theophrastus is the example and possibly the short explanation which follows.

Someone may ask how the scholion came to be misplaced. Perhaps it is sufficient to point to the misplaced scholion on chapter 9 18a34–5. Our scholiast is capable of serious error; the Theophrastean scholion is only another example. Nevertheless, I think we can say more if we take account of a scholion on 7 17b7, for it appears to offer a clue. Aristotle is concerned with cases in which something is said of a universal, but not universally: e.g., "A man is white." The scholiast begins his remarks by quoting the first two words of Aristotle (ὅταν δὲ xxxiii.23) after which he paraphrases or rather freely expresses Aristotle's thought. He speaks of unquantified propositions (ἀπροσδιόριστοι προτάσεις 23). There is nothing wrong here, but the scholiast goes on to say that Aristotle is accustomed to call quantifiers like "all" and "no one" προσδιορισμοί (24–5).[37] That is mistaken and may explain in part at least how the Theophratean scholion got misplaced. The scholiast had a commentary or other source before him in which the noun προσδιορισμός or, as I prefer to imagine, the verb προσδιορίζεσθαι occurred. He construed the word wrongly and understood Theophrastus to be making a point about quantification. That would be a foolish error, but hardly surprising in the case of a scholiast who mixes notes on chapters 8 and 9 and says that Aristotle calls quantifiers προσδιορισμοί.

---

[35] The verb προσδιορίζεσθαι is attested for Theophrastus. See FHS&G 650.39, where it is translated "add the determination."

[36] Of course Aristotle uses συναληθεύειν at *De int* 10 19b36, and Theophrastus may have done so on occasion. Nevertheless, considering lines 11–12 together, I think it most likely that συναληθεύειν should be attributed to the scholiast.

[37] ταῦτα γὰρ Ἀριστοτέλης εἴωθε καλεῖν προσδιορισμούς (xxxiii.24–5).

III. Conclusion

If the preceding argument is correct, persons interested in the history of logical theory may feel some disappointment, for Waitz' scholion—now no. 84 FHS&G—offers nothing new. It concerns contradiction and provides no evidence concerning Theophrastus' treatment of the logical quantifier. In particular, we cannot say on the basis of the scholion that Theophrastus opposed Aristotle: the former accepting and the latter rejecting quantification of the predicate.[38] Still less can we make a connection with Ammonius' rejection of the quantified predicate. When the commentator discusses the statement "Every man is capable of every science," he may have a particular opponent in mind, but our text provides no reason for believing that the opponent is Theophrastus.[39] Furthermore, we shall not be tempted to describe the scholion as futile and unworthy of Ammonius.[40] Once we recognize that the scholion is misplaced and that the topic is contradiction, we can see that the scholion contains an apt example which could be worked into Ammonius' comments on contradiction.[41]

What should be faulted is not the content but the placement of scholion. The scholiast entered the Theophrastean material as a note on 17a14; and in doing so he made a mistake which has adversely affected

---

[38] Bocheński (above, n.6) 44.

[39] Mignucci (above, n.16) 38–40. In private correspondence, Prof. Mignucci has suggested to me that the length and detail of Ammonius' discussion is best explained by supposing a group of deviant Peripatetics who endorsed quantification of the predicate and may have tried to refer back to Theophrastus. The suggestion may well be correct. I leave discussion to those better versed in ancient logic and offer only two brief comments. First, it is striking that Ammonius writes at such length without naming Theophrastus. Were the Eresian the putative source for a theory concerning the quantification of the predicate, we might expect him to be named. Second, whatever the truth concerning deviant Peripatetics, the scholion, on my interpretation, offers no evidence, for it is out of place and not concerned with the quantification of the predicate.

[40] Busse, CAG 4.5, p. xxxi n.3.

[41] If we allow for the brevity of the scholion and recognize that it probably refers to De interpretatione 6 17a36, we can say that both the scholiast and Ammonius offer closely related analyses. They share the same vocabulary (ὅρος schol. line 18, Ammon. 84.22 etc.; συναληθεύειν schol. line 12, Ammon. 84.34; ὁμωνυμία schol. line 17, Ammon. 85.4; παραλογίζεσθαι schol. line 15, Ammon. 85.31 [cf. Arist. SE 1 165a16]), make use of an example with an individual as subject (schol. lines 12–13, Ammon. 84.31) and take account of Aristotle's insistence that the same fact be affirmed and denied (schol. lines 18–19, Ammon. 84.16).

modern scholarship. The word προσδιορισμός has been wrongly understood; the same is true of κατηγορούμενον. In the latter case, confused usage has been suspected, but that suspicion loses its textual basis when the scholion is properly connected with contradiction. Both Aristotle and Theophrastus hold that contradiction depends upon opposed statements having the same subject and predicate. Our scholion makes the point negatively with special reference to the predicate. This is not to deny all confusion. The scholiast certainly was confused, and he has caused us to be similarly affected. Let's hope we can now approach the scholion freed from inherited error.[42]

---

[42] I want to thank Dr. Josip Talanga for discussing with me almost every aspect of this paper. His criticisms have been most instructive.

12

Alexandria, Syene, Meroe: Symmetry in Eratosthenes' *Measurement of the World*

A.S. Gratwick

Ian Kidd many years since gave a short talk on Eratosthenes' famous measurement to the St. Andrews Student Classical Society which I attended as a then young member of staff. He well knows that I have a keen interest in the history of mathematics; but he does not know that it was that talk of his which sparked that interest in the first place, and I return to the subject here in grateful thanks to him. My case is that there was more to Eratosthenes' argument than appears in our principal source Cleomedes, that what is unsatisfactory in the premises as reported by him can be elucidated from allusions in Martianus Capella and in Strabo, and that information obtained by the Hellenistic explorer Philo, an elder contemporary of Eratosthenes largely forgotten in the modern doxography, was crucial for the deductions which Eratosthenes made. It will be convenient first to quote the relevant passages in translation, citing Cleomedes at length to put his discussion of Eratosthenes in its context.

I. The Key Passages

1. Cleomedes *De circulari motu corporum caelestium* 1.10 pp. 91–102 Ziegler, 1.7 pp. 33–7 Todd (c. A.D. 370):

Various opinions have been expressed by natural scientists concerning the circumference of the world, but those of Posidonius and Eratosthenes are better than the rest, the latter establishing its circumference by a geometrical approach, while Posidonius' is simpler.[1] Each of them assumes certain postulates and arrives at his conclusion by following the postulates. We shall first discuss Posidonius' approach.

He states that Rhodes and Alexandria lie on the same meridian. Meridian circles are those drawn through the poles of the universe and a point which lies vertically over any terrestrial observer. So the poles of all meridian circles are the same, but the zenith point varies; hence an infinite set of meridian circles may be drawn. So Rhodes and Alexandria lie under the same meridian and the distance between the cities is thought to be 5,000 stades. Suppose this to be the case. All meridian circles belong to the class of great circles on the cosmos cutting it in equal halves and drawn through its poles.

Assuming these postulates, Posidonius next divides the circle of the zodiac (i.e., the ecliptic) into forty-eight parts, that circle being equal in size to a meridian circle since it too divides the universe into equal halves, thus quartering each of the twelve signs of the zodiac. Now if the meridian through Rhodes and Alexandria is divided into the same 48 parts as the zodiac-circle, its sections too will be equal to those of the zodiac-circle. For when equal magnitudes are divided into equal parts, the parts of the one must be equal to the parts of the other.

Assuming these further postulates,[2] Posidonius next states that the star called Canobus is the brightest in the South on the rudderboard of the constellation Argo.[3] This star is not visible in Greece at all, hence Aratus makes no mention of it in his *Phaenomena*. For those travelling from North to South it starts to become visible in Rhodes and once seen on the horizon it immediately sets as the celestial sphere revolves. But when having sailed the five thousand stades from Rhodes we get to Alexandria, this star is found to have an elevation of a quarter of a sign above the horizon when it is exactly on the meridian, that is one forty-eighth of the meridian passing through Rhodes and Alexandria.

---

[1] διὰ γεωμετρικῆς ἐφόδου ... ἁπλουστέρα: the antithesis may rather mean "by a land-measuring (surveyor's) approach ... a more direct approach," for obviously both assume the same geometrical model.

[2] τούτων τοίνυν οὕτως ἔχειν προ(σ)υποκειμένων ASG: προϋποκειμένων MSS and edd., but ineptly after τούτων τοίνυν οὕτως ἔχειν ὑποκειμένων as the introduction of the previous paragraph; there are two sets of postulates, one set general, one particular. Clearly a compound meaning "in addition," not "first," is wanted. The same confusion of these particular words occurs in the MSS of Galen *UP* 3.8.

[3] Cf. Geminus 3.15, Pliny *Nat.* 2.178.

Now the section of the same meridian overlying the distance between Rhodes and Alexandria must also be one forty-eighth of that circle because the Rhodians' horizon-circle is also one forty-eighth of the ecliptic circle distant from the Alexandrians' horizon circle. So since the part of the earth underlying this section is thought to be 5,000 stades the other sections must also be of 5,000 stades. So the great circle of the world is found to be 240,000 stades if the distance from Rhodes to Alexandria be 5,000 stades; if not, then (it will be found) in that proportion to the (true) distance.

Such is Posidonius' approach to the problem of the circumference of the world; that of Eratosthenes involves a geometrical approach and may seem somewhat obscure.[4] Our following introductory remarks will clarify what he says. Let us suppose first that Syene and Alexandria lie on the same meridian and next that the distance between the cities is 5,000 stades; third, that the rays sent from different parts of the sun to different parts of the earth are parallel; for mathematicians assume them to be so. Let there be a fourth postulate, proved by the mathematicians, that straight lines meeting parallel lines make equal alternate angles.[5] Fifthly, that arcs over equal angles are similar, that is have the same relation and proportion with respect to their respective circles, this too proved by the mathematicians;[6] for when arcs are constructed over equal angles, if any one of them is a tenth of its particular circle, the rest are also tenths of their particular circles.

Having grasped these points one will have no difficulty in understanding Eratosthenes' approach, which goes like this. He states that Syene and Alexandria lie under the same meridian. Since meridian circles are as great as any in the cosmos, the circles on earth underlying them must also be as great as any on earth. So the magnitude of the circumference of the circle through Syene and Alexandria that this approach indicates matches the circumference of a great circle of the world.[7]

Now he states, and it is the case, that Syene lies under the circle of the summer tropic. So when the Sun has entered Cancer and in making his summer turn is exactly on the meridian, the gnomons of hour-counters[8]

---

[4] ἡ δὲ τοῦ Ἐρατοσθένους γεωμετρικῆς ἐχομένη καὶ δοκοῦσά τι ἀσαφέστερον ἔχειν: I suspect that Cleomedes means "in its unabridged form."

[5] Euclid *El.* 1.29.

[6] Euclid *El.* 3.def.11.

[7] ὥστε ἡλίκον ἂν τὸν διὰ Συήνης καὶ Ἀλεξανδρείας ἥκοντα κύκλον τῆς γῆς ἡ ἔφοδος ἀποδείξηι (ἐπιδείξηι, ἀποδείξει, ἀποδείξοι variant readings of the MSS) αὐτή, τηλικοῦτος ὁ μέγιστός ἐστι τῆς γῆς κύκλος. Since Syene lies SSE of Alexandria three degrees to the East this is a very crude approximation. But if the interpretation given below is right, this rather inelegant step in the argument is unnecessary. Cleomedes may be "cutting the corner" here if in fact Eratosthenes showed first that the meridian distance between *the parallels* through Syene and Alexandria should be five thousand stades, whatever (if anything) passed as the figure for the direct route, which is more like 5,350 stades. The assumption made by Cleomedes and others that 5,000 stades is the *direct* distance may easily be a misunderstanding; it is easy to see how in the context of ancient geography the distance between *the parallels* through A and B might be confused with the direct distance between A and B, especially when A is more or less due north of B.

[8] Here and *passim* I render ὡρολόγιον "hour-counter" and ὡροσκοπεῖον "hour-

necessarily become shadowless, the Sun being stationed exactly overhead; and there is report that this happens over a belt of three hundred stades. But at the same time in Alexandria, the markers of hourcounters do cast shadows since this city lies further to the north than Syene. Now given that the cities lie under a great meridian circle, if we draw an arc to the foot of the gnomon of the hourcounter in Alexandria from the tip of the gnomon's shadow, this arc will be a section of a great circle in the bowl, since the bowl of the hourcounter lies under a great (celestial) circle.

So if we next imagine straight lines produced from each of the two gnomons they will cross at the centre of the world. Since the hourcounter at Syene lies vertically under the sun, if we further imagine a straight line from the sun arriving at the tip of the gnomon of the hourcounter there will be one straight line from the sun coming to the centre of the earth. If we imagine another straight line drawn from the tip of the shadow of the gnomon of the hourcounter at Alexandria to the sun, this and the aforementioned straight line will be parallel, arriving as they do from different parts of the sun at different points on the Earth.

Now the straight line coming from the centre of the earth to the gnomon at Alexandria intersects these parallel lines so that it makes equal alternate angles, one of which is at the centre of the earth at the meeting of the straight lines which were drawn from the hourcounters to the centre of the earth, and the other at the meeting of the tip of the gnomon at Alexandria and of the line drawn from the tip of the shadow to the sun through its point of contact with the gnomon. Over this angle there is the arc drawn from the tip of the shadow of the gnomon to its base, over the one at the centre of the world there is the arc from Syene to Alexandria. Now these arcs are similar the one to the other, going as they do over equal angles. So the ratio which the arc in the bowl has to its own circle is the same as the ratio which the arc from Syene to Alexandria has to its full circle. The arc in the bowl is found to be one fiftieth of its circumference. Therefore the distance from Syene to Alexandria must also be one fiftieth of any great circle of the world, and this distance is 5,000 stades. Therefore the full circle works out as 250,000 stades. Such is Eratosthenes' approach.

2. Martianus Capella *De nuptiis Mercurii et Philologiae* 6.596-9:

...We next have to show what position and magnitude are Earth's portion. As for the circumference, it is 252,000 stades as was deduced by gnomonical reckoning <from *scaphia*>[9] by the great scholar Eratosthenes.

I should explain that the name *scaphia* applies to round bowls of bronze which distinguish hour-lines by the tip of a (radial) stilus erected on the bottom centre (of the bowl); this stilus is called the gnomon; the curving length of its shadow measured out by the reckoning (in degrees) of its own

watcher"; these and σκάφια "bowls" are all the same thing, but I think it misleading to translate as "sundials."

[9] *ut ab Eratosthene doctissimo gnomonica supputatione discussum. quippe scaphia* .... MSS, edd.; but *quippe* and the subsequent gloss on *gnomon* implies that <*ex scaphiis*> or the like has dropped out at the end or near the end of the prior sentence.

particular compass-span for an equinox, on being inclined twenty-four degrees, will deliver[10] the limit of a double arc.

Now Eratosthenes, being informed by Ptolemy's royal surveyors about the count of stades from Meroe to Syene and noting what (angular) part of the Earth this was and multiplying in proportion, unhesitatingly settled respecting the circumference and measure of the Earth how many thousands of stades were its full compass.

The size of the earth has been found by the succinctness of calculation: now let her position be imparted. That she is set absolutely centrally in the deepest part of the universe is shown by manifold proofs ... .

3. Strabo 17.1.48 (c. 10 B.C.; an eyewitness report)

(There is a "Nilometer" well at Elephantine near Syene which measures the rise and fall of the river and serves as a sort of calendar), and in Syene there is the well that indicates the summer solstice, since these regions lie under the summer tropic and render gnomons shadowless at mid-day ... and the sun coming to the zenith necessarily casts beams as far as the water of wells even if they are very deep ... .[11]

4. Pliny Nat. 2.183–6

...In similar fashion they tell that in Syene, a town which is 5,000 stades above Alexandria, no shadow is cast on midsummer's day and that a well made there for the sake of the experiment is totally illuminated ... it is also well established that in Berenice the city of the Troglodytes and 4,820 stades from there in Ptolemais, a town of the same nation which was founded on the coast of the Red Sea for the earliest elephant-trade, the same thing happens forty-five days before the before the solstice and as many again after it, and that for these ninety days shadows are cast southwards. (184) Again in Meroe — this island and capital of the Aethiopian race is commonly held to be 5,000 stades from Syene — shadows disappear twice a year when the sun occupies the eighteenth step of Taurus and the fourteenth of Leo[12]...

---

[10] *reddid<er>it* (597) ASG; a past tense seems to make no sense here. The text reads *cuius umbrae prolixitas aequinoctio centri sui aestimatione dimensa uicies quater complicata circuli duplicis modum reddidit* (*reddit* L), Willis conjectures a lacuna before *reddidit*, Martianus seems to be trying to make the elementary point that the equinoctial shadow-arc gives the local latitude φ measured on the meridian of the bowl from the foot of the gnomon, and this plus 24 degrees delivers the longest shadow-arc (the winter solstice). If that is all, then *duplicis* means "a two-stage arc" symmetrical only if φ = 24 degrees. But the word itself and the context imply that Martianus ought also to mention the arc of shortest day: *hinc illinc* or the like seems wanted before *reddidit*.

[11] ἐν δὲ τῆι Συήνηι καὶ τὸ φρέαρ ἐστὶ τὸ διασήμαινον τὰς θερινὰς τροπάς, διότι τῶι τροπικῶι κύκλωι ὑπόκεινται οἱ τόποι οὗτοι καὶ ποιοῦσιν ἀσκίους τοὺς γνώμονας κατὰ μεσημβρίαν ... ἀνάγκη δὲ κατὰ κορυφὴν ἡμῖν γινόμενον (sc. τὸν ἥλιον) καὶ εἰς τὰ φρέατα βάλλειν μέχρι τοῦ ὕδατος τὰς αὐγάς, κἂν βαθύτατα ἦι ...

[12] With 30 days to a sign, this gives 13 + 30 + 30 + 14 = 87 noons for the latter part

(185) and Eratosthenes has handed down that all over the land of the Troglodytes shadows are cast in the opposite direction for twice forty-five days in a year ...[13]

5. Strabo <u>Geog</u>. 2.1.20 (Hipparchus fr. 17 Dicks)

(As to the parallel of latitude through Meroe Hipparchus says that) Philo the writer of *The Voyage to Ethiopia* finds that the sun is in the zenith forty-five days before the summer solstice and states the gnomon-ratios both for the solstices and the equinoxes, and that Eratosthenes himself agrees very closely with Philo (but that no-one, not even Eratosthenes investigates the (continuation of the) parallel in India ...).[14]

---

of Taurus, Gemini, Cancer, and the first part of Leo with 43 before the first noon of Cancer and 43 after; there is a slippage of one at each end in the count, because Cancer 1 should have been counted as day 0, not day 1 in the reckoning, if the aim was to identify the the dates of shadowlessness at Meroe as exact quadrant-points, as well as symmetrical around the first point of Cancer.

[13] I quote this amazing chapter, so typical of its author, in full: simili modo tradunt in Syene oppido quod est supra Alexandriam quinque milibus stadium solstiti die medio nullam umbram iaci, puteumque eius experimenti gratia factum totum inluminari; ex quo apparere tum solem illi loco supra uerticem esse, quod et in India supra flumen Hypasin fieri tempore eodem Onesicritus scribit. constatque in Berenice urbe Trogodytarum et inde stadiis IIII milia DCCCXX in eadem gente Ptolemaide oppido, quod in margine Rubri maris ad primos elephantorum uenatus conditum est, hoc idem ante solstitium quadragenis quinis diebus totidemque postea fieri et per eos XC dies in meridiem umbras iaci. (184) rursus in Meroe — insula haec caputque gentis Aethiopum V milibus stadium a Syene in amne Nilo habitatur — bis anno absumi umbras, sole duodeuicesimam Tauri partem et quartam decimam Leonis tunc obtinente. In India gente Oretum mons est Maleus nomine, iuxta quem umbrae aestate in austrum, hieme in Septentrionem iaciuntur. quindecim tantum noctibus ibi apparet Septentrio. In eadem India Patalis celeberrimo portu, sol dexter oritur, umbrae in meridiem cadunt. (185) Septentrionem ibi Alexandro morante adnotatum prima tantum parte noctis aspici Onesicritus dux eius scripsit, quibus in locis Indiae umbrae non sint, septentrionem non conspici et ea loca appellari ascia nec horas dinumerari ibi. et tota Trogodytice umbras bis quadragenis quinis diebus in anno Eratosthenes in contrarium cadere prodidit. (186) sic fit ut uario lucis incremento in Meroe longissimus dies XII horas aequinoctiales et octo partes unius horae colligat, Alexandriae uero XIIII horas, in Italia XV, in Britannia XVII, ubi aestate lucidae noctes haut dubie se promittunt, id quod cogit ratio credi solstiti diebus accedente sole propius uerticem mundi angusto lucis ambitu subiecta terrae continuos dies habere senis mensibus, noctesque e diuerso ad brumam remoto. quod fieri in insula Thyle Pytheas Massiliensis scribit, sex dierum nauigatione in Septentrionem distante; quidam uero et in Mona quae distat a Camaloduno Britanniae oppido circiter CC milia adfirmant.

[14] τὸ μὲν οὖν κατὰ Μερόην κλίμα Φίλωνά τε τὸν συγγράψαντα τὸν εἰς Αἰθιοπίαν πλοῦν ἱστορεῖν ὅτι πρὸ πέντε καὶ τεσσαράκοντα ἡμερῶν τῆς θερινῆς τροπῆς κατὰ κορυφὴν γίνεται ὁ ἥλιος, λέγειν δὲ καὶ τοὺς λόγους τοῦ γνώμονος πρός τε τὰς τροπικὰς σκιὰς καὶ τὰς ἰσημερινάς, αὐτόν τε Ἐρατοσθένη συμφωνεῖν ἔγγιστα τῶι Φίλωνι, τὸ δ' ἐν τῆι Ἰνδικῆι κλίμα μηδένα ἱστορεῖν, μηδ' αὐτὸν Ἐρατοσθένη ...

6. Aelius Aristides 48.347 (*Aegyptios*, c. A.D. 150)

...In Elephanine everything is illuminated, the temples, the people, the monuments, and nothing has a shadow at midday when the sun is filling his greatest circuit; and in Syene at the same time on the same day the disc of the sun is seen shining perfectly centrally in the holy well like a stopper fitting evenly all round to the mouth of the well ...[15]

7. Heliodorus *Aeth*. 9.22.4 (? c. A.D. 375)

...They also pointed out that the gnomons of hourcounters are shadowless at mid-day, the sun's ray standing exactly in the zenith in the region of Syene and disbarring the casting of the gnomon's shadow by its being illuminated on all sides, just as the water at the bottom of wells is illuminated for the same reason. Hydaspes did not wonder at these things as anything particularly unfamiliar; for he said the same things happened at Meroe in Ethiopia ...[16]

8. Servius ad V. *Ecl*. 3. 105 (c. A.D. 400)

(answers to the riddle *dic quibus in terris – et eris mihi magnus Apollo – tris pateat caeli spatium non amplius ulnas* [Virgil *Ecl*. 3.104–5])
...others want the well meant to be the one which is in Syene, a region of Egypt, which philosophers dug to be of exceptional depth with the particular purpose of proving that place to be the only one which the sun beamed on with a perpendicular gaze: for eight days before the kalends of July when the sun is on its centre...[17]

9. Macrobius *Comm. Somn. Scip*. 2.7.16:

The town of Syene, which is the first in the province of the Thebaid after the southerly mountain wastes, is set under the summer tropic and on the day when the Sun enters a certain[18] part of Cancer at the sixth hour of

---

[15] ἐν μὲν Ἐλεφαντίνει λάμπεται πάντα καὶ νέωι καὶ ἄνθρωποι καὶ στῆλαι καὶ οὐδὲν ἔχει σκιὰν τῆς μεσημβρίας, ἐπειδὰν τὴν μεγίστην ὁ ἥλιος πληροῖ· ἐν Συήνηι τῆς αὐτῆς ἡμέρας τε καὶ ὥρας μέσος ἐν μέσωι τῶι ἱερῶι φρέατι ὁ κύκλος τοῦ ἡλίου φαίνεται ὥσπερ ἐπίθεμα ἴσον πανταχόθεν πρὸς τὸ χεῖλος ἔλλαμπον ...

[16] ἐδείκνυσαν δὲ καὶ τοὺς τῶν ὡρολογίων γνώμονας ἀσκίους κατὰ μεσημβρίαν ὄντας τῆς ἡλιακῆς ἀκτῖνος κατὰ τροπὰς θερινὰς ἐν τοῖς περὶ Συήνην εἰς ἀκρίβειαν κατὰ κορυφὴν ἱσταμένης καὶ τῶι πανταχόθεν περιφωτισμῶι τὴν παρέμπτωσιν τῆς σκιᾶς ἀπελαυνούσης, ὣς καὶ τῶν φρεάτων τὸ κατὰ βάθος ὕδωρ καταυγάζεσθαι διὰ τὴν ὁμοίαν αἰτίαν. καὶ ταῦτα μὲν ὁ Ὑδάσπης οὐ σφόδρα ὡς ξένα ἐθαύμαζε· συμβαίνειν γὰρ τὰ ἴσα καὶ κατὰ Μερόην τὴν Αἰθιόπων...

[17] ...alii uero uolunt puteum significari qui est in Syene, parte Aegypti, quem ad hoc nimiae altitudinis philosophi effoderunt ut probarent locum illum esse solum quem recto intuitu sol inradiaret: nam VIII K. Iul. die quando in centro suo est sol ... The expression *in centro suo* here (cf. Martianus Capella quoted above in n.10) seems to mean "at zero degrees."

[18] *certam* MSS, but surely *primam* is meant.

day since the sun is found in the zenith over the city now shadow can be cast there by any body and even the stilus (called the gnomon) of a hemisphere showing the hours cannot of itself make a shadow. And this is what the poet Lucan meant to say but did not actually bring off quite right. For in saying "...and never-shadow-bending Syene" (BC 2.587) he touched the matter, but muddled the truth. For Syene does not fail to bend shadows *ever*, but only at the one time which we have reported along with its cause.[19]

II. Eratosthenes' Measurement of the Circumference of the World

The result of the reasoning in the work of Eratosthenes called *The Measurement of the World*[20] was endorsed by Hipparchus and is well fixed in the later ancient geographical tradition: the circumference is 252,000 stades. But we owe our only comparatively coherent account of Eratosthenes' reasoning to Cleomedes in his elementary textbook known as *De circulari motu corporum caelestium* written about six centuries later (passage 1). He (and Philoponus quoting Arrian) attest 250,000 stades, which was evidently the penultimate step[21] in the argument., an argument which has been severely pruned in other respects. For the rest, there is an even more obviously truncated version or rather allusion in Martianus Capella's *De nuptiis Mercurii et Philologiae* dating from the early fifth c. A.D. (passage 2). This is usually discredited as garbled, but it is I believe not without independent value. Neither Cleomedes nor Martianus say anything about a well at Syene, but there was a popular belief first attested in Strabo (passage 3) and in Pliny

---

[19] ciuitas autem Syene, quae prouinciae Thebaidos post superiora montium deserta principium est, sub aestiuo tropico constituta est, et eo die quo Sol certam partem ingreditur Cancri hora diei sexta, quoniam Sol tunc super ipsum inuenitur uerticem ciuitatis, nulla illic potest in terram de quolibet corpore umbra iactari, sed nec stilus hemisphaerii monstrantis horas quem gnomona uocant tunc de se potest umbram creare. et hoc est quod Lucanus dicere uoluit nec tamen plene ut habetur absoluit. dicendo enim "atque umbras numquam flectente Syene" rem quidem attigit, sed turbauit uerum. non enim numquam flectit, sed uno tempore quod cum sua causa rettulimus. The majority of the MSS of Lucan as well as Priscian *GL* 2.511 have *numquam*, but V is right against these with *nusquam*, see Housman *ad loc.*

[20] περὶ τῆς ἀναμετρήσεως τῆς γῆς Hero *Dioptra* 35; cf. Macrobius *Somn. Scip.* 1.20.9 quoting Eratosthenes *in libris dimensionum*.

[21] 252,000 stades: Strabo 2.5.7 and 2.5.34, Galen *Inst. log.* 12.2, Theon *Expos.* 124.10–12 and the Latin tradition, Vitruvius 1.6.9, Pliny *Nat.* 2.112, 2.247, Martianus Capella 6.596. Philoponus *in Ar. Mete.* 1.3.2 p. 15 ed. Hayduk quotes 250,000 stades from Arrian's lost περὶ μετεώρων.

(passage 4, whence no doubt Servius in passage 8) that part of Eratosthenes' argument depended on the observation that this well was wholly illuminated at midsummer noon, proving that the sun was in the zenith, and therefore that Syene was a place exactly on the tropic latitude. In Aelius Aristides, the well is said to be holy (passage 6), and Heliodorus (passage 7) implicitly contradicts the idea that gnomon-shadowlessness and glistening wells are unique to Syene; for between the tropic and the equator, gnomon-shadowlessness, and therefore the total illumination of any well, occurs everywhere twice a year so many days before and after the summer solstice; Strabo (passage 5) and Pliny (passage 4) show that Eratosthenes knew about this.

If that well featured at all in Eratosthenes' account, its role in the argument was peripheral. On the other hand, I shall suggest that the information in 4 and 5 is both pregnant and neglected, and that Martianus in 2 was right to refer to Meroe and the distance from Meroe to Syene as having an integral part in Eratosthenes' basic argument. Pliny in 4 is vague and somewhat garbled, but Strabo in passage 5, though he quotes no figures, clearly shows that Eratosthenes agreed closely with the gnomon readings of the early Hellenistic explorer Philo for Meroe at the confluence of the Nile and its last tributary the Astaboras. Quite a lot seems to follow from that.

III. Cleomedes' Account

It has often been pointed out in modern times that the specific purpose of the final adjustment to 252,000 stades was to enable the equation

$$\text{one degree of latitude} = 700 \text{ stades}$$

and since Eratosthenes himself made a geometrical division into sixtieths the basis of his mathematical geography[22] it would indeed have

---

[22] Strabo *Geog.* 2.5.7, cf. O. Neugebauer, *History of Ancient Mathematical Astronomy*, Stud. in the Hist. of Math. and Phys. Sc. (New York & Berlin: Springer 1975), vol. 2, 590. This was important as representing the union of Greek geometry of the circle and the regular enclosed figures with Babylonian sexagesimal arithmetic. Dividing a circle into sixty parts depends upon combining the geometrical constructions for the inscribed triangle and pentagon, that is, the regular figures which start with the fifteen-agon; evaluating the chords of involves the irrationals $\sqrt{3}$ and $\sqrt{5}$ in product sum and difference. 252,000 allows one to assign simple numerical values to the chords

been natural to make the angular units of any circle commensurable with a standard number for the length of the circumference to facilitate among other things the arithmetical evaluation of chords in the circle. The particular equation is only one illustration of the obliging nature of the non-prime number $252 = 2^2 \times 3^2 \times 7$; in his *Laws* Plato had made 5040 the ideal number for the households of Magnesia because it divides by any of the nine digits, making life easier for the civil servants in the ideal city.[23]

Cleomedes' omission of the adjustment already shows that his summary is drastic, and it would be hazardous to assume that any of it is still in Eratosthenes' own words. It is even doubtful whether Eratosthenes' book was still even extant in its original form when Cleomedes was writing in the mid to late fourth century.[24] The immediate source is unknown. The simplest but uncertain assumption is that he was using a summary made by Posidonius in the first c. B.C. which went with Posidonius' own alternative argument about the size of the world, also quoted by Cleomedes, from the different altitudes of the star Canobus as observed from Rhodes and from Alexandria.

The beautifully simple and most spectacular part of Eratosthenes' argument is, however, certainly well preserved — the application of elementary Euclidean geometry in contexts at once tiny and immense. That needs no further comment than a diagram (see Fig. 1); essentially, the zenith distance at midsummer noon at Alexandria measures the difference in latitude between Alexandria and the tropic of Cancer; if that distance is known, then so is the circumference of the world. But there are some neglected peculiarities and difficulties in the premises and in the way that Cleomedes comments and reports.

---

of more regular inscribed figures than 360,000, and in certain respects more arithmetical facility in reducing complex ratios to relatively simple approximations.

[23] Plato *Leg.* 737e–744d. We see here the Platonist as well as the arithmetician in Eratosthenes.

[24] See Neugebauer (above, n.22) 960f., on internal astronomical evidence. This dating is significantly later than many older studies suppose. But the only ground for a date in the earlier centuries A.D. was that Cleomedes has a "thing" about Epicurus, which however does not prove that Cleomedes must have written at a time when Epicureanism was still actually flourishing. Neugebauer further argues that Cleomedes belonged to northern Asia Minor rather than to the Alexandria of Theon and Hypatia.

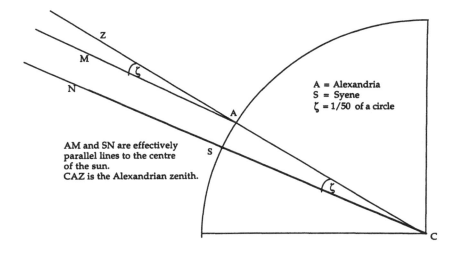

Figure 1

First, Cleomedes begins by extracting five "helpful" postulates. But the third of these is unsatisfactory.[25] He makes it sound as though shadow-tips may be cast by rays from any part of the sun's disc. Here I think Cleomedes was oversimplifying, whether out of confusion or deliberately, to make things "easier" than in Eratosthenes himself.

For lines from the centre of the sun to the disc of the earth are virtually parallel even when measured on some fine scale because the source is a point, the earth is very small, and the distance great. So lines from the centre of the sun to any two places on earth are virtually parallel: what is theoretically a cone with its base in the earth and vertex in the sun is in effect a straight line.

But lines from the rim of the sun's disc to a particular place on earth may only be deemed parallel if the angular scale by which their incidence on earth is observed is itself so coarse that it is as great or greater than the angular measure of the sun's disc, which is about a half of a degree. In that case we shall effectively be treating the sun as a point source like the star Canobus in Posidonius' account. In other words

---

[25] καὶ τρίτον τὰς καταπεμπομένας ἀκτῖνας ἀπὸ διαφόρων μερῶν τοῦ ἡλίου ἐπὶ διάφορα τῆς γῆς μέρη παραλλήλους εἶναι p. 96 Ziegler = p. 35 Todd, cf. in the account itself p. 98 = p. 36 αὐτὴ καὶ ἡ προειρημένα εὐθεῖα παράλληλοι γενήσονται, ἀπὸ διαφόρων γε τοῦ ἡλίου μερῶν ἐπὶ διάφορα μέρη τῆς γῆς διήκουσαι.

cones which have their base in the sun's rim and their vertices in or on earth are non-negligible and may not except for very coarse measurements be interpreted as straight lines.

The tip of any shadow is composite: the far end is cast not by rays from the centre of the sun's disc but from its southern rim, and the boundary between the penumbra and the darker umbra is made by rays from the upper rim of the sun's disc.

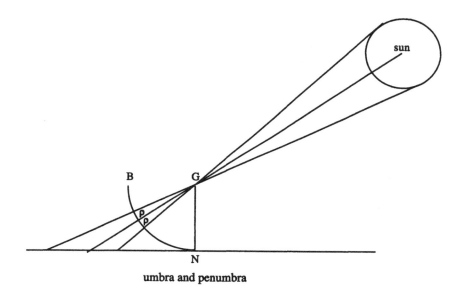

umbra and penumbra

Figure 2

Simply measuring the full penumbral length of a shadow cast in a bowl must therefore involve a systematic underestimation of the sun's altitude properly defined as the line from the top of the gnomon to the *centre* of the sun's disc. This point is fudged in Cleomedes' account.[26]

---

[26] In explaining his own (alleged) measurement of the obliquity in *Almagest* 1.12 pp. 61–3 Toomer, Ptolemy implicitly acknowledges the problem: instead of using the σκάφιον, he describes two devices in which the shadow is created by an object having magnitude, not by the tip of a gnomon. The first of these automatically aligns to the centre of the sun, while his other simpler and preferred device casts a shadow formed by the rim of the sun, and we are to read "the middle of the shadow" so formed against the scale. That is scarcely an improvement on the procedure suggested above for using the σκάφιον.

But in reading shadow-lengths in a simple *scaphium* of the kind which Cleomedes and Martianus Capella attest for Eratosthenes the penumbral region is at least constant and the true line to the centre of the sun is always given by the midpoint of the penumbra. So although it would be no easier to observe the penumbra distinctly than on a plane surface, it would be sound practice to read the full lengths of shadows, and to subtract a set correction factor in recording the result: a quarter of a degree would be optimal. There are many contexts in which such precision would be superfluous; but the smaller the angle one is trying to measure, the more critical the correction factor becomes in proportion, and it is certainly not negligible in reading the midsummer zenith distance at a place like Alexandria relatively close to the tropic; a quarter-unit in a magnitude of only seven or eight is considerable.

I assume Eratosthenes must have realised this from the further evidence of Cleomedes' own account.

For the other main peculiarity in Cleomedes concerns the assumption that Syene is exactly on the tropic and the "report" about shadowlessness there. It is of course just as important that the line from the tropic should be drawn to the *centre* of the sun's disc, because it is only thus that the two critical solar lines may legitimately be taken to be virtually parallel. And yet Cleomedes reports in passing that shadowlessness is a phenomenon observed over a belt of three hundred stades straddling the tropic latitude. The geometrical explanation of this is elementary: the cone of sunlight from the sun's rim drawn to the centre of the earth is intercepted by the earth's surface and the radius of the earth is here clearly non-negligible, cf. Fig. 3.

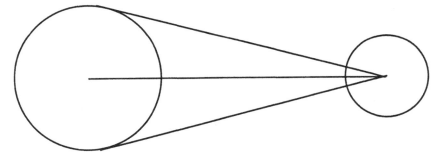

Figure 3

Cleomedes returns to this "datum" twice later on in other connections;[27] but it is introduced here in a way that ought to flummox the reader, for it seems either to be irrelevant or to detract seriously from the precision of the whole method. The absence of an explanatory gloss on this in Cleomedes' introduction is striking and suggests that he himself or his source was confused. The question is, what point did the acknowledgment that the sun's disc has a certain magnitude serve in Eratosthenes' original argument?

Evidently noontide shadowlessness on midsummer's day does not uniquely locate the tropic (as supposed for example by Servius and Macrobius, passages 8 and 9) except as a broad band which *a posteriori* on Eratosthenes' final figure should represent

$$300/252000 = 1/840 = 3/7 \text{ of a degree}$$

i.e. 30 miles or 48 kilometres on the ground and on the low side if pressed as a definition of the sun's angular diameter. But how then do we know that Syene really is in the middle of that band and not displaced more or less north or south? For Cleomedes, the identification of Syene as a place *on* the tropic is so self-evident as not to need elaboration.[28] But in Eratosthenes' account, some more positive evidence was surely required to justify it as a postulate. For otherwise there is a potential error of about ± quarter of a degree in the definition of the zenith of the tropic, and another of + quarter of a degree in the line from the gnomon at Alexandria, if it reads the uncorrected penumbral shadow. At one extreme these errors would by luck cancel out, but at the other extreme, they would add up.

IV. Eratosthenes' Argument

Setting the question of the size of the zenith distance aside for the moment, I suggest that Eratosthenes' original argument was as follows.

---

[27] 2.1.76 and 79, pp. 140 and 144 Ziegler = pp. 51 and 53 Todd; see I.G. Kidd, *Posidonius* II: I. *Testimonia and Fragments* 1–149 (Cambridge: Cambridge University Press 1988) 443–7 on F 115 = Cleomedes 2.1.79–80 on the argument from this to an absolute estimate of the size of the sun.

[28] *umbras nusquam flectente Syene*, Lucan *BC* 2.587 (not *numquam*, the v.l attested by Macrobius quoted above, passage 9; cf. n.19 *ad fin.*). It is clearly one of those things which every schoolboy knew.

Alexandria, Syene, Meroe   191

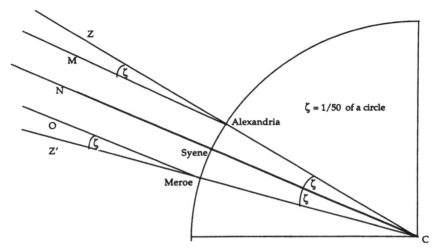

(a) The midsummer noontide shadow at Meroe matches the Alexandrian but points south. Therefore Meroe is as far from Syene as Syene is from Alexandria.
(b) Meroe is as far from Syene as Syene is from Alexandria. Therefore the midsummer noontide shadow at Meroe matches the one at Alexandria but points south.
(c) The midsummer noon-tide shadows at Alexandria and Meroe match and the distance is 10,000 stades. Therefore Syene is equidistant from both and lies on the tropic.

Figure 4

1. "It is reported by Philo[29] that the midsummer shadow at Meroe points south and whether measured as an arc in a scaphium or (more likely) on the ground as a tangent[30] his measurement matches the north-pointing Alexandrian shadow on that day. So this is the mirror-image of the phenomena at Alexandria (cf. Fig. 4) and it follows that the latitude of the tropic is half-way between the latitudes passing through Meroe and through Alexandria."

---

[29] ap. Strabo 2.1.20 quoted above passage 5; an elder contemporary of Eratosthenes, for Hipparchus evidently reckoned that Eratosthenes agreed with Philo about the Meroe-shadows, not the reverse, while he is mentioned as a "praefectus" apparently in the time of Ptolemy I by Pliny *Nat.* 37.108. Also mentioned as the author of τὰ Αἰθιοπικά by Antigonus of Carystus 160. Modern doxographers, e.g. Neugebauer (above, n.22) and Dilke in his *Greek and Roman Maps* (London: Duckworth 1985) regularly overlook him altogether, but he was as important in his way as was the better known Pytheas of Massilia in his.

[30] i.e., as the ratio of shadow-length to gnomon height, which would have been pretty accurately defined as 1 : 8 at both places.

2. "It is reported by someone else that midsummer shadows cease to point northwards some 150 stades north of Syene and that over a belt of three hundred stades which includes Syene there is more or less fleeting noontide shadowlessness on midsummer day; further south, shadows are again observed, pointing south, and symmetrical with shadows at corresponding latitudes further north. This means that light is arriving from the sun's disc perpendicular to tangents to the earth's surface and aimed at the centre of the world over a belt of latitude equal to the angular diameter of the sun's disc.

It is further said that there is a well at Syene which is for a moment uniformly illuminated at noon precisely on midsummer's day. If that is strictly true, then Syene is indeed on the tropic latitude; but all wells within the band just defined must also be the fleeting recipients of vertical beams of light and be totally but not uniformly illuminated, so this is not diagnostic." [31]

3. "It follows that the meridian distances between the latitudes of Meroe and Syene and between the latitudes of Syene and Alexandria are practically the same, whether or not they are all three places are on the same meridian."

4. "The royal surveyors report that the distance SM from Syene to Meroe is 5,000 stades; the orientation of this distance is almost north-south and may be safely taken as the distance on any meridian between the latitudes through Meroe and Syene, and therefore, from (3), as the distance on any meridian between the latitudes through Syene and through Alexandria, making 10,000 stades in all. *If* the Royal Surveyors quote a figure of 5,000 stades for the distance Alexandria-Syene as well as for Syene to Meroe, then the three places are on the same meridian; but the journey to Syene takes one SSE from Alexandria, and true distance must be greater than 5,000 stades."

---

[31] On this, see further below, pp. 194–6. In theory, a crude way of testing this would have been to install a couple of rods at right angles east-west and north-south in the well near or at water-level to quarter its disc, and to cover the well-head with corresponding symmetrical cross pieces to serve together as "sights" for the central line of the well. If there is any residual zenith distance at midsummer noon, the shadow cast on the water by the upper east-west bar should remain distinct from the lower bar when the shadow of the north-south bar coincides with its counterpart. But I imagine that the heroic researcher scrutinizing any wells in the region at midsummer would have been dazzled if not permanently blinded.

Alexandria, Syene, Meroe 193

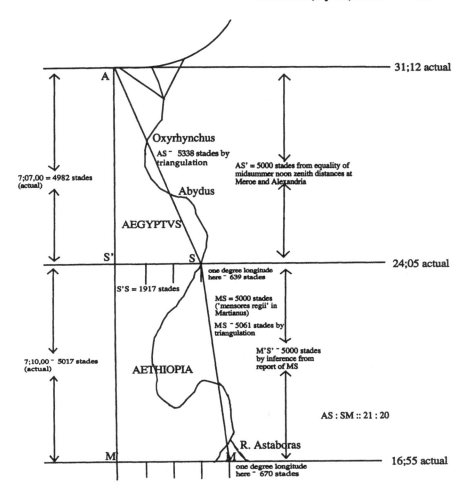

Figure 5

This seems to be the most economical way of filling in the background to Eratosthenes' account and of explaining the cruder features in Cleomedes. Primacy goes to a simple argument from symmetry which seems to follow directly from Hipparchus' remarks about the close agreement of Philo and Eratosthenes as to the midsummer zenith at Meroe; the crucial point is that the angles are taken to be the *same*, however measured. Cleomedes says nothing about this, presumably because he does not wish to discuss the phenomenon of south-pointing shadows beneath the tropic. Essentially the same argument from symmetry applied much more locally is then used to identify the location of Syene on the tropic, and we give direct credence here to what Martianus Capella says in passage 2 about the measurement in stades of the distance from Meroe to Syene. The map of Egypt shows that the most direct route from Syene to Meroe, though not for the tourist, is also the only practical alternative to the lengthy detour following the line of the Nile. It is the route taken by 18th and 19th century explorers. It remains to consider the angle of the Alexandrian midsummer zenith distance on which Eratosthenes settled; but first it is convenient to digress and consider the matter of the well at Syene a little further.

V. The Well at Syene

As pointed out above, total *and uniform* illumination of a well at midsummer noon would diagnose its being precisely on the tropic latitude, and the theoretical instance makes a pretty set of three mathematical solar arguments directing us to Syene from opposite sides of the tropic. But it is obviously only theoretical. Similar and only imperceptibly different phenomena would be observed in wells anywhere in the belt of noontide shadowlessness, and indeed beyond, as is proved by the figures for Syene, which in Eratosthenes' time was nearly 250 stades north of the then true tropic latitude[32] and thus did not even lie within the belt which Eratosthenes defines.

Any well-head is as a point to the sun, but in the human scale has size; if any rays from the sun can enter a well vertically, it must already be strongly illuminated to a potentially very great depth by rays which are not quite vertical. This applies when the zenith distance of the sun south or north of the well is equal to or less than its own angular radius (cf. Fig. 6).

It is clear that even in June the water-table at Syene can never have been very far from the surface, so that the wells at Syene and Elephantine seen and described by Strabo cannot have been very deep affairs. At a depth of 25 feet the ray *af* would be half an inch from the wall *ab*, at a depth of 50 feet, one inch, and so on. The consequent imperfection in the circularity of illumination would be quite imperceptible.

---

[32] About 23;43,30, see below, n.34, whereas Syene is on lat. 24;05, more than a third of a degree to the north.

Alexandria, Syene, Meroe 195

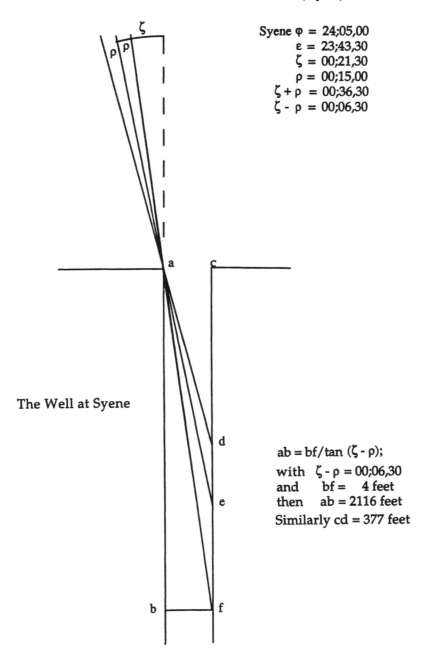

Syene φ = 24;05,00
ε = 23;43,30
ζ = 00;21,30
ρ = 00;15,00
ζ + ρ = 00;36,30
ζ − ρ = 00;06,30

The Well at Syene

ab = bf/tan (ζ − ρ);
with   ζ − ρ = 00;06,30
and   bf =   4 feet
then   ab = 2116 feet
Similarly cd = 377 feet

Figure 6

It is of course nonsense to imagine with Pliny (passage 4) that the well at Syene was dug *experimenti causa*. It was a holy well (Aristides, 6), and no doubt its special fame (as opposed to that of the well at Elephantine) was not scientific but religious.

VII. Halving the Quarters of the Year

We return to the question of the zenith distance of the sun at midsummer. In Heliodorus' novel (passage 7), Hydaspes was quite right not to be particularly impressed. For everywhere between the tropic latitudes there are two days in the year when the sun stands in the local zenith at noon. At the equator, this happens at noon on both the equinoxes; from late March to September shadows point south, from late September to March, they point north. As one goes north from the equator the period during which shadows point south in the summer months decreases so that the days of shadowlessness converge symmetrically around midsummer as the latitude increases, and the tropic of Cancer is the limiting case — shadows never point south, and there is only one day when shadowlessness occurs. The rate of change is proportional to the sines of the obliquity of the ecliptic ε and of the latitude φ; as a function of sines, the rate of decrease is sinusoid, slow at first and then increasingly rapid. Using trigonometry it is easy to determine the latitude at which shadowlessness occurs so many days before and after midsummer or *vice versa*.[33]

In Fig. 7 the arc BN is the celestial meridian at summer solstice and D is the northern limit of the sun's annual motion. H is the plane projection of a point K on the more southerly celestial latitude AP. It stands away from A at an angle λ and the angle $(90-\lambda)$ is the number of days until the sun will be in the zenith at A on the latitude AP. This is also the number of days that the sun was in the zenith at the same latitude before midsummer. Since

$$\sin \lambda = KP/HP = KP/PA = LQ/AQ = LM/AC$$
$$= LM/MK = MK/MJ = AC/DG = \sin \varphi / \sin \varepsilon$$

the number of days is given by $\cos \lambda$ but that is the same as $\sin \lambda$ when $\lambda = 45$ degrees and $HK = KP = 1/\sqrt{2}$ which is the case for Meroe.

---

[33] We may ignore here the inequality of the seasons and the true length of the year in equating one "day" with one degree in the rotation of the celestial sphere, so that 45 days = 45 degrees of rotation.

Alexandria, Syene, Meroe   197

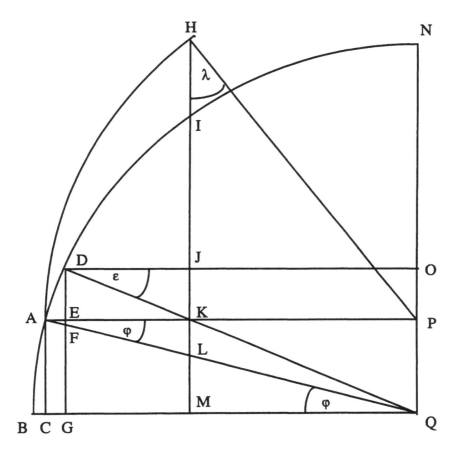

Figure 7

It is not impossible that Eratosthenes understood the geometrical part of this argument, but he could scarcely apply it without a table of chords like Ptolemy's, and it is in any case unnecessary to suppose that he did understand the geometry, for there is a simpler route to a less general conclusion. Since the rays from the centre of the sun's disc which define the local zenith distance may be taken as parallel, it follows that when there is shadowlessness at Meroe, then the zenith distance at noon at Syene must now be ζ, and at Alexandria it must be 2ζ, since the sun's "angle of attack" is evidently less than it was at midsummer by ζ, as is shown in Figure 8.

198 The Passionate Intellect

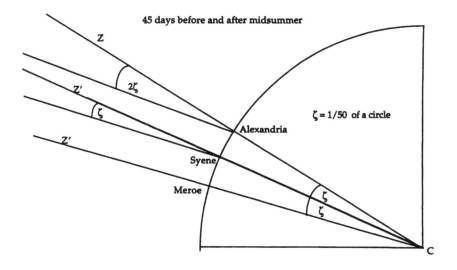

Figure 8

The zenith distances at any latitude φ are by definition

spring equinox	φ
summer solstice	φ - ε
autumn equinox	φ
winter solstice	φ + ε

where ε is the obliquity of the ecliptic. Further at midsummer noon

$$\varphi = \varepsilon + \zeta$$

where ζ is the shortest zenith distance ever observed at the particular latitude. Hence we have zenith distances in terms of ε and ζ

spring equinox	ε + ζ
summer solstice	ζ
autumn equinox	ε + ζ
winter solstice	2ε + ζ

Now it follows directly from Philo's information about shadowlessness at Meroe occurring at the midpoints between the equinoxes and midsummer (passage 5), from Eratosthenes' close agreement with Philo (passages 4 and 5), and from the argument which we have attributed above to Eratosthenes that the noontide midsummer shadows at Alexandria and Meroe are equal and opposite, that we have the following array of magnitudes for zenith distances on the latitudes of Alexandria Syene and Meroe for the summer months:

| | noontide zenith distances at | | | |
	Alexandria	Syene	Meroe	any lat. φ
Spring equinox	$\varepsilon + \zeta$	ε	$\varepsilon - \zeta$	φ
45th day	2ζ	ζ	0	
Midsummer	ζ	0	$-\zeta$	$\varphi - \varepsilon$
45th day	2ζ	ζ	0	
Autumn equinox	$\varepsilon + \zeta$	ε	$\varepsilon - \zeta$	φ

and the continuation is completed by symmetry and inversion as follows:

45th day	2ε	$2\varepsilon - \zeta$	$2\varepsilon - 2\zeta$	
Midwinter	$2\varepsilon + \zeta$	2ε	$2\varepsilon - \zeta$	$\varphi + \varepsilon$
45th day	2ε	$2\varepsilon - \zeta$	$2\varepsilon - 2\zeta$	
Spring equinox	$\varepsilon + \zeta$	ε	$\varepsilon - \zeta$	φ

The seasonal rise and fall in the noontide zenith distances at each of the three equidistant latitudes are constant and equal to ζ which we now define specifically as the zenith distance at midsummer noon at Alexandria. Part of the cycle is illustrated in Figure 9, in which, with Eratosthenes, we are making

$$\zeta = 1/50 \text{ of a circle} = 7.2 \text{ degrees} = 7;12,00$$

and from which one may see how by inversion and symmetry the cycle of a whole year would appear.

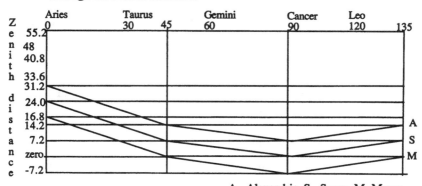

Figure 9

Reverting to the tabulation, one notes among other things that, symmetrically corresponding to the three occasions and two places where shadowlessness occurs in summer, there are likewise three occasions and two places in winter when and where the zenith distance is equal to twice the obliquity of the ecliptic. Hence the most obviously direct way of measuring ζ at midsummer noon at Alexandria is by no means the only way of reading that angle or of estimating ε — though it is very doubtful whether Eratosthenes or anyone else ever bothered to check much of this systematically, given that the whole table follows logically from the combination of Philo's information about shadowlessness at Meroe with the report of shadowlessness at midsummer at Syene.

Given that $0 < \zeta < \varepsilon$ the question arises what proportion of ε should be subtracted and added to φ to fill in the empty cells in the column at the right of the tabulation above so as best to match the sinuosity of the curve which describes the annual cycle of decrease and increase in the zenith distances observed at a particular latitude halfway between the "cardinal points" of equinox and solstice; the simplest answer is

$$\varphi \pm 7\varepsilon/10$$

and with

$$\varepsilon = 1/15 = 10/150 \text{ of a circle}$$

that becomes

$$\varphi \pm 7/150 \text{ of a circle}.$$

That in turn favours our defining

$$\zeta = 1/50 = 3/150 \text{ of a circle}$$

for purely arithmetical reasons, for thus we have the pattern in 150ths:

	noontide zenith distances at			
	Alexandria	Syene	Meroe	$\varphi_{A, S, M}$
Spring equinox	13	10	7	φ
45th day	6	3	0	$\varphi - 7\varepsilon/10$
Midsummer	3	0	- 3	$\varphi - \varepsilon$
45th day	6	3	0	$\varphi - 7\varepsilon/10$
Autumn equinox	13	10	7	φ
45th day	20	17	14	$\varphi + 7\varepsilon/10$
Midwinter	23	20	17	$\varphi + \varepsilon$
45th day	20	17	14	$\varphi + 7\varepsilon/10$
Spring equinox	13	10	7	φ

This involves the simple arithmetical ratios

$$\varphi : \varepsilon : \zeta :: 13 : 10 : 3$$

and has the advantage of giving a good value for the latitude of Alexandria. But in Eratosthenes' day the true value of ε was about 23;43,30,[34] and the true latitude of Alexandria is 31;12,00, making ζ = 7;29,30, which, measured as a proportion of a circle, is very close to 1/48, and that is what Eratosthenes' ought to have found, if he really depended exclusively on a midsummer noon reading for ζ at Alexandria without prior assumptions as to the value of ε or without any awareness of the the pattern apparent in the table. But if we do make

---

[34] For the formula used to calculate the slow shift in the value of the obliquity, see S. Newcomb, *A Compendium of Spherical Astronomy* (New York: Macmillan 1906) 237.

$$\zeta = 1/48$$

then the ratios become a little less simple — the common denominator goes up to 240 — and one places the latitudes of Alexandria and Meroe a little too far apart:

$$1/15 + 1/48 = 7/80 = 31;30$$
$$1/15 - 1/48 = 11/240 = 16;30$$

whereas

$$1/15 + 1/50 = 13/150 = 31;12$$
$$1/15 - 1/50 = 7/150 = 16;48$$

is exact and leads to a table in which the numbers are smaller and therefore simpler. Certainly some such purely arithmetical juggling was involved in Eratosthenes' choice of $\zeta = 1/50$ to go with $\varepsilon = 1/15$, for there is no way that the fraction 1/50 can directly represent a reading from a scale; one cannot construct divisions in fiftieths by strict geometrical methods, any more than one can construct a scale in say 83ds. But that is another story.[35]

---

[35] A version of this paper was given as one of the Research Seminars of the School of Greek, Latin and Ancient History, University of St. Andrews, on Oct. 14, 1994. My thanks are due to my colleagues for their comments, in particular to Mr. P.G. Woodward.

13

Seneca's *Natural Questions* — Changing Readerships

Harry M. Hine

I. Antiquity

In this paper I shall attempt a brief outline of the different sorts of readership that Seneca's *Natural Questions* has attracted from antiquity to the early modern period. After Aristotle's *Meteorologica*, this work of Seneca's is the most extensive ancient treatise on meteorology that has survived from antiquity (though one should not forget the substantial commentaries on Aristotle's work by Alexander, Olympiodorus and Philoponus). The word meteorology today has a more restricted sense than it had in antiquity, when it covered not only what we mean by it but also other phenomena that were then believed to occur in the atmosphere — including meteors and comets — or to be caused ultimately by the activity of air — including rivers, seas, and earthquakes. Seneca's treatise proceeds by critical discussion of the theories of his predecessors, and so is a valuable, though sometimes fallible, source of information about his many Greek and few Roman predecessors, most of whose works are now lost. Source-criticism has in recent times been one of the most important areas of investigation of the *Natural Questions*, and here we have no more judicious and reliable guide than Ian

Kidd in his work on Posidonius, who is regularly cited by Seneca. But source-criticism is not my theme in this essay. Nor am I directly concerned with the other great area of scholarly debate about the work, which is the relationship between the scientific[1] sections of the work on the one hand, and on the other, the prefaces and conclusions to individual books, and the digressions, which are often devoted to ethical or theological themes. However, as we shall see, the coexistence of scientific, ethical and theological material in the work has been an important factor in its survival and in its ability to attract different readerships.

Seneca wrote the *Natural Questions* during the last few years of his life, in the early 60s AD (he was writing Book 6 late in AD 62), at the same period as he wrote the *Moral Letters* and worked on a treatise on moral philosophy. It is a tempting speculation that these works were intended as a sort of philosophical last bequest, for in AD 62 Seneca withdrew from Nero's court, and may well have calculated that his years might be numbered, not just because of his age but because of the political dangers he might be in — and indeed he did die because he was implicated, perhaps falsely, in the Pisonian conspiracy of AD 65. The treatise on moral philosophy does not survive, and may never have been finished, but a substantial proportion of the *Letters* survives, and so does the *Natural Questions*, though in a damaged and perhaps incomplete state.[2]

It is reasonable to suppose that the *Natural Questions* owed its survival from antiquity mainly to the author's reputation as a moral philosopher and as the nearest thing the pagan world could produce to a Christian;[3] just as the tragedies most likely survived, when those of other Roman writers perished, because they were Seneca's. In the case of the *Natural Questions* the supposition is supported by examination of the known readers of the work in antiquity, who are singularly few: all

---

[1] In view of the slipperiness of the word, I should perhaps say that in this paper I use the word "scientific" to describe the subject-matter of Seneca's work — which falls within the sphere of several of our modern-day natural sciences — and not to imply anything about Seneca's methodology.

[2] On the chronology, and the final years of Seneca's life, see M.T. Griffin, *Seneca: a Philosopher in Politics* (Oxford: Clarendon Press 1976) chs. 2 and 11, appendix A1; on the incompleteness, H.M. Hine, *An Edition with Commentary on Seneca*, Natural Questions, *Book Two* (New York: Arno Press 1981) 32–4.

[3] Cf. Tertullian, *De Anima* 20.1 ... *Seneca saepe noster* ...; G.M. Ross, "Seneca's Philosophical Influence," C.D.N. Costa (ed.), *Seneca*, Greek and Latin Studies (London & Boston: Routledge 1974) 116–65.

one can be sure of is that Lucan had read his uncle's treatise almost as soon as it was written, and drew on it in detail when writing about the Nile in Book 10 of the *Civil War*;[4] then one must jump to the fourth century, when Ammianus Marcellinus — or his source — shows knowledge of the work; and then to the sixth century, when John the Lydian — or *his* source — produced a summary in Greek of what Seneca had to say about the Nile.[5] None of these three authors is writing a scientific treatise: each is including scientific material in a quite different sort of work, Lucan in his historical epic, Ammianus in his history, John the Lydian in his treatise *De Mensibus*. By contrast there is no sure evidence that the elder Pliny used this particular work of Seneca in his *Natural History*, and it is unknown to the series of late antique and early mediaeval writers of handbooks and encyclopaedic works covering scientific topics, from Calcidius and Macrobius in the fourth century, via Martianus Capella and Boethius, to Isidore of Seville in the seventh and Bede in the eighth centuries.[6] The elder Pliny's *Natural History* was copied throughout these centuries, and was familiar at least to Bede,[7] but of Seneca's work there is no trace.

II. The Middle Ages

Since the *Natural Questions* was not in the main stream of Latin scientific writing in late antiquity, it is reasonable to suppose its preserva-

---

[4] H. Diels, "Seneca und Lukan," *Abhandlungen der Preussischer Akademie der Wissenschaften* 1885, Phil.-hist. Abh. 3 (Berlin 1886); reprinted in W. Burkert (ed.), *Kleine Schriften zur Geschichte der antiken Philosophie* (Hildesheim 1969) 379–408.

[5] A. Gercke, *Seneca-Studien*, Jahrb. f. class. Philol., Suppl. 22 (Leipzig 1896) 94–103. Whether the unknown author of the poem *Aetna* had read Seneca's work, indeed whether he wrote before or after Seneca, is open to question: the resemblances are no closer than one might find in any two Latin writers applying themselves to similar topics; nor, to my mind, is Seneca's silence about the work a decisive argument against its priority. But for a less sceptical view see F.R.D. Goodyear, "The Aetna: Thought, Antecedents, and Style," H. Temporini (ed.), *ANRW* II.32.1 (Berlin, New York 1984) 344–63.

[6] See W.H. Stahl, *Roman Science: Origins, Development, and Influence to the Later Middle Ages* (Madison WI: University of Wisconsin Press 1962) for a survey of these and other writers.

[7] L.D. Reynolds, *Texts and Transmission: A Survey of the Latin Classics* (Oxford: Clarendon Press 1983) 307–16; M. Chibnall, "Pliny's *Natural History* and the Middle Ages," T.A. Dorey (ed.), *Empire and Aftermath: Silver Latin II*, Greek and Latin Studies (London & Boston: Routledge 1975) 57–78.

tion depended on its author's reputation. It survived independently of the other works of Seneca, and lagged precariously behind his other philosophica: our earliest complete manuscripts are from the twelfth century; prior to that there are only the briefest of extracts from the ninth century from the circle of Alcuin,[8] the mention of a manuscript at Reichenau in the ninth century,[9] and speculations about other signs of influence. In the middle ages we can detect two quite different sorts of reader, when we look at the numerous different sets of excerpts that survive, and at the use made of the work by mediaeval writers. The ninth century excerpts just referred to consist of just three brief passages from the preface to Book 1, all of them on the nature of god — and these or similar excerpts may have suggested to Anselm the phrasing of a central idea in his *Proslogion*.[10] The twelfth-century Florilegium Duacense contains a more varied range of extracts — most of them very short, and in total barely three printed pages — including parts of the same passage about god, but also passages on ethical topics, such as the goal of human life, death, freedom, and flattery. Significantly, the extracts all come from the prefaces or conclusions of individual books of the *Natural Questions*.[11] The Florilegium Gallicum, another, and rather more extensive, twelfth-century set of excerpts, also confines its interests to ethical and theological extracts, though the excerptor has not merely read the prefaces and conclusions, but has read the scientific sections with sufficient attention to extract one or two isolated sentences embedded in a scientific context.[12] But the creators of such sets of ex-

---

[8] H.M. Hine, "The Manuscript Tradition of Seneca's *Natural Questions*: Addenda," *CQ* 42 (1992) 558–62.

[9] On this and other aspects of the mediaeval manuscript tradition see Hine in Reynolds (above, n.7) 376–8.

[10] Hine (above, n.8) 559 gives a text of the excerpts. Compare *Proslogion* 2 *aliquid quo nihil maius cogitari possit* with *Nat.* 1.pr.14 ... *magnitudo* ... *qua nihil maius cogitari potest*, a sentence included in the excerpts.

[11] There is a text of the excerpts in H.M. Hine, "The Manuscript Tradition of Seneca's *Natural Questions*: Some Manuscripts Related to Z," *Prometheus* 5 (1979) 63–72.

[12] Thus the extracts include 4b.3.6 *Inter nullos magis quam inter philosophos esse debet aequa libertas* and 4b.5.1 *Si omnia argumenta ... uincunt litigant*; though it is significant that these two come from Book 4b, which in the excerptor's copy was the first book (for the excerpts come from a manuscript with the book order 4b–7, 1–4a; on the book order of the manuscripts, see e.g. Hine (above, n.2) 2–23; for a different view of the original order, see most recently N. Gross, *Senecas Naturales Quaestiones: Komposition, naturalphilosophische Aussagen und ihre Quellen*, Palingenesia 27 (Stuttgart: Franz Steiner 1989) 306–20). The complete excerpts are as follows (as

cerpts show no interest in the scientific content of the work at all. Other later excerptors, though, were different. In the margin of Leiden, Bibliotheek der Rijksuniversiteit, Voss. Lat. F.69 (12th cent), somebody has marked the beginning and end of an extensive series of passages that turn up, copied from L (perhaps via an intermediate manuscript), in a 15th century manuscript, Paris, Bibliothèque Nationale lat. 16591, and this excerptor was certainly interested in the scientific content.[13]

But from early in the twelfth century, and maybe earlier, there is clear evidence of interest in the scientific content of the work in the way that mediaeval writers draw on the *Natural Questions*. It has been suggested that the author of the first Old English riddle in the Exeter Book was acquainted with Stoic cosmology through reading the *Natural Questions*; if correct, this suggestion implies the work was available in England perhaps as early as the eighth century, though there is no other evidence of this.[14] The treatise *De mundi coelestis terrestrisque constitutione*, falsely attributed to Bede, is more clearly influenced by Seneca. Its date is uncertain: the extant manuscripts are twelfth century, and maybe that is when it was written, but it survives in two versions, and an earlier date, somewhere between the ninth and twelfth century, cannot be ruled out for the original treatise.[15] Be that as it may, the great burst of copying of the *Natural Questions* that began in the early twelfth century coincided with a renewed interest in scientific matters. At first

---

contained in Paris, Bibliothèque Nationale, lat. 17903, 13th cent.; I ignore minor omissions and rephrasing): 6.32.1–12; 1.17.1–10; 4b.3.6 *Inter nullos magis quam inter philosophos esse debet aequa libertas*; 4b.5.1 *Si omnia argumenta ... uincunt litigant*; 4b.13.9 *Facile est extinguere sitim sanam*; 4b.13.11 *Quis non intelligit omnia consuetudine uim suam perdere*; 5.18.5–16; 6.1.4–3.4; 7.1.1–5; 7.30.5–32.4; 7.9.3 *Nulla tempestas magna perdurat ... minus temporis*; 7.30.1; 1.pr.3–17; 2.59.2–13; 3.pr.2–18; 3.30.8 *Cito nequitia ... uitia discuntur*; 3.18.3 *Cotidie aliquid subtilius aliquid elegantius excogitat luxuriae furor usitata contemnens*; 3.27.2 *Iam non sunt homines ad popinam ... quoque gulosi sunt*; 3.27.2 *Nihil difficile est naturae ... momento fit cinis, diu silua*; 4a.pr.1–5 (with several omissions); 4a.pr.14–18.

[13] The excerpts begin with passages on snow and hail: 4b.3.3–4 *Quare autem ... cauantur aqua*; 3.6 *Quare non ... grandinem interesse*; 5.1 *Pauca enim ... uincunt litigant*.

[14] M. Lapidge, "Stoic Cosmology and the Source of the First Old English Riddle," *Anglia* 112 (1994) 1–25.

[15] One version is edited and translated by C. Burnett, *Pseudo-Bede:* De mundi celestis terrestrisque constitutione: *A Treatise on the Universe and the Soul*, Warburg Institute Surveys and Texts 10 (London: Warburg Institute 1985); on Senecan influence see Hine, "Seneca and Anaxagoras in Pseudo-Bede's De mundi celestis terrestrisque constitutione," *Viator* 19 (1988) 111–27.

Seneca was the sole source available for ancient learning on meteorology — for instance in the *Dragmaticon* of William of Conches, which draws extensively on Seneca's discussions of meteorological phenomena.[16] Soon Aristotle's *Meteorologica* was available in Latin, as were Arabic works, but Seneca was still important, for, besides on occasion engaging critically with Aristotle, he passed on the ideas of a number of later thinkers, and covered topics not covered by Aristotle. Thus in the thirteenth century Robert Grosseteste, Roger Bacon, Albert the Great and Vincent of Beauvais all drew on the work.[17]

Another indicator of changing patterns of readership is the company that the *Natural Questions* keeps in surviving manuscripts. The work was preserved independently of Seneca's other works, and twelfth-century manuscripts regularly contain the work on its own[18] or combined with totally unrelated works,[19] though already in the twelfth century we find the *Natural Questions* in manuscripts containing larger collections of Seneca's works.[20] But there is also a small group of manuscripts that combine Seneca's *Natural Questions* with the *Natural Questions* of Adelard of Bath.[21] This combination, of Seneca's account of the Greco-

---

[16] See C. Picard-Parra, "Une utilisation des *Quaestiones Naturales* de Sénèque au milieu du XIIe siècle," *Revue du moyen âge latin* 5 (1949) 115–26; K.-D. Nothdurft, *Studien zum Einfluss Senecas auf die Philosophie und Theologie des zwölften Jahrhunderts* (Leiden: Brill 1963) 162–75.

[17] Nothdurft (above, n.16) 178–81.

[18] On its own: Génève, Bibliothèque Publique et Universitaire, lat. 77 (Z); Leiden, Bibliotheek der Rijksuniversiteit, Voss. Lat. O.55 (A); Oxford, Merton College, 250 (F); Oxford, St John's College, 36 (J). I have ignored cases in which the original manuscript of the *Natural Questions* has subsequently been bound together with another manuscript.

[19] With unrelated works: Bamberg, Staatsbibliothek, Class. 1 (M.IV.16) (B); Heiligenkreuz, Bibliothek des Zisterzienserstifts, 213 (C); Paris, Bibliothèque Nationale, lat. 8624 (H); Vatican City, Biblioteca Apostolica Vaticana, Pal. lat. 1579 (V) (the *De remediis fortuitorum* is also included).

[20] Combined with other works of Seneca: Cambrai, Bibliothèque Municipale, 555 (K); Leiden, Bibliotheek der Rijksuniversiteit, Voss. Lat. F.69 (L); Montpellier, Bibliothèque de la Faculté de Médicine, 116 (G); Montpellier, Bibliothèque de la Faculté de Médicine, 445 (S); Trier, Bibliothek des Priesterseminars, 66 (R.IV.2) (k).

[21] The works were both contained in a lost manuscript bequeathed by Philippe d'Harcourt, bishop of Bayeux, 1142–64, to the library at Bec (see G. Becker, *Catalogi Bibliothecarum Antiqui* (Bonn 1885) 202; *Catalogue général des manuscrits des bibliothèques publiques de France: Départements*, Octavo series, Vol. 2 (Paris: Plon 1888) 398). Surviving manuscripts with the combination are Paris, Bibliothèque Nationale, lat. 6628 (P), and the closely related El Escorial, Real Biblioteca, O.III.2, which also contains *De Beneficiis* and *De Clementia* (13th cent.; R); also a descendant of R, Paris, Bibliothèque Nationale, lat. 6385 (14th cent.).

Roman tradition and Adelard's account of Arabic ideas, shows an interest in the scientific material for its own sake.

III. The Early Modern Period

"Collected works" of Seneca are increasingly frequent among the manuscripts of the fourteenth and fifteenth centuries, and the *Natural Questions* first got into print in the 1490 Venice edition of Seneca's works — as usual it lagged behind the other philosophical works, which had been in print since 1475. From the editio princeps onwards, the *Natural Questions* was most commonly printed together with the other prose works of Seneca, though there were also occasional editions of the *Natural Questions* alone.[22] We might surmise that it was now once more being read because of Seneca's reputation, and that may have been largely true, but it was still from time to time read for its scientific content. M. Fortunatus, in his Aldine edition (Venice 1522), equipped with extensive notes, was as interested in expounding the scientific subject matter as in the ethics. A century later Liebert Froidmont (or Froidment), known as Libertus Fromondus, also produced extensive interpretative and critical notes to the *Natural Questions* that were first printed in the 1632 Antwerp edition of Seneca, and reprinted in later editions. Fromondus also wrote a popular *Meteorologicorum Libri Sex* (1627, second edition, slightly revised, 1639, and further reprints down to 1670), in which he dealt with the whole of meteorology in the ancient sense, and frequently discussed the views of Seneca amongst others. He once introduces a quotation (from *Nat.* 5.9) with the words: *Vere et eleganter, id est, ut solet, Seneca* — and that despite regular disagreements with Seneca's views. He was professor of philosophy and theology at Louvain, author of anti-Copernican works, and in meteorology his is a conservative, Scholastic approach, frequently citing Seneca as one of the long line of authorities stretching from Aristotle and earlier down to his own day;[23] thus there are several chapter headings along the

---

[22] E.g. Leipzig ca. 1492–5 (per Arnoldum de Colonia); Venice 1522 (M. Fortunatus); Paris 1540 (L. Strebaeus).

[23] See C.B. Boyer, *The Rainbow: from Myth to Mathematics* (Princeton NJ: Princeton University Press 1987²) 197–9; Boyer shows how Fromondus, and others in the early modern period, neglected some of the best of late mediaeval meteorological writing. Theodoric of Freiberg, early in the fourteenth century, came closer than anybody else before Newton to explaining the formation of the rainbow, but his work was totally neglected for several centuries (110–25).

lines of *Causae tonitrui, Anaxagorae, Senecae, Paracelsi, Bodini, reiectae* (*Meteor.*, 1627 ed., p. 59). However, Fromondus was not unaware of the implications of recent observational work. He accepted Tycho Brahe's demonstration that the comet of 1577 was above the moon, which disproved the Aristotelian view that all comets were sublunary; but he argued that some comets are sublunary, and that celestial comets are maybe not coeval with the stars and planets, but formed from celestial exhalations just as sublunary comets are formed from terrestrial exhalations.

But within a few years of the first edition of Fromondus's *Meteorologica*, the whole field was beginning to be transformed by new experimental techniques, new observations, and new theories; and ancient meteorology was breaking up into distinct scientific disciplines. In the first half of the seventeenth century Galileo and others were devising rudimentary thermometers, and the first sealed glass thermometers were invented around the middle of the century. Torricelli invented the mercury barometer in 1643. Newton explained the formation of rainbows in his lectures on optics of 1669–71 (first published in the *Opticks* of 1704), and accounted for the motions of comets in the *Philosophiae Naturalis Principia Mathematica*, first published in 1687. Of course these were just the beginnings of long processes of discovery that are still continuing, but for our purposes Fromondus is a suitable stopping-point, as one of the last writers to regard meteorology in the classical sense as a single discipline, and one of the last who could turn to Seneca and other classical writers expecting to learn some meteorology from them.

I end with a quotation that neatly illustrates the change that took place in the seventeenth century. With Fromondus's regular use of Seneca, contrast the sole reference to Seneca in the earliest work of Robert Boyle, published in 1660: "But this (as we lately intimated) proceeds upon the supposition, that the air is every where of the same consistence that we found it near the surface of the earth; but that cannot with any safety be concluded, not only for the reason I find to have been taken notice of by the ancients, and thus expressed in *Seneca* [*Nat.* 4.10]: *Omnis aër* (says he) *quo propior est terris, hoc crassior; quemadmodum in aqua et in omni humore faex ima est, ita in aëre spississima quaeque desidunt*. But much more, because the springy texture of the aërial corpuscles makes them capable of a very great compression, which the weight of the incumbent part of the atmosphere is very sufficient to give those that be undermost and near the surface of the earth."[24] In that one passage the sense of the distance between Boyle and the ancients, the confidence in the progress that has been made, is very clear. Seneca from then on was not part of science, but part of the history of science. He himself would not have minded, in fact he might have been dismayed that it had taken so long,[25] for he foresaw that his own ideas would be superseded: *ueniet tempus quo posteri nostri tam aperta nos nescisse mirentur* (7.25.5, referring to the motion of comets), and: *multa uenientis aeui populus ignota nobis sciet, multa saeculis tunc futuris, cum memoria nostri exoleuerit, reseruantur* (7.30.5). Nor does this last sentence mean that he would have felt he had no right to be remembered in subsequent ages, for, as he says elsewhere, to explain why he devotes space to the views of his earliest predecessors: *plurimum ad inueniendum contulit qui sperauit posse reperiri. cum excusatione itaque ueteres audiendi sunt: nulla res consummata est dum incipit* (6.5.3).

---

[24] *New Experiments Physico-Mechanical Touching the Spring of Air, and its Effects*, The Works of the Honourable Robert Boyle (London 1744) i.57. In this work Boyle refers only three times, and briefly, to Aristotle; in his complete works there are another half dozen quotations from Seneca, mostly from his other philosophical works; see the index to the collected works.

[25] Cf. *Nat.* 7.31-2, where he deplores the lack of interest in philosophy among his contemporaries.

14

Crates of Mallos, Dionysius Thrax and the Tradition of Stoic Grammatical Theory

Richard Janko

It is a pleasure to write in honour of Professor Kidd, my first Head of Department when I taught at St Andrews for a brief but memorable year in 1978–9. He set a fine example to a young scholar, as a teacher, a conscientious administrator, a truly Apamean polymath, a considerate colleague and a warm friend, even though neither of us then had any reason to believe that this particular neophyte would or could acquire more than a passing interest in Hellenistic thought. I have appreciated his guidance and amity ever since, and welcome this opportunity to express to him openly my admiration and gratitude.

I. From the Stoics to Dionysius Thrax

Among ancient traditions of learning, that of Hellenistic grammatical theory has proved peculiarly hard to reconstruct. The main difficulty is of course the almost complete loss in their original form of the grammatical and literary-critical writings of the second century B.C., apart from the *Techne* of Dionysius Thrax. We will be unable definitively to settle the controversy over the authenticity of the *Techne* until someone does a careful edition of the fragments of Aristarchus, to see whether the grammatical terms used in sources like Aristonicus go back to the great Alexandrian critic. Even whether Aristophanes of Byzantium pursued systematic investigations into grammar remains disputed.[1] In any case, Alexandria may not be the appropriate place in which to seek such a grammatical theory at this date; for these scholars, grammatical principles were a means to another end — the *diorthosis* of the texts of Homer's poems and other classics. Important though their observations may have been, they did not, it appears, pursue a systematic investigation into grammar for its own sake. Neither did the Stoics regard grammar as an autonomous, autotelic science: they treated it as a part of dialectic, in connection with their theory of signs and signification. In their case too we are hampered by the loss of the original texts, which is worsened by the lack of a complete collection of Stoic grammatical fragments since that of Schmidt in 1839.[2] A third locus for linguistic theory was treatises on diction (*lexis*), going back as far as Aristotle, whose treatments of rhetoric and poetics include the most pertinent observations on grammar which he made. Again, the loss of such works as Theophrastus' Περὶ λέξεως is a grave impediment.

The converse of the problem of sources is also a serious nuisance: we must have many fragments of Hellenistic grammatical theory which are transmitted anonymously and with no date. Given the chronological obstacles to reconstructing the history of Hellenistic philosophy, it has proved difficult to establish how language-science evolved except in broadest outline. The latest studies, while they exhibit much disagreement, do at least concur in arguing that the Stoics contributed more to grammatical theory than did the Alexandrians, whose interests, being

---

[1] For a balanced view see Daniel J. Taylor, "Rethinking the history of language science in classical antiquity," Daniel J. Taylor (ed.), *The History of Linguistics in the Classical Period* (Amsterdam and Philadelphia PA: John Benjamin 1987) 9, and Dirk M. Schenkeveld, "Studies in the History of Ancient Linguistics IV: developments in the study of ancient linguistics," *Mnemosyne* 43 (1990) 289–306, esp. 290–8. Christopher K. Callanan, *Die Sprachbeschreibung bei Aristophanes von Byzanz*, Hypomnemata 88 (Göttingen: Vandenhoeck & Ruprecht 1987), goes too far in denying that Aristophanes had a grammatical system, while Hartmut Erbse ("Zur normativen Grammatik der Alexandriner," *Glotta* 58 (1980) 236–58), goes to the other extreme by arguing that they not only had a grammatical theory, but also codified it in a systematic form.

[2] Rudolf Traugott Schmidt, *Stoicorum Grammatica* (Halle: Anton 1839; Repr. Amsterdam: Hakkert 1967).

more purely philological, less readily induced them to undertake a systematic exposition of the subject.

A central figure among the Stoics who wrote on these topics was Diogenes of Babylon, scholarch in Athens in the middle of the second century and a colleague of Carneades on the celebrated embassy to Rome of 155 B.C.[3] Clear lines of transmission lead from Diogenes to two scholars who contributed greatly to the discipline. Apollodorus of Athens constitutes the missing link between him and Dionysius Thrax: after studying with Diogenes, Apollodorus moved to Alexandria, where he became, together with Dionysius, Aristarchus' most important pupil (Ps.-Scymnus, *Periegesis* 16–24). Indeed, Frede has plausibly suggested[4] that Apollodorus influenced Dionysius: it is thrice recorded that Dionysius' grammatical doctrines at some time diverged from those of the *Techne*, and Frede well observes that each divergence is in the direction of Stoic doctrine. In particular, Diogenes, Apollodorus and the *quondam* Dionysius agree in classifying pronouns as demonstrative articles.[5] Apollodorus must have known Diogenes' doctrines, and surely did play a major role in introducing them to Alexandria. Accordingly, we should see Dionysius' *Techne* not as simply a codification of the observations of Aristophanes and Aristarchus, as has been the standard view,[6] but as a combination of insights derived from the Stoa with that philological precision and understanding of poetry which had been the goal of these Alexandrians. The *Techne* aims to provide a basic work of

---

[3] On the importance of Diogenes' theory of language see Michael Frede, *Essays in Ancient Philosophy* (Oxford: Clarendon Press 1987) 358–9, and Wolfram Ax, *Laut, Stimme und Sprache: Studien zu drei Grundbegriffen der antiken Sprachtheorie*, Hypomnemata 84 (Göttingen: Vandenhoeck & Ruprecht 1986) 138–211; Dirk Obbink and Paul A. Vander Waerdt, "Diogenes of Babylon: The Stoic Sage in the City of Fools," *GRBS* 32 (1991) 355–96, esp. 355. Much new material will emerge from Delattre's reconstruction of Diogenes' *On Music* as critiqued by Philodemus in the latter's *On Music* IV: see Daniel Delattre, "Philodème, *De la Musique*: livre IV, colonnes 40* à 109*," *Cron. Erc.* 19 (1989) 49–143; Id., *Philodème, De la Musique Livre IV*, Diss. University of Paris IV (Sorbonne) 1993.

[4] Frede (above, n.3) 358–9.

[5] For Apollodorus and Dionysius, see A.D. *Pron.* 5, 18–19; for Diogenes, see D.L. VII 58.

[6] For bibliography see Daniel J. Taylor, "Rethinking the history of language science in classical antiquity," Taylor (above, n.1), 1–14, to which should be added Rudolf Pfeiffer, *History of Classical Scholarship from the Beginnings to the End of the Hellenistic Age* (Oxford: Clarendon Press 1968) 203.

reference for literary scholarship like that of Dionysius.[7] That such was its aim is made clear by the opening, as Frede notes.[8] A casual aside on patronymics (*Techne* 12), which has passed unremarked,[9] confirms this: ἀπὸ δὲ μητέρων οὐ σχηματίζει πατρωνυμικὸν εἶδος ὁ "Ομηρος, ἀλλ' οἱ νεώτεροι, "Homer does not form a patronymic from mothers' names, but those later than him do." By the *neoteroi* Aristarchus and his followers always meant the poets after Homer,[10] as is evident here; they were concerned to distinguish Homeric from post-Homeric usage. Moreover, this passage is not from the introduction, the only part of the work generally accepted as genuine. This not only supports the authenticity of the entire *Techne*, contrary to recent doubts,[11] but also confirms that its author had specifically Homeric exegesis in mind, exegesis such as Dionysius himself practised.[12] As Frede says,[13] if we wish to uphold the genuineness of the *Techne* we should entertain his suggestion that Dionysius at first adhered to the Stoic doctrines derived from Diogenes, but later modified them to the form seen in the *Techne* in the light of his own understanding of language.

II. Crates of Mallos in the Herculaneum Papyri

Another contemporary of Diogenes of Babylon had an equally significant place in the evolution of this tradition, and was indeed influenced by him, as we shall see. Crates of Mallos, called "the grammarian" by many (apparently including Posidonius[14]) but "the critic" by

---

[7] As witness the collection of his fragments by Konstanze Linke, *Die Fragmente des Grammatikers Dionysios Thrax* (Berlin and New York: de Gruyter 1977).

[8] Frede (above, n.3) 340.

[9] Even in the recent commentary by Jean Lallot, *La Grammaire de Denys le Thrace* (Paris: Editions du CNRS 1989).

[10] This was shown by Alexandre Severyns, *Le Cycle épique dans l''école d'Aristarque* (Paris: Champion 1928).

[11] On the controversy see Taylor (above, n.6) 8–11. Vincenzo Di Benedetto had accepted only Chs. 1–5 ("Dionisio Trace e la techne a lui attribuita," *ASNP*, Ser. II, 27 (1958–9) 169–210, 28 (1959) 87–118; Id., "La techne spuria," *ASNP*, Ser. III, 3 (1973) 797–814). Lallot (above, n. 9) 19–26, is willing to accept the authenticity of Chs. 1–10, but not that of the remainder.

[12] Dionysius was not afraid to challenge even Aristarchus' interpretations of Homer, not always rightly: for examples see R. Janko, *The Iliad: A Commentary. IV: Books 13–16* (Cambridge: Cambridge University Press 1992) 305, 340, 415, 420.

[13] Frede (above, n.3) 359.

[14] Ap. Geminus *Elem. Astron.* 16.21 = Crates fr. 34a in H.J. Mette, *Sphairopoiia:*

himself (S.E. *Adv. Math.* I 79), became the leading scholar at the Attalid court at Pergamum and the chief rival of Aristarchus.[15] He may have helped to organise the royal library,[16] and like Diogenes he went on a celebrated embassy in about 168 B.C. to the Senate of Rome, where he broke his leg and gave influential lectures while he recuperated (Suet. *Gram.* 2). Here we have again been handicapped by the lack of a reliable edition of his fragments, which are numerous; the collection by Hans-Joachim Mette is purposely incomplete and speculative.[17] Moreover, one major source for Crates' views on language has been neglected until very recently.

The library of the Epicurean Philodemus of Gadara, originally consisting of hundreds of complete papyrus-rolls, was rediscovered at Herculaneum in 1752–4. In recent decades there has been tremendous progress on the surviving papyri, under the aegis of Marcello Gigante. This progress, combined with that heightened interest in Hellenistic philosophy to which Professor Kidd's oeuvre attests and has contributed, has greatly improved our comprehension of these texts.[18] Moreover, a new method of papyrological reconstruction, developed independently by Delattre[19] and Obbink,[20] offers real prospects of recomposing entire *volumina* from the detached and jumbled fragments. Accordingly, a new text and translation of all three of Philodemus' major aesthetic treatises, *On Poetry*, *On Music* and *On Rhetoric*, is in prepara-

---

Untersuchungen zur Kosmologie des Krates von Pergamon (Munich: Beck 1936), cf. I.G. Kidd, *Posidonius II: II. Fragments 150–293* (Cambridge: Cambridge University Press 1988) 458–60.

[15] See James I. Porter, "Hermeneutic Lines and Circles: Aristarchus and Crates on the Exegesis of Homer," Robert Lamberton and John J. Keaney (eds.), *Homer's Ancient Readers* (Princeton NJ: Princeton University Press 1992) 67–114, esp. 85–6.

[16] Pfeiffer (above, n.6) 235.

[17] *Parateresis: Untersuchungen zur Sprachtheorie des Krates von Pergamon* (Halle: Max Niemeyer 1952), with the remarks of Pfeiffer (above, n.6) 239 n.7. Thus David L. Blank has shown that Mette is wrong to equate Crates' position with that seen in Sextus Empiricus and the empirical physicians (*Ancient Philosophy and Grammar* (Chico CA: Scholars' Press 1982) 3–4).

[18] For an excellent overview see Mario Capasso, *Manuale della papirologia ercolanese* (Lecce: Congedo 1992).

[19] Delattre 1989 (above, n.3).

[20] Dirk Obbink, *Philodemus: De Pietate I* (Diss., Stanford University 1986), to be published in revised form by Clarendon Press, Oxford, 1995. See also R. Janko, "*Philodemus resartus*: progress in reconstructing the philosophical papyri from Herculaneum," John J. Cleary (ed.), *Proceedings of the Boston Area Colloquium in Ancient Philosophy* 7 (Lanham MD: University Press of America 1991) 271–308.

tion.²¹ Because of Philodemus' style of polemic, in which he often gives first a summary of opposing views and then a refutation, with extensive quotations (some repeated), these works offer our best hope of recovering new information about Hellenistic aesthetics in general, and the theories of the second century B.C. in particular.

Near the end of Book V of *On Poetry*, Philodemus offers his criticisms of an important theory of poetry which Crates had somewhere propounded.²² The passage has recently been much discussed,²³ and has been reliably reedited by Cecilia Mangoni.²⁴ Crates' views were originally represented at greater length, since the Epicurean had summarised the theory which he was to rebut in some fragments which belong earlier in the same Book.²⁵ Furthermore, Philodemus notes that he had already refuted Crates' views on the euphony of the letters earlier, specifically in Book II.²⁶

The potential significance of Philodemus' treatise for our understanding of the ancient grammatical tradition is even larger because, as the Epicurean makes clear, Crates himself passed in review the doctrines of various earlier writers. At col. xxiv 24ff. Mangoni, Philodemus begins to review 'the opinions in Crates' (τὰ πα[ρὰ] τῶι Κράτ[ητι).²⁷ Crates

---

²¹ See R. Janko, "Introducing the Philodemus Translation Project: Reconstructing the *On Poems*," *Proceedings of the XXth International Congress of Papyrology* (Copenhagen 1993) 367–81, esp. 373–4.

²² Cols. xxiv 24–xxix 23 in the edition of Cecilia Mangoni, *Filodemo. Il Quinto Libro della Poetica* (Naples: Bibliopolis (La Scuola di Epicuro XIV) 1993) = cols. xxi–xxvi in the edition of Christian Jensen, *Philodemus Über die Gedichte fünftes Buch* (Berlin 1923).

²³ James I. Porter, "Philodemus on material difference", *Cron. Erc.* 19 (1989) 149–78; Porter (above, n.17) 112; Elizabeth Asmis, "Crates on Poetic Criticism", *Phoenix* 46 (1992) 138–69; Nicola Pace, *Problematiche di Poetica in Filodemo di Gadara* (Diss., University of Milan 1992) esp. 120–9.

²⁴ Above, n.22.

²⁵ See my review of Mangoni (above, n.22) in *CPh* 89 (1994) 282–9, esp. 282 n.4.

²⁶ Col. xxix 7–18 Mangoni: τὰ δὲ περὶ τῶν στοιχείων, ἐν ο[ἷς] τὴν κρί[σ]ιν εἶναί φησι (sc. ὁ Κράτης) τῶν σπου[δ]α[ίων] ποιημάτων, τίνος αὐτῶι καὶ πόσης ἡδονῆς γέμε[ι π]αρεστακότες ἐν τ[ῶ]ι δευτέρωι τῶν ὑπομνημάτων, διὰ τὸ καὶ περὶ ποιήματος εἶναι κοινῶς, ἀποδοκιμά[ζομ]εν παλιλλογε[ῖ]ν, ὥσ[τε] τὰς παρὰ Ζήνωνι δόξας ἐπικόψαντες ἤδη μεμηκυσμένον τὸ σύγγραμμα καταπαύσομεν. "But as for his remarks on the letters, in which he (sc. Crates) claims that the judgement of good verses resides, we have shown in his regard in the second of our treatises (since it is also about verse in general) of what and of how much absurdity they are full, and we decline to repeat it, so that, after refuting the opinions found in Zeno (sc. of Sidon), we can bring to a close a work that has already become long."

²⁷ The phrase has always been taken as "the opinions *of* Crates," but see my review of Mangoni (above, n.25) 283 n.7.

discussed, first, Heracleodorus and those of similar outlook, next Andromenides, and lastly certain "philosophers," by whom, Philodemus speculates, he may or may not have meant Epicurus and his followers (τ]οὺς περὶ τὸν Ἐπίκουρον). A new supplement to the text by Annick Monet[28] makes clear that, in Philodemus' judgement, Crates had in fact misunderstood his predecessors:

ἀπο[τυγ]χάνει τοιγα[ρ]οῦν [τῆ]ς Ἡρακλεοδώρου καὶ τῶν ὁμοίων δόξης — [οὐ γ]ὰρ τὴν σύνθεσιν, ἀλλὰ τὴν ἐπιφαινομένην [α]ὐ[τῆι] φωνὴ[ν] ἐπ[αι]ν[οῦσιν (suppl. Monet: ἐπ[αι]ν[εῖ Kentenich) — ὡς κ]αὶ τῆς Ἀνδρομενίδ[ου, πά]ντη⟨ι⟩ γε νομίζων ὁ[μολ]ογεῖν αὐτὸν καὶ διὰ [πα]ντὸς τοῖς εἰρημένοις.

He misunderstands[29] the doctrine of Heracleodorus and those like him, since they praise not the word-order (*synthesis*) but the sound that supervenes upon the word-order, just as he also misunderstands that of Andromenides, although he believes that he is always totally in accord with what Andromenides said.

Philodemus is making the ironic point that Crates in fact agreed with Heracleodorus and company when he thought he differed, and disagreed with Andromenides when he thought they were in full accord! One is reminded of Varro's claim[30] that Crates misunderstood the views of both Chrysippus and Aristarchus when he exploited the former's doctrine of anomaly to rebut the latter's view of analogy.

Crates' name appears at least twice in papyri derived from the fragmentary opening Books of Philodemus' *On Poetry*.[31] In the first pas-

---

[28] Oral seminar communication, "First International Colloquium on Philodemus' *On Poems*," Los Angeles, May 1994.

[29] ἀποτυγχάνει, "misses the point of," has always been mistranslated: it was rendered "hat nicht derselbe Ansicht" by Jensen (above, n.22) and "è in disaccordo" by Mangoni (above, n.22), but see LSJ s.v. II (I thank D. Delattre for this point).

[30] *De Ling. Lat.* IX 1: Crates, nobilis grammaticus, qui fretus Chrysippo, homine acutissimo qui reliquit περὶ ἀνωμαλίας III libros, contra analogian atque Aristarchum est nixus, sed ita, ut scripta indicant eius, ut neutrius videatur pervidisse voluntatem, i.e. "the distinguished scholar Crates, relying on Chrysippus, a most penetrating man who left behind three books *On Anomaly*, argued against analogy and Aristarchus, but in such a way, as his writings show, that he seems not to have understood completely the intent of either." On the alleged controversy see Blank (above, n.17) 1–4; W.J. Slater, *Aristophanis Byzantii Fragmenta* (Berlin and New York: de Gruyter 1986) 137–9; Daniel J. Taylor, Taylor (above, n.1) 6–8; Schenkeveld (above, n.1) 290–3.

[31] *PHerc.* 1073 fr. 1, *PHerc.* 1676 col. ii (= Tr. B fr. 25 col. ii 19, C col. ii 24 in Francesco Sbordone, *[Φιλοδήμου Περὶ Ποιημάτων] Tractatus Tres* (Naples: Giannini

sage it is conjoined with that of Andromenides, as we might expect; in fact, Crates is agreeing with Andromenides that the three parts of the poetic art are πόησις, πόημα and ποητής ("poetry," "verse" and "poet"), a bizarre tripartition acquired from Neoptolemus of Parium[32] and passed down to Lucilius[33] and perhaps to Posidonius.[34] (The latter was after all the pupil of Crates' pupil Panaetius.) The second passage refers to Crates' *Sphairopoiia*.[35] Accordingly, we may reasonably hope to detect further traces of Crates' thought in these Books, once they are reconstructed. If we could recover his thought on euphony, we would certainly be dealing with his opinions on vocal sound (φωνή), precisely the context in which Diogenes and other Stoics (at least Archedemus) presented their grammatical theory.[36]

Experimenting with the new method of reconstruction, I was able to establish the sequence of over sixty columns from the fragmentary *volumen* called Treatise B by Sbordone[37] (Herculaneum papyri 460 and 1073, now columns 74–101 in the complete roll as provisionally reconstructed). This sequence, determined on papyrological grounds, was confirmed by the discovery of a set of parallels in the same order in a different roll, papyrus 994, named Treatise A by Sbordone.[38] Since Treatise A was unwound continuously, the order of its columns is certain. These parallels must be explained by Philodemus' method of offering a summary and then a refutation, which here occupies Treatise A.

1976)). I suspect that there is a third reference in *PHerc.* 460 fr. 23.21 (= Tr. B fr. 30 Sbordone), beside a possible mention of Pausimachus in line 24 of the same column; this represents the start of the discussion of euphonic letters. A fourth reference is possible in a passage where Philodemus begins his refutation, and appears to claim that Crates distorted the views of Heraclides of Pontus (*PHerc.* 1074a fr. 3a.1–11, = Tr. D fr. 40 in Maria Luisa Nardelli, *Due Trattati filodemei* Περὶ ποιημάτων (Naples: Giannini 1983)). For a new text see R. Janko, "Reconstructing Philodemus' *On Poems*", Dirk Obbink (ed.), *Philodemus and Poetry* (Oxford and New York: Oxford University Press 1994) 69–96, esp. 80–1 with n.37.

[32] Phld. *Poem.* V col. xiv 5–11 Mangoni.
[33] *Remains of Old Latin* III 404–6 Warmington.
[34] For his definitions of ποίημα and ποίησις from his *On Diction* see D.L. VII 60, = fr. 44 Edelstein-Kidd.
[35] See Porter (above, n.15) 89–90.
[36] See now Ax (above, n.3), and Dirk M. Schenkeveld, "Studies in the History of Ancient Linguistics III: The Stoic ΤΕΧΝΗ ΠΕΡΙ ΦΩΝΗΣ," *Mnemosyne* 43 (1990) 86–107; id. (above, n.1) 298–306.
[37] Above n.31.
[38] For a tabulation with provisional column-numbers see Janko (above, n.31), Table 6.1 on p. 74.

Their great extent, where (uniquely) the summary fills much of one book-roll and the refutation occupies what appears to be the book following, suggests that he is summarising and critiquing the doctrines on euphony of a major opponent. I have argued elsewhere[39] that this is the refutation of Crates' euphonic doctrines which Philodemus says he had provided in *On Poetry* II, and that Crates is himself examining the views of Heracleodorus and his fellows, specifically those of a certain Pausimachus.

III. Crates' Grammatical Terminology

Until the planned new edition of the book-roll to which these materials belonged can be completed, the reader must be content with a discussion of the context of the grammatical terms found in Treatise B.[40] In the opening 73 columns of the roll (formerly called Treatise E[41]), before the section on euphony where these terms appear (Treatise B), Crates is critiquing the views of those who, he claims, held that the excellence of a verse (ποίημα) lies in either its "word-choice" (ἐκλογή) or its "word-order" or "composition" (σύνθεσις).[42] These critics are respectively Andromenides, and Heracleodorus and company, whom we met above. Thus, Philodemus reports, he asks those who praise the *synthesis* "with regard to what criterion they praise it or what effect a fine composition will have," since "the composition does not create the fine sound."[43] Crates complains that his predecessors do not "present a systematic set of precepts about combination in speech that is to be chosen or es-

---

[39] (Above, n.38) 89–92. My conclusion was anticipated by C. Jensen in. J. Stroux, *Antidoron: Festschrift für J. Wackernagel* (Göttingen 1923) 312 n.3.

[40] For the meantime, I refer to these texts using the inventory-numbers of the papyri together with the fragment-numbers of the previous editions by Sbordone and Nardelli (above, n.31), with the caution that their numeration bears almost no relation to the true sequence.

[41] First published by Nardelli (above, n.31), but now joined with *PHerc*. 444 (see next note).

[42] Cf. his statement at *PHerc*. 444 fr. 4 (first published by F. Sbordone, "Il papiro ercolanese 444," *RAAN* 35 (1960) 99–110, reprinted in his *Sui Papiri della Poetica di Filodemo* (Naples: Giannini 1983) 239–50): "some, he says, claim that the good verse arises from beautiful and poetic words, but according to others it is the case that inferior verses often arise from commonplace and ordinary words, but that, when such words are beautifully arranged, good verses arise."

[43] *PHerc*. 444 fr. 8 (above, n.42).

chewed, since excellence and inferiority lie in this alone."[44] After a possible appearance of the names of both Crates and Pausimachus,[45] the opponent promises to discuss "sounds in themselves."[46] He argues that verses are pleasing only because of the sounds which they contain, and that various sounds, accents, syllables or words, especially if repeated, please or displease the ear. This argument forms the core of Treatise B, and includes an impressive array of grammatical terms. Whether the opinions are those of of Crates' predecessor Pausimachus or of Crates himself (as I believe more likely), they have a secure *terminus ante quem* in the middle of the second century B.C. Treatise B therefore offers a point of unusual fixity in our fluid knowledge of the grammatical tradition, and should give us a clearer picture of the progress of linguistic science down to the first half of the second century B.C. I shall present these terms in the order corresponding to that of the *Techne* ascribed to Dionysius Thrax.

First, the terms for the Greek accents differ markedly from Dionysius'. Although Crates uses the standard term περισπᾶσθαι for "to have a circumflex accent,"[47] he employs ἄνεσις "laxness" for "grave" and ἐπίτασις "tenseness" for the acute.[48] These two terms appear together thrice. The corresponding verbs are ἀνίεσθαι "to be lax," i.e. to have a grave accent, and ἐπιτείνεσθαι "to be tense," i.e. to have an acute accent.[49] Dionysius, of course, uses βαρεῖα and ὀξεῖα (τάσις) for "grave" and "acute" (*Techne* 3). The metaphor of the tension in a stringed instrument or a bow[50] supplies the source for both Crates' and Dionysius' terms;[51] the same origin underlies τάσις and τόνος.[52] This is of course an apt nomenclature, since Greek then had a tonic accent, and

---

[44] *PHerc.* 460 fr. 25, = Treatise B fr. 18 Sbordone.
[45] *PHerc.* 460 fr. 23.21–4, = Treatise B fr. 30 Sbordone.
[46] *PHerc.* 460 fr. 24.23–4, = Treatise B fr. 19 Sbordone.
[47] *PHerc.* 460 fr. 19.21, = Tr. B fr. 5 col. i Sbordone. This term is first attested in Aristophanes of Byzantium (schol. on Hom. *Od.* 7.317).
[48] *PHerc.* 444 fr. 7.22, *PHerc.* 460 fr. 16.17–18 (= Tr. B fr. 10 col. ii Sbordone) and *PHerc.* 1073 fr. 15b.23–24 (= Tr. B fr. 10 col. i Sbordone, restored). ἄνεσις also appears in *PHerc.* 460 fr. 16.3.
[49] *PHerc.* 460 fr. 16.5, 9, 10, 12 (= Tr. B fr. 10 col. ii Sbordone).
[50] Crates spells this out in an analogy with "an instrument or a bow" at *PHerc.* 1073 fr. 15b.19–24 (= Tr. B fr. 10 col. i Sbordone), where this pair of terms recurs.
[51] Aristoxenus already applied them to musical pitch (*El. harm.* 15.15, 15.20, 16.4, 18.1, 18.19).
[52] On the terminology see also G.B. Pecorella, *Dionisio Trace* ΤΕΧΝΗ ΓΡΑΜΜΑΤΙΚΗ, Rome n.d. 85ff.

the pitch of a string is raised when it is tightened and lowered when it is slackened. Crates' terms are paralleled in only two places. First, a scholium on Dionysius Thrax (p. 130 Hilgard) calls the grave accent ἡ ἀνειμένη τάσις. Secondly, they are used in a critique of Isocrates' monotonous style by the Peripatetic Hieronymus of Rhodes (fr. 52 Wehrli), who is quoted by Philodemus[53] and summarised by Dionysius of Halicarnassus (*Isocr.* 13.3–5).[54] Hieronymus (ca. 290–30 B.C.) held that repetitions of similar accents on successive words should be avoided; this position, here applied to poetry by Crates, was to be echoed by Cicero (*de opt. gen. orat.* 4.10), Dionysius of Halicarnassus (*Comp.* 12.3)[55] and an anonymous writer in Walz, *Rhet. Gr.* III 589.22.

The letters are classified into vowels, semi-vowels (which modern linguists call continuants) and consonants. The terms are φωνῆεν for vowel,[56] defined as in Dionysius Thrax (*Techne* 6) by its ability to be sounded without other letters; second, the ἡμίφωνον or continuant;[57] and last, the ἄφωνον or stop.[58] This classification is standard,[59] but it has escaped notice that Dionysius too is interested in euphony. Crates and Heracleodorus both detect and praise euphony in the letters,[60] and Crates' other predecessor Andromenides ascribed excellence in poetry to words made up of letters of a certain quality and quantity.[61] Now

---

[53] *Rhet.* IV (*PHerc.* 1007) cols. xvi* 13–xviii* 8 Sudhaus: "Hieronymus says that Isocrates' speeches can be read easily, but cannot be delivered in public in a loud voice and high pitch, and cannot be spoken at all in this style with the appropriate manner of delivery. For Isocrates neglected the most important thing, which moves the masses most: for his diction is lifeless and impossible to listen to and, as it were, composed for a single pitch, but he rejected the style broken up and varied with high and low pitch" (*epitasis* and *anesis*) "and with emotive transpositions, but he is enslaved to smoothness throughout."

[54] Dionysius is argued to have plagiarised Philodemus by P. Costil, *L'Esthetique littéraire de Denys d'Halicarnasse* (Diss., Paris 1949) 369 (cited by G. Aujac, *Denys d'Halicarnasse, Opuscules rhétoriques*, Budé t.1 (Paris: Les Belles Lettres 1978) 193–4). But is it also possible that Crates quoted Hieronymus, and both Philodemus and Dionysius of Halicarnassus drew on Crates? See also G. Indelli, "Testimonianze su Isocrate nel *PHerc.* 1007," *Cron. Erc.* 23 (1993) 87–92.

[55] μηδὲ δὴ ὁμοιότονα παρ' ὁμοιοτόνοις.

[56] *PHerc.* 1073 fr. 12.4 (= Tr. B fr. 32 Sbordone, where Crates claims that "we cannot utter anything without vowels, since nothing rests on these, but the sound in itself"), and *PHerc.* 460 fr. 7.6–7 (= Tr. B fr. 8 col. i Sbordone, a reference to "those vowels that are indivisible," i.e. perhaps not diphthongs or long vowels).

[57] *PHerc.* 460 fr. 7.14–15 (= Tr. B fr. 8 col. i Sbordone).

[58] *PHerc.* 460 fr. 7.24–5 (= Tr. B fr. 8 col. i Sbordone).

[59] Cf. e.g. D.H. *Comp.* 14.2–4.

[60] *On Poems* V col. xxiv 24ff., quoted above, n.31.

224 The Passionate Intellect

Dionysius classifies the letters in a descending order according to their euphonic qualities: vowels are most euphonious, continuants in the middle, and consonants least (*Techne* 6):

> ἡμίφωνα δὲ λέγεται, ὅτι παρ' ὅσον ἧττον τῶν φωνηέντων εὔφωνα καθέστηκεν ἔν τε τοῖς μυγμοῖς καὶ σιγμοῖς... ἄφωνα δὲ λέγεται, ὅτι μᾶλλον τῶν ἄλλων ἐστὶν κακόφωνα, ὥσπερ ἄφωνον λέγομεν τὸν τραγῳδὸν τὸν κακόφωνον.

> Semi-vocalic elements are so called, because they are to some extent less euphonious than the vowels in their mooings and hissings ... Non-vocalic elements are so called, because they are more cacophonous than the rest, just as we say a cacophonous tragic actor has no voice.[62]

This hierarchy can now be shown to have an antecedent in Crates, who states that sounds ending with vowels are superior to sounds ending with continuants or stops, because the former "signify most" (?).[63] Thus he prefers an open light syllable with an acute accent (as in ὅ-πλον or κύ-κλος) to a closed heavy syllable with a grave accent (as in χὰλ-κόν).[64]

What is more, Crates' preferences for different sounds can, where we have information as to the details, be shown generally to correspond to those found in what is usually regarded as the most original work of Dionysius of Halicarnassus, the *Peri Syntheseos onomaton*. Among long vowels, Dionysius ranks eta second-best, but long iota fifth and worst (*Comp.* 14.10–13). Crates greatly prefers eta to long iota,[65] which he calls "narrow and hard to pronounce";[66] he exemplifies this by altering several Homeric verses to show why Homer "avoided" the iota.[67]

---

[61] *PHerc.* 460 fr. 2.25–6 (= Tr. B fr. 25 col. iii Sbordone), where Philodemus tells us that he is quoting Andromenides verbatim.
[62] Cf. *PHerc.* 1073 fr. 8a.2–7 (= Tr. B fr. 4 col. ii Sbordone), where Crates accepts the claim that a person with a poor voice, an ἰσχνόφωνος, will not be a good poet.
[63] *PHerc.* 460 fr. 7.21–6 (= Tr. B fr. 8 col. i Sbordone): τῶν γὰρ ἤχων ὅσοι εἰς αὐτὰ τὰ φωνήεντα τελευτῶσιν, εὐσημότατοί εἰσιν, οἱ δ' εἰς ἄφωνα ἢ ἡμίφων[α οὐ]χ ὁμοίως.
[64] *PHerc.* 460 fr. 20.4–11 (= Tr. B fr. 12 Sbordone) beside fr. 19.18ff. (= Tr. B fr. 5 col. i Sbordone).
[65] *PHerc.* 1073 fr. 7a.2 (= Tr. B fr. 9 col. i Sbordone), 460 fr. 14c.11ff. (= Tr. B fr. 6 col. i Sbordone), 1073 fr. 5 (= Tr. B fr. 6 col. ii Sbordone).
[66] *PHerc.* 1073 fr. 5.2–4 (= Tr. B fr. 6 col. ii Sbordone); cf. how Dionysius calls long hypsilon, superior only to long iota, "narrow" (*Comp.* 14.12).

Among the continuants, Dionysius prefers lambda to the sibilants, with the nasals occupying an intermediate position (*Comp.* 14.19). Crates gives no hierarchy, but praises the word *lotos*[68] and likes a syllable containing no nasal but an unaspirated stop plus lambda plus alpha, e.g. *pla-* or *kla-*.[69] Conversely he disparages the syllables *ma* and *man*, apparently suggesting that they have a Phrygian ring.[70] The sibilants sigma and xi are problematic for him, especially when used to excess,[71] just as for Dionysius (*Comp.* 14.20). Among the stops, Crates distinguishes between the effect of an unaspirated voiced or voiceless stop (preceding lambda plus alpha) and that of an aspirated stop (apparently in the same phonetic environment).[72] His reasoning is lost, but this time he certainly did not share Dionysius' preference for aspirated stops,[73] because elsewhere he objects to a properispomenon preceded by a sibilant and an aspirate (σχῆ-μα).[74] In all other respects, however, the new material throws into doubt the originality of the euphonic theory in the *De Compositione Verborum*; Dionysius is, at best, applying to prose a method which others had developed in the context of poetry.

As for the "accidents" or transformations of letters, syllables and words (glossed συμβεβηκότα by Philodemus[75] in his refutation), Crates catalogues a number of terms in a brief passage:[76]

τὰ μὲν [γὰ]ρ ἀνομ[οί]ως θεωρ[εῖσθαι]" φησὶν "[δεῖν ἕνεκα τῶν ὑπ]οκειμένων, [τὰ] δὲ κα[τ]ὰ τὸν ἦχον ἀνέσει καὶ [ἐ]πιτάσει καὶ προσπνε[ύ]σει καὶ ψιλότητι καὶ ἐ[κτ]άσει καὶ συσ[το]λ[ῆι καὶ] προθέσει καὶ πτώσει, [ὧ]ν πάντων ὀρθῶς [εὑρισ]κομένων ἑλλην[ισ]μὸς ἀποτελεῖται καὶ ἁρμογή τις.

---

[67] Perhaps in *PHerc.* 460 fr. 13.15ff. (= Tr. B fr. 2 Sbordone), 1073 fr. 4 (= Tr. B fr. 31 Sbordone), certainly in *PHerc.* 460 fr. 14c.11ff. (= Tr. B fr. 6 col. ii Sbordone), 460 fr. 12 (= Tr. B fr. 13 Sbordone).
[68] *PHerc.* 460 fr. 22.5–8 (= Tr. B fr. 7 col. i Sbordone).
[69] *PHerc.* 460 fr. 6.8–16 (= Tr. B fr. 9 col. ii Sbordone), cf. 1073 fr. 2a.1–5 (= Tr. B fr. 8 col. ii Sbordone).
[70] *PHerc.* 460 fr. 17.3–12 (= Tr. B fr. 11 col. ii Sbordone).
[71] *PHerc.* 460 fr. 22.8ff. (= Tr. B fr. 7 col. i Sbordone)
[72] *PHerc.* 460 fr. 6.8–27 (= Tr. B fr. 9 col. ii Sbordone).
[73] *Comp.* 14.27. See further David L. Blank, "Stop or Spirant: a note on the division of Nonvocal and Semivocal Elements," to appear in *Glotta*.
[74] *PHerc.* 460 fr. 19.18ff. (= Tr. B fr. 5 col. i Sbordone)
[75] Treatise A col. b 7 Sbordone.
[76] *PHerc.* 460 fr. 16.13–25 (= Tr. B fr. 10 col. ii Sbordone).

Some <verses?> must," he says, "be regarded in a dissimilar way by reason of the subject-matter, but others according to the sound, with laxness and tenseness, aspiration and lack of aspiration, lengthening and shortening, prefixing and modification of endings. When all these things are correctly devised, pure Greek and a kind of harmony ensues.

The pairs are thus falling and rising pitch (discussed above), aspiration and lack of aspiration (πρόσπνευσις and ψιλότης),[77] lengthening and shortening (ἔκτασις and συστολή),[78] and lastly prefixation and suffixation (πρόθεσις and πτῶσις).[79] These terms too are somewhat unusual. Whereas ψιλότης is standard, πρόσπνευσις is rare instead of δασύτης; it recurs only in the Emperor Julian (Or. 2.72a), although προσπνέω is found in this sense in Seleucus (ap. Ath. IX 398b)[80] and Apollonius Dyscolus (Pron. 55.23, Synt. 141.4). ἔκτασις, συστολή and their related verbs ἐκτείνειν and συστέλλειν are standard by this date, as is βραχύς for a short syllable.[81] As well as in the *Techne* (6, 8, 9), they appear in Dionysius of Halicarnassus (Comp. 14.12, 25.41), Sextus Empiricus (Adv. Math. I 108) and Apollonius Dyscolus (Synt. 281.7). On the other hand, πρόθεσις is used to mean "prefixation" only by Apollonius (Pron. 58.16, Synt. 311.1), whereas in Dionysius Thrax (*Techne* 18) and in Dionysius of Halicarnassus this term signifies "preposition." [82] However, since a true preposition is not accented separately in Greek, and belongs to the same unit as the word which it precedes (by proclisis), prepositions could be seen as a species of "prefixing." Crates uses πτῶσις in its basic sense as a logical term for "modification" that "falls under" (πίπτει)[83] another form (an alteration almost

---

[77] This pair also appears at *PHerc.* 460 fr. 21.11–12 (= Tr. B fr. 29 Sbordone, restored); πρόσπνευσις recurs alone at 460 fr. 6.20 (= Tr. B fr. 9 col. ii Sbordone), fr. 4.1 (= Tr. B fr. 28 Sbordone), with πνεῦμα at fr. 6.25–6.
[78] This pair recurs at *PHerc.* 1073 fr. 18.11 (= Tr. B fr. 34 Sbordone), and the corresponding verbs may appear at *PHerc.* 460 fr. 20.16–17 (= Tr. B fr. 12 Sbordone); they are used together at D.H. *Comp.* 14.7.
[79] LSJ s.v. IV.3 improbably take this pair of terms as "stem" (or "root") and "ending."
[80] Seleucus may have derived this term from Crates, whose Ἀττικὴ διάλεκτος he cites elsewhere (below, n. 125).
[81] *PHerc.* 460 fr. 20.9–10 (= Tr. B fr. 12 Sbordone).
[82] *Comp.* 2.3.
[83] Cf. *PHerc.* 460 fr. 16.1–3 (= Tr. B fr. 10 col. ii Sbordone): κ[ἂν τῶι] "τε⟨ί⟩χεος [ἔξω" ἀμφό]τεραι αἱ πτώ[σεις πί]πτουσιν εἰς ἄνεσ[ιν, i.e. "in the phrase τείχεος ἔξω both endings fall into (or 'under'?) a lax accentuation," where πτώσεις means "declined forms."

exclusively to the end of a word, whether by declension, conjugation or compounding); this is Aristotelian in origin,[84] but Crates' usage seems identical with the Stoics'.[85]

The so-called πάθη τῆς λέξεως "modifications of diction," which involved the addition, subtraction, alteration or rearrangement of letters, are often described as the "quadripertita ratio:" the invention of the terms πρόσθεσις, ἀφαίρεσις, ἐναλλαγή and μετάθεσις was ascribed by Karl Barwick[86] to the Stoics' τέχνη περὶ φωνῆς "handbook on sound," and specifically to the τόπος περὶ βαρβαρισμοῦ καὶ σολοικισμοῦ ("section on barbarism and solecism"). However, Ax[87] has recently denied the likelihood of Stoic influence and instead has traced the schema, at least in its first three items, to Aristotle's *Poetics* and even to Plato's *Cratylus*.[88] The presence of its terms here sheds some light on the controversy. Crates pairs the verbs προσλαμβάνω "add" and (probably) ἀποβάλλω "remove" (both applied to letters);[89] he also uses ἐναλλάττω "exchange" for swapping two words equivalent in sense and scansion but different in accent,[90] ἀλλαγή for altering a verse by inserting a different noun and verb,[91] and παραλλαγή to refer to the "slight" (βραχεῖα) "variation" between a voiceless and a voiced

---

[84] *Int.* 16b1, 16, *Poet.* 1457a18, etc., with Pfeiffer (above, n.6) 77–8. On the Stoic concept of "case" see Frede (above, n.3) 304–5; A.A. Long and D.N. Sedley, *The Hellenistic Philosophers*, vol. 1 (Cambridge: Cambridge University Press 1987) 201.

[85] Its meaning is obscure at *PHerc.* 1073 fr. 6.21 (= Tr. B fr. 23 col. iii Sbordone); it may mean "suffix" at *PHerc.* 460 fr. 19.10 (= Tr. B fr. 5 col. i Sbordone), if it is correctly read there.

[86] *Remmius Palaemon und die römische ars grammatica, Philologus Suppl.* 15:2 (Leipzig: Dieterich 1922) 94–8.

[87] "Quadripertita ratio: Bemerkungen zur Geschichte eines aktuellen Kategoriensystems (Adiectio - Detractio - Transmutatio - Immutatio)," Taylor (above, n.1) 17–40, esp. 29ff. In fact πρόσθεσις, ἀφαίρεσις, ὑποκορισμός and ἐξαλλαγή are the four kinds of jokes from paronymy in the *Tractatus Coislinianus* V 4, which, I have argued, is a summary of *Poetics* II: see *Aristotle on Comedy: Towards a Reconstruction of* Poetics *II* (London: Duckworth 1984) 175–81, with numerous parallels. Cf. also Blank (above, n.17) 43, Dirk Schenkeveld, "Pap. Hamburg 128: a Hellenistic *Ars Poetica*," ZPE 97 (1993) 67–80, esp. 71, and Ineke Sluiter, *Ancient Grammar in Context* (Amsterdam: VU University Press 1990) 12.

[88] 394b (πρόσκειται γράμμα ἢ μετάκειται ἢ ἀφῄρηται), 432a1ff. (ἐάν τι ἀφέλωμεν ἢ προσθῶμεν ἢ μεταθῶμέν τι).

[89] *PHerc.* 460 fr. 21.2–4 (= Tr. B fr. 29 Sbordone), cf. Treatise A col. b 2 Sbordone (ἀπο[βαλλόμενα is my restoration — Sbordone had supplied ἀ[ποτιθέμενα in Treatise A).

[90] *PHerc.* 1073 fr. 15b.16–17 (= Tr. B fr. 10 col. i Sbordone).

[91] *PHerc.* 460 fr. 12.9 (= Tr. B fr. 13 Sbordone).

consonant.⁹² Whereas ἐναλλάττω is standard, προσλαμβάνω is mainly a mathematical and logical term, by which the Stoics meant "add as a minor premiss."⁹³ However, Apollonius Dyscolus uses the equivalent noun πρόσληψις of adding letters and words (*Synt.* 170.3, *Pron.* 87.13). Similarly, he employs ἀποβάλλω in the sense of "to drop" a letter.⁹⁴ Crates' use of these terms proves that, even if its origin is Peripatetic, the "quadripertita ratio" still formed part of Stoic grammatical theory in the second century B.C. This is as we would expect from the testimony of Varro, who ascribes it both to the Alexandrian scholars and to the Stoics.⁹⁵ Here the schema may be completed by the verb μετατίθημι, which is not found of altering the order of letters but is applied by Crates to his technique of "rearranging" the words in a verse.⁹⁶

Lastly, Crates names four parts of speech, which are glossed μέρη τοῦ λόγου by Philodemus in his refutation.⁹⁷ These are ὄνομα "noun," twice paired with ῥῆμα "verb,"⁹⁸ a part which must be restored as πρ[ό]θεσις "preposition" (πρ[ο]σηγορία "appellative" would exceed the space), and (paired with the previous term) σύνδεσμος "conjunction."⁹⁹ These terms are all known to Dionysius Thrax (*Techne* 11, 18), but πρόθεσις does not appear in the systems of either Chrysippus or

---

⁹² *PHerc.* 460 fr. 6.19 (= Tr. B fr. 9 col. ii Sbordone). Cf. Chrysippus, *SVF* III 182 von Arnim, and for 'interchange' A.D. *Pron.* 110.3, *Synt.* 214.9.

⁹³ LSJ s.v. I.4.

⁹⁴ *Pron.* 36.21, cf. LSJ s.v. ἀποβολή 1.

⁹⁵ *Ling. Lat.* VI 1.2: huius rei auctor satis mihi Chrysippus et Antipater et illi in quibus, si non tantum acuminis, at plus litterarum, in quo est Aristophanes et Apollodorus, qui omnes verba ex verbis ita declinari scribunt, ut verba litteras alia assumant, alia mittant, alia commutent, i.e. "I find sufficient authority for this in Chrysippus, Antipater and those scholars in whom there is, if not so much brilliance, at least more learning, including Aristophanes and Apollodorus. They all write that words can be modified from other words, in such a way that some words take on extra letters, others drop them, and others alter them."

⁹⁶ *PHerc.* 466 fr. 7.3 (= Tr. E fr. 10 Nardelli), 466 fr. 6.12 (= Tr. E fr. 9 Nardelli), 1073 fr. 19.1 (= Tr. B fr. 35 Sbordone), 1073 fr. 11.1 = Tr. B fr. 7 col. ii Sbordone (my supplement in three cases). The technique of μετάθεσις is already applied to prose in Demetrius, *De Eloc.* 45–6, and Cic. *Orat.* 214–15, even before its extensive use by Dionysius of Halicarnassus in his *De compositione verborum*; its first use in verse is here, followed by D.H. *Comp.* 4.1–4 (for the replacement of a word in a verse see already Aristotle, *Poet.* 1458b15–31).

⁹⁷ Treatise A col. b 4–5 Sbordone.

⁹⁸ *PHerc.* 460.21.4–5 (= Tr. B fr. 29 Sbordone, with the parallel at Treatise A col. b 4–5 Sbordone), and *PHerc.* 460 fr. 12.9–10 (= Tr. B fr. 13 Sbordone).

⁹⁹ *PHerc.* 460 fr. 21.8–10 (= Tr. B fr. 29 Sbordone).

Diogenes of Babylon.[100] In his synopsis of the order in which these terms were distinguished and came into use, Dionysius of Halicarnassus[101] states that πρόθεσις was among the latest additions to the system, when it was distinguished from σύνδεσμος. Quintilian[102] offers similar information.[103] Seemingly the term was added during the second century, which accords with our *terminus ad quem* for the text here summarized.

IV. Crates and the Linguistics of Diogenes of Babylon

We may ask, finally, in what context Crates presented his discussion of word-choice, word-order and euphony. The influence of handbooks of rhetoric and especially of Stoic treatments of dialectic is apparent in his emphases. Dionysius of Halicarnassus[104] tells us that, within the λεκτικὸς τόπος ("section on diction"), the discussion of word-choice preceded that of synthesis. Similarly, Diogenes Laërtius says that the Stoics divided rhetoric into expression, sequence and delivery.[105] This accords with the apparent order of topics in Treatises E and B.

Moreover, although Crates' terms for parts of speech do not correspond to those of Diogenes of Babylon, his treatise contains a striking parallel with Diogenes' theory of φωνή. Crates is arguing that the sound (which he calls both φωνή and ἦχος)[106] is the primary element in Homer's verses which enchants us and arouses us to exaltation:[107]

---

[100] D.L. VII 57–8: cf. the five-part "Stoic" system in the scholia to Dionysius Thrax, p. 517.33ff. Hilgard.

[101] *Comp.* 2.3: οἱ δὲ καὶ τὰ ἐπιρρήματα διεῖλον ἀπὸ τῶν ῥημάτων καὶ τὰς προθέσεις ἀπὸ τῶν συνδέσμων ("others too distinguished adverbs from verbs and prepositions from conjunctions"). "Praepositio" first appears in Cicero, *Orat.* 158.

[102] *Inst. Or.* I 4.19: paulatim a philosophis ac maxime Stoicis auctus est numerus, ac primum convinctionibus articuli adiecti, post praepositiones, nominibus appellatio, deinde pronomen, deinde mixtum verbo participium, ipsis verbis adverbia ("their number was gradually increased by philosophers, especially Stoics, and first articles and then prepositions were added to connectives, appellatives and then pronouns were added to nouns, and then participles were drawn from nouns and verbs, and adverbs were added to verbs"). See further Frede (above, n.3) 341–2.

[103] The appearance of πρόθεσις in this sense in a fragment of Chrysippus, *SVF* II 45 von Arnim, is surely doubtful.

[104] *Comp.* 2.6–7; cf. Cic. *De Orat.* III 149, and for further parallels Frede (above, n.3) 322.

[105] D.L. VII 43 (φράσις, τάξις and ὑπόκρισις).

[106] With this interchangeability cf. the Stoic distinction, probably derived from Diogenes of Babylon, at D.L. VII 57: διαφέρει φωνὴ καὶ λέξις, ὅτι φωνὴ μὲν καὶ ὁ ἦχός ἐστι, λέξις δὲ τὸ ἔναρθρον μόνον, "a word differs from speech, because sound

ὅτι δ' ἀρχηγὸν ἡ φωνὴ καὶ ἐκ τῶν ὀρνέων ἔστιν ἰδεῖν. καὶ γὰρ ἐπ' ἐκείνων χωριστοῦ ἐκπίπτοντος ἤχου ἀποτελεῖταί τις καὶ ἔναρθρος φωνή, καθάπερ καὶ ἐπὶ τῆ[ς ἀη]δ[όν]ος φέρεται. τὴν δ' ὑπο[τετα]γμένην ἔνν[οιαν ἀ]φῶμεν νῦν. οὐδ[ὲ γὰρ ὁ] σίττακος οἶδεν ε[ἰ τρα]γῳδίας λέγει στί[χον, ἀλ]λ' ὅμως ἀποτελεῖ[ται] τοὺς ἤχους οὕτω[ς ὡς] ὁ ἄνθρωπος.

... One can see from the case of birds too that the word is a principal element. For, in their case, a kind even of articulated word is produced from the separable sound which pours forth, just as is held to be true of the nightingale. Let us now leave aside the underlying intent. For a parrot does not know whether it is speaking a line from a tragedy, but it produces the sounds all the same, just as a person does.

In Diogenes' linguistic theory, it is the articulation of the sounds which makes language distinct from mere noise such as most animals produce. Yet, he argues, articulation alone is not a sufficient condition for intelligent speech, since birds like parrots produce articulated speech, yet do not understand it at all:[108]

ἄνθρωπος οὐ τῶι προφορικῶι λόγωι διαφέρει τῶν ἄλλων ζώιων (καὶ γὰρ κόρακες καὶ ψίττακοι καὶ κίτται ἐνάρθρους προφέρονται φωνάς), ἀλλὰ τῶι ἐνδιαθέτωι.[109]

A human being differs from other animals by using not speech which is pronounced (for crows, parrots and jays can pronounce articulated words), but speech which is internalised.

---

can be a word, but speech is only that which is articulate." Crates also used the Stoic term διάλεκτος at *PHerc.* 460 fr. 25.8 (= Tr. B fr. 18 Sbordone), even if not all the other references to it in Treatises E and B are his (*PHerc.* 444 fr. 16.22, 460 fr. 32b.20 (= Tr. B fr. 40 Sbordone), 460 fr. 31.14–15 (= Tr. B fr. 1 Sbordone), 444 fr. 2.21, 26 (τῶν [τ]ῆς διαλέκτ[ου] μερῶν); for this term cf. D.L. VII 56.

[107] *PHerc.* 460 fr. 9 19–1073 fr. 3.8 (= Tr. B fr. 26 cols. i–ii Sbordone).
[108] S.E. *adv. Math.* viii 275 (= *SVF* II 135, 223 von Arnim).
[109] Cf. his distinction between animal and human φωνή at D.L. VII 55–6: ζώιου μέν ἐστι φωνὴ ἀὴρ ὑπὸ (read ἀπὸ?) ὁρμῆς πεπληγμένος, ἀνθρώπου δ' ἔστιν ἔναρθρος καὶ ἀπὸ διανοίας ἐκπεμπομένη ... λόγος δέ ἐστι φωνὴ σημαντικὴ ἀπὸ διανοίας ἐκπεμπομένη ("the voice of an animal is air which has been struck as the result of instinct, that of a human being is articulate and emitted as a result of thought ... speech is a meaningful voice emitted as a result of thought"), and also that between speaking and pronouncing (ibid. VII 57): διαφέρει δὲ καὶ τὸ λέγειν τοῦ προφέρεσθαι· προφέρονται μὲν γὰρ αἱ φωναί, λέγεται δὲ καὶ τὰ πράγματα, ἃ δὴ καὶ λεκτὰ τυγχάνει ("saying differs from pronouncing, since sounds are pronounced, but things, which are the same as sayables, are said").

The similarities between these passages could be owed to a common source, but, since Diogenes and Crates were contemporaries, influence from one to the other seems likely. Now Diogenes' role in the evolution of linguistics turns out to have been fundamental; for, as Ax has shown, he updated Stoic theory about noise, voice and speech in the light of Aristotle's biology, with parrots as a prime example.[110] Since Crates seems not to have been interested in animals, whereas Diogenes was not only concerned with their intellectual capacities but also exploited the biological treatises of Aristotle, who notes parrots' ability to speak,[111] Crates seems more likely to depend on Diogenes than *vice versa*. His adoption of Diogenes' theory of sound (φωνή) makes him more a Stoic than anything else.

Now the theory of φωνή was central to Stoic dialectic, and the context in which Crates uses it sheds some light on that theory. The order shared by several Stoic treatises on dialectic is known from Diogenes Laërtius, who presents both a general outline at VII 43ff. and a combined summary of the treatises of Diogenes of Babylon, Posidonius and others at VII 55–62. Now in both summaries the first part of dialectic is the τόπος περὶ φωνῆς ("section on sound"), which comprised φωνή itself with its definition and the parts of speech. After this the first summary (VII 44) offers a peculiar set of topics, to which Schenkeveld has called attention.[112] He notes that, after the first topic, φωνή and the parts of speech (τὰ τοῦ λόγου μέρη), there then follows a heading, as delimited by the use of περί, entitled περὶ σολοικισμοῦ καὶ βαρβαρισμοῦ καὶ ποιημάτων καὶ ἀμφιβολίας ("on solecism, barbarism, verse and ambiguity"). This strange collocation of subjects is then followed by a distinct topic, περὶ ἐμμελοῦς φωνῆς ("on musical sound"). The common factor linking the items under the second heading is the use of language.[113] Solecisms and barbarisms are misuses of language, verse (specifically in Greek) contains peculiar uses of language, and ambiguities are equally problematic.

---

[110] Ax (above, n.3) 138–211; Schenkeveld, (above, n.1) 298–306. Ax has missed the parallel in Philodemus.
[111] *H.A.* VIII 12.597b27, cf. IX 13.615b19ff. on jays.
[112] Schenkeveld (above, n.36) 91.
[113] So Schenkeveld (above, n.36) 94, following Marc Baratin and Françoise Desbordes, *L'Analyse linguistique dans l'antiquité classique. I. Les Théories* (Paris: Horizons du langage 1981) 30–1.

I think we can go a step further and say that the common thread holding these topics together is *hellenismos* ("good Greek"). This, of course, is the first (and surely the most important)[114] of the "virtues of speech" (ἀρεταὶ λόγου), which in Diogenes Laertius' combined summary of the τόπος περὶ φωνῆς (VII 59–60) are defined after the parts of speech and before three of the four members of that same odd set, barbarism, solecism and poetry (ποίημα and ποίησις).[115] As Schenkeveld[116] has argued, the "virtues of speech" are limited to prose. For the Greeks poetic diction, and especially that of Homeric verse, presented a problem in relation to *hellenismos*.[117] The Homeric forms of the language were not in current use, and could not be restored to current use, yet how could one deny that the most canonical works of Greek literature were in correct Greek? Indeed, Aristarchus claimed that Homer was the author παρ' ὧι τὰ τοῦ ἑλληνισμοῦ ἠκρίβωται ("by whom good Greek has been perfected"),[118] and his pupil Ptolemy Pindarion went so far as to argue that Homeric Greek be revived as a spoken language.[119] That there were whole treatises on *hellenismos* is evident from Sextus Empiricus' lengthy treatment of the question "Is there a *techne* of *hellenismos*?" (*adv. Math.* I 176ff.), from references to works like Seleucus' Περὶ ἑλληνισμοῦ and from Varro's analogous *De Lingua Latina*.[120]

---

[114] Cf. Frede (above, n.3) 320. Contra: Schenkeveld (above, n.36) 97.

[115] As Schenkeveld observes (above, n.36) 89, 95–8), the postponement of ἀμφιβολία to follow the set of definitions from ὅρος to μερισμός is probably an error on Diogenes Laërtius' part, perhaps connected with a switch in his sources, from Diogenes of Babylon (chs. 55–8, 59?) to Posidonius (chs. 59?, 60a), then to Antipater (60b–61), and then back to Posidonius (62). But his exact procedure remains unclear.

[116] Above (n.36) 98–9.

[117] See Kees Versteegh, "Latinitas, Hellenismos, 'Arabiyya," Taylor (above, n.1) 251–74, esp. 264–7.

[118] Quoted in A.D. *Pron.* 71.20 Schn.

[119] Ap. S.E. *adv. Math.* I 202–3: ἀναλογία, φασίν (sc. οἱ ἀπὸ Πινδαρίωνος), ὁμολογουμένως ἐκ τῆς συνηθείας ὁρμᾶται· ἔστι γὰρ ὁμοίου καὶ ἀνομοίου θεωρία, τό τε ὅμοιον καὶ ἀνόμοιον ἐκ τῆς δεδοκιμασμένης λαμβάνεται συνηθείας. δεδοκιμασμένη δὲ καὶ ἀρχαιοτάτη ἐστὶν ἡ Ὁμήρου ποίησις· ποίημα γὰρ οὐδὲν πρεσβύτερον ἧκεν εἰς ἡμᾶς τῆς ἐκείνου ποιήσεως· διαλεξόμεθα ἄρα τῆι Ὁμήρου κατακολουθοῦντες συνηθείαι ("analogy, it is agreed, arises from approved common usage; for it is the observation of what is like and unlike, and what is like and unlike is taken from usage. But Homer's poetry is approved and the most ancient; for no verse has come down to us older than his poetry. So, then, we will converse in accord with Homer's usage.") See Franco Montanari, "Il Grammatico Tolomeo Pindarione, i poemi omerici e la scrittura," *Ricerche di Filologia Classica* I (Pisa: Giardini 1981) 97–114.

[120] Cf. Frede (above, n.3) 312.

Now for Crates, the primary virtue of diction is *hellenismos* or pure Greek, as we saw in the passage quoted above where he listed the "accidents."[121] A reference, apparently, to the converse of good Greek, βαρβαρισμός "barbarism," follows in the next column.[122] Soon afterwards, moreover, Crates argues that the need for good sound in poetry may override those of *hellenismos*, e.g. when Sophocles and Homer diverge from good Greek when they call, respectively, an anchor an ἰσχάς (normally "fig") or a column "long" (normally "tall").[123]

I have argued elsewhere[124] that the work of Crates which Philodemus is here summarising overlapped in content with Crates' 'Αττικὴ διάλεκτος or Περὶ τῆς 'Αττικῆς λέξεως ("On Attic speech"), in which *hellenismos* was the central focus.[125] His attention to *hellenismos* in the context of the Stoic theory of φωνή accords with and clarifies the results of recent research into the structure of the Περὶ φωνῆς. In response to the question "why should verse differ from normal Greek?," Crates formulated the answer that poets' apparent offences against normal Greek were to be justified by the overriding need for good sound, by which all good poets excel. The new material promises to confirm that Crates' views on poetry and language were of central importance in the tradition of Hellenistic grammatical science.

---

[121] *PHerc.* 460 fr. 16.13–25 (= Tr. B fr. 10 col. ii Sbordone).
[122] *PHerc.* 1073 fr. 10b.17–18 (= Tr. B fr. 37 Sbordone).
[123] *PHerc.* 460 fr 15 and fr. 14 (= Tr. B fr. 23 col. ii and fr. 6 col. i Sbordone).
[124] Janko (above, n.38) 94 n.145. It may be that this work is itself the object of Philodemus' attack.
[125] See frr. 65–70 Mette, with Mette (above, n.17) 48–55. It reached Athenaeus, significantly, via Seleucus' Περὶ ἑλληνισμοῦ (ap. Ath. IX 366d–367a): cf. above, n.79. Its authenticity is rejected, without reasons, by Pfeiffer (above, n.6) 243 n.4.

15

Aenesidemus and the Academics

Jaap Mansfeld

I. Photius on Aenesidemus: The Issue

In a brilliant and learned recent article[1] F. Decleva Caizzi argues that Photius' information concerning the founding father of Neopyrrhonism, Aenesidemus,[2] does not permit us to infer so to speak automatically that he was an Academic, though this has been the common view, and that there are reasons for believing that in fact he was not an Academic. She further argues that he was born at Cnossos not Aegae, and that it was at Aeolean Aegae, in the province of Asia, that he met the Lucius Tubero to whom he dedicated the book summarized by Photius. She uses this argument to buttress up the *opinio communis* that this person is L. Aelius Tubero,[3] *legatus* of Cicero's brother Quintus in Asia in 58 BC. In

---

[1] "Aenesidemus and the Academy," *CQ* 42 (1992) 176–89.
[2] Cf. Aristocles *ap.* Eus. *p.e.* XIV xviii.29: "nobody payed any attention to these people" (sc. Pyrrho and Timon) "just as if they had not existed at all, until rather recently a certain Aenesidemus in Alexandria in Egypt began to breathe new life into this nonsense." Aristocles' affirmation is not entirely correct, see below, text to nn. 48–51.
[3] Generally believed to be the dedicatee of Varro's *Tubero de origine humana* as well.

the present paper, dedicated to the good friend and exemplary scholar whom I first met some fifteen years ago at the German spa of Bad Homburg, I argue that the evidence found in Photius does not permit us to infer that Aenesidemus was *not* an Academic. I further argue that it is plausible that he actually began his career as an Academic, though strictly speaking this cannot be deduced from Photius' testimony. A *non liquet* remains a definite option.

Photius begins by advising us[4] that he read a treatise in eight books by Aenesidemus (ἀνεγνώσθη Αἰνησιδήμου Πυρρωνίων λόγοι η'). He then gives a summary of the "general theme of the work" (ἡ μὲν ὅλη πρόθεσις τοῦ βιβλίου), viz. the Pyrrhonist doctrine as distinguished from those of the other schools. He continues by telling us that Aenesidemus dedicated the work to an upper-class Roman who was "from the Academy."[5] A rather substantial and according to Photius virtually verbatim abstract (μικροῦ γλώσσῃ αὐτῇ ταὐτά φησιν) from the first book follows, concerned with the difference between Academics and Pyrrhonists. The Academics are dogmatic; they posit some things indubitably and unambiguously reject others. The Pyrrhonist position is described next, whereupon the author again turns to his opponents. "The Academics, he [sc. Aenesid.] says, of today in particular (οἱ δ' ἀπὸ τῆς 'Ακαδημίας, φησί, μάλιστα τῆς νῦν), in several respects agree with Stoic doctrines and in fact look like Stoics fighting (other) Stoics." They introduce virtue and stupidity, assume good and evil and true and false, and define probable and improbable, being and non-being as well as a lot of other things, affirming to disagree (sc. from the Stoics) only as to the cataleptic presentation. The Pyrrhonist position is again described as being very much different. The Academics contradict themselves by on the one hand arguing pro and contra anything, and on the

---

[4] In what follows I summarize Phot. *Bibl.* cod. 212 pp. 169b18–70a41 B. (A.A. Long and D.N. Sedley (tr.), *The Hellenistic Philosophers* I (Cambridge: Cambridge University Press (1987); hereafter LS) 71C). The edition used is R. Henry, *Photius: Bibliothèque*, Budé t.III (Paris: Les Belles Lettres 1962).

[5] γράφει δὲ τοὺς λόγους Αἰνησίδημος προσφωνῶν αὐτοὺς τῶν ἐξ 'Ακαδημίας τινὶ συναιρεσιώτῃ Λευκίῳ Τοβέρωνι, γένος μὲν 'Ρωμαίῳ, δόξῃ δὲ λαμπρῷ ἐκ προγόνων καὶ πολιτικὰς ἀρχὰς οὐ τὰς τυχούσας μετιόντι. The words 'with a distinguished political career' look more like flattery than description, as is only meet and proper in a letter of dedication. *Pace* Decleva Caizzi I believe that this does not help us to identify the dedicatee with certainty, though one has to admit that Q. Cicero's *legatus* may be our man if (a quite large if, see pt. II) Photius is not mistaken and if the Aegae mentioned by him is the Aeolian city. See also below, n.7, n.44.

other affirming that things are "cataleptic in a loose way" (κοινῶς ὑπάρχειν καταληπτά⁶).⁷

Photius concludes his introduction by telling us that this is what "Aenesidemus from Aegae" (ὁ Αἰνησίδημος ὁ ἐξ Αἰγῶν) writes about the difference between Pyrrhonists and Academics at the beginning of his work. He continues his abstract by listing the contents of the rest of book I and those of the following books.

II. Where Aenesidemus was Born

The first thing to be established is the nature of the material at Photius' disposal. It is clear that he had come across a codex containing this work of Aenesidemus,[8] perhaps *inter alia*. This sported a *subscriptio* stating the name of the author and the title of the work, but clearly lacked a *bios* or biobibliography. Accordingly it was not a learned edition. The work itself began with a dedicatory epistle from

---

[6] To introduce (μή> with Sandbach, followed by LS, or to read <ἀ>κατάληπτα with Hirzel, seems unnecessary.

[7] The contemporary Academics who so to speak betray the original Academic position whom Aenesidemus has in mind and seems to lump together are Philo of Larissa († 84/3) and his followers and, perhaps, Antiochus († 68/7, 16 years after Philo's death). For reports about Philo's view of the cataleptic presentation which agree with Aenesidemus' description of those of his anonymous opponents see Sext. *P.* I 235 = LS 68T and Cic. *Ac.Po.* II 18 = LS 68U. Texts concerning Philo's position are quoted and discussed by J. Glucker, *Antiochus and the Late Academy* (Göttingen: Vandenhoeck & Ruprecht 1978) 64 ff. For Antiochus' Stoicism likewise see Sext. *P.* I 235; cf. Cic. *Ac.Pr.* II 132 *appellabatur Academicus, erat quidem, si perpauca mutavisset, germanissimus Stoicus*, and Plut. *Cic.* iv *ad init*. This reference to his contemporaries dates Aenesidemus to the 1st half of the 1st cent. BC, see Glucker 118. J. Barnes, "Antiochus of Ascalon," M. Griffin and J. Barnes (eds.), *Philosophia togata: Essays on Philosophy and Roman Society* (Oxford: Clarendon Press 1989) 93–4, argues that Aenesidemus thinks of Philo only, because Antiochus "did not fight with the Stoics"; see also Glucker 117f. But Antiochus clearly still wanted to be called an *Academic*, and Philo, as far as I know, is never accused of being a crypto-Stoic (cf. Antiochus according to Cic. *Ac.Pr.* II 18: Philo's softening of the Stoic criterium leads to the position he wants to avoid, viz. *nihil posse comprehendi*). Ancient polemics are often crude, so one cannot be sure either way. If Antiochus is not included in Aenesidemus' criticism, the latter's treatise may perhaps be dated to about the same time as Antiochus' critique of Philo. This would give 68/7 as *t.a.q.*; L. Aelius Tubero was in Asia 10 years later. For the dates of Philo and Antiochus I of course follow T. Dorandi, *Ricerche sulla cronologia dei filosofi ellenistici* (Stuttgart: Teubner 1991) 60, 66ff., 74.

[8] On the titles ascribed to Aenesidemus see V. Brochard, *Les sceptiques grecs* (Paris: Vrin 1959²) 247f.

which Photius derived his information concerning the circumstances under which the treatise was published.[9]

According to Photius Aenesidemus is "from Aegae," whereas Diogenes Laertius, who mentions both his name and the title[10] of the work epitomized by Photius in his *diadoche* of Pyrrhonists (IX 116, a late fabrication[11]), says he is "a Cnossian" (Κνώσιος). Decleva Caizzi believes that this means "born at Cnossos" and argues that Diogenes' information should be accepted. She refers to Goedeckemeyer,[12] who she says is the only scholar to have been aware that "the expression ἐξ Αἰγῶν does not necessarily signify the place of birth, and so does not have to be taken as alternative to Cnossos." [13] I have checked the reference to Goedeckemeyer, who tells us that he bases his view that "ein hinzugefügter Stadtname nicht notwendig den Geburtsort bezeichnet" on a remark of Sprengel, according to whom Erasistratus (born at Ioulis in the isle of Ceos) was called a Samian because he was buried near Mykale, opposite Samos.[14] This clearly will not do. Adjectives derived from geographical names as a rule pertain to the place of birth but need not do so, whereas the preposition ἐκ followed by the name of a city (or country etc.) in the genitive must denote the place of provenance, or the place one has travelled from.[15] The *Suda* entry mentions both

---

[9] Two similar cases have been analyzed by J. Schamp, *Photios: historien des lettres. La* Bibliothèque *et ses notices biographiques,* Bib. de la Faculté de Phil. et Lett. de l'Univ. de Liège 248 (Paris: Les Belles Lettres 1987) 101ff., "Le bon usage des titres (codd. 97, 96, 98)," 103ff., "Hiéroclès: Le bon usage des dédicaces."

[10] Also mentioned at Sext. *M*. VIII 215, who quotes from book IV.

[11] F. Decleva Caizzi, *Pirrone: Testimonianze,* Elenches 5 (Napoli: Bibliopolis 1981) 271.

[12] A. Goedeckemeyer, *Die Geschichte des griechischen Skeptizismus* (Leipzig: Dieterich'sche Verlagsbuchhandlung 1905) 210 n.7.

[13] Decleva Caizzi (above, n.1) 179.

[14] He refers to "Sprengel, Versuch einer Gesch. der pragm. Arzneikunde [sic] I S. 540 f." without indicating the edition used. But in the one available to me (i.e. that in two fat volumes which Goedeckemeyer seems to have had in mind), *Kurt Sprengel's Versuch einer pragmatischen Geschichte der Arzneikunde,* 4. Aufl., m. Ber. u. Zus. vers. v. J. Rosenbaum, *Aelteste Geschichte der Medicin bis zur empirischen Schule,* Bd. I (Leipzig: Gebauersche Buchhandlung 1846) 521–3 on Erasistratus' biography, this is not found. In his "Vorrede," p. viii, Rosenbaum points out that "Sprengel, welcher überhaupt in vielen Stücken Autodidakt war, [...] eine gründliche grammatische Kenntnis des Griechischen abging."

[15] See LSJ *s.v.* ἐκ III 3. Decleva Caizzi fails to produce a parallel for ἐκ + the name of a city (or country) in the genitive which fails to do this. In the list of Arian bishops who attended the synod of Nicaea in the excerpt (not by Photius) from book I of Philost. *h.e.* (I 8a, p. 9) expressions such as ἐκ ... τῆς ἄνω Λιβύης, ἐκ ... Θηβῶν τῶν 'Αἰγυπτίων,

Erasistratus' place of birth, using and explaining the ethnicon ('Ιουλιήτης, ἀπὸ 'Ιουλιάδος πόλεως Κέω τῆς νήσου), and his place of burial (τέθαπται δὲ πρὸς τῷ ὄρει τῇ Μυκάλῃ καταντικρὺ Σάμου).[16] In the two passages where Erasistratus is called "Samian" the formula is the ethnicon Σάμιος, not the expression ἐκ Σάμου. These are Jul. *Mis.* 17.13–14 ἆθλος ἰατρῷ προύτέθη τῷ Σαμίῳ (Erasistratus' name is mentioned subsequently), and Steph. *in Progn.*, *CMG* XI 1,2 p. 58.30–1 ἐγνώσθη τῷ βασιλεῖ Σελεύκῳ περὶ Ἐρασιστράτου τοῦ Σαμίου.[17] What we have here are versions of the story of prince Antiochus' infatuation with his father's wife Eurydice which was diagnosed by Erasistratus. Another apparent parallel is the formula "Posidonius, Apamean from Syria or Rhodian" (adjectives again).[18] Other testimonia however show that Posidonius, born at Apamea, was called Apamean because this was his place of birth and Rhodian because he became a citizen of Rhodes and made his living there.[19] He is never said to be ἐκ 'Ρόδου.

We may therefore infer that, when taken *au pied de la lettre*, Diogenes' ethnicon Κνώσιος may pertain either to Aenesidemus' place of birth, or to a city of which he became a citizen or where he was active for a certain period of time, or to a place where (or near which) he was buried. But it is by no means certain that Κνώσιος is correct in some sense or other. Diogenes may have erred, or the tradition he follows may have been mistaken.[20] Photius' unambiguous ἐξ Αἰγῶν can only refer to a place of birth. If this designation was based on documentary evidence it will have been the *subscriptio* of the book he excerpted.[21] I have done a *TLG*-search for αἰγων, from which I have had to eliminate numerous

---

ἐκ ... Παλαιστίνης etc. denote the provinces the bishops travelled from. Their individual sees are as a rule indicated by the ethnicon. The edition referred to is Philostorgius: *Kirchengeschichte* ed. J. Bidez, *GCS* 68 (Leipzig: J.C. Hinrichs'sche Buchhandlung 1913), 3rd rev. ed. F. Winkelmann (Berlin: Akademie-Verlag 1981).

[16] *Suda* 2 p. 402.25ff. = Erastr. fr. 1A Gar. (I. Garofalo, *Erasistrati fragmenta* (Pisa: Gardini 1988)).

[17] The first passage = Erasistr. fr. 26C Gar., the second is lacking in this collection. Garofalo (above, n.16) 17 n.130 suggests that Julian's 'Samian' may derive from the story of the place of burial (cf. above, text to n.14).

[18] Ποσειδώνιος 'Απαμεὺς ἐκ Συρίας ἢ 'Ρόδιος, *Suda* 4 p.179.22 = Pos. T1a E.-K.

[19] T2a, 2b and 4 E.-K. At F81 E.-K. he is called Ποσειδώνιος ὁ 'Ρόδιος without further explanation.

[20] See above, text to n.11.

[21] Decleva Caizzi (above, n.1) 179 suggests that the expression ἐξ Αἰγῶν was found in the dedicatory epistle, but fails to indicate how it figured there.

goats in the genitive plural and a few proper names. Little remains that is of some use. Dioscurid. *Mat.Med.* I 26.1 speaks of a drug ἐξ Αἰγῶν τῆς Αἰτωλίας, i.e. gives Aetolian Aegae as its place of provenance. Damasc. *Vit.Isid.* fr. 69 *ap.* Phot. *Bibl.* cod. 242 speaks of someone who got his wife from Cilician Aegae (ἐξ Αἰγῶν δὲ κατήγετο τῶν Κιλικίων ἡ γυνή). But the *subscriptio* in the codex used by Photius may have been wrong or have lacked the ethnicon. It also remains a definite possibility that Photius made a mistake, because the author of the book excerpted before that of Aenesidemus is "Dionysius the Aegaean" (cod. 211, p. 186b21 B.: Διονυσίου Αἰγέως). Decleva Caizzi appeals to the authority of Schamp, who states that Photius hardly ever makes mistakes of this nature.[22] But hardly ever is not good enough. An example of such a mistake is provided by Hägg in his methodically exemplary study of Photius' methods and practice.[23] At cod. 44 (p. 9b20–1 B.) Photius says that Philostratus is a Tyrian (Φιλοστράτου Τυρίου), whereas all our other evidence, including that of the subscriptions of the extant manuscripts of the *Vita Apollonii*, presents him as a Lemnian.[24]

On the basis of the available evidence one can only conclude to a *non liquet*. We cannot really be sure whether Cnossus or Aegae was Aenesidemus' place of birth or a place where he worked and/or was buried.[25] Aristocles in unambiguous terms mentions Alexandria (not Aegae or Cnossus) as the city where he was active, but his expression "a certain Aenesidemus" reveals that he knew next to nothing about the man.[26] There is no reason, however, to deny that Aenesidemus may have spent some time at Alexandria; this, at any rate, offers a sound explanation for the fact that Philo came to know the tropes used at *Ebr.* 169–202.

---

[22] Decleva Caizzi (above, n.1) 176 n.3, referring to Schamp (above, n.9).
[23] T. Hägg, *Photios als Vermittler antiker Literatur. Untersuchungen zur Technik des Referierens und Exzerpierens in der Bibliotheke* (Uppsala/Stockholm: Almqvist & Wiksell International 1975). This study is exemplary because the author argues from the known to the unknown; he studies Photius' excerpts from extant originals, so that we are in a position to check what he did.
[24] Hägg (above, n.23) 17 and n.2, with references to attempts at explaining the mistake. A work by another Φιλοστράτου Τυρίου is briefly mentioned cod. 150, p. 99b4 B.
[25] Alternative *ethnica* may be listed in a single source, see e.g. D.L. IX 30 (Leucippus) and IX 34 (Democritus).
[26] See above, n.2.

III. The Meaning of Συναιρεσιώτης

Aenesidemus' original philosophical allegiance is of more importance than his place of birth. Is the contention justified that the description of the dedicatee as τῶν ἐξ 'Ακαδημίας τινὶ συναιρεσιώτῃ has to be translated "a member of the Academic sect" and that this merely is a formula which is expressive of Photius' critical attitude towards Scepticism in general?[27] Or, to put it more strongly, should we interpret συναιρεσιώτῃ as meaning "to a member of a *different* sect," viz. of the Academy as different from Aenesidemus' own Pyrrhonist school?

It has to be granted that συναιρεσιώτης is a rare word, used by Photius and a few other Christian authors to designate Arians or other heretics. It is also feasible to compare it with the astrological term συναιρετίστης found in Vettius Valens and others, but *pace* Decleva Caizzi it should not be called a "variant" of the latter. Its closest relative is the equally rare term συστασιώτης, already found in Herodotus. These words are compounds of αἱρεσιώτης and στασιώτης, which in their turn derive—by means of the suffix -(ω)της—from nouns on -σις, viz. αἵρεσις and στάσις, whereas αἱρετίστης and its compound συναιρετίστης derive from the verb αἱρετίζω. Συστασιώτης means 'member of the same faction' or "fellow-conspirator" at Hdt. V 70 and 124.[28] Simpl. *in Cael.* 91.8 interestingly uses it to indicate Aristotle's followers (τοὺς ἑαυτοῦ συστασιώτας), that is to say those belonging to his school.[29] One of the meanings of στάσις besides that of (seditious) "faction" is (philosophical) "position,"[30] just as αἵρεσις may mean (philosophical, or medical) "viewpoint" or "school" as well as "quarrelsome view" or even "heresy." In fact, these words and their derivatives may be used in both in a neutral and a pejorative sense ("sect" *vs* "heresy"). The word αἱρετίστης is used for "partisan" or "follower" in a

---

[27] Decleva Caizzi (above, n.1) 182ff., also for what follows.
[28] Cf. e.g. Strab. XIV v.14, Proc. *Bell. Pers.* I xxiv.5. Damasc. *Vit. Isid.* fr. 258 οἱ τῆς ἀλλοφύλου δόξης ἑταῖροι καὶ συστασιῶται *ap.* Phot. *Bibl.* cod. 181 is unclear.
[29] Cf. the similar formulas at Gal. *Adv. Jul.* XVIIIA 258 K., οὕτως Πλάτων ἅμα τοῖς ἀπ' αὐτοῦ πᾶσιν, οὕτως 'Αριστοτέλης ἅμα τοῖς ἐκ τοῦ Περιπάτου, οὕτως Ζήνων καὶ Χρύσιππος ἅμα τοῖς ἄλλοις Στωϊκοῖς ἐγίγνωσκον.
[30] Sext. P. I 222, II 48, III 33, III 37. At Plut. *Cic.* iv *ad init.*, on Antiochus who "seceded from what is called the New Academy ... and left the faction of Carneades (τὴν Καρνεάδου στάσιν ἐγκατέλειπεν)" the meaning of στάσις is close to that of αἵρεσις in the sense of "school."

political sense.[31] It may also denote the purported founder of a philosophical sub-sect (Ariston at D.L. VII 161) or the followers of a particular philosopher (the Heracliteans at D.L. IX 6, the followers of Socrates, Plato, Aristotle and Zeno respectively at Clem.Al. *Strom.* VI xviii.167.3). The earliest instances of the term in this meaning are in the famous passage[32] about the three main Jewish "philosophical schools" at Jos. *B.J.* II 119, 124 and 141. Other terms that may be compared in this context are συσχολαστής,[33] "fellow-pupil" or, more rarely, "younger colleague," and συνουσιαστής, "pupil."[34]

I have looked at Decleva Caizzi's instances for συναιρεσιώτης meaning "sectarian," or (Arian) "heretic" in general, rather than "fellow-sectarian."[35] These are to be found in Photius' extensive excerpts of the Arian church historian Philostorgius, *damnatae memoriae*, a separate work,[36] in the brief excerpt from this author at *Bibl.* cod. 40, in the treatment of Eunomius in cod. 137, and in the *Amphilochiae*. She points out that some among these passages show that this word may be used absolutely, viz. without an accompanying genitive, and so could mean "member of a sect." In the passage about Tubero, she argues, "the compound word with συν- pertains quite naturally to τῶν ἐξ Ἀκαδημίας and does not need an external reference such as Aenesidemus."[37] My first objection is that this makes the word συναιρεσιώτῃ superfluous. The expression τῶν ἐξ Ἀκαδημίας τινί by itself already means "to a member of the Academy," the preposition ἐκ (or ἐξ) + the name of a school denoting the affiliation[38] and τινί the

---

[31] Polyb. I 79.10, II 38.7, II 55.8, XXI 23.11, D.S. XVIII 75.2.
[32] Cribbed by Porph. *Abst.* IV 11–13, which in its turn is transcribed at Eus. *p.e.* IX iii.
[33] "Fellow-pupil:" Strab. XIII i.67 (ἐκ δὲ τῆς Πιτάνης ἐστὶν Ἀρκεσίλαος ὁ ἐκ τῆς Ἀκαδημίας, Ζήνωνος τοῦ Κιτιέως συσχολαστὴς παρὰ Πολέμωνι, cf. XIV i.34), Plut. *Rect. rat.* 47E, D.L. IV 30, Epiph. *haer.* (*Panarion*) I 247.19, 255.19, 256.23, II 189.17, II 333.18. "Younger colleague:" D.L. VII 9.
[34] Xen. *Mem.* I 6, [Plat.] *Min.* 319e, Jos. *Ap.* I 164, D.H. *Lys.* 3, [Plut.] *Lib. ed.* 8B, Iust. *dial.* 2.4, Phot. *Bibl.* cod. 158, p. 100b28 B. (cf. cod. 229, p. 253a8).
[35] Decleva Caizzi (above, n.1) 183–5.
[36] See above, n.15.
[37] Decleva Caizzi (above, n.1) 185.
[38] Ephipp. *Nauag.* fr. 1 *ap.* Ath. XI 509c τῶν ἐξ Ἀκαδημίας τις, Strab. I xiii.66.4–5 προσποιούμενος δ' ἅμα τῶν τε ἐξ Ἀκαδημίας φιλοσόφων εἶναι, Strab. XVII iii.22.18–20, Καρνεάδης (οὗτος δὲ τῶν ἐξ Ἀκαδημίας ἄριστος φιλοσόφων ὁμολογεῖται), Simpl. *in Cat.* 212.8 οἱ δὲ ἐξ Ἀκαδημίας, Plut. *An seni* 798B τινα τῶν ἐκ τοῦ Κήπου φιλοσόφων, Plut. *Frat. am.* 485A <ὡς τὸν> ἐκ τῆς Στοᾶς σοφόν, Plut.

individual concerned. Photius himself, in the same codex (p. 170a24 B.), uses οἱ δ' ἐξ 'Ακαδημίας for "Academics." So if he had wanted to say that Tubero was an Academic without implicating Aenesidemus he might simply have omitted συναιρεσιώτῃ. What is more, the genitive τῶν depends on τινί and συναιρεσιώτης is a further qualification of this τινί.[39]

The evidence adduced by Decleva Caizzi in favour of her translation of συναιρεσιώτης is in my view insufficient and at any rate does not entail that the word *must* have this meaning.[40] The excerpt at Philost. *h.e.* II 8, which p. 19.11 B. begins with the words ὅτι περὶ 'Αγαπητοῦ τοῦ συναιρεσιώτου, is about this Agapetos. The name is a rather common one; what Photius wants to emphasize, or so I believe, is that this person was a follower of Arius *just like* Philostorgius; hence "belonging to the same heresy." *Ibid.* IV 4 p. 60.14–16 the Arian Eudoxios (a per-

---

St. abs. 1058D ὁ δ' ἐκ τῆς Στοᾶς βοῶν μέγα, [Gal.] *Qual.Incorp.* XIX 473 K. (*SVF* II 386) ἐκ τῆς Στοᾶς, Gal. *MM* X 17 K. κατὰ τοὺς ἐκ τοῦ Περιπάτου καὶ κατὰ τοὺς ἐκ τῆς Στοᾶς, Asp. *in EN* 44.13 οἱ μὲν οὖν ἐκ τῆς Στοᾶς (cf. *ibid.* 44.23, 45.16; texts at *SVF* III 386), *ibid.* 44.20 τῶν δὲ ἐκ τοῦ Περιπάτου, Simpl. *in de An.* 217.36–7 (*SVF* II 395) παρὰ τοῖς ἐκ τῆς Στοᾶς λέγεται, Polyb. V 93.8 ἦν δὲ τῶν ἐπιφανῶν ἀνδρῶν ἐκ τοῦ Περιπάτου καὶ ταύτης τῆς αἱρέσεως, D.H. *Amm.* 1.3–4 τῶν φιλοσόφων τις τῶν ἐκ τοῦ Περιπάτου, Strab. XIV v.4 ἄνδρες ἀξιόλογοι τῶν ἐκ τοῦ Περιπάτου φιλοσόφων 'Αθήναιός τε καὶ Ξέναρχος, Luc. *Demon.* 54 τὸν χωλὸν τὸν ἐκ τοῦ Περιπάτου, *Eun.* 3 τοῖς ἐκ τοῦ Περιπάτου, *Philops.* 6 Κλεόδημός τε ἦν ὁ ἐκ τοῦ Περιπάτου, Ath. VI 249a Νικόλαος δ' ὁ Δαμασκηνὸς (εἷς δ' ἦν τῶν ἐκ τοῦ Περιπάτου), Ael. *NA* XII 34 (= Clearch. fr. 103 W). λέγει δὲ Κλέαρχος ὁ ἐκ τοῦ Περιπάτου, Gal. *Nat.Fac.* II 88 K. τοῖς ἐκ τοῦ Περιπάτου φιλοσόφοις (cf. *ibid.* II 90 K., 116 K.), Gal. *PHP* II 3.24 τοὺς ἐκ τοῦ Περιπάτου, Gal. *MM* X 15 K. οἱ ἐκ τοῦ Περιπάτου κριταί, Gal. *Inst.Log.* vii.2 καὶ μέντοι καὶ τῶν ἐκ τοῦ Περιπάτου τινὲς ὥσπερ καὶ Βόηθος (cf. *ibid.* 19.2 οἱ ἐκ τοῦ Περιπάτου γεγράφασιν), Clem.Al. *Strom.* II vii.34.1 τοῖς ἐκ Περιπάτου (cf. *ibid.* II xxiii.138.6, V ix.59.2), Sext. *P.* III 181 οἱ ἐκ τοῦ Περιπάτου (cf. *M.* IX 334), Eus. *p.e.* VII 14.1 τινες εἰρήκασι τῶν ἐκ τῆς αἱρέσεως ὄντες τοῦ Περιπάτου, Jul. *Adv.Cyn.* viii.38 οἵ τε ἐκ τοῦ Περιπάτου, Porph. *Intr.* 1.15 οἱ ἐκ τοῦ Περιπάτου (cf. Procl. *in R.* I 237.8, I 252.24, I 253.12, Procl. *in Alc.* 296.13, Procl. *in Prm.* 888.1, 892.10, 1024.9, Ammon. *in Porph.* 46.21, Ammon. *in APr.* 10.20, Ascl. *in Metaph.* 178.20, Simpl. *in Ph.* 579.28, 923.3, 1036.4, Simpl. *in de An.* 268.10, David *in Porph.* 190.14, Steph. *in Int.* 10.31).

[39] I cite a few parallel constructions: Aesch. *Pr.* 897 μηδὲ πλαθείην γαμέτᾳ τινὶ τῶν ἐξ οὐρανοῦ (cf. scholia *ad loc.*), Strab. VIII vi.22.36 χρησμὸς ὁ δοθείς τινι τῶν ἐκ τῆς 'Ασίας ἐρωτῶντι, Gal. *Aff.Dig.* V 18 K. συνωδοιπόρησά τινι φίλῳ τῶν ἐκ Γόρτυνος τῆς Κρήτης ἀνδρί, Greg. Nyss. *Eun.* I 50.6 συνῆν τὰ πρῶτα τῶν ἐκ τοῦ γένους οἶμαί τινι.

[40] At Hipp. *Ref.* IX 23.20–1 Marc. μηδὲν ἀποκρύπτειν τοὺς συναιρεσιώτας (listed at Decleva Caizzi (above, n.1) 183 n.24), the word *must* mean "members of the same sect."

son who plays a rather large role in the *h.e.*), on becoming bishop of Antioch as successor of Leontios, is persuaded to change his mind about an important point of doctrine; those who persuade him are οἱ συναιρεσιῶται. The translation "fellow-heretics" seems to have more point than "(Arian) heretics," though the latter is possible (actually, it is hard to distinguish the meaning of the first of these translations from the second). *Ibid.* V 5 p. 69.13–14 (bishop Meletios) μεταπέμπεται ... ἐξ Ἀλεξανδρείας τὸν συναιρεσιώτην Ἀρείου Εὐζώϊον, the translations "member of the heretic sect of Arius" and "fellow-member of the heretic sect of Arius" are equally feasible, though one cannot help feeling that Photius wants us to understand that Meletios summons a fellow-partisan, or rather fellow-heretic. *Ibid.* X 12 p. 131.4 (Philostorgius) λέγει γὰρ περί τινος Εὐδοξίου, συναιρεσιώτου μὲν κτλ., Photius again seems to wish to emphasize that this Eudoxios—who is to be distinguished from the above-cited bishop Eudoxios and is mentioned for the first time here—was an Arian too, like Philostorgius himself. Phot. *Bibl.* cod. 40 p. 8a6ff. (also printed as Philost. *h.e.* IV 12b p. 65.34ff. B.)[41] is about the famous Arian Aetius who is deposed ὑπ' αὐτῶν τῶν συναιρεσιωτῶν, as according to Photius Philostorgius is forced to admit *malgré lui* (καὶ μὴ βουλόμενος). The scandal, of course, is that Aetius was deposed by *his own* people, "ses propres frères en hérésie" (tr. Henry). At *Bibl.* cod. 137 p. 97b2–3 B. τοῖς συναιρεσιώταις Εὐνομίου διὰ θαύματος μὲν ἤγετο, both "the heretic followers of Eunomius" and "Eunomius' fellow-heretics" (i.e. fellow-Arians) are possible translations. Phot. *Amphil.* Qu. 154.18ff. West. is about the edition of the Bible by Theodotion, who belonged to the sect of Marcion. He published this edition to spite his "fellow-heretics" (τοῖς συναιρεσιώταις μηνίων) rather than "the heretics" in general. *Ibid.* Qu. 312.23ff. is about a person called Asterius who is "rewarded by his fellow-heretics" (rather than "by the (Arian) heretics"—μισθὸν ... παρὰ τῶν συναιρεσιωτῶν) and becomes bishop.

In whatever way one translates, there can be no doubt that the sectarians, or heretics, at issue belong to the same sect or heresy as the protagonist (or, in Philostorgius' case, the excerpted author). It is also significant that the word αἱρεσιώτης is not found in the excerpts from the *h.e.* But it does occur three times in the *Bibl.*, where each time it means

---

[41] Twice quoted by Decleva Caizzi (above, n.1) 183, viz. both among the five texts taken from the *h.e.* and among the two from *Bibl.* cod. 40.

"heretic:" cod. 120 (brief excerpt from Iren. *haer.*), p. 94a2, cod. 177 (substantial excerpt from a work by Theodore of Antioch), p. 122b14, and cod. 228 (excerpts from various works of Ephrem of Antioch), p. 246b2 B. It is hard to see why Photius, assuming he wanted to call Tubero a "heretic" from the Academy rather than an Academic "fellow-heretic" of Aenesidemus, refrained from using αἱρεσιώτης instead of συναιρεσιώτης at the beginning of cod. 212.

IV. Aenesidemus and the Academy: The Tradition Transformed

My conclusion is that Photius meant to say that Aenesidemus dedicated his work to Aelius Tubero, an Academic who belonged to his own sect, viz. Aenesidemus' sect. Photius' abstract from the first book of Aenesidemus' treatise pays ample attention to the distinction between Academics and (Neo)Pyrrhonists. Though Photius may well have believed that these varieties of Scepticism are two of a kind, the assumption that when calling Tubero a fellow-sectarian of Aenesimus he failed to distinguish between the two schools is implausible.[42]

The following hypothesis in my view is a more likely solution of the puzzle. Both Aenesidemus and Tubero originally were Academics. Aenesidemus did not at all like the dogmatist turn taken by the Stoicizing Academics who were his contemporaries. He rejected the

---

[42] Yet this distinction may be ignored by ancient authors. Epict. *Diss.* I 27.2 speaks of σοφίσματα ... Πυρρώνεια καὶ Ἀκαδημαϊκά, cf. *ibid.* 27.15 ἐρχέσθω καὶ ἀπαντάτω Πυρρώνειος καὶ Ἀκαδημαϊκός, though I 5 is entitled Πρὸς τοὺς Ἀκαδημαϊκούς. Gal. *Opt.Doct.* I 48 K. speaks of Ἀκαδημαϊκοί τε καὶ Πυρρώνειοι in one and the same breath, cf. *Pecc.Dig.* V 60 K. κατὰ μὲν τοὺς Ἀκαδημαϊκούς τε καὶ Πυρρωνείους. Luc. *Icar.* 25 *ad fin.* says τὸ Ἀκαδημαϊκὸν ἐκεῖνο ἐπεπόνθει καὶ οὐδέν τι ἀποφήνασθαι δυνατὸς ἦν, ἀλλ' ὥσπερ ὁ Πύρρων ἐπεῖχεν ἔτι καὶ διεσκέπτετο, for which he is rebuked in the scholia *ad loc.*: οὐκ ἀκριβῶς τὴν Ἀκαδημίαν τοῖς Πυρρωνείοις ἤτοι Ἐφεκτικοῖς ἀπονέμεις, Λουκιανέ· ἀντιδιαστέλλονται γὰρ τούτοις οἱ ἐξ Ἀκαδημίας, ὡς αὐτῶν ἔστιν ἐκείνων τῶν Πυρρωνείων ἀκοῦσαι ἐν ταῖς Ὑποτυπώσεσιν. Cf. also Phil. *QG* III 33, lumping together 'those which are now called Academics and Sceptics', and Sen. *Ep.* 88.43 *circa eadem etiam fere Pyrrhonei versantur et Megarici et Eretrici et Academici*. The difference between the Academics and the Pyrrhonists would never have been the theme of numerous ancient studies (Gell. XI v.5, who cites a book by Favorinus as an example and might have added the monograph by Plutarch listed as no. 64 in the *Lamprias Cat.*; see further e.g. C. Lévy, *Cicero Academicus: Recherches sur les Académiques et sur la philosophie cicéronienne*, Coll. École française de Rome 162 (Rome: École française de Rome 1992) 22ff.) if there had been no problem.

position of the sceptic Academics in general but, as we have seen, disagreed *"mostly"* with "those of today," which entails that his critique of their great predecessors will have been less strong. He argued for a return to the earlier sceptic Academy (viz. that of Arcesilaus) and more specifically for a return to the Pyrrho who according to contemporaries of Arcesilaus, viz. the Stoic Ariston of Chios and Pyrrho's follower Timon, had been an important source of inspiration for Arcesilaus.[43] The historical reliability of these affirmations is irrelevant in this context. Aenesidemus so to speak started a Pyrrhonist current in the Academy and was able (or at least attempted)[44] to win over the upper-class dedicatee of his treatise to this point of view. Neopyrrhonism began its career as a αἵρεσις within a αἵρεσις, that is to say as an anti-Stoic subsect in what out of courtesy one might still have called the Academic sect, or if you wish as a sub-school of thought within an already pluriform school of thought. This explains the sense in which a follower of the Academy such as Tubero could be a fellow-sectarian of Aenesidemus. The original terminology used by the latter to describe this situation has been replaced by Photius' συναιρεσιώτῃ, but we need not doubt the material accuracy of this designation.

What happened to the Academy in the first century BC is that it split up into various factions, or sub-sects: that of its last scholarch,[45] Philo of Larissa, who made concessions to the Stoic theory of knowledge, that of Antiochus of Ascalon, who went much further and tried to restore an ideal earliest Academy, incorporating Aristotelianism and Stoicism into Platonism,[46] the one-man faction of Cicero, who—not without overstating his case—considered himself practically the sole remaining representative of the Academy of Arcesilaus and Carneades,[47] and that of

---

[43] See the cento of Ariston's witty and well-known parody of a Homeric line (*SVF* I 343) and of lines of Timon (fr. 16 Diels) at both Num. fr. 25.19ff. des Places (*ap.* Eus. *p.e.* XIV v.13) and D.L. IV 33.

[44] Aenesidemus' Tubero may have been a lukewarm follower of the Academy. For the lukewarm relations to Epicureanism of Memmius, the dedicatee of Lucretius' epic, see B.K. Gould, *Literary Patronage in Greece and Rome* (Chapel Hill/London: The University of North Carolina Press 1987) 51ff., and L. Canfora, *Vita di Lucrezio* (Palermo: Sellerio 1993) 44ff., 52ff.

[45] See Glucker (above, n.7) 105f., 111, 120.

[46] For Antiochus' return to the *veteres* see e.g. Barnes (above, n.7) 78ff., also for references to the literature.

[47] *N.D.* I 11–12, where he states that there is almost no Academic left in Greece; *Ac.Po.* I 43, *Ac.Pr.* II 7–11. See further e.g. E. Rawson, *Cicero: A Portrait* (London: Allan Lane 1975) 233ff. That he either did not know about Aenesidemus or failed to

Aenesidemus, who argued for a return to undiluted scepticism and sought to affiliate himself with Pyrrho's legacy. This appeal to Pyrrho is entirely comparable to Antiochus' appeal to Socrates, Plato, Aristotle and Zeno of Citium.[48]

As a matter of fact, attempts were made by others to connect Pyrrho with the section of the Ionian succession[49] deriving from Socrates: via Stilpon of Megara (D.L. IX 61, citing the *Successions* of Alexander Polyhistor,[50] who, it should be noted, is a contemporary of Aenesidemus),[51] via Euclides of Megara (*Suda* 4 p. 404.19–21, no source cited), or via Phaedon of Elis (Strab. IX i.8, no source cited). The historical truth of these constructions, which has bothered scholars no end, is of course not the issue.[52] History was being rewritten to a definite purpose.

Of these first-century BC Academics, only Aenesidemus eventually became the founding father of a new and successful school (which, however, posed as a venerably old one). In this context it is important to note that in his discussion of the differences between (Neo)Pyrrhonism and the other schools Sext. *P.* I 232 says that Arcesilaus' views are virtually indistinguishable from Pyrrhonism.[53] The hypothesis that this view

---

take notice is no more mysterious than the absence of references in the philosophical treatises to Lucretius, (parts of ?) whose epic he knew and admired (*Ad fam.* II 9[11].3, *Lucretii poemata*). For *poemata* (which may be translated 'poetry') designating an entire epic, *pace* the arguments adduced by Canfora, *o.c.* 19f., see e.g. Plato *Parm.* 128a (not in DK), *Akt.* (Stob. *Ecl.* I 52.6 only) IV 13.10 = Parm. fr. 28A48 DK, Plut. *Quom. adul.* 16CD = Parm. fr. 28A15 DK (on the epics of among others, Parmenides and Empedocles), Clem. *Strom.* V xiv 101.4, Diog. Laert. VIII 55 = Parm. fr. 28A9 DK and Emp. fr. 31A1 DK, VIII 59 = Emp. fr. 31A1 DK (note that each of Empedocles' epics contained more than one book), IX 22 = Parm. fr. 28A1.

[48] On this search for archegetes O. Gigon, "Die Erneuerung der Philosophie in der Zeit Ciceros," *Recherches sur la tradition platonicienne*, Entr. Hardt 3 (Vandœuvres & Genève: Fondation Hardt 1955) 23–59 is still worth reading.

[49] The usual position of the early Pyrrhonists is in the Italian (*cum* Eleatic) succession; this for instance is where D.L. VIII–X posits them. The three passages which place Pyrrho among the followers of Socrates are conveniently accessible at Decleva Caizzi (above, n.11), T 1 A (where p. 83 the transl. "Brisone, figlio di Stilpone" should be replaced by "B., allievo" or "compagno di S."), T 2 and T 3.

[50] *FGrH* 273F92.

[51] For the date see R. Goulet, "Alexandre de Milet, dit Polyhistor," R. Goulet (ed.), *Dictionnaire des philosophes antiques* I (Paris: Editions du CNRS 1989) 144 and R. Giannatasio Andria, *I frammenti delle <<Successioni dei filosofi>>* (Napoli: Arte Tipografica 1989) 115f.

[52] For the problematic aspects of Alexander's affirmation see Giannatasio Andria (above, n.49) 127, with references to the discussion.

[53] LS 68I. But at *P.* I 233–4 Sextus lists arguments in favour of making a distinction.

derives from Aenesidemus seems feasible. Numenius fr. 25.72ff. des Places *ap*. Eus. *p.e.* XIV vi.6[54] is even quite gossipy about Arcesilaus' (crypto)-Pyrrhonism. He states that that he was "a Pyrrhonist in actual fact and an Academic in name only,"[55] and that his only motive for calling himself an Academic was his esteem for his lover. Numenius too will have availed himself of Neopyrrhonist sources, but from the perspective of the Platonic *diadoche* apparently liked to stand on its head what he found in these works.

---

[54] LS 68F.
[55] Cf. the similar formula describing Antiochus quoted above, n.7.

16

The Pathology of Ps.-Hippocrates, *On Ancient Medicine*

Robin Waterfield

It was Ian Kidd who first made me read *On Ancient Medicine* thoroughly, by asking me to teach on it, while I was a young lecturer in his Department of Greek at the University of St. Andrews. So I am delighted to have the opportunity to offer him some thoughts on this important treatise, in memory of three happy years at St. Andrews and of the subsequent congenial co-authorship of a book.

The general theme of this collection of essays is the influence of an individual ancient author on the transformation of the tradition within which he worked. The influence of the author of *On Ancient Medicine* (I shall refer to both the treatise and the author as VM, for short) on medical tradition has perhaps been exaggerated at times. Gomperz, for instance, hailed VM as the forerunner of positivism.[1] That this is far from being the case has been shown most persuasively by Lloyd.[2] One might say at the most that the author has an intuitive understanding of the importance of empiricism, and that he brings forward some good

---

[1] T. Gomperz, *Greek Thinkers* 1 (London: John Murray 1901) 297ff.
[2] Especially G.E.R. Lloyd, *Magic, Reason and Experience* (Cambridge: Cambridge University Press 1979) 147ff.

arguments against the common non-empirical trend in Greek medicine; but it must also be said that his own theories are equally liable to the same or similar arguments, and thus that he fails to live up to his intuition. In particular, it is hard to see how he feels he can get away with attacking aetiologies of disease which depend on the hot, cold, wet and dry (chapters 13–19), while relying himself on factors such as "the salty, the bitter, the sweet, the acidic, the astringent, the insipid, καὶ ἄλλα μυρία" (14.31–5).[3] Perhaps it is because VM's theory is more complex and less generalized, since it allows for a larger number of factors, that he feels it is better (see 19.18–21); it is capable of allowing a doctor more precision, and it is more accessible to a layman (see 2.13ff.). Or perhaps his theories are more commonsensical, at least in the sense that they correspond more to common Greek pre-scientific cultural information.[4]

In any case, VM's execution falls short of his aspiration. Nevertheless, the importance of his intuitions must be re-emphasized in the face of Lloyd's critique.[5] VM knows that exactitude is not—or not yet—attainable (e.g. 2.3–5, 9.19ff., 12.7–16), but still he insists on the priority of experience and physical feelings (τοῦ σώματος τὴν αἴσθησιν, 9.17–18) over ὑπόθεσις (2 and *passim*), on induction over deduction, on medicine as dietetics against the background of common sense rather than the kind of pet theories espoused by the Harley Street doctors in George Bernard Shaw's play *The Doctor's Dilemma*. He even has an experimental method to recommend (24.11–13): first discover what happens to χυμοί under certain conditions *outside* the body, and then

---

[3] I refer throughout to the edition of W.H.S. Jones, *Hippocrates*, Loeb 1 (London: Heinemann 1923), as being the most accessible text which has sequential line numbers for each chapter for ease of reference. But better texts are: J. Jouanna, *Hippocrates: L'ancienne médecine*, Budé (Paris: Les Belles Lettres 1990); W.H.S. Jones, *Philosophy and Medicine in Ancient Greece, Bulletin of the History of Medicine*, Suppl. 8 (Baltimore: The Johns Hopkins Press 1946); and A.J. Festugière, *Hippocrate: L'ancienne médecine* (Paris: Libairie C. Klincksieck 1948).

[4] See W.D. Smith, "The Development of Classical Dietetic Theory," M.D. Grmek (ed.), *Hippocratica* (Paris: Editions du CNRS 1980) 439–48. However, it is also true that VM has been influenced by fifth-century rationalistic thinking on progress and on the origins of civilization: see H.W. Miller, "*On Ancient Medicine* and the Origin of Medicine," *TAPA* 80 (1949) 187–202, and "*Techne* and Discovery in *On Ancient Medicine*," *TAPA* 86 (1955) 51–62.

[5] See also, for instance, J. Longrigg, *Greek Rational Medicine* (London: Routledge 1993) 84–5.

apply the results to treating the invisible insides of the body. All this is important for medicine, which should be the empirical science *par excellence*.

Nevertheless, there are obstacles to viewing VM as an early scientist. It is not the purpose of this paper directly to further the debate outlined in the previous paragraphs, but to focus on another potential obstacle — one which has had less attention paid to it in the secondary literature on the treatise. What I want to explore is an aspect of the treatise which is peripheral to this debate, at least in the sense that it is not unimportant in contributing to our assessment of VM's coherence. In chapters 9–11 we are told that the cause of disease is πλήρωσις and κένωσις, repletion and depletion, in the human body. However, elsewhere in the treatise (chapters 3ff., 14ff.), diseases are said to be caused not by having too much or too little food in one's system, but food of the wrong sort, which upsets the balance of the powers (δυνάμιες) of the human body. In fact, at 19.26–8, it is confidently asserted that *all* diseases arise from these powers. Nevertheless, at 22.1–3, we seem to be told that *some* diseases arise from the shape or structure (σχῆμα) of the internal organs.

At first sight, then, there are three views in the treatise of the origin of disease: one concerned with repletion and depletion, one with powers (and this is claimed to be exhaustive), and one with shapes. It is noteworthy that they are all broadly consistent in that they focus on dietetics and the human body, rather than on factors such as the climate, as is familiar from elsewhere in the Hippocratic corpus (e.g. *Airs Waters Places, The Sacred Disease, The Nature of Man*); but it is also clear that there is apparently considerable uncertainty within the treatise on the aetiology of disease. Nevertheless, I believe that closer study of the text reveals that we are not faced with another instance of lack of coherence here: the apparent inconsistencies can be resolved.

I. Powers

I propose to start with the doctrine of "powers," since that seems to me to be the fundamental aspect of VM's pathology. This strand of VM's pathology is relatively well known, and I shall merely be rehearsing the familiar picture. Chapter 3 introduces us to a cornerstone of the author's medical theory, which is that foods (and drinks) can be classified along a scale of weakness and strength. The key words in this chapter, as elsewhere, are "power" (δύναμις), "strong" (ἰσχυρός) and "uncompounded" or "unmixed" (ἄκρητος). The two basic tenets of his dietetics are (i) that men cannot eat the same food as animals, and (ii) that sick men cannot eat the same food as healthy men. Observation of these points, in VM's view, led to the development of dietetics, which is to say, in his case, of medicine.

Curiously, "strong" and "uncompounded" are used simply as alternative ways of describing the same phenomenon. The idea is that food taken straight from nature is strong because it is uncompounded. I say that this is a curious notion because it implies that lettuce, say, is a strong food and only suitable in an unmixed form for animals, not men. It is of course true that a diet consisting solely of lettuce or the like would not sustain a human being very effectively, but that is not what VM means by "in an unmixed form." Rather he means that even lettuce should be cooked with other foods so as to weaken its natural strength. One sentence, however, is ambiguous on this score. The author is discussing how medical men of the past (the practitioners of "ancient medicine") developed foods suitable for the human constitution: "They occupied themselves with this and boiled, baked and mixed many other foods [sc. other than the staple wheat which has just been mentioned], combining the strong, uncompounded foods with weaker ones" (3.39–42). What are these weaker foods? They could be weaker *natural* foods. But if it were the case that there are weak foods occurring in nature, this would undermine VM's crucial argument about the origin of medicine, which is that dietetics and cooking arose in order to develop foods which are more suited than strong, natural ones for the weaker constitution of humans.

Of course, it is not impossible that the author's logic is shaky, but there is another possible interpretation of the sentence, which makes better sense. This is that boiling and baking of foods is what weakens them, so that you then have weaker foods to mix in with the stronger, natural ones. That this interpretation is correct is confirmed by the rest of the treatise. At 5.23–4, for instance, the assertion is that the strength of foods is removed "by blending and boiling" (see also 13.19–23). The basic doctrine of chapter 5 is that the weakest constitutions (i.e. those of sick people) need the weakest foods (i.e. those which have been processed most); the result is slops or soups, the traditional diet of the sick.

The idea, then, is that *all* foods taken straight from nature are strong, *qua* unmixed, and that you weaken them by boiling them — that is, by mixing them at least with water, and often with other things too.

Just as "strong" and "uncompounded" often go together, so "strong" is glossed as "possessing great powers" (μεγάλας δυνάμιας ἔχων, 3.23–4). This might seem obvious: to say that something is "strong" seems to be the same as saying that it "possesses great powers" VM certainly means us to get this impression. But lettuce as well as pepper must possess great powers, since it is "strong" when uncompounded. Actually, VM has a technical doctrine of δύναμις, which, to be sure, he takes to be simply a spelling-out of *his* idea of strength. The δύναμις of a thing is closely allied with its nature: it is, if you like, its predominant characteristic. "A *dynamis* is a simple real entity which is characterized by its specific activity and whose specific essential nature is revealed to the senses by its activity."[6] Thus it is the δύναμις of salt to be salty, of lemons to be acidic, and so on. But you can even have a δύναμις of being insipid (14.33), and this explains how VM can maintain that all natural foods are strong, even lettuces, since they all have their δυνάμιες in an unadulterated way. There are said (14.34) to be innumerable such powers, not all of which are tastes: there are also the powers of heat and cold, and of causing flatulence (chapters 13–15, *passim*). Cooking, then, is in effect the toning down of the natural powers of a thing by blending, as is said at 13.32–5.

We can now turn to consider the pathology of VM. He explains the actual process of disease in some detail. Man's physical nature too consists of or incorporates δυνάμιες (14.31ff.). Just as the best food is that in which the powers have been blended, so in man, when the powers of his body are well blended with one another, he is healthy. The relationship between the powers of foods and those of the human body explains his pathology. At 14.35–57, he argues that taking in foods whose powers are uncompounded and strong upsets the balance of the powers blended in the body. The result is that some power in the body is separated off and isolated (ἀποκρίνειν, ἀπόκρισις). He does not explicitly go on to say exactly why such ἀπόκρισις of the bodily powers is dis-

---

[6] H.W. Miller, "*Dynamis* and *Physis* in *On Ancient Medicine*," *TAPA* 83 (1952) 184–97; the quotation is from p. 191. On δύναμις in our treatise, see also Jones (1946) (above, n. 3) 93–6, and G. Plamböck, *Dynamis im Corpus Hippocraticum* (Wiesbaden: Akademie der Wissenschaften und der Literatur 1964) esp. 74–89.

ease, nor whether the taking in of sweet food, for instance, separates off the sweet δύναμις of the body, or some other δύναμις, perhaps the opposite, sour. Most probably his point is that the ingestion of strong acid foods "separates off" the acid in the body, making it dominant and causing diseases which can be identified by the acidity of whatever discharges they involve — the discharge being what has been separated off.[7]

II. Repletion and Depletion

The second strand in VM's nosology, that of repletion and depletion, is introduced in chapters 9 ff. The basic idea here is that habituation creates disposition (an idea that was to flourish in Aristotle's ethics).[8] If Smith's habit is to take a single main meal a day, and Brown's is to take two main meals a day, then under certain conditions[9] they will suffer if they break their routine. Smith will suffer because his system is accustomed to digest slowly, so he is still in a state of repletion when he takes his extra meal. Brown will suffer because his system is accustomed to digest quickly, so his state of unusual depletion will cause him problems.[10]

In chapter 10 VM attributes the cause of some diseases, at least, even severe ones, to repletion and depletion. Our task, then, is to reconcile

---

[7] There are, probably, two main influences on the theory here: Alcmaeon and Anaxagoras. The Alcmaeonic influence is obvious from a consideration of his fragment 4 (Diels-Kranz): his theory of health is that it is equal distribution (ἰσονομία) of the δυνάμεις, of which there are, as in VM, an unspecified number. Disease is autocracy (μοναρχία) of a δύναμις, as in VM. In Anaxagorean cosmogony, in the beginning everything was conglomerated with nothing distinct. Creation begins with the ἀπόκρισις of the opposites which then become distinct from one another. Similarly, in VM the notion of κρῆσις seems to imply a complete fusion as opposed to mere association, so that when the bodily powers are in this state, none is distinct, but after ἀπόκρισις, one or more becomes distinct. On these philosophic debts in VM, see Jouanna (above, n. 3) 57–61.

[8] On Aristotle's use of this and other medical analogies in his ethics, see G.E.R. Lloyd, "The Role of Medical and Biological Analogies in Aristotle's Ethics," *Phronesis* 13 (1968) 68–83.

[9] For the proviso, see 10.9–12. The conditions are unspecified, but are probably conditions of ill health, which makes it likely that we should be looking for a prior nosology. This will be confirmed in what follows.

[10] For the symptoms immediately caused by breaking one's routine, see also *Regimen in Acute Diseases* 27–30 (W.H.S. Jones, *Hippocrates*, Loeb 2 (London: Heinemann 1923) 84f.) with Jones (above, n. 3) 96–8.

this, if possible, with the assertion in chapter 19 that *all* diseases are caused by the powers. In my opinion, the two nosologies are related, although the text does not specifically relate them. We must consider the theory about the strength of foods and their action in separating off the bodily powers in relation to what is said about digestion. Many passages in the treatise make it clear that the definition of a food that is too strong for a person is that the person's digestive system is unable to cope with it (ἐπικρατέειν; see e.g. 3.45 ff., 5.20, 7.12–13). The powers of foods are harmful when they are unable to submit to πέψις, coction (chapter 19), and the result of coction is κρῆσις, the beneficial blend of powers, those of the food harmonizing with those of the body.

This can be applied to Smith and Brown. To say that someone is full is to say that his digestive system has not completed the coction, the assimilation of food (11.6–7). Therefore, the influx of new powers from more food is too much for his system to cope with, and ἀπόκρισις will take place.

That is straightforward, but my reconstruction looks at first sight less plausible in the case of those who are empty. If they are empty, then surely they are ready for the intake of new food, and no ἀπόκρισις and no illness should follow. In fact, however, this simple story is not the case, and the fact that we have firm grounds for denying it confirms my reconstruction. It is expressly said at 10.32–3 that the problem in this case is that the digestive system becomes weaker, so that the person is no longer able to assimilate his food. Since he cannot assimilate it, it follows once again that ἀπόκρισις will occur, and hence sickness.

III. Structures

So far, then, we can attribute to VM a coherent pathology. We come next to the problem of chapters 20–4.[11] The problem is whether or not they are interpolations, or perhaps appendices to the text. The treatise so far has been systematic and has fulfilled its purpose of criticizing the new method of medicine[12] and expounding the correct, traditional

---

[11] There are good discussions in Jones (above, n.3) 89–92, and Jouanna (above, n.3) 18–22. Jouanna takes as his target the rejection by Plambӧck (above, n.6) of these chapters as inauthentic.

[12] On VM's attack on philosophical medicine, see G.E.R. Lloyd, "Who is Attacked in *On Ancient Medicine*?," *Phronesis* 8 (1963) 108–26. This article is reprinted, with

method. Chapter 19 ends neatly, but chapter 20 starts abruptly. These last chapters contain a rag-bag of material which jars with the rest of the treatise in the looseness of its arrangement and, if it provides an alternative nosology, in content as well. The style of these last chapters, however, is of a piece with that of the rest of the treatise. If the nosological difficulty can be satisfactorily overcome, it seems best to conclude that these chapters are an appendix, written by the original author himself, but not included in the original lecture.[13]

Chapters 22–3 briefly develop the idea that the internal organs of the body have various structures (σχήματα), which the doctor should be aware of. We do not here need to go into his anatomical views; the issue with which we are presently concerned is raised right at the beginning of chapter 22: "I think the following knowledge is also necessary, namely which human παθήματα arise as a result of powers and which as a result of structures."[14] Jouanna accepts this statement at face value; the final position of VM, he says, is that some diseases are due to δυνάμιες and others to σχήματα. In chapter 19 he mentions only diseases caused by δυνάμιες because he is there combating the similar theory that diseases are caused by hot and cold; then in chapters 22–4 he goes on to mention additonal diseases caused by σχήματα. Festugière[15] too is quite content to accept that chapters 22–3 do give an alternative aetiology for some diseases. He claims that we should see the assertion in chapter 19 as something of an overstatement, and that we should not expect the same standards of precision in an ancient piece of writing.

However, this solution does not do justice to the strength of the statement at 19.26–8. VM has been discussing diseases due to the δυνάμιες of heat and cold, and then he says that *all other* diseases (τἄλλα ὅσα κακοπαθεῖ ὁ ἄνθρωπος πάντα) are also due to δυνάμιες. This is an unequivocal, blunt assertion, which is hard to explain away as being due merely to the surrounding context.

---

a new introduction, in G.E.R. Lloyd, *Methods and Problems in Greek Science: Selected Papers* (Cambridge: Cambridge University Press 1991) 49–69. See also Jouanna (above, n.3) 22–34. It is worth noting that a similar attack is adumbrated in the first chapter of *Precepts*.

[13] The treatise was possibly originally delivered as a lecture. See in particular the rhetorical touches in 1.25, 13.28–9, and 17.1.

[14] Plamböck (above, n.6) also claims that χυμοί play a larger part in these final chapters than earlier in the treatise, but this is simply not so: see Jouanna (above, n.3) 19–20.

[15] Festugière (above, n.3) xxx–xxxi.

Jones[16] is rather more subtle. He claims that chapters 22-3 have a very limited aim, that of explaining symptoms rather than diseases. So, for instance, at 22.47ff. belching as a symptom of certain disorders is explained by the hollow bowl shape of the stomach. This is an attractive view and would resolve the potential inconsistency in the sense that our author would still be maintaining that all diseases are caused by powers, but that certain symptoms are caused by the shapes and structures of the internal organs.

There are objections to Jones's view, however, one of which is less cogent than the other, but I mention it here all the same because it could also have been an objection to the solution I will shortly be suggesting. The weak objection is that παθήματα in the opening sentence of chapter 22 (quoted above) *must* be translated as "diseases" (cf. 2.16–18), so that Jones's interpretation fails to square with the author's avowed intention. But in fact πάθημα does not *mean* "disease"; it means "what a person experiences," usually implying unusual or unpleasant experiences. It is a contextually determined word. Its context in chapter 2, for example, determines that its sense there *is* "disease." The context of chapters 22-3, then, may indicate that the required sense here is "symptoms." In any case, a non-prejudicial translation of the sentence should not include the word "disease," so that the author is not committed to saying that structures cause diseases as the powers do.

There is, however, a stronger objection to Jones's view, which is enough on its own to be fatal to it. It arises from considering 22.61ff. There the author explains that because of the structure of the liver, it is peculiarly liable not just to symptoms ("pain," 22.67), but also to abscesses and tumours. He then makes a similar point about the diaphragm. Now, abscesses and tumours are not symptoms of a disease; they are themselves diseases, as the Greeks were very well aware. Symptoms and diseases are easily distinguishable by treatment: if you successfully treat a rash and that does not get rid of the ailment, then the rash was merely a symptom; if, on the other hand, the ailment ceases, the rash was all there was to the disease.

So Jones's view collapses, not because there is no mention of symptoms, but because there are more than just symptoms in the text. Nevertheless, I do not think we are left with Festugière's and Jouanna's weak solution. We need to accommodate the significant fact that symptoms

---

[16] Jones (above, n.3) 89.

and diseases are both discussed in these final chapters. I suggest that the most economical and charitable way to do this is to allow the author an implicit distinction between main causes and contributory causes. Thus the main cause of all diseases, including abscesses, can still be the ἀπόκρισις of powers; but the secondary cause, imported to explain no more than the particular form the disease will take, and therefore including symptoms, can be the structures of the organs. This distinction, between a general nosology and an explanation of the particular form of a disease, is in fact what distinguishes the remarks on disease in earlier chapters from those of the final chapters.

Whenever one dates the composition of VM,[17] examples of the distinction between main and contributory causes can be found, with developed vocabulary, in contemporary literature.[18] But this also misses the point. It is not a technical distinction at all. Every time one person helps another person, but contributes less towards the final result than the main agent, or every time an allied force reinforces a main army, the distinction is acknowledged. It is therefore not hard to claim that this is the tacit distinction which explains the apparent inconsistency between the final chapters of VM and the earlier chapters. The final chapters are, as already remarked, a rag-bag of material, so if we find the need to import a tacit distinction, that should not occasion surprise. It is probably best to see these final chapters as an appendix to the original lecture.

I conclude, then, that it is possible to see that VM has a single, coherent pathology. He does not overstate his case when he says that all diseases, in his opinion, are caused by the separation off of powers.

---

[17] Estimates vary from the middle of the fifth century (Festugière (above, n.3) and J. Longrigg, "[Hippocrates] Ancient Medicine and Its Intellectual Context," F. Lasserre and P. Mudry (eds.), *Formes de pensée dans la collection hippocratique* (Geneva: Librairie Droz 1983) 249–56) to the middle of the fourth century (H. Diller, "Hippokratische Medizin und attische Philosophie," *Hermes* 80 (1952) 385–409; reprinted in H. Diller, *Kleine Schriften zur antiken Medizin* (Berlin: de Gruyter 1973) 46–70). Jouanna's cautious dating of around 420–10 is probably best.

[18] Starting, I think, with Aeschylus, *Agamemnon* 810–11, 1116.

IV. The Classical and the Christian

17

The Discipline of Self-knowledge in Augustine's *De trinitate* Book X

Lewis Ayres

Augustine's thoughts on self-knowledge are, for some historians of ideas and philosophers, one of the key building blocks of the modernist notion of "the self."[1] My strong disagreement with this understanding of Augustine's work is one of the main factors which forms the background to this paper.[2] For me, and for some other recent writers on Augustine, this perception is in part founded on a failure to attend to the style, genre and intention of Augustine's texts. It is only when one looks at the theological structure and purpose of his arguments, and when one re-reads, in that light, the interaction of the Christian and the Classical in his work that a more accurate picture may emerge. Recent work by ancient historians and other scholars of the early Church on the emer-

---

[1] One of the clearest presentations of this view is to be found in Charles Taylor's *Sources of the Self. The Making of the Modern Identity* (Cambridge: Cambridge University Press 1989) esp. ch. 7, 127–42.

[2] Of course, demonstrating that this is a radical misunderstanding of Augustine himself does not resolve the question as to whether the Augustinian tradition contributed to features of modern thought which Augustine's modern critics emphasise — but it does demand from those critics a more nuanced view of the development of western tradition.

gence of a "Christian discourse," a complex of rhetorical strategies able to provide a cultural language for the late antique world as it gradually became "Christianized," has some parallels with what I am hinting at here.[3] To understand the nature of Christian theology in this period scholars need to become much more aware of the subtlety with which Christians adapted and refocused their classical heritage, and how that heritage played a complex and intimate part in the development of peculiarly Christian ways of thinking.[4]

In this paper I have examined one of the key books of Augustine's central dogmatic work, the *De trinitate* (*trin.*),[5] a work which has often served not only as the key evidence in the attempt to demonstrate Augustine's anticipation of modern self-hood, but also as proof of his supposed attempt to found the doctrine of the Trinity on a conception of a divine *substantia* preceeding the three *personae* of classical Trinitarian *formulae*. The work has a multi-layered and complex structure which makes detailed treatment of any one argument or any one passage extremely difficult. Accordingly, in the first section of this paper, I have offered an account of the place of Bk X within the overall argument of *trin.*, then indicated something of the different levels on which the book operates, and finally made clear the level of argument which I am primarily examining. In the rest of the paper I have attempted to produce a reading of Bk X as a whole; I have not attempted to consider in detail the picture of Augustine's understanding of self-knowledge one finds in modern thought, hoping that my examination of the book speaks for itself. I have commented on the various sections of Bk X in order, hoping thus to make clear something of the texture and style of Augustine's argument as well as describing its overall thrust.

---

[3] Good examples are provided by the general approach of Averil Cameron's *Christianity and the Rhetoric of Empire. The Development of Christian Discourse* (Berkeley CA: California University Press 1991) and Robert Markus's *The End of Ancient Christianity* (Cambridge: Cambridge University Press 1992). One could also note the description of the *social* function of allegory in D. Dawson, *Allegorical Readers and Culutral Revision in Ancient Alexandria* (Berkeley CA: University of California Press 1992).

[4] I have set out my view of the theological work involved in this task more fully in my "The Future of Patristics: Questions of Theological Hermeneutics," L. Ayres and G. Jones (eds.), *Christian Origins I: Theology, Rhetoric and Community*, forthcoming (London: Routledge).

[5] All abbreviations of Augustine's works are those of the *Augustinus Lexicon*, (ed.) C.P. Mayer (Basel & Stuttgart: Schwabe & Co. 1986–).

My interest in Augustine was the result of the teaching of the recipient of this volume, but my reasons for originallly taking up the study of Augustine would seem ironic — or even worrying — to many fellow Augustinian scholars. Inspired by Ian Kidd's presentation of the *Gorgias* and *Republic* I resolved to replace (as was allowed) one of my finals papers with a dissertation on Plato. Unfortunately the rules dictated that such a dissertation should be written under the auspices of the Latin department and so I needed to find a figure in the Latin speaking world who would allow me to explore some similar themes. It was thus Ian Kidd who unwittingly inspired me to study Augustine, as a substitute for Plato! I have much to thank him for, and hope that he will take my attempt to be a little clearer about where Augustine differs from his Classical predecessors as a tribute to his ability to convey the thoughts of the first Master.

I. Book X and the *De trinitate*[6]

My brief sketch of the argument which leads to Bk X is itself a little at odds with some accepted trends of scholarship on the work, and while some defence of this reading is made in the footnotes, that argument will have to be made in full in another forum.[7] In the second half of *trin.*

---

[6] My understanding of Bk X and especially of the need to situate it in context is closely allied to the argument of R. Williams, "The Paradoxes of Self-Knowledge in the De trinitate," J.T. Lienhard et al. (eds.), *Collectanea Augustiniana. Augustine: Presbyter Factus Sum* (New York & Frankfurt: Peter Lang 1993) 121–34. His emphasis on the way in which Augustine builds up paradox in order to concentrate our minds on the *discipline* of Christian life is central to my own attempt to discuss the book.

[7] Much of what follows is drawn from my Oxford DPhil thesis, *The Beautiful and the Absent: Anthropology and Ontology in Augustine's De trinitate.* The basic argument of that thesis is that the unity of the work is to be found in an embyronic theological anthropology which becomes increasingly explicit as the book progresses. This overall theme lies behind my brief portrayal in the text above. I would like to thank my examiners Prof. R.A Markus and Fr. A. Meredith S.J., for their help and encouragement. The traditional interpretation is still founded on the two seminal works of M. Schmaus, *Die psychologische Trinitätslehre des Heiligen Augustinus*, Munster. Beitr. z. Theologie 11 (Munster: Aschendorff 1967: repr. of the 1927 original) and A. Schindler, *Wort und Analogie in Augustins Trinitätslehre*, Herm. Untersuch. z. Theologie 4 (Tübingen: J.C.B. Mohr 1965). Of the large body of literature on *trin.*, and in the context of this paper, my position is also developed in distinction to the thesis of E. Booth published as "St. Augustine's 'notitia sui' related to Aristotle and the early neo-Platonists," *Augustiniana* 27 (1977) 70–132, 364–401; 28 (1978) 183–221; 29 (1979) 97–124. Booth's account does not seem to do justice to the sophistication of either

(Bks VIII–XV) Augustine turns from a detailed consideration of the faith which one must hold in order to interpret biblical reference to God (Bks I–IV) and from discussion of how one should construct the philosophical logic of trinitarianism (Bks V–VII) to an examination of the nature of faith itself — to an examination, that is, of faith in the Trinity. The examination of Books VIII–XV of *trin.* is most accurately characterised as a consideration of the *process* of Trinitarian analogy, where that consideration is understood to be also of the place of theological thought within the process of reformation/redemption.[8] I have offered further discussion of this theme in consideration of Book IX below. The actual analogies which occupy a considerable part of the material of these books thus need to be carefully situated within the overal thrust of the work before their significance and function can be understood.[9]

---

account; he discusses the analogy of *memoria, intellegentia* and *uoluntas* (1979: 106f.) without looking at the particular arguments through which Augustine comes to his formulation, missing the import of the Ciceronian parallel (see 1979: 106, n.36), and simply parallels the "enneadic" structue of Augustine's analogy (1979: 110) with triads in Plotnius, again not really attempting to deal with the markedly different structures of the "intelligible universe" in the two thinkers. His account, though important, seems to rely too strongly on the assumption of a Plotinian parallel without noting the central philosophical and theological differences.

[8] Detailed attention needs to be paid to exactly what is at issue at the beginning of Book VIII. The prologue to the book (VIII, *proem.*, 1) clearly idenitifies the unity of the Trinity as that which the human mind is unable to comprehend and which results in endless discussion of the Trinity, and hence it is this which demands attention, *modo interiore*. Understanding the trinitarian unity is in large part understanding the unity of Father and Son in salvation — or at least it begins at this point. This is evident from the discussion of Book VII, where the central question, whether one can call Christ the "Wisdom" of the Father is a question of the nature of their unity (e.g. VII, 1,2 following the question posed at VI, 1,1). In turn that unity appears as it does to us because scripture wishes to teach us about the relationship of that unity and our own with God in a certain way (VII, 3,4). The way in which we imitate Christ is conditioned by our understanding of the nature of the trinitarian unity (VII, 6,12; 3,5). Thus we are both examing how we may understand the intra-trinitarian unity, and how that understanding affects the way in which imitiate it: see Ayres (above, n.7) 38–52.

[9] My description of the work operates largely external to the debate about the overall structural pattern of the books of *trin.*, esp. as evident in the work of E. Hill, "St. Augustine's 'De trinitate': the doctrinal significance of its structure," *Revue des Etudes Augustiniennes* 19 (1973), 277–86, and most recently E. Hill (tr.), *The Trinity*, The Works of Saint Augustine I/5 (New York: New City Press 1991) 21–7, 263–5. See also E. Muller, "Rhetorical and Theological Issues in the Structuring of Augustine's *De trinitate*," *SP* 27 (1994) 356–63.

In Book VIII Augustine first sets out the paradoxical problem of knowledge of Goodness and Truth in terms of human inability to perceive God because of our fallen condition.[10] This allows him to turn to consideration of how we love a good human being, coming to the initial conclusion that we love them because of the presence of the truth (that is God) to the human mind.[11] This position enables Augustine to conclude that we must come to know the truth through learning to love our neighbour and God in an appropriate order.[12] I purposely avoid here the language of "use" and "end" in describing this love;[13] Augustine in Book VIII is concerned primarily with setting out the paradoxical nature of our knowledge of truth: we must learn both that our love of each other is ultimately dependent on our love of God, and that we can only restore the correct order in our love through correctly loving our fellow human beings.[14] This theme is backed up by a strong appeal throughout *trin.* to the connection between God's creation of the world through his *logos*, and Christ's fittingness as *logos* to be incarnated into the world made through him.[15] These themes are the background to Augustine's use of the analogy of love towards the end of Book VIII. However, failure to notice the situation of Augustine's actually quite brief *direct* discussion of that analogy might lead us to conclude that it is only an initial offering soon to be discarded.

Augustine's aim throughout the latter half of Book VIII has been to indicate that the presentation of the Trinity in Scritpure is attentive to the

---

[10] See the parallel statements at the end of *trin.* VIII, 2,3; 3,5 and 4,8.

[11] *Trin.* VIII, 3,5. For two treatments of this book which fit in closely with my own summary see R. Dodaro, *Language and Justice: Political Anthropology in Augustine's De Ciuitate Dei* (Oxford DPhil, 1992) and R. Williams, "*Sapientia* and the Trinity: reflections on the *De trinitate,*" B. Bruning et al. (eds.) *Melanges T.J. Van Bavel* (Leuven: Leuven U.P. 1990) 317–32.

[12] *Trin.* VIII, 6,9; 8,12.

[13] I accept the position of O.M.T. O'Donovan, "*Usus* and *Fruitio* in Augustine, *De doctrina christiana* I," *JThS* n.s. 33 (1982) 361–97 that Augustine came to avoid this language because of its implications about the nature of love so described. O'Donovan's perception of Book VIII, *The Problem of Self-Love in Augustine* (New Haven CT: Yale University Press 1980) 75–81 differs considerably from my own.

[14] *Trin.* VIII, 8,12 (CCSL 50, 288): *cum ergo de dilectione diligimus fratrem, de Deo diligimus fratrem; nec fieri potest ut eamdem dilectionem non praecipue diligamus, qua fratrem diligamus.* Cf. the relationship betwen faith and the two objects of love in VIII, 9,13.

[15] Most apparent in the paralleling of the Christology of Bk XIII (and Bk IV) with the anthropology of Bk XII, see below sec. V.

problems of human knowledge. Every aspect of doctrine is, for Augustine the *rhetor*, "addressed" to an aspect of our humanity, and through such address corectly formulated doctrine is able to draw us to the goals it espouses. The Trinity is no exception: the Trinity provides a doctrine of God founded in the economy of God's self-communication, and the form of that comunication is addressed to an aspect of human being.[16] "Being" in this case refers especially to human possibility and to the possible directions that we take through the course of life. The Trinity presents a particular problem because, unlike Paul or Christ, who provide clear examples which can be understood by accord with the normal structures of our existence, the Trinity seems necessarily outside any *species* known to the human mind.[17] If we cannot know the Trinity then it lies outside the bounds of our love. Our task then must be (and note that this difficulty is not spelled out so well simply for an easy answer to be extracted from a hat) to identify those aspects of human existence which will allow us to have a faith which is not a worldly delusion (*non ficta*).[18]

One of the themes in what follows in Book VIII (VIII, 6.9ff.) pursues again the nature of our knowledge and love even of those exemplars which previously seemed so much easier to comprehend and follow. Initially Augustine says that we love Paul because of our common humanity; but later refines this position by saying that we in fact love him because of his *iustum animum* — our common humanity gives us common access to the standards of *iustitia*. However, knowing his mind to be just presents particular difficulties because justice cannot be known through any type of knowledge *in corpore* (which covers here all types

---

[16] *Trin.* VIII, 5,8 (CCSL 50, 278–9): *An quemadmodum in Domino Iesu Christo, Quod resurrexit a mortuis, ita Trinitatem quam non uidemus, et qualem nullam umquam uidimus, possumus credendo diligere? Sed quid sit uiuere et quid sit mori, utique scimus; quia et uiuimus et mortuos ac morientes aliquando uidimus atque experti sumus... sed ex qua rerum notarum similitudine uel comparatione credamus, quo etiam nondum notum Deum diligamus, hoc quaeritur.* Cf. VIII, 4,7. The traditional argument between a psychological explanation for Augustine's turning to the trinitarian analogies (Schmaus) or an explanation based on Plotinian parallel (Benz) this misses at least part of the point; for a discussion of these two options see Booth (above, n.7) 97. There is something of a parallel with the discussion of the *Christus medicus* image in *doc.*, where the aptness of Christ's salvific action fits our ability to understand, see *doc.* I, 12,13ff.

[17] *Trin.* VIII, 5,8.

[18] See *trin.* VIII, 3,5, Ayres (above, n.7) 64f. For our faith to be *non ficta* is for it to rely on the right earthly images for its point of departure.

of mental picturing). In a complicated passage Augustine seems to say that any account of the true knowledge of justice must locate the ability to describe and discuss justice within an account of the possibility of moving towards justice (not to take this view would involve the paradox of the unjust person having accurate knowledge of true justice).[19] The *love* of justice must be an integral part of the *knowledge* of justice if that knowledge is to be real. This argument is ultimately founded in an account of the presence of justice to us through our created status, but how such "participation" is to be understood forms one of the key themes of this paper.

Sidestepping for a moment the direct question of knowledge, Augustine turns in more detail to the relationship between loving justice and acting justly. He offers a different angle on the problem of of our normally perceiving *in corpore* by critiquing inter-mundane power structures at VIII, 7,11. Here confusion of knowing God and contact with "powers" below God is again the confusion of some thing for that "in which" it was created. The central example is Christological: to understand Christ's miracles we need to understand Christ himself. Understanding "Christ himself" here is to understand the centrality of his *humilitas* (a theme that points back to and is more easily understood in the light of *doc.*) to all his other actions — thus the miracles are understood properly when they are understood to point to the nature of God as love.[20] Making this leap brings out how we may love that which we do

---

[19] *Trin.* VIII, 6,9 (CCSL 50, 283): *neque omne ualent; et qui intueri ualent, hoc etiam quod intuentur non omnes sunt, hoc est, non sunt etiam ipsi iusti animi sicut possunt uidere ac dicere quid sit iustus animus. Quod unde esse poterunt, nisi inhaerendo eidem ipsi formae quam intuentur, ut inde formentur et sint iusti animi...* [so far: not everyone with the power to see a just mind is also what they see, and the only way to become what one sees is to strive for that which one sees] *cur ergo alium diligimus quem credimus iustum, et non diligimus istam formam... An uero nisi et istam diligeremus, nullo modo eum diligeremus quem ex ista diligimus, sed dum non iusti sumus, minus eam diligimus quam ut iusti esse valeamus? Homo ergo qui creditur iustus ex ea forma et ueritate diligitur... ipsa uero forma et ueritas non est quomodo aliunde diligatur* [when we love someone we believe to be just we also love the form of justice, but not sufficiently to be just ourselves; hence we need to learn to love the form itself if we are to become just]. In what follows (VIII, 7,10–8,12) Augustine redraws the necessary direction of our love so that we come to love our neighbour as a way of turning inward to contemplate the form of justice.

[20] *Trin.* VII, 7,11 (CCSL 50, 286): *...non dixit "Discite a me quia quatriduanos mortuos suscito"; sed ait: "Discite a me quia mitis sum et humilis corde."* Cf. *doc.* I, 36, 40.

not know: by loving our neighbour we love God, *Nemo dicat: "non nouit quod diligam." Diligat fratrem, et diliget eamdem dilectionem... dilectionem autem necesse est ut diligat, qui diligat fratrem.*[21]

A few last steps are then necessary: we truly love others when we love the love which they show, and to love thus is both to love and to know God. Hence we can perhaps anticipate the structure of Books IX–XV of *trin.* by saying that the Trinity addresses in us the capacity of our nature to grow in knowledge and love of God.[22] Appropriately loving another increases in us the love of God. *This* is the background to Augustine's assertion at the end of Book VIII that love has a threefold structure. Book IX does not simply abandon this analogy, but begins the proces of fulfilling its potential.[23]

Book IX also begins what is taken to be a famous series or progression of analogies for the Trinity from corporeal to incorporeal. I do not have space here to demonstrate the inadequacy of this view in its simpler forms, it must suffice to say that attention to the flow of the text demonstrates that Augustine continually plays with the dynamic of corporeal and incorporeal all the way through these books, and that the differing analogies he uses are usually variations on one or two standard themes. Elsewhere I have tried to indicate that there are two levels to the use of these analogies:[24]

1) On the first level Augustine intends to discuss and describe the process by which Christians can draw analogies for the Trinity, and thus to examine the nature of theological analogy itself. Augustine builds a succession of analogies for the Trinity all of which need to be understood as individual stages within an argument, either commenting on what has gone before or introducing new themes into the discussion. This investigation of the role of analogy in trinitarian theology centres around a reconsideration of the relationship between love and knowledge in Christian life, and the possible necessity of mediation in the

---

[21] *Trin.* VIII, 8,12 (CCSL 50, 286–8).
[22] See Ayres (above, n.7) 160–7.
[23] Key to my interpretation of the relationship between Bk VIII and the rest of Bks VIII–XV is Williams (above, n.11).
[24] Ayres (above, n.7) 83–4: my description of the levels here is not quotation and involves revision, for the sake of clarity.

mind's knowledge.²⁵ This level can best be described as the *flow* of the argument.

2) On the second level, this attempt to describe how we might understand the Trinity is formed by discussion of one central model or analogy for the Trinity itself, and the theological anthropology concomitant with that picture. That model is formed on the premise (not fully evident until Book XIV) that the human person is in the image of God when she or he has a life centred around the attempt to discern how a Christian must live in order to fulfill God's command of love. Through making progress in such a life one comes to understand the trinitarian mystery more closely.²⁶ In the context of *trin.* one of the key aspects of such discernment is to be able to distinguish between God and the world in terms both metaphysical and moral, and thus learning not to think of God as imaged in physical things is in part to begin the process of turning ourselves away from an obsession with desire in the sense of *cupiditas*.²⁷ This level can perhaps be described as the *structure* and *purpose* of the argument.²⁸

The two levels are of course closely interlinked, but one can usually see fairly clearly an emphasis on one strand or another at the various stages of the argument. It is with aspects of *both* the levels of trinitarian analogy that this paper is concerned. My consideration of Book X

---

²⁵ Cf. Williams (above, n.11) 323: "*this* is why the enormous digression of IX to XIV is necessary: we must discover whether there is anything we can say about the subject relating to itself without the mediation of anything outside itself if we are to try to say anything about *God...* There is nothing that can be said of the mind's relation to itself without the mediation of the revelation of God as its creator and lover."

²⁶ It is here that, while I have found his essay extremely frutiful in my own research I begin to diverge from the findings of J. Cavadini's recent "The Structure and Intention of Augustine's *De trinitate*," *Augustinian Studies* 23 (1992) 103–23. His assertion that Bks IX–XIV are a Plotinian attempt at ascent to the contemplation of the Creator (105) *and* that this attempt is predicated on failure (106), seems to under emphasise the subtlety of the treatment of our knowing which one finds from the very outset of Bk VIII. These books are not an attempt at some sort of "ascent" which Augustine knows will fail, but a continual consideration of the process by which we come to know God. Of course, it may be that our two considerations simply have differing emphases.

²⁷ An introduction to the nature of desire in Augustine and especially the distinction between *cupiditas* and *caritas* is provided I. Bochet, *Saint Augustine et le Désir de Dieu* (Paris: Etudes Augustiniennes 1982) 36–44 (*cupiditas*), 275–94 (*caritas*).

²⁸ See Ayres (above, n.7) 80–4.

emphasises at beginning and end that one needs to see the analogy under consideration there as part of a larger argument, and the last section of this paper looks in detail at one key shift in the progress of analogies (level *one*). However, such an emphasis also facilitates my wider examination of aspects of Augustine's consideration of the *discipline* of self-knowledge as part of his emerging theological anthropology (level *two*).

Returning to my introductory summary of the Books leading to Bk X, Bk IX can be said to concern the relationship between knowledge and love against the background of a increasingly sophisticated discussion of the nature of our desire for God. This latter discussion emphasises that our desire must take shape as a desire about to be fulfilled even while we are aware that in this life it will never be. This eschatological perspective is the situation of all the analogies for the Trinity:[29] Learning to reject analogies which fail simply because of their lack of logical accord with the "rules" of Trinitarian theology, and moving to more sophisticated analogies, does not allow us to understand more deeply the nature of God unless we *also* come to see more clearly how only eschatological fulfilment of any analogy will allow it to image God absolutely appropriately.[30] Learning to see the problems with simpler analogies leads us into a deeper and more focused consideration of the problem of any created analogy. This, finally, is not intended to lead to agnosticism but to a deeper understanding of the process of analogy within Christian life.

In Book IX itself these themes are apparent in the discussion of knowledge and the *uerbum mentis* against the background of a discussion of the nature of desire.[31] All acts of knowing or deciding involve

---

[29] In this regard the prologue to Bk IX (CCSL 50, 292) is all important: the point is made in three stages, first Ps. 68. 33 and 104. 4 are quoted to emphasise that we must *Quaerite faciem eius semper*. Second, I Cor. 8.2 and Gal. 4.19 indicate that we cannot know God directly in this life but only be known by him, *Nec sic quidem dixit "cognouit illum"; quae periculosa paesumptio est; sed: Cognitus est ab illo*. Third, we are told that perfection in this life is *sequor ad palmam supernae uocationis Dei...* (Phil. 3.13–15).

[30] As is also evidenced by the movement from discussing our renewal in this life at XIV, 17,23 to the discussion of our perfection in the final vision of God at XIV, 18,24.

[31] Again there is a great deal of secondary literature here. See G. O'Daly, *Augustine's Philosophy of Mind* (London: Duckworth 1987) 140f. His emphasis on the role of the will in the production of a *uerbum* is important, contra the account of B. Bubacz, *St. Augustine's Theory of Knowledge: A Contemporary Analysis* (New York & Toronto:

the production in the mind of a *uerbum mentis* through assent to some
trace in the memory or perceived sensory stimuli. The assent we give is
an aspect of our desire and may be part of either *amor* or *cupiditas*.[32]
Cutting the argument ridiculously short, to "discover" something is to
bring forth an "appropriate" knowledge which produces a unity (of intention) in the mind, and in so doing we discover that the unifying love
was there all along, prior even to the knowledge which also, in some
sense, already exists.[33] Perhaps we might say that the theme of the
uerbum mentis is here not primarily concerned with elucidating further
a theory of perception *per se*, but is rather being used to draw out some
of the inter-relationship — and unity — between knowledge and love.
Augustine's contribution to the ancient discusson of unity and knowledge is to insist, as perhaps is clear by now from this short survey, that
unity in this context is only understood by understanding the unity of
Father and Son, and hence the unity of the trinitarian persons. This in
turn we learn through our being drawn into "union" (which here remains purposely vague) with the Trinity. Our self-knowledge can only
begin to serve as an analogy for the Trinity once we discover where we
might "look" in ourselves to grow in knowledge and love of God.[34]

Edwin Mellon 1981). Also helpful is U. Duchrow, *Sprachverständnis und biblisches Hören bei Augustin*, Herm. Untersuch. z. Theol. (Tübingen: J.C.B. Mohr 1965) 122–44.

[32] At IX, 6,11–7,12 forming a *uerbum* occurs ideally when we see something and also see the form within us and are then able to produce a "word" of judgement or assessment. The example around which the section focuses is the recognition, approval and imitation of a good person. In 7,13–8,13 the word is said to be formed by *cupiditas* or *caritas*; if from the former then one has become unaware of the source of judgement in the act of judging, a point strengthened by Augustine's uses of the metaphor of the mountains and the clouds at the beginning of 6,11.

[33] *Trin.* IX, 9,14: *Conceptum autem uerbum et natum idipsum est, cum uoluntas in ipsa notitia conquiescit, quod fit in amore spirtualium*. This theme points both back to Augustine's use of the *logos prophorikos / logos endiathetos* theme at VII, 3,4, and forward to the unity of *scientia* and *sapientia* in the Incarnation at XIII, 19,24f.

[34] *Trin.* IX, 12,18. The discussion here of the way in which love effects a unity in knowledge follows the complicated sentences of IX, 11,16 (CCSL 50, 307) where knowledge according to species is always like the thing known (*similis est rei*). We too are like God when we know him, and become more like him when we learn to live and love appropriately (producing appropriate "words") as created beings, when we adopt the correct "place" in creation: *ita cum Deum nouimus, quamuis meliores efficiamur quem eramus antequam nossemus, maximeque cum eadem notitia etiam placita digneque amata uerbum est, fitque aliqua Dei similitudo illa notitia; tamen inferior est, quia in inferiore natura est; creatura quippe animus, Creator autem Deus.* Importantly also cf. XI, 6,10.

II. Book X, 1,1-7,10

In the reading of Book X which follows I have placed great emphasis on the need to read the discrete sections of Augustine's text in the context of the argument as a whole. This is important in two particular areas: first, the argument of Book X needs to be seen in the context of the work as a whole — and I have remarked on this in the previous section. Secondly one needs to pay detailed attention to the way in which Augustine employs some fairly traditional argumentative tropes. In this regard one needs to cultivate an "intratextual *Tendenzkritik*," becoming aware not only of the interests served by a particular argument, but also of the direction in which one argument leads the overall structure. Perhaps my meaning is most evident in Augustine's adaptation of or contribution to traditional philosophical and rhetorical arguments by the addition of a theological "twist"; in such cases concentration simply on his place in a particular tradition can obscure to us the particular purpose the argument serves in *this* text.

The argument of Bk X takes place on a number of levels, perhaps best explained in this order: first, Augustine is following through the shift from the analogy of *mens*, *notitia* and *amor*, which he has considered through the course of Bk IX, to that of *memoria, intelligentia* and *uoluntas* (which has occurred at the end of Bk IX). At this level he attempts to show how the second formulation is a better tool for the exploration of the mind's self-knowledge than the first, in particular it allows him to focus on discussion of the *process* of knowledge, the process of seeking and studying. Second, Augustine is finding new ways of illustrating the basic problem of *any* human attempt at knowing the mind and understanding the Trinity through, third, linking the refutation of academic scepticism to the need to grasp the nature and possibilities of human knowing if we are to understand how we might grow in knowledge of God. With reference to the last point, Augustine's refutation moves from showing how perception is trustworthy because of the standards by which we judge, to showing that this argument (which may initially seem weak and confusing) implies our place in a web of possible truthful connections related to God's presence in creation.[35] These three levels in Bk X also provide one instance of how Augustine moves

---

[35] I have commented below on the relationship between his treatment of Scepticism in *trin.* and his treatment in *acad.*

from the first to the second level of trinitarian analogy in the latter half of *trin.* as described above.

The inquiry seems at first to follow well-trodden paths, a reconsideration of the ancient inquiries into our ability to search for that which we do not know. Augustine's three tiered solution may, on first reading, also seem somewhat predictable: we search for something because we already know something of it; we feel something of our goal because of a felt lack; and we are also able so to search because of our participation in truth. However Augustine's main concern here is not actually the philosophy of knowledge *per se*, he is most interested in understanding the sort of love or desire that arises in our attempt to discover something "new."[36] Something new here means, as will become clearer, the presence of God to the mind.

This love or desire increases the more we know of that which we seek and yet realise that we do not yet know all. Thus to know something to be a sign and yet not understand what it signifies increases our desire to find out its meaning. The reason given for this increase in desire is important: we know and perceive "in the reason of things" the importance of knowledge of signs, and hence of the value of communication:

> *Quid ergo amat, nisi quia novit atque intuetur in rationibus rerum quae sit pulchritudo doctrinae, qua continentur notitiae signorum omnium; et quae sit utilitas in ea peritia... ne sibi hominum coetus deteriores sint quauis solitudine, si cogitationes suas colloquendo non misceant? Hanc ergo speciem decoram et utilem cernit anima, et nouit, et amat; eamque in se perficit studet, quantum potest, quisquis vocum significantium quaecumque ignorat, inquirit. Alius est enim quod eam in ueritatis luce conspicit, aliud quod in sua facultate concupiscit.*

> What then does he love, unless he knows and perceives in the reason of things what beauty there is in teaching, in which the knowledge of all signs is contained, and what is the benefit of being skilled in these... unless a meeting together of men was actually worse than solitude, if they did not mix their thoughts together by conversation? The soul, then, discerns this useful and beautiful *species*, knows it and loves it: and whoever asks after the meaning of signs of which he is ignorant studies to perfect that *species* in himself, as far as is possible.[37]

In discussing this statement I want to avoid the general debate about the exact character of Augustine's understanding of the "illumination"

---

[36] *Trin.* X, 1,1. The twist comes at the beginning of X, 1,2 where Augustine shifts from the general process of learning to someone who hears a *signum incognitum*.
[37] *Trin.* X, 1,2 (CCSL 50, 313).

of the mind by truth (although my discussion will eventually have bearing on that debate),[38] and point instead to a particular feature of this theory's use in *trin*. When Augustine uses language associated with illumination in *trin*. X he is most importantly concerned with knowledge which helps either to indicate the goodness and purpose of general themes in human life, or particular goals towards which we should aim. Augustine does use such language in situations where we are talking about the simple processes of judging our perceptions or memory images, but he makes his most important observations in connecting this language with our search for justice, or for God. One simple pointer to this emphasis is the vital part played by moral analogies or examples in the flow of arguments that formally seem to depend only on analogies drawn from theories of perception.[39] I have already indicated — and will draw out further — that something of the key to the selection of these examples lies first in the interplay between the double logic of trinitarian analogy which Augustine draws up and second in the complex links between the evolution of an analogy of the Trinity in the mind and the description of the process by which self-knowledge and knowledge of God are linked.

Augustine's terminology of "illumination" is also rarely precise (a fact that so far does not seem to have informed discussion of this topic)

---

[38] The literature is of course vast, a basic bibliography to 1973 is provided by Andresen, *Bibliographia Augustiniana* (Darmstadt: Wissenschaftliche Buchgesellschaft 1973) 103–5. The basic models of interpretation are provided by R.H. Nash, *The Light of the Mind: St. Augustine's Theory of Knowledge* (Lexington KY: The University Press of Kentucky 1969) 94–124. See also the account of B. Bubacz (above, n.31) 133–61 and C. Harrison, *Beauty and Revelation in the Thought of St. Augustine* (Oxford: Clarendon Press 1992) 146–8. I have found none of these accounts to be much help in the case of *trin*. O'Daly's account is extremely astute but, as with his book in general, makes no attempt to distinguish development or particular situations, see (above, n.31) 204–7 and the discussion of the refutation of scepticism at 92–102. Bubacz's account of the active role of the mind (partly following Nash) is important, but his ultimate "non-theistic" approach (esp. 152ff.) seems largely to miss the point of the theory in Augustine's post 396 AD works (and may well do so in those written before). Most importantly these traditional theories do not really provide a flexible framework that might demonstrate how the theory is put to theological use in different circumstances (the one that comes nearest is R. Lorenz's "Gnade und Erkenntnis bei Augustinus," *ZKG* 75 (1964) 21–78). The terminology of illumination does not represent a fixed "theory" but rather is a collection of ideas under examination and exploration: once the end of this paper has been reached it should be clearer that the necessity of a *discipline* of self-knowledge precludes us approaching "illumination" as an easily comprehensible "theory."

[39] See e.g VIII, 6,9 and IX, 6,9.

and he carefully adapts it to particular circumstances.⁴⁰ Here, for instance, at X, 1,2 *doctrina* "as such" is taken as an example of a *species*, an equation which makes most sense when we consider Augustine's specific intentions in this text. *Pulchritudo doctrinae* here is the beauty of teaching itself, a *species* which is thus not an example of a fixed physical reality, or a fixed act, but the beautiful form of a particular possibility in human life which has been ordained by God. In fact a "form" is very often in *trin.* something which indicates an appropriate direction for our lives. An important parellel is to be found at *trin.* IX, 6,9, where knowing the *inuiolabilem uertitatem* is also knowing *non qualis sit uniuscuisque hominis mens sed qualis esse sempiternis rationibus debeat*, knowing how human beings *ought* to live.⁴¹ Similarly Augustine's use of the triad *mensura, numerus* and *pondus* (founded on its appearance at Wisd. 11, 21) at *Gn. litt.* IV, 3,7 (for example) is designed to show that in perceiving these three we perceive God's work of limiting, forming and ordering.⁴² Again, at *trin.* VI, 10,12 we see the *unitas, species* and *ordo* in all things: but to see this is to see an image of the Trinity where the three persons *a se inuicem determinari* — by analogy the "traces" we see in creation are also striving to represent in a finite way the mutual determination of their heavenly, trinitarian exemplar and cause.⁴³ In seeing the ordering work of God the relationships established between things, and the overall direction in which things mutually naturally "point" is as important as the brute fact of their simple existence as examples.⁴⁴ Returning to *trin.* X,

---

⁴⁰ One important constant in the differing metaphors and similes is insistence that God is the light which enlightens our minds (John 1.9: see e.g. *conf.* IX, 10), the light is not simply a natural capacity of the human mind. See F. Körner, " 'Deus in homine uidet.' Das subjekt des menschlichen Erkennens nach der Lehre Augustins," *Philosophisches Jahrbuch* 64 (1956) 166–217.
⁴¹ *Trin.* IX, 6,9 (CCSL 50, 301).
⁴² *Gn. litt.* IV, 3,7 (PL 34, 299): *An secundum id quod nouimus mensuram in eis quae metimur, et numerum in eis quae numeramus, et pondus in eis quae appendimus, non est ista Deus. Secundum id quod mensura omni rei modum praefigit, et numerus omni rei speciem, et pondus omnem rem ad quietem ac stabilitatem trahit.*
⁴³ *Trin.* VI, 10,12 (CCSL 50, 242).
⁴⁴ The traditional literature on this question is perhaps flawed by a failure to relate the theme to the theological context in which it usually appears, and in particular to the trinitarian and "relational" themes which pervade its use. This literature is fairly comprehensively noted by C. Harrison (above, n.38) 101f. In connection with the trinitarian location of the language their is a great difference between my position and Du Roy's, cf. *Intelligence de la foi en la Trinité selon saint Augustin* (Paris: Etudes Augustiniennes

1,2 we seek to know and to understand signs because we have an innate sense of the value of such knowledge in promoting the realisation of our natures. To seek to understand a sign must at some level be to understand the value of being part of a communicating human community. The soul should seek to put this perception into action in the way most suited to its capacity, forming an appropriate desire to learn language and understand words whose meanings are unknown. Particular successes that we may have on the way to a new knowledge increase our desire to put the *species* which we perceive into action and increase our hope of realising what we know "in the reason of things" to be beautiful. Thus we proceed only on the basis of what is already known to us, and kowledge is thus always related to desire (because we may only desire an object if we in some sense know it).

The ultimate test of this view is the mind's search for self-knowledge. The majority of sections X, 3,5–4,6 consists of an attempt to heighten the paradoxes involved in the mind's knowledge of itself in preparation for the account of how we can know ourselves at X, 8,11. One of the most important stages in this process is the comment that the mind cannot know itself *in part*: for the mind to know itself it must know its participation in living and understanding because this is what separates it from animals.[45] It is not possible to isolate or objectify the mind in the process of self-knowledge, because the mind is part of a living and intelligent being. Thus, at the end of X, 4,6 the mind's position as a process in the individual renders any account of self-knowledge on the model of our knowledge of things impossible.[46] Augustine has here taken up what he has proved at such length in the first sections of the book, the necessity of coming to know through a gradual and appropriate progress from part to whole, beginning always from what is known, and used that theme to create a paradox in the case of the mind's self-knowledge. Be-

---

1966) 269–308. Du Roy does not make any attempt (as one would expect given his approach) to tie the theme into a specifically trinitarian metaphysic of relationality. For some hints towards a different approach see R. Williams, "'Good for Nothing'? Augustine on Creation," *Augustinian Studies* 25 (1994) 9–24.

[45] *Trin.* X, 3,6 (CCSL 50, 318–19): *cum itaque aliquid de se scit... totam se scit. Deinde quid eius et tam notum est, quam se uiuere?*

[46] *Trin.* X, 4,6 (CCSL 50, 319): *At si nouit quid quaerat, et se ipsam quaerit, se ipsam utique nouit. Quid ergo adhuc quaerit? Quod si ex parte se nouit, ex parte autem ad huc quaerit, non se ipsam, sed partem suam quaerit. Cum enim ea ipsa dicitur, tota dicitur.*

cause the mind is non-isolatable and indivisible it cannot be known in this way. The only solution is that if we can only seek for the mind as a whole, then the mind *as a whole* must be already present, otherwise the seeking would not be possible. Any attempt to provide a logically coherent language which relies on talking as if one "part" of the mind is known while another remains unknown is refused.[47]

Having set up the problem of self-knowledge in this way, Augustine turns, at X, 5,7, to an attempt to explain the reasons for the Delphic injunction to self-knowledge. Following the Ciceronian interpretation, to know oneself, is to know one's mind.[48] He begins by asserting that the injunction exists so that we will be able to live according to our natures, which means entering into our true place as created beings, both aware of our true direction and purpose and hence aware of our position under God (*sub eo scilicet cui subdenda est*).[49] From this beginning Augustine outlines the problems involved in the fallen mind's self awareness, beginning with a description of our present incapacities. The fallen mind, in its passion to hang onto that with which it is best accustomed, makes images of exterior things which it can use as a self-representation (*...imagines eorum conuoluit, et rapit factas in semetipsa de semetipsa*). The degree of our fallenness is revealed by the extent to which we are still able to judge and understand with our *rationalis intelligentia* the *species* which ground the things we see around us.[50] In the worst case scenario we think our minds not to be the images (for we

---

[47] Cf. *Gn. litt.* 7, 21,28 (PL 34, 365–6): *neque enim aliunde se quaerit, quam a seipsa. Cum ergo quaerentem se nouit, se utique nouit; et omne quod nouit tota nouit, cum itaque se quaerentem nouit, tota se nouit, ergo et totam se nouit: neque enim aliquid aliud, sed seipsam tota nouit.* At this point Augustine seems to parallel the type of discussion evident at Plotinus *Enn.* V, 3,1 and 5. This theme is taken up in the next section of the paper.

[48] *Tusc.* V, 25,70. This tradition of interpreting the injunction could of course come to Augustine from many sources, the importance of the *Tusc.* parallel lies in the linkage there between self-knowledge and the struggle involved in the life of virtue. The coincidence of themes closely mirrors Augustine's own use. This will become clearer in the following sections of the paper.

[49] *Trin.* X, 5,7 (CCSL 50, 320): *Credo, ut se ipsam cogitet, et secundum naturam suam uiuat, id est, ut secundum naturam suam ordinari appetat...* The theme of desiring to be ordered according to our created nature, follows up the discussion of my previous paragraph: to know ourselves is to be aware of the divinely intended structure and purpose of human life.

[50] The nature of the correctly ordered soul is taken up in detail in Books XII and XIII, see below, sec. V.

could not understand them to be images if we could not distinguish the mind and the things within it) but to be the things of which they are images. The images themselves which we hold within us as self-perception thus stand a risk of becoming all that we know, we think as if we were asleep or mad.[51]

At this point Augustine proceeds to demonstrate the error of those who refuse to think of the mind as incorporeal (X, 7,9–7,10), aware that his argument — especially in the last sentences of X, 6,8 — has come to hinge on that assumption. Thus, in X, 7,9 Augustine offers a list of traditional philosophical theories about the nature of the soul. However real these options are for Augustine in the fifth century, he uses his list to argue that a whole variety of traditional ancient philosophical discussions fail not because of their failure to provide convincing pictures of the soul as such, but because of their failure to engage in the correct method of discovery.[52] The importance of this short section for my investigation lies in the description (in X, 7,10) of searching with which Augustine draws it to a close: "finding" (*inuenire*) is "going into" something that is already present (as all knowable things must in some sense be on the basis of his previous argument) — a seemingly obvious but extremely elusive concept. This analogy for our knowing relies in part on a concept of knowledge by participation, and makes most sense when we think of judging corporeal images (*imaginibus corporum*): we know such things by "coming into" the images impressed in our minds through the sense organs. The theme of "coming into" knowledge thus depends strongly on Augustine's discussion of the *uerbum mentis* in Book IX, where the phrase is used with particular relationship to the link between our knowledge and the direction of our love. To produce a "word" about something there is centrally to produce a judgement or assent about something we perceive internally; in many cases the "word" produced is a judgement about how something known should be acted on — what part it will play in the structure or pattern of our lives. As the linking of knowing with *cupiditas* and *caritas* in Bk IX shows, to know something is also to allow it a place in the overall structure of our desires and acts of will. Thus *inuenire* at X, 7,10 is a metaphor which focuses upon the process of assessing the images present in the mind

---

[51] *Trin.* X, 5,7 (CCSL 50, 321).
[52] *Trin.* X, 7,10 (CCSL 50, 323): *...non ob hoc errare, quod mens desit eorum notitiae, sed quod adiungunt ea sine quibus nullam possunt cogitare naturam.*

(whether from memory as commonly understood or from immediate sense data) and making judgements. In this sense "finding" something is here the same as producing a "word" about something. From this understanding of "coming into" corporeal judgements Augustine is also able to speak about our knowledge of God. When we come into knowledge of non-corporeal things we cannot do so unless we understand something of the mechanism by which this happens: we must "come into" knowledge of the mind through the mind, through a substance of the same type as the mind (to put it very crudely). The mind is really that which is behind all sensual perception and so must be the organ through which it seeks itself.[53]

Augustine counters the Academic challenge largely by asserting they misunderstand the nature and role of the senses. The argument that their suspicion of any claim to certain knowledge is incoherent, an argument which plays a prominent part in *acad.* Bk III (esp. III, 9,20f.), appears here in close connection with a more developed concentration on the method by which one searches for a thing. As there, Augustine ultimately claims that the *search* for knowledge or truth *is* possible, but that we need to think very carefully about the method by which we might search.[54] Augustine here believes that we do not begin to search from a position of ignorance, and in understanding the very command "know thyself," we already have some sense of the object's presence. However if we are to follow through this most basic and barely formed awareness we will need to cultivate what we might call a discipline of discernment,[55] and it is that discipline which occupies the remainder of Book X (X, 8,11–X, 12,19). Discovering that we can search is not itself the problem for Augustine, it is the difficulty involved in coming to understand the *discipline* of searching that lies at the heart of his argument, and it is the character of that discipline which places the discussion of self-knowledge firmly in a trinitarian context.

---

[53] *Trin.* X, 7,10.
[54] Cf. *acad.* III, 20,43: At that time Augustine had not yet developed the Christological structure of his argument to the extent found in *trin.* XII and XIII, and hence in *acad.* we find a much less sophisticated account of *how* we learn to search for truth.
[55] *Trin.* X, 8,11 (CCSL 50, 324): *Ergo se ipsam quemadmodum quaerat et inueniat, mirabilis quaestio est, quo tendat ut quaerat, aut quo ueniat ut inueniat.*

III. Book X, 8,11–10,16

That this is a "discipline" is clear from the emphasis on *methods* of searching: the mind here is being exhorted not simply to see in a certain way but to *seek to see* in a certain way. The mind becomes accustomed to being "in" the objects which it most immediately loves, and thus to escape our attatchment to material things will take the effort of a discipline, it will not be evident simply through a once and for all act of thinking differently. The deceptively simple *non se tamquam sibi detracta sit quaerat; sed id quod sibi addidit detrahat*[56] is actually the key to much of the argument of Book X. When we search for things that we *can* think of as *detracta* we are searching for things as if they were objects in the material world or as if they could be thought about according to our normal canons of thought. This I think is clear from his description of what happens normally: *hinc ei oboritur erroris deducus, dum rerum sensarum imagines secenere a se non potest, ut se solam uideat... quoniam dum se solam nititur cogitare, hoc se putat esse sine quo se non potest cogitare,*[57] and after the sentence in question, *cum ergo sit mens interior, quodam modo exit a semetipsa, cum in haec quasi vestigia multarum intentionum exserit amoris affectum.*[58] In normal circumstances to think about something is to go "out from oneself" and look to the images that we create of things in our minds; this action creates a duality (hence the use of *detraho*) which enables us to see objects in their character as objects even when they are only images in the mind. However, the corporeal or perhaps more subtly *worldly* character of those images affects the way in which we are able to think about things not in the same class. If we think about the mind as if it were separate from us then we are thinking about it as if it were an object in the world like the other things that we perceive.

However, at this point Augustine does not go on to present us with an alternative way of thinking using another faculty or style of thought which is easily analogous to our normal thoughts. We are told instead to turn round the *intentio uoluntatis* which had been wandering around in "other" things (*uagabatur*) and to stand and concentrate on ourselves (*statuat in semetipsam*).[59] The outworking of this rather gnomic injunc-

---
[56] *Trin.* X, 8, 11 (CCSL 50, 324).
[57] *Trin.* X, 8, 11 (CCSL 50, 324).
[58] *Trin.* X, 8, 11 (CCSL 50, 325).
[59] *Trin.* X, 8, 11 (CCSL 50, 325).

tion is an analysis of the *process* by which this statement or command might itself be understood — in effect a continuation of Augustine's attempt to explain the meaning of the Delphic injunction to self-knowledge. X, 9,12 focuses this discussion and reinforces some points which have already been made: knowing one's mind is not like knowing angels because we believe things about absent beings — however incorporeal — by assenting to certain propositions; in the same way it is not like knowing our faces because they too are known in a mirror, as if absent. Nor are we looking for some "thing" which could serve as an analogy for the mind: as is clear in X, 10,16, any thing about which we were uncertain could not be proposed as being the mind or as being like the mind, because it would thus be something which had been thought about as if it were absent. We would have had to think of it as something separate even to think of it as a possible answer to the search, and it could only have been known to us through an imaginary phantasm (*imaginalis figmentum*). Thus X, 10,16 attempts to rule out a whole variety of methods of searching through labelling them all — however sophisticated — as involving an artificial separation of mind and object known.

Going back a little to the start of this present section of the essay, Plotinus, *Enn.* I, 6,9, has often been indicated as a possible "parallel" with *trin.* X, 8,11.[60] Consideration of this parallel will help to illustrate ways in which Augustine and Plotinus are *not* attempting the same exercise. Plotinus indicates that in order to see ourselves we must work like a sculpture who cuts away (ἀφαιρῶ and ἐργάζῶ) at a block of marble,[61]

---

[60] E.g. in all three modern editions of the work, the CCSL, Bibliotheque Augustinienne and Nuova Biblioteca Agostiniana.

[61] Augustine's use of *detraho* seems to mirror well the middle platonic and Plotinian use of ἀφαιρῶ (and to a *much* lesser extent ἀνάλυσις): I am grateful to Dr. B. Capper for first indicating the possible link. Elsewhere *detraho* and ἀφαιρῶ do seem to be used similarly, e.g. *Enn.* 6.8.11 and 6.8.21. The parallel would certainly seem to be with Plotinus's use of the term, following Martley, indicating a process of mental abstraction as much as a full-blown "apophatic" theology, and thus slightly different from the usage of ἀφαιρῶ one finds in e.g. Gregory of Nyssa, e.g. *De an. et res.* PG 46, 40C. However, the parallel at X, 8,11 is uncertain simply because Plotinus's simile functions so differently from Augustine's techincal usage here. Much more work on Augustine's use of *detraho* is needed than is possible here: for the combination of mathematical and grammatical uses of the verb see *TLL* 5. 828–9. On the philosophical and mathematical senses of ἀφαιρῶ see R. Mortley, "Negative Theology in Plotinus," *AJPh* 96 (1975) 363–77, esp. the literature cited in n.1, and J. Whittaker, "Neopythagoreanism and Negative Theology," *Symbolae Osloenses* 44 (1969) 109–

clearing away darkness (σκοτεινά) until a face is revealed bright and beautiful. This metaphor is followed by an indication of how the pure will be able to see the forms, and that purity here is a moral quality. It is also the case that what one perceives in looking at oneself is non-corporeal and part of the intelligible world. Lastly, Plotinus does use the language of "oneness" to describe the resultant quality of self-perception (...οὐδὲν ἔχων ἐμπόδιον πρὸς τὸ εἷς οὕτω γενέσθαι...) when this feat of seeing in oneself has been acomplished. However to assert this as a parallel without further comment actually misses much of the point Augustine is trying to make. Plotinus's language of revealing a beautiful face through a process in something which is objectified, as the statue imagery suggests, does not simply go against the intention of Augustine's picture, it betrays a different thrust to the argument.

Perhaps my point is clearest in two stages: first, there is a clash of images between these two passages — very differing connotations are evident in the choice of metaphorical language chosen, even if Plotinus in the end comes close to using similar language of a discovered unity (we need constantly to bear in mind how carefully Augustine prepares the ground for his argument by ruling out of court any sort of style of knowing which involves such an objectifying procedure).[62] Secondly, these two passages reveal different interests in what appears to be — and what to some extent obviously *is* — a similar process. The thrust of Augustine's argument focuses upon the different styles of knowing necessary in knowing objects which are separate from us and in knowing our minds. for this reason he pays much more attention to the actual method by which one comes to such knowledge (as we shall see). Plotinus, on the other hand does not consider *how* we can understand and interpret the experience of trying to know ourselves, and thus is able to make effective but philosophically loose use of the sculptor simile, of

---

25, esp. 121ff. On the subject of ἀνάλυσις I have been much influenced by Colin Macleod's essay "'Ἀνάλυσις: a Study in Ancient Mysticism," as printed with extra notes in *Collected Papers* (Oxford: Clarendon Press 1983) 292–305.

[62] For an earlier discussion of the importance of attending to the metaphors used by Augustine and ancient writers in general see my "Between Athens and Jerusalem: Prolegomena to Anthropology in *De trinitate*," *Modern Theology* 8 (1992) 53–73, and R.J. O'Connell's recent *Soundings in St. Augustine's Imagination* (New York: Fordham University Press 1994). Note also that what one comes to see is radically different in the two writers, Plotinus ends *Enn.* I. 6,9 by discussing the relationship of the Good and Beauty, the metaphor of ascent and the Neoplatonic hierarchical intelligible world are absent from Augustine's picture.

allusions to the famous *Phaedrus* myth of the soul's chariot being pulled by two horses (esp. here with reference to the section of the story at *Phaedrus* 252d–254), and of allusions to the ascent to the Good in *Symposium* and *Republic*. If I might put my case in an equally metaphorical way, the faultlines of Plotinus's argument, the points at which Plotnius himself strains to make sense, are not concerned with the problems and mechanics of our own self-perception in the same way as is Augustine's argument.[63]

In many ways equally convincing parallels with the emphasis of Augustine's argument at X, 8,11 are provided by some of the material in *Enn.* VI.4–5, ("On The Presence of Being Everywhere"), *Enn.* V, 6 ("On the fact that that which is beyond being does not think"), and very clearly at *Enn.* V, 3 ("On the Knowing Hypostases").[64] I don't want here to suggest these as actual references, that is a task beyond the scope of my argument, but I do want to suggest that they function just as well in indicating similarities and the particular character of the differences between the Augustinian and Plotinian understanding of self-knowledge at this point. At VI, 4,2 Plotinus comments on our willingness to raise questions of space about Being simply because in normal perception we associate space with beings. We need instead to realise that an encounter with Being is an encounter with "the All" (τὸ πᾶν) and that it is never possible to tear Being from itself, which must lead to a radical reconception of our knowing in this case. At VI, 5,8 Plotinus comments on crude understandings of the process of illumination (ἐλλάμψις); we talk as if space were an integral part of the process of illumination (here πόρρω and χωρίς) when in fact we need to use such language only to indicate metaphorically some key facets of what happens in the process of illumination. As he goes on to tell us, because of the difference between form as archetype and object as "image," illumination seems to involve a keeping "separate" (χωρίς), although of course it cannot actually involve a separation in space.[65] At *Enn.* V, 6,1, (according to Porphyry the

---

[63] My interpretation of *Enn.* I. 6,9 is much indebted to J. Rist's discussion in the two relevant chapters of his *Plotinus: The Road to Reality* (Cambridge: Cambridge University Press 1967) 38–65; in particular one needs to note that the strong emphasis on the similarities between good things and the Good is to some extent particular to *Enn.* I, 6,9.

[64] Booth (above, n.7) 212 notes the similarity with *Enn.* V, 3,1 but does not examine the comparison in any detail.

[65] My understanding here is much indebted to J. Rist's "The Problem of 'Other-

treatise next in chronological order after *Enn.* VI, 4–5) something thinking itself is that which most nearly escapes being a duality in a way that something thinking another thing never can. Lastly, *Enn.* V, 3 presents a series of parallels with Augustine's argument.[66] Plotinus asks whether that which thinks itself must be complex, and whether one part of the soul is able to know another (*Enn.* V, 3,1). Gradually our reason is isolated and the dual soul spoken of, the sensual part aware of the corporeal world and the higher able to be aware of νοῦς and able gradually to become more like it (*Enn.* V, 3,3). From here we are able to begin to understand the self-thinking qualities of the νοῦς, able to think of itself and aware of the link between the Intelligibles and the Intellect. If knowledge is not to involve division (μερισμὸς) then νοῦς and τὸ νοήτον must be the same (*Enn.* V, 3,5).

However, in all of these passages there are clear differences with Augustine's account. First, Plotinus's presentation does not seem designed to construct a doctrine of analogy which will *necessarily* be part of a practice in the world in the same way as Augustine understands "practice." In a number of the above mentioned passages the discussion of the nature of self-thinking νοῦς is designed to provide part of a proof for the existence of a higher hypostasis which is beyond thought. The unity in duality which must characterise all thinking in some sense can only be conceived if there is something which is beyond such duality and hence beyond thought. It is important also to remember that Plotnius's Neoplatonic radicalism, with reference to middle Platonism, often denies the possibility of participation between the different hypostases (least clear in V,6 of those *Enneads* mentioned above).[67]

---

ness' in the Enneads," *Le Néoplatonisme. Colloque international du C.N.R.S., Royaumont, juin 1969* (Paris: Editions du CNRS 1971) 77–87. There Rist sets out some essentials of the theme: the "otherness" which characterises all things separate from the One is in some sense a mark of their movement (see *Enn.* III, 8,1: and their tendency to non-being), and in unity with the One it must disappear. This last theme is evident from the famous contrast of νοῦς thinking and νοῦς loving at *Enn.* VI, 7,35: the soul in union has no movement and hence no otherness. At that point the soul remains different perhaps because it differs in strength from the One although essentially similar. However one hedges matters it does seem that there is something of a disjuncion between the metaphysics of Plotinus and his understanding of mystical union.

[66] It is worth noting that despite the lack of this parallel in the relevant Augustinian literature A.H. Armstrong notes an "apparent parallel" with *trin.* IX, 3,3 and X, 3,5 in his Loeb edition, *Plotinus*, Loeb 5 (London: Heinemann 1984) 75.

[67] There is a very useful summary of the differences between Plotinus and the middle

Plotinus uses some common Neoplatonic themes to persuade us first to see the different implications of the dualities present in our thinking, thus encouraging us to reason to the existence of something beyond thinking, and second to persuade us to see the need for the Good to be prior to the Beautiful if we are to understand the relationships between the different hypostases. The theme of duality and unity in thinking is put to very different use in these passages of Plotinus from the situation we find in *trin.* X, depending to a large extent on a different basic picture of the "intelligible universe," if such a phrase is at all appropriate in Augustine's case. Plotinus's use of the theme of unity and duality in thinking depends upon his understanding of the structure of the universe and his understanding of how all things are characterised by their natural difference from the One. Augustine's understanding is some ways takes place in a "flattened" intellectual universe, there being no place for the intellectual hierarchy of Neoplatonism, and is designed to illustrate our place in a fallen yet potentially perfectly ordered universe. It is possible for Augustine to "think ourselves" without abandoning all knowledge of our secondary position: there is a relationship between creator and creature which permits an awarenes of the presence of God to us while still being aware — while necessarily also being aware — of our created status.[68]

The second difference between these two authors lies in the different uses to which these conceptions of duality and unity are put. For Plotinus there is a dialectic which allows us to understand (naturally with some paradox) the unity which must characterise the One (and arrival at that unity will in the end result in the soul divesting itself of logic and dialectic[69]). Although there are very few ways in which we can

---

platonic outlook with reference to participation and analogy, and the theological use of these themes in R.D. Williams, *Arius: Heresy and Tradition* (London: DLT 1987) 215ff., esp. 219–22. I say "often" because of the question of Plotinian mysticism, see Rist (above, n.63) 213f.

[68] In some senses the key theme in Augustine's transformation of Neoplatonism is his understanding of the necessary and intended difference between God and creation which facilitates love in a way markedly difference from all conception of difference in Plotinus.

[69] See esp. *Enn.* I, 3, 4. It is of course impossible to do just to the sophistication of Plotinus's account here, but it is important to note that his account of the presence of the intelligibles in the intellect is a central part of how he can hold together these themes of separation and ultimate participation, see esp. A.H. Armstrong, *The Architecture of The Intelligible Universe in the Philosophy of Plotinus* (Cambridge: Cam-

make direct use of the language of participation, the language of emanation and of the different hypostases seems to guarantee the possibility of reasoning through the order of the cosmos (however difficult it is to draw any direct link between the good we see around us and Good itself).[70] Plotinus is able to be make use of what we can know about the structure of the cosmos as a "trace"[71] of the One to show how we may reason through it. We can also speak of a mystical ascent to the One in which our normal sense of duality is transcended, and even our searching must give way to stillness in order to join the One's perfect rest (V, 5,8). The two languages of return are linked through the centrality of dialectic and reason (as a Plotinian *exercitatio animi*) to the process of return.[72]

For Augustine the purpose of the contrast between unity and duality is markedly different. First, it indicates the problems fallen people have in separating their normal modes of thought from the type of thinking necessary to think the mind and to understand how they are able to judge at all. Second, to understand the presence of God to the mind — and in some sense our participation in God's self-giving — we need to move beyond objectification. Third, in *trin.* the purpose of overstepping the "duality" of perception is intended to allow us to make further progress at imagining how the intra-trinitarian logic works. We can only understand the unity of our mind's self-presence once we learn to understand the perfect mutual presence of the Trinity. Understanding the Plotinian One is markedly different from understanding the unity in difference of the Trinity and the continual immediacy of its self-communication to the mind. Ultimately, because of Augustine's eschatological location of the vision of God, we can only live *towards* fulfillment of our searching self in union with God — a theme which will become clearer in the next section of the paper. The unity that we come to know in this life can only ever provide an analogy of the unity for which we strive.

bridge University Press 1940), and the discussion of the One in the first two chapters of the work. The question of the One's knowledge is well summarised in Rist (above, n.61) 65ff.; 38ff.

[70] In this regard the optimism of *Enn.* I, 6 stands out, see in general terms A.C. Lloyd, *The Anatomy of Neoplatonism* (Oxford: Clarendon Press 1990) 140f.

[71] Cf. for example *Enn.* VI, 7,17 and V, 5,5. Perhaps here the late tolerance and acceptance of Stoic themes by Plotinus is evident.

[72] This is presented at its most seamless by A.H. Armstrong in his ch. 16 of A.H. Armstrong (ed.), *The Cambridge History of Later Greek and Early Medieval Philosophy* (Cambridge: Cambridge University Press 1967) 250–68.

Thus moving beyond the easy parallel of *trin.* X, 8,11 and *Enn.* I, 6,9 enables us to explore at more length other parallels which seem to demonstrate closely related terminologies of unity and duality in thinking and self-thinking. However, this more difficult exercise begins to show up the complexities of any easy equation of the two thinkers' techniques and intentions, and demonstrates the care with which we need to compare Plotinian and Augustinian views on self-knowledge. We can only understand where their positons are similar once we begin to place their views on this particular subject in the context of their wider use of any particular theme. This comparison has particular importance here because of the relationship between self-knowledge and knowledge of the Trinity in Augustine.

IV. Book X, 10,13–12,19

Returning to our original text, and starting at X, 10,13 (thus returning over some of the ground traversed in the last section), we see again that to know ourselves, we need to undertake a process of thought, we need to think about *how* we will seek, not simply for what we will seek. Augustine seeks through X, 10,13–10,16 to identify things which are irremovable from our self-perception, and at the end of X, 10,16 he asserts that beneath all our activity we need to suppose something as the subject of the verbs of living (knowing, understanding, and willing). We can give no content to these verbs in the sense of filling out their subject as yet: we can simply assert the existence of a subject engaged in these activities.[73] The particular three things on which he picks are also of significance: they do not constitute simply three functions or faculties of the mind, but the three verbs which seem necessary to Augustine (and which necessarily go together) to facilitate the conscious progress of life of which we are all aware.[74] If we follow the logic of Book X as I have indicated then it is clear that we can think of the action of the mind in the world (and note that no other kind is envisaged) but we cannot give any

---

[73] A helpful parallel is provided by the probably slightly later discussion in *an. et or.* IV, 6,7–7,10 where we are often not aware of the capacities of these three "parts" of us, even though we are aware of them in some basic form. Even Peter, ready to lay down his life for Christ is depicted here as unaware of the powers and resources of his own will.

[74] *Trin.* X, 9,13 (CCSL 50, 326): *Sed est et cadauer, uiuit et pecus; intellegit autem nec cadauer, nec pecus. Sic ergo se esse et uiuere scit, quomodo est et uiuit, intelligentia.*

imaginary/perceptible content to "things" such as *uoluntas*. Their status is as yet purposely unexplained and we must take *uoluntas*, for example, as referring to "the activity of will in conjunction with... ," not thinking of will as if it were a separable thing; we know of our need to think of it *etsi non detracta* but cannot yet do so. The attempt to describe a discipline which will facilitate awarenes of our active presence in the world again forms the background to what follows.

Augustine finishes Book X by returning to the question which formed the context of the whole discussion (carried over from Book IX), how are we to understand the trinity of the mind, its knowledge and love?[75] Discussion of X, 11,17 will complete my understanding of the shift in the trinitarian analogy under consideration, the shift from a triad of *mens*, *notitia* and *amor* to one of *memoria*, *intelligentia* and *uoluntas* mentioned briefly at the beginning of the paper. As with many other places where Augustine produces a "new" analogy or shifts terminology he does so extremely abruptly, with very little warning. For the majority of the book, as will have become apparent from my reading, he simply does not discuss "head on" the nature of his picture of the mind as analogy, but now he returns to that aspect of his discussion, leaving it up to us to follow the threads of the discussion, and to place the brief discussion at the end of the book in its context.

The shift happens ostensibly because these three new terms provide a better way of understanding progress in knowledge (which *has* been a major theme of the book). We can see in these three the *ingenia paruulorum*: this trinity brings out the quick reactions of one who studies and especially the close relationship between increase in memory and increase in desire.[76] The better someone remembers, the better they understand and the better a person they are likely to be or to become. There is a fairly obvious parallel intended between the person who begins a search for God inspired by an initial understanding, and the child eager to learn. This is apparent both from the use of the picture of our ultimate loves which has been established as a fundamental division between the fallen and the being-redeemed person, and from the discus-

---

[75] *Trin.* X, 11,17.
[76] *Trin.* X, 11,17 (CCSL 50, 329): *In his enim tribus inspici solent etiam ingenia paruulorum cuiusmodi praeferant indolem.*

sion of learning *doctrina* (mirroring the discussion of *pulchritudo doctrinae* at X, 1,2).[77]

But that is not all, for this new trinity also points to Cicero and to a formulation of the rhetorical tradition. At *inu. 2, 53, 160* Cicero turn to the question of describing things which one can class as *honestum* (as part of the *inuentio* of character). *Honestum* is divided into four parts, *prudentia, iustitia, fortitudo* and *temperantia:*

> *Prudentia est rerum bonarum et malarum neutrarumque scientia. Partes eius: memoria, intellegentia, prouidentia. Memoria est per quam animus repetit illa quae fuerunt; intellegentia, per quam ea perspicit quae sunt; prouidentia, per quam futurum aliquid uidetur ante quam factum est.*
>
> Wisdom is knowledge of good, of bad and of things which are neither. Its parts are memory, intelligence and foresight. Memory is that through which the mind recalls what has happened; intelligence that through which the mind ascertains what is; foresight, that through which something that will happen is seen before it does.

The allusion at *trin.* X, 11,17 is not accidental. Augustine's introduction of the trio *memoria, intellegentia* and *uoluntas* replacing Cicero's third-place *prouidentia*, not only allows him to link *usus* and *uoluntas* and *amor*, but also picks up and refocuses the meaning of *prouidentia*. However, before looking directly at Augustine's use some background will prove helpful.

Despite its importance and usefulness as a description of the divisions of the moral life, the Ciceronian phrase is used remarkably infrequently by Christian authors before Augustine (and perhaps this lack of frequency has contributed to the importance of its use here being neglected in secondary scholarship).[78] One interesting and instructive parallel

---

[77] *Trin.* X, 11,17 (CCSL 50, 329): *Cum uero de cuiusque doctrina quaeritur, non quanta firmitate ac facilitate meminerit, uel quanto acumine intellegat; sed quid meminerit, et quid intellegat quaeritur. Et quia non tantum quam doctus sit, consideratur laudabilis animus, sed etiam quam bonus; non tantum quid meminerit et quid intellegat, uerum etiam quid uelit attenditur... Tunc enim laudandus est animus uehementer amans, cum id quod amat uehementer amandum est.* The love imagery of Bk VIII is spelled out in terms of the final analogy of Bks X–XIV.

[78] The only scholar to discuss the parallel at any length is Schindler (above, n.6) esp. 58–60. He remarks on the importance of the allusion but does not seem to find a way of satisfactorily incorporating it into his account of *trin*. His summary (p. 60) is helpful:

"Daß hier wirklich diese Tradition von Einfluß ist, deutet Augustin ja an und bestätigt sich auch bei der Durchsicht Ciceros und Quintilians, wobei (and the only parallel which clearly develops the phrase theologically) is to be found in Victorinus's commentary on Eph. 3.1–4. Victorinus's text of those verses read: *Huius rei gratia ego Paulus uinctus Christi pro uobis gentibus, si tamen audistis dispositionem dei gratiae. Notum mihi factum est mysterium, sicut ante scripsi in modico, prout potuistis legentes intellegere prudentiam meam in mysterio Christi.*[79] The providential translation of the Greek's οἰκονομίαν as *dispositionem* (as against the vulgate's *dispensationem*) and τὴν σύνεσίν μου as *prudentiam meam* (a translation in common with the vulgate, but cf. Col. 2.2, where the same noun in different context is translated by the more predictable *intellectus*) allows Victorinus to draw the Ciceronian

> wierderum bemerkenswert ist, daß schön da die drei als wirkliche dreiheit auftauchen und somit die Dreiheit gerade dieser 'Seelenvermögen' einigermaßen präformiert war, bevor Augustin die Sache aufgriff. Bezeichnend ist ebenfalls, daß im dritten Glied, beim usus, Augustin den Willen und die Willensrichtung mit ins Spiel bringt und sein uti-frui-Schema in Erinnerung ruft, während dieser Terminus bei Quintilian z. B. nicht den Gebrauch zum Guten oder Bösen meint, sondern die Ubung, die zu Natruanlage und Wissen hinzutreten muß. Was schon für das Schema der drei Fragen galt, gilt hier natürlich noch mehr: das vorgegebene Schema wird von Augustin mit fast völlig neuem Inhalt gefüllt, und es fliessen nicht nur typisch augustinische, sondern auch weitergehende geistesgeschichtliche Ströme in das Flußbett der rhetorischen Formeln, die Augustin dazu erwählt hat, einer weit über solche Traditionen hinausdrängen geistigen Bemühung zu dienen."

While Schindler is right that Augustine fills a traditional rhetorical scheme with new content, and incorporates it entirely into his theology, he is perhaps too global in his judgement that Augustine provides entirely new content: Augustine manipulates the content so as to effect a reorientation of the scheme, tying our moral lives directly into our growing in knowing and loving the Trinity. It is important that Schindler does not see how this adaptation fits into the overall structure of what Augustine is attempting in *trin*. His account remains helpful for its clear emphasis on the tradition from which this formulation arose. Apart from the doubt about Augustine's reading of Quintilian, I have concentrated here on the Ciceronian parallel, believing it to be paramount. Schindler provides texts in his notes illustrating some other uses in the tradition.

As a parallel (and one much more fully developed) for this theological adaptation of Cicero and the rhetorical tradition see the first two chapters of R. Dodaro's thesis (above, n.11) 1–81 on the transformation of the orator. The philosophical use of the theme is not commented on in M. Testard's *Saint Augustin et Cicéron* (Paris: Etudes Augustiniennes 1958), nor in A. Michel's *Rhétorique et Philosophie chez Cicéron* (Paris: Presses Universitaires de France 1960).

[79] Vict., *In Eph.* I, 1262A–1263B Teubner. Previous to his conversion Victorinus had of course dealt fairly descriptively in his commentaries on Cicero. Of his treatement one should note especially that he equates the three words with the three parts of time, e.g. *Expl. in Cic. rhet.* 2, 52: *Nam praeteriti temporis est memoria, praesentis,*

parallel. First Victorinus is able to state that grace is presented in an order to us (*disposita sit*) through the presence of God in Christ and Christ's *uirtus*, just as the gospel was presented to the Ephesians through Paul: whatever happens as part of this ordering happens through revelation. Then, commenting on the latter end of this passage, he draws attention to the *prudentiam* which has been revealed to him: when we want to know the content of this insight we are told: *in eo, quod tibi reuelatum est, uel memoria uel scientia uel intellegentia. haec enim partes prudentiae.* Victorinus connects the Christian understanding of what is *honestum* with the Ciceronian definition of *prudentia* but transforms it through the context of revelation in Christ: Christ's *uirtus* reveals our *prudentia*. This parallel does not seem to indicate any direct borrowing of themes for two simple reasons: first, the passage is not matched elsewhere in Victorinus's writings, and in particular the theme is not linked in directly with his christology or with his trinitarian terminology. Secondly one does not find extensive discussion of Eph 3.1–4 in *trin*. However, the passage, by its very lack of direct relationship to Augustine's own independent use indicates the possibility of direct borrowing from Cicero by two similarly trained late Roman orators: but it is Augustine's use which is the more sophisticated and the more closely integrated into an overall theological position.

That Augustine *intentionally* alludes to Cicero in this trinitarian analogy seems evident from his later direct discussion of Cicero's text at *trin*. XIV, 11,14. There *prouidentia* will not do in any Christian trinity which describes the nature of the mind because humans have no foresight (quoting Wisd. 9.14). In this life we can only turn towards the future by concentrating our *uoluntas* on God.[80] Augustine also attempts to show that the three terms are all present simultaneously, and that all are vital to present self-awareness. That which makes it possible for us to be aware of ourselves now can be called memory, and without this "memory" it would not be possible for the will or love to assent to our present self-awareness. If we are to understand the self-presence and self-giving of the Trinity we need to see these three not as representing

intellegentia, futuri providentia: has similiter definit. As one might expect, *after* Augustine one finds the phrase reasonably frequently in well known Augustinians, e.g. Arnobius Iunior, Fulgentius and Faustus of Riez.

[80] Perhaps here one can see similar reasoning to that employed at *retr.* I, 1,2; 1,4, commenting on *acad*. where Augustine is unhappy with his earlier emphasis on speaking of providence as it can only be understood in connection with God.

three different phases of time (as in Victorinus) but as all being necessary for the process of present self-knowledge. The direct discussion of Cicero's definition is preceded by quotation from *Hortensius* in favour of the permanence of the virtues in the next life (if only, in some cases, as memory). This passage thus indicates to us that the isolation of that within us which facilitates a virtuous life is the identification of that which is permanent within us.[81] After the discussion of *inu.* at XIV, 11,14, and following a discussion of the need for the image of God within us to be renewed through a process of graceful worship of God, and not through self-absorption (XIV, 12,15–18,24), Augustine turns again to Cicero at the end of Book XIV. There the *Hortensius* is again quoted, this time to demonstrate that one only becomes wise through attention to the teaching of Christ and not simply through attention to human philosophical searching. In making this statement Augustine contradicts Cicero's mention of a possible extinction of ourselves at death as a legacy of his dalliance with the new Academy, souls are immortal and he should have stated so unambiguously.[82]

The Ciceronian allusion at X, 11,17 is, then, designed to provide a picture of the mind or soul which concentrates directly on our ability to grow in the love of God. Augustine comes to this final image of Book X through the discussion of the triad of the mind's knowing, understanding and living, a triad which concentrates on the mind's innate and inescapable awareness of itself in all its actions. Thus *memoria, intellegentia* and *uoluntas* offers a triad which focuses directly on what we must discern if we are to see how we are already present to ourselves. At the same time this trinity is both able to explain how we become obssessed with created things to the exclusion of God[83] and is able to explain how we might "return" to God. In the latter case this trinity picks up on the theme of our need to return to our appropriate created "place" and ties in closely with the forthoming discussion of how the Christian moves from *scientia* to *sapientia* (discussed below); this trinity is able to form the core of a discussion of how we come to understand our lives as the sphere of redemption in Christ. This trinity enables us to look at how we might come to see ourselves *etsi non detracta*, coming to an increasing awareness of ourselves through reori-

---

[81] *Trin.* XIV, 9,12.
[82] *Trin.* XIV, 19,26. Augustine repeats the intellectual history of *acad.* III.
[83] There is an excellent analysis of just this point at XIV, 13,17.

enting ourselves towards God. Note finally that in being aware of this trinity extracted, in the flow of Augustine's argument, from the verbs of remembering, knowing and willing/loving we do not know ourselves as self-sufficient or as in any complete, we are rather aware of a process of self-presence which constantly leads us towards or away from our true "place."[84]

In the last section of Bk X (12,19) Augustine poses a question: should we now ascend (*ascendendum est*) to contemplate the highest *essentia* of the three persons, or should one make further use of models in the soul which is the point at which we form impressions of corporeal bodies? I think the gerunds here are vital: this is not a posing of alternatives either of which are acceptable (Augustine simply going on to choose the more laborious route!), Augustine asks a question about the necessary route one must follow if progress is to be made. Two reasons are given for preferring the second choice: first the difficulty of separating the operations of the mind from the things which it perceives — once again we have great difficulty in separating ourselves from the images by which we know corporeality, and a further exploration of the problem is necessary; second, because of this first difficulty we are not able to see fully the difference between *memoria* and *intelligentia*, and without an understanding of their separate qualities we cannot understand the necessary role of love in this analogy and thus in the Trinity. Augustine thus builds on his analysis of the difficulties of seing ourselves *non detracta*, but does not offer an easy solution, he has told us that to see ourselves thus is to understand the interaction of *memoria, intellegentia* and *uoluntas*, but he also states that this in itself cannot be accomplished simply by stating the triad and saying "there, look." Augustine's argument began as an insistence that there must be a discipline of self-knowledge. Much of the book consisted in an attempt to highlight the difficulty with any such discipline and the difficulty with any appropriate self-knowledge. The book ends with the evolution of a new analogy for the trinity within a picture of what is permanent in the mind. These permament features are the features which guarantee the permanent process of our existence towards or away from God whether or not we are aware of them. At the very end of the book Augustine has only *begun* to set the scene for the discussion of how we can become involved in the discipline itself, through Bks XIII–XIV.

[84] Cf. Williams (above, n.7) 127.

V. Conclusion

At this point Book X ends, and it might seem that the attempt to examine one book of such a complex work as *trin.* in isolation is always a virtually impossible task, simply because of the difficulty of bringing one's conclusions to full development. Perhaps one might have more success attempting to present an overall sketch of the work rather than beginning to look at the issues raised in one section without being to relate them in detail to the rest of the argument. However, it is important to note that there are two good reasons for looking in detail at this part of the work. First, one begins to get a feel for the style of Augustine's argument, in particular a feel for the different layers on which the argument operates. Here there has been no direct discussion of the Trinity itself, and yet that lies always below the surface. The discussion of the mind's self-knowledge only makes sense when we understand that it is part of a wider consideration of how we may come to know and love God. Following this statement directly, my second reason is that without going through the argument about self-knowledge here in some detail we might miss the essential fact that it is *not* complete. Book X does not offer Augustine's views on self-knowledge, but simply one part of a wider argument which links theological anthropology with the theology of the Trinity. As we have just seen, Augustine ends the book by reasserting the difficulty of attaining the sort of self-knowledge that he has tried to establish as being the only sufficient self-knowledge. Being fully aware of this virtual, if temporary *aporia* in the argument of *trin.* is the most important corrective to the assumption that it is possible to abstract from Augustine's text an account of self-knowledge not tied in to an account of how one comes to know God, and how one may think of God as Trinity.

The *aporia* is only temporary, and Augustine does go on to provide an answer to the situation as it is left at the end of Book X. That answer is provided in three stages — though remember again that each of these stages should also be the subject of a detailed commentary. First Book XI returns over the ground of the difference between our awareness of things and our awarenes of each other, concentrating on and expanding Augustine's view of how this new triad actually operates. Second, Book XII offers an understanding of the two parts of the soul, the lower and the higher and explains that it is only when our souls (which remain an inseparable unity) operate in the correct order that we are able to see the true purpose and place of the various things which we perceive, and hence begin to set right our absorption with worldly corporeal images. This order is illustrated through the important pairing of *scientia* and *sapientia*.[85] Book XIII mirrors and completes this discussion with its picture of Christian *scientia* and *sapientia*, two modes of human knowing — not simply the knowlede of two separate sets of objects — which find their unity in the person of Christ. He is both divine and human and the examples which he presents to us lead into the *sacramentum* of his divine nature.[86] Thus it is only through attention to our life in this world, through the example which Christ presents to us that we may come to understand the divine nature. The *aporia* of needing to understand the mind's self-presence and yet not being able to escape from corporeal ways of thought is solved through our slow progress in a life which relies on God's grace taking us through Christ as *exemplum* to Christ as *sacramentum*. This last step is rightly part of the third stage of the answer, which one finds in books XIV and XV. There we find that contrary to Cicero's picture we only come to wisdom and to know our state as *imago Dei* when we strive to know, love and understand God. In so doing we properly love ourselves (XIV, 14,18) and come to see how we as created can never truly understand the Trinity itself. At this final

---

[85] See Ayres (above, n.7) 129–46. Key to my examination there is the analogy of men and women for the lower and higher parts of reason is just that, and that whatever that book reveals about Augustines' understanding of men and women (much less than is supposed on a quick reading of the passage) we miss the point of its appearance in *trin.* if we do not look at the part it plays in the structure of this work, especially in combination with Bk XIII. On the question of the book as allegory see T.J. Van Bavel, "Women as the Image of God in Augustine's *De Trinitate* XII," A. Zumkeller (ed.), *Signum Pietatis: Festgabe für Cornelius Mayer o.s.a. zum 60* (Würzburg: Augustinus Verlag 1989) 267–88. For *scientia* and *sapientia* see the following note.

[86] On Bk XIII see Ayres (above, n.7) 146–56. The seminal interpretation of the *scientia/sapientia* pairing in terms of Christology remains that of G. Madec, "Christus, scientia et sapientia nostra. Le principe de cohérence de la doctrine augustinienne," *Recherches Augustiniennes* 10 (1975) 77–85. This account, while provocative leads something to be desired in terms of analysis of the actual textual location of Augustine's particular use of the theme. The pairing needs to considered in conjunction with that of *sacramentum* and *exemplum*. For this see B. Studer, "Sacramentum et Exemplum," *Recherches Augustiniennes* 10 (1975) 87–141, but also R. Dodaro, "*Sacramentum Christi*: Augustine on the Christology of Pelagius," *SP* 27 (1993) 274–805. Contra Studer, Dodaro insists that the pairing is not an antithesis, one passes through *exemplum* to *sacramentum*. His analysis fits closely in with my own concentration on the link between the discipline necessary in this life to follow the *exemplum Christi* as a necessary part of our growth in knowledge and love of the Trinity itself.

point of *trin.* it becomes clear that no conception of self-knowledge will ever be complete in so far as it fails to understand that we will only come to be aware of ourselves when we are granted the final vision of the Trinity after the judgement — and that will be a vision of Christ *both* crucified *and* in glory.[87] This however, is to look too directly at another level of the argument in *trin.*!

---

[87] See *trin.* I, 13, 30–1.

18

Melanchthon's First Manual on Rhetorical Categories in Criticism of the Bible

C.J. Classen

I. Introduction

Biblical exegesis is as old as the Bible itself. For some more recent parts of the Old Testament are based upon and make use of older parts, whether they adapt them to their own time or reinterpret them in accordance with their own theological views or religious beliefs.[1] Later one finds in the Jewish tradition the *Torah* both as object and standard of interpretation, also e.g. in the Qumran texts, while both Jesus and St. Paul as well as other authors of the New Testament support their own

---

[1] See for example volumes in the series Compendia Rerum Iudaicarum ad Novum Testamentum (CRINT), esp. II 1: M.J. Mulder, H. Sysling (eds.), *Mikra. Text, Translation, Reading and Interpretation of the Hebrew Bible in Ancient Judaism and Early Christianity* (Assen: Von Gorcum 1988), also II 2: M.E. Stone (ed.), *Jewish Writings of the Second Temple Period* (Assen: Von Gorcum 1984) (on apocrypha and pseudepigrapha). See also H. Graf Reventlow, *Epochen der Bibelauslegung I. Vom Alten Testament bis Origenes* (Munich: Beck 1990) esp. 11–23; B. Uffenheimer and H. Graf Reventlow (eds.), *Creative Biblical Exegesis, Journal for the Study of the Old Testament*, Suppl. Ser. 59 (Sheffield: Sheffield Academic Press 1988); H. Fuchs, "Schrifterklärung," G. Herlitz and B. Kirschner (eds.), *Jüdisches Lexikon* I–IV (Berlin 1927–30) col. 262–9; "Hermeneutik," TRE 15, 108–56.

teaching by means of references to, quotations from and interpretations of the Old Testament.[2]

I cannot, here, characterize the various forms of Jewish exegesis, Halakha and Haggadah, or Philo's allegorizing together with their respective aims.[3] Nor can I illustrate at length the various types of exegesis practised in the New Testament and later by the earliest Fathers of the Church: one meets with a great variety of approaches, of methods (grammatical, historical, philological) and of intentions, partly due to different kinds of influences (e.g. philosophical ones).[4] What matters is that during the imperial period, as for pagan texts, also for the Holy Scriptures rhetorical criteria and categories begin to play an increasing role, as has been shown e.g. both for Origen and for St. Augustin, who even recommended the Bible as a sourcebook for rhetoric.[5]

However, for reasons not to be analysed here, the medieval exegetes and commentators — broadly speaking — replaced rhetoric by dialectic, so that rhetoric, as a tool for interpreting the Bible, lost its place (except for being used within the framework of the *ars concionandi*).[6]

---

[2] On the *Torah* as norm see Reventlow (above, n.1) 15–17; 20–2; 29–36 et saep.; on the Qumran texts pp. 32–7, on the New Testament pp. 52–103; on the Qumran texts see also Mulder (above, n.1) 339–77 and Stone (above, n.1) 483–550; on the New Testament see also Mulder (above, n.1) 691–725. On the oral *Torah* see Sh. Safrai in Sh. Safrai, P.J. Tomson (eds.), *The Literature of the Sages* I (Assen: Von Gorcum 1987) 35–120.

[3] On Halakha and Haggadah see Reventlow (above, n.1) 17–20, 29–35, 106–16; on Halakha see Safrai and Tomson (above, n.2) and P.J. Tomson, *Paul and the Jewish Law: Halakha in the Letters of the Apostle to the Gentiles*, CRINT III 1 (Assen: Von Gorcum 1990); on Philo see Stone (above, n.1) 233–82; Mulder (above, n.1) 421–53; P. Carny in Uffenheimer (above n.1) 31–8; D.T. Runia, *Exegesis and Philosophy: Studies on Philo of Alexandria* (Aldershot: Variorum Reprints 1990).

[4] See nn. 2 and 3 above and on the Church Fathers see Mulder (above n.1) 727–87; Reventlow (above, n.1) 116–93; Ch. Schäublin, *Untersuchungen zu Methode und Herkunft der antiochenischen Exegese* (Cologne 1974); see also n.5 below.

[5] See R.R. Bolgar, *The Classical Heritage and its Beneficiaries* (Cambridge 1954) 53 with reference to August. *doc.* 4.2 and 4.20; see rather 4.3, 4, 5, 11, 12 etc. On Origen see B. Neuschäfer, *Origenes als Philologe*, 2 vols. (Basle: Reinhardt 1987); further literature is listed by H.J. Sieben, *Exegesis Patrum: Saggio bibliografico sull' exegesi biblica dei Padri della Chiesa*, Sussidi Patristici 2 (Rome: Istituto Patristico 'Augustinianum' 1983).

[6] Cf. Th. J. Wengert, *Philip Melanchthon's Annotationes in Johannem in Relation to its Predecessors and Contemporaries* (Geneva: Droz 1987) 107. On the medieval exegesis in general see B. Smalley, *The Study of the Bible in the Middle Ages* (Oxford: Clarendon Press 1985[3] (first ed. 1941)); H. de Lubac, *Exégèse médiévale*, 2 vols., Théologie 41–2 (Paris: Aubier 1959–64), on the fate of rhetoric during this period B. Vickers, *In Defence of Rhetoric* (Oxford: Clarendon Press 1988) 214–53.

In the West the Latin text of the Bible formed the basis of spiritual and allegorical interpretation, sometimes influenced by the scholastics, and also of literal exegesis, as practised e.g. by Nicholas of Lyra (1270–1349) in his *Postilla*, a paraphrase which benefitted from the author's knowledge of Hebrew.[7] But the Greek text was virtually unknown in the West, nor was the Greek rhetorical tradition applied there, while in the East, where the Bible was read in Greek, speculative and homiletic exegesis prevailed.[8]

It was the earliest humanists who gradually applied the methods they developed for pagan texts to the Bible, and especially to the New Testament. Lorenzo Valla (1407–55), scholar at the court of Alfonso I, king of Naples, and later papal secretary, famous for his interest in and work on the Latin language (*Sex elegantiarum libri*), had the advantage of knowing Greek and being in a position which enabled him to use and collate several manuscripts (seven Greek, four Latin ones).[9] He became aware of different readings and the need of establishing a correct text; therefore, he started to compare the Vulgate with the Greek text and to correct the Vulgate with the help of the Greek, whether he thought the Vulgate corrupted conscientiously or unconscientiously or mis-translated. Thus, his approach was basically philological; but we do not find

---

[7] See de Lubac (above, n.6) I 23–6, II.2 344–67 et saep.; J.H. Bentley, *Humanists and Holy Writ* (Princeton NJ: Princeton University Press 1983) 21–31; Wengert (above, n.6) 96–118. Of the *Postilla* I have consulted the editions Venice 1481 (no title page, fol. 2ʳ: *Prologus primus Venerabilis fratris Nicolai de lyra ordinis seraphyci Francisci: in testamentum vetus...*; Hain N° 3164, *Gesamtkatalog der Wiegendrucke* N° 4286) and Strasbourg 1492 (*Prima pars venerabilis fratris Nicolai de lyra ordinis seraphici francisci (in testamentum vetus)...*, correspondingly for the *secunda, tertia* and *quarta pars*; Hain N° 3169, *Gesamtkatalog* N° 4292 (also reprinted Frankfurt 1971).

[8] Cf. Bentley (above, n.7) 15–17 (with further literature); to avoid a misunderstanding I should emphasize that Greek was, of course, known by some scholars in the West. On the East see H.-G. Beck, *Kirche und Theologische Literatur im Byzantinischen Reich*, Byzantische Handbuch 12/1 (Munich: Beck 1959), esp. 413–22, 467–72, 514–15, 591–7, 649–55, 789–93.

[9] See Bentley (above, n.7) 32–69, on the manuscripts p. 38; see in general S. Camporeale, *Lorenzo Valla. Umanesimo e teologia* (Florence: Istituto Nazionale di Studi sul Rinascimento 1972); also Ch. Trinkaus, *In Our Image and Likeness. Humanity and Divinity in Italian Humanistic Thought*, 2 vols. (London: Constable 1970) esp. 571–8, also 674–82 and P.G. Bietenholz, Th. B. Deutsch (eds.), *Contemporaries of Erasmus*, 3 vols. (Toronto: University of Toronto Press 1985–87) III 371–5. Valla wrote his *Collatio Novi Testamenti* 1442–48 (not published till 1970 in Florence by A. Perosa) and rewrote it 1453–57, printed by Erasmus as *Laurenti Vallensis...in Latinam Novi testamenti interpretationem...Adnotationes apprime utiles...* (Paris 1505).

him reflecting upon the methods he was applying, nor does he seem to "employ (sc. for the New Testament) some of the methods he used in his textual scholarship on classical works."[10] While he gained fame by proving the *Donation of Constantine* to be a forgery (also the correspondence between St. Paul and Seneca), he refrained from discussing authorship or authenticity of New Testament books. However, occasionally his careful examination of the text led him to corrections or improvements with important doctrinal consequences.

Valla's *...in Latinam Novi testamenti interpretationem... Adnotationes...* were published by Erasmus who regarded Valla together with his contemporary Jacques Lefèvre d'Etaples as his predecessors.[11] Lefèvre, a Frenchman, trained and first active in Paris, influenced later by Aristotelianism through his friend Pico della Mirandola and by mysticism through the writings of Nicholas of Cusa, translated, interpreted and preached the word of God. He regarded the Holy Scriptures as a gift of God transmitted by the Holy Spirit through the various authors of the Bible as *instrumenta*, to be further elucidated with the help of God through commentators as *subinstrumenta*, provided they approached their task in an attitude of humility and belief; most important for the interpretation is, he thought, the Holy Spirit, as whose instrument the exegete has to understand himself. Starting from certain assumptions about the nature of the Word of God, especially its dignity, Lefèvre was primarily concerned with its literal meaning, which he tried to determine by philological methods, making use of the Greek text, explaining etymologies or adding parallels from other books of the Bible or from the Fathers of the Church.[12]

---

[10] Bentley (above, n.7) 39.
[11] See G. Bedouelle, *Lefèvre d'Etaples et l'Intelligence des Ecritures*, Travaux D'Hum. et Ren. 152 (Geneva: Droz 1976); H. Heller in Bietenholz (above, n.9) II 315–17. His exegetical works: *Epistole divi Pauli apostoli cum commentariis preclarissimi viri Jacobi Fabri Stapulensis* (Paris 1512) and *Commentarii initiatorii in quatuor evangelia...* (Meaux 1522).
[12] See his dedicatory letter to the (younger) Guillaume Briçonnet (1472–1524), introducing his commentary on St. Paul's epistles of 1512 (above, n.11: fol. aI^r–aII^r), in part reprinted by Bedouelle (above, n.11) 141–5, see also 146–51 and his *praefatio* for the commentary of 1522 (above, n.11: fol. aII^r–aIV^v), in part reprinted by Bedouelle pp. 152–7, see also E.F. Rice, *The Prefatory Epistles of Jacques Lefèvre d'Etaples and Related Texts* (New York: Columbia University Press 1972) 295–302 (text of 1515) and 434–42. On the role of the Holy Spirit see Bedouelle (above, n.11) 185–9, on his philological method p. 27, on his exegetical principles see further F. Hahn, "Faber Stapulensis und Luther," *ZKG* 57 (1938) 356–432, esp. 396–424; S. Hausammann,

Erasmus, born and educated in the Low Countries and influenced by the *Devotio moderna*, the Brethren of Common Life, and more especially by the beginnings of humanistic studies north of the Alps, early developed a keen interest in Greek language and literature.[13] The encounter with John Colet in Oxford made him turn to religious matters:[14] Well versed in Greek he soon realized the need for a careful examination or reexamination of the basis of the Christian faith, the text of the Bible, and after writing a commentary on the epistles of St. Paul, which was never printed, in 1516 he published the Greek text of the New Testament together with an important methodological introduction and *Adnotationes*, since 1517 *Paraphrases* on most parts of the New Testament, and in 1519 a new Latin translation (to replace the Vulgate). Thereby he revolutionized the study of the New Testament and paved the way for Melanchthon's work and for that of many others.[15]

Römer-briefauslegung zwischen Humanismus und Reformation, Studien 2. Dogmen. und Syst. Theol. 27 (Zürich: Zwingli 1970) 88–117; J.B. Payne, "Erasmus and Lefèvre d'Etaples as Interpreters of Paul," *Archiv für Reformationsgeschichte* 65 (1974) 54–82.

[13] See e.g. C. Augustijn in *TRE* 10, 1–18; O. Herding in *Lexikon des Mittelalters* 3 (Munich 1986) col. 2096–100; H. Holeczek in W. Killy (ed.), *Literatur Lexikon* 1–15 (Gütersloh 1988–93) 3 273–81.

[14] 1467–1519, see J.B. Trapp in Bietenholz (above, n.9) I 324–8. His commentaries remained unpublished for a long time: J.H. Lupton (ed.), *Ioannis Coleti Enarratio in Epistolam S. Pauli ad Romanos* (London 1873) and *in primam Epistolam S. Pauli ad Corinthios* (London 1874) (both reprinted Farnborough 1965 and 1968); see now B. O'Kelly, C.A.L. Jarrott (eds.), *John Colet's Commentary on First Corinthians* (Binghamton NY: Center for Medieval and Early Renaissance Studies 1985).

[15] Cf. *Novum Instrumentum omne, diligenter ab Erasmo Rotterodamo recognitum et emendatum* (Basle 1516) (with *Methodus*: fol. bbb1ʳ–bbb5ᵛ and, following the text, *Adnotationes* pp. 231–675, reprinted with corrections as *Novum Testamentum omne, multo quam antehac diligentius ab Erasmo Roterodamo recognitum, emendatum et translatum* (Basle 1519, again 1522, 1527, 1535); *Tomus primus Paraphraseon D. Erasmi Roterodami, in novum testamentum* (Basle 1524) and *Tomus secundus continens Paraphrasim D. Erasmi Rot. In omneis epistolas apostolicas...* (Basle 1523) (this edition here used); cf. also J. Clericus (ed.), *Desiderii Erasmi Roterodami Opera Omnia...* I–X (Leyden 1703–6) 5: on various psalms (col. 171–556), 6: *Novum Testamentum*, 7: *Paraphrases in N. Testamentum*: *Opera Omnia Desiderii Erasmi Roterodami* (Amsterdam: North-Holland 1969–) esp. 5.2 and 5.3, 1985–86: *Enarrationes in Psalmos; The Collected Works of Erasmus* (Toronto: Toronto University Press 1974–) esp. 42: *New Testament Scholarship. Paraphrases on Romans and Galatians* (1984) 46: *Paraphrase on John* (1991) 49: *Paraphrase on Marc* (1988). For the two versions of the *Methodus* see A. and H. Holborn (eds.), *Desiderius Erasmus Roterodamus. Ausgewählte Werke* (Munich: Beck 1933) 150–62 (1516) and 177–305 (expanded version: *Ratio seu methodus* 1518 and later with additions). See further, A. Reeve, M.A. Screech (eds.), *Erasmus' Annotations on the New Testament: Acts, Ro-*

Erasmus was familiar with rhetorical theory (e.g. Quintilian) and regarded rhetorical training as useful for a future theologian; he referred to St. Augustin not only to support this view, but also for the observation that St. Paul employed rhetorical schemata, in his own exegesis rhetoric played virtually no part.[16] His method, too, was basically philological, his aim was to establish a correct text (in his edition) and to justify it and to make it intelligible through his *Adnotationes* and his translation. He collated manuscripts, and with their help examined the text carefully, corrected corruptions (also wrong translations), or solved linguistic difficulties by explaining words or phrases, with the classical Greek authors serving as standard, while not unaware of the special nature of the language of the New Testament. In doing this, Erasmus showed great care not to ignore earlier exegetes, especially the Fathers of the Church, naming his sources most diligently and using them invariably with great acumen. This he also applied to the works of the Bible, pointing both to grammatical flaws and to discrepancies in the various accounts of the apostles. Sometimes he considered historical questions or the authenticity of particular works, occasionally he indulged in allegorical interpretation or addressed himself to moral or doctrinal issues. But his main "purpose was to render the text more accurate and lucid, and to improve the Latin";[17] in paying special attention to these aspects he showed himself aware of the basic rules and principles of rhetoric; but in analysing and interpreting the texts he did not resort to its particular categories or terms.

II. Melanchthon's First Manual on Rhetoric

This is the background against which one has to see and evaluate Melanchthon's use of rhetorical categories in the study of the Bible.[18]

---

mans, *I and II Corinthians* (Leiden: Brill 1990). On Erasmus' exegesis see e.g. Hausammann (above, n.12) 117–44; Bentley (above, n.7) 112–93; F. Krüger, *Humanistische Evangelienauslegung. Desiderius Erasmus von Rotterdam als Ausleger der Evangelien in seinen Paraphrasen*, Beitrage zur historischen Theologie 68 (Tübingen: Mohr 1986); E. Rummel, *Erasmus' Annotationes on the New Testament* (Toronto: University of Toronto Press 1986); see also Wengert (above, n.6).

[16] Rhetorical training: *Methodus* (ed. Holborn, 1933 (above, n.15)) 154, 185, 187 (Quintilian), 190–1; St. Augustin: p. 153 = 184; St. Paul's rhetorical schemata: pp. 155, 190.

[17] Cf. Rummel (above, n.15) 89.

[18] The literature on Melanchthon is too vast to be listed here, see W. Hammer, *Die*

Born in 1497 in Bretten (Germany), Melanchthon became acquainted with humanistic ideas at a very early stage in his family through his great-uncle Reuchlin and as a student at the universities of Heidelberg and Tübingen. A reading of Rudolf Agricola's *De inventione dialectica* (published in 1515) made him study the ancient orators more carefully and methodically and to pay more attention to their rhetorical technique; and soon after being appointed professor of Greek at Wittenberg at the age of 21, he published a handbook of rhetoric (1519: *De Rhetorica libri tres*, to be followed by two others in 1521: *Institutiones rhetoricae* and in 1531 *Elementorum rhetorices libri duo*) and began to make use of rhetorical theory in lecturing on various books of the Bible.[19]

In the handbook of 1519 one meets Melanchthon after polemical remarks against *Lyrani, Carrucani* and *Sententiarii* and after a word of praise for Erasmus, *qui primus etiam doctorum iudicio Theologiam ad fontes revocavit*,[20] first stressing the importance of dialectic and rhetoric

---

Melanchthonforschung im Wandel der Jahrhunderte, Qu. und Forsch. zur Reformationsgeschichte 35–6, 40 (Gütersloh: G. Mohn 1967–81), important: K. Hartfelder, *Philipp Melanchthon als Praeceptor Germaniae* (Berlin 1889) with lists of his works (pp. 579–620) and his lectures (pp. 555–66), see also R. Keen, *A Checklist of Melanchthon Imprints through 1560* (St. Louis MO: Center for Reformation Research 1988); for the works see C.G. Bretschneider, H.E. Bindseil (eds.) *Philippi Melanchthonis Opera* I–XXVIII (Halle: Schwetschke 1834–60), recent brief account with further literature: H. Scheible in *TRE* 22 (1992) 387–410; special studies: W. Maurer, *Der junge Melanchthon*, 2 vols. (Göttingen: Vandenhoeck & Ruprecht 1967–69); H. Sick, *Melanchthon als Ausleger des Alten Testamentes* (Tübingen: Mohr 1959); A. Sperl, *Melanchthon zwischen Humanismus und Reformation*, Forsch. zur G. und lehre des Protestantismus 15 (Munich: C. Kaiser 1959); A. Schirmer, *Das Paulusverständnis Melanchthons 1518–1522* (Wiesbaden: F. Steiner 1967); Hausammann (above, n.12) 145–61, 211–315; S. Wiedenhofer, *Formalstrukturen humanistischer und reformatorischer Theologie bei Philipp Melanchthon*, Regensburger Studien zur Theologie 2 (Frankfurt: Lang 1976); Wengert (above, n.6); J.R. Schneider, *Philip Melanchthon's Rhetorical Construal of Biblical Authority. Oratio Sacra* (Lampeter: Edwin Mellon 1990); see also my own papers: "Cicero orator inter Germanos redivivus II," *Humanistica Lovaniensia* 39 (1990) 157–76; "Paulus und die antike Rhetorik," *Zeitschrift für die Neutestamentliche Wissenschaft* 82 (1991) 1–33; "St. Paul's Epistles and Ancient Greek and Roman Rhetoric," *Rhetorica* 10 (1992) 319–44.

[19] The reprints of the two earlier works (Wittenberg and Basle 1519 and Hagenau 1521) are listed in Bretschneider (above, n.18) 13 col. 413–14, the third (Wittenberg 1531) is reprinted there col. 417–506, other editions listed: col. 413–16, see also Keen (above, n.18) 50–4; edition here used: Wittenberg 1536. Cf. in addition the *Dispositiones rhetoricae* of 1553, lecture-notes, published in H. Zwicker (ed.), *Supplementa Melanchthoniana* II, *Philologische Schriften* 1 (Leipzig: R. Haupt 1911) 1–172.

[20] P. 4. *Lyrani* are no doubt those who follow Nicholas of Lyra (s. above), *Sententiarii* those who accept Petrus Lombardus' *Sententiae*; it should not be forgotten that

in general. He continues with definitions and descriptions of various basic concepts, before he gives a rather long account of the demonstrative genus with *termini technici* as well as quotations and examples from ancient, i.e. pagan sources. In this context he deals i.a. with the *enarratorium genus* of which he distinguishes two types, paraphrasis and commentary. The former he illustrates by referring to Erasmus' *Paraphrasis in Pauli epistolam* and recommends it for the training of the young, explicitly emphasizing, that when he himself lectured on St. Paul's letter to Titus,[21] he encouraged his students to practice this kind of exercise, as this epistle is particularly suitable for it, because it contains many *loci communes*; he even indicates here how what St. Paul says briefly may be paraphrased more elaborately, starting himself with one or two actual examples.[22]

In the following section *De commentandi ratione* (On the method of commenting upon a text), he deals with the other form of *enarratio*, commentary.[23] Having distinguished various forms of *oratio*, he discusses first the *ad docendum composito*, next the historical *enarratio* and identifies as two essential elements *circumstantiae* (particulars) and *loci communes*; to these he adds figures of intensification and of variation (*augendi variandique figurae*) as especially important in sacred writings and refers to St. Paul's letter to the Hebrews as an example.

---

sententiarius denoted a degree and corresponding position in the university at the time, cf. Th. Muther (ed.), *Die Wittenberger Universitäts- und Facultäts-Statuten vom Jahre MDVIII* (Halle 1867) 7, 8, 9, 19, 20 (oath), 21; p. 19: *Sententiarius legat quatuor libros Petri Lombardi...*; he was assigned new duties in 1533, cf. C.E. Foerstemann, *Liber Decanorum Facultatis Theologiae Academiae Vitebergensis* (Leipzig 1838) 155. No satisfactory explanation seems to have been offered hitherto for *Carrucani*; I wonder whether Melanchthon is playing with the proverbial καρικὴ Μοῦσα which he refers to a little later (p. 19) and which Erasmus comments upon at some length in his *Adagia* (I 879).

[21] See p. 30, cf. Hartfelder (above, n.18) 76, 555; Bretschneider (above, n.18) I col. 49–51 and XI p. 25 (*De artibus liberalibus oratio*: 1517; for details see Horst Koehn, Philipp Melanchthons Reden, *Archiv für Geschichte des Buchwesens* 25 (1984) col. 1320–1). Melanchthon edited the text of the letter for this lecture: *Epistola Pauli Ad Titum qua Compendio vere Christiani Hominis Vitam ac Mores Format* (Wittenberg 1518).

[22] P. 30: *ut si inde incipias: Oportere episcopum non praefractum esse: non ociosum est, cur hoc primo loco admoneat: deinde quam sit pestilens vitium administrantibus rempublicam pervicacia, vel exemplis declaretur iisque contrariis, ut si quis componat malos pontifices cum bonis etc.*

[23] Cf. pp. 31–41; p. 31: *omnis oratio est, aut ad docendum composita, aut historica, aut suasoria, aut allegorica.*

Under this heading he deals with the manner of *sacra enarrare*, to relate and interpret holy matters, warns against immoderate praise and explains what the story of Abraham and Isaac means and how it should be commented upon. He criticizes several allegorical interpretations of some of his contemporaries and at the end of this section approves of St. Chrysostom for his interpretation of stories, and of Origen and Tauler for their allegorizing.[24]

I cannot, and need not, here discuss all references to and examples from the Bible in the first book of Melanchthon's rhetorical manual of 1519, even though they are not too numerous. Suffice it to say that the theory of rhetoric he offers is that of pagan antiquity, both rules and examples, but Melanchthon's new and special concerns is the interpretation of the Bible, together with the preaching of the word of God (as shown by the section *De sacris concionibus*[25]) and the training of the young in rhetoric.

Interestingly, there seems to be hardly any reference to the Holy Scriptures in the second book which is devoted to *dispositio* (arrangement), while in the third on *elocutio* (style) St. Paul's epistle to the Romans is named together with epic poetry and some of Cicero's and Demosthenes' speeches as example of the grand style; and not infrequently in this last book Melanchthon illustrates both figures of thought and of speech from the Bible. He quotes Galatians 1.6 as an example for the (rare) opposite of *amplificatio* (he himself uses the verb *minuimus*) and Galatians 3.1 ("Who has bewitched you that ye should not obey the truth:" *quis vos fascinavit non oboedire veritati*), adding as comment that "in the earlier word there is less emphasis than in the later one."[26] Later he quotes Romans 5.20 ("Where sin abounded, grace did much more abound:" *ubi abundavit delictum, superabundavit et gratia*) and then 6.1 ("What shall we say then? Shall we continue in sin that grace may abound?:" *Quid igitur dicemus? Manebimus in peccato?*) as examples of a question (*interrogatio*), emphasizing the manner in which it supports the *dispositio* (arrangement) and paves the way for other figures, in this case the *praesumptio*, i.e. the anticipation of an opponent's objection, which he elucidates a little later with the help of two ex-

---

[24] Cf. pp. 31–3; 33–4.
[25] For other examples from the Bible see pp. 35; 39–40 (Abraham); 53–4; 60; 85–7 et saep. *De sacris concionibus:* pp. 103–7.
[26] See p. 119: *in priore verbo minor est emphasis quam in posteriore; caeterum res est eadem*.

amples, one from Cicero (*pro Milone* 3), one from St. Paul's letter to the Romans 9.6 (incorrectly quoted with an addition from Romans 4.12: "For they which are of the circumcision Israel, are not all Israelites:" *non enim omnes qui sunt ex circumcisione Israel, hi sunt Israelitae*). The *subiectio* (a question of the speaker with a suggestion how the argument should proceed) and the *dubitatio* (an orator's simulated indecision) are illustrated by examples from the same letter (Romans 6.2: *Absit*, and 4.9-10).[27]

In summarizing one may state that in composing this first rhetorical manual Melanchthon clearly had the text of the Bible constantly at the back of his mind, especially St. Paul's epistles (mainly that to the Romans), drawing on it primarily where he discusses the form of presentation in general (*genus*) or specific elements of style, but not the *dispositio*.

III. The *Institutiones Rhetoricae*

Melanchthon's second handbook on rhetoric, published without his permission two years later from lecture notes, taken by his students, is much shorter (*Institutiones Rhetoricae*). Here the fourth type of *genus* besides demonstrative, deliberative and judicial, foreshadowed already in the earlier work, is now fully established as *genus dialecticum* (concerned in fact less with logical reasoning than with teaching),[28] and a shift of emphasis from judicial and political rhetoric towards teaching and preaching becomes obvious from *causa* being supplemented by

---

[27] See p. 119 for Gal. 1.6 and 3.1, for Romans 5.20 and 6.1 p. 125, for Cic. *pro Milone* (quoted not verbatim) and Romans 9.6 pp. 125–6, for the *dubitatio* see p. 125, for the *subiectio* p. 127; brief references to Cicero's *pro Milone* occur frequently, see e.g. pp. 11, 50, 69, 75, 76, 88, 90, 95, 99–100, et saep.

[28] Fol. AII^r (also *dialecticum thema*); 1519: pp. 11–13, 64–5 (*didacticon seu dialecticum*), 91; see also the *Elementorum rhetorices libri duo* of 1531 (here cited the edition Wittenberg 1536) fol. A8^v–B1^r and B3^r–6^r = Bretschneider (above, n.18) 13, col. 421–9; see also below n.48. The four-fold division may have been suggested to Melanchthon by the four qualities which Maximus of Tyre expects the philosophically trained orator to display in the four areas of his activity (*or.* 25.6 p. 304 Hobein); for he refers to Maximus' explanation of Homer's μῶλυ (*Od.* 10.305: *or.* 26.9 and 29.6 pp. 320 and 346 Hobein) in a letter to Bernard Maurus in 1519 (Bretschneider (above, n.18) 1, col. 62–6, reference: col. 65–6), see also *De Rhetorica* p. 7. For other possible sources for Melanchthon's new *genus* see my paper "Paulus und die antike Rhetorik" (above, n.18) 16–17 n. 54.

[29] *Sicut caussarum ita thematum genera quatuor sunt* (fol. AII^r).

thema right at the beginning ("There are four kinds as of cases so also of themes, subjects"[29]).

In his discussion of the judicial kind Melanchthon points out that one can employ almost the same arguments as in lawsuits also in literary disputes, and he illustrates this by St. Paul's argument in Romans 4.9–12. It should be noted that here not the text of the Bible is being quoted; rather we find a wording very similar to that in his *Artifitium (!) Epistolae Pauli ad Romanos* or his *Theologica Institutio*, both exegetical works, based like the *Institutiones Rhetoricae* on notes of his students.[30]

Next in the work of 1521 Melanchthon deals with *status* (i.e. in traditional rhetoric "what is at stake"), for which he gives several definitions. To the first of them ("status is a summary statement of what exactly a dispute is about:" *est summaria sententia de qua proprie litigatur*) he adds: "For instance Faith justifies; that summary statement of Paul's dispute is said to be the *status*."[31] Also for several types of arguments Melanchthon adduces examples from St. Paul's epistles, e.g. for *inversio* (which he defines as that "by means of which we show the evidence that speaks against us to work in our favour:" *qua docemus signum quod contra nos producit, pro nobis facere*) Galatians 3.21b, again with St. Paul's argument rephrased in manner very similar to that found in the lecture notes on Galatians.[32] Similarly to show how to argue about an ambiguous text (*de ambiguis scriptis*, see also *ex*

---

[30] Text in the *Institutiones* (fol. BII˅): *Abraham ante circuncisionem iustificatus est, ergo non ex circuncisione*, in the *Artifitium* (p. 23): *Abraam est iustificatus ante circumcisio-nem Ergo non ex circumcisione*, in the *Institutio* (p. 98): *Abraham iustificatus est ante circumcisionem; ergo iustificatio non est ex operibus*. Both the *Artifitium Epistolae Pauli ad Romanos* and the *Theologica Institutio...in Epistolam Pauli ad Romanos* may be found in E. Bizer (ed.), *Texte aus der Anfangszeit Melanchthons* (Neukirchen-Vluyn: Neukirchener 1966) 20–30, 90–9 and 102–31 = Bretschneider (above, n.18) 21, col. 49–60 and 11–46; for corrections of Bizer's text see the review by H. Scheible, *ZKG* 79 (1968) 417–19.

[31] *Ut, Fides iustificat, haec summaria sententia disputationis Paulinae dicitur status* (fol. BII˅).

[32] *Nunquid lex adversus promissiones, si non iustificat, Imo si lex iustificaret, esset adversus promissiones dei* (fol. BIII˅); text in the *Exegesis in Epistolam Pauli pros tous Galatas* (see Bizer (above, n.30) 34–7) p. 36: *Inversio, Respondeo: Imo si per legem esset iustitia foret contra promissionem*. On *inversio* see also *De Rhetorica* of 1519 p. 100 with the same standard example as in the later work of 1521 (*si occidissem in sepeliendo non fuissem occupatus*), but not with the additional examples from Thucydides and St. Paul; cf. also *Elementa* (above, n.19) KI˓ (= Bretschneider (above, n.18) 13, col. 488–9).

ambiguo) arguments of St. Paul's are adduced from his epistle to the Romans, but not in his own words ("works do not justify:" *cum...opera non iustificent* and *opera legis non iustificare*).³³

In the following sections one finds various figures of style illustrated by examples from the Bible, for metaphors e.g. *crux pro mortificatione* ("cross instead of tribulation"), or "Satan has sought you that he may sift you as wheat" (*Satanas expetivit vos, ut cribaret: Luc.* 22.31) or "I will make you fishers of men" (*Faciam vos piscatores hominum: Matt.* 4.19; *Marc.* 1.17); for *antonomasia* he cites "saviour" (*salvator*) for Christ, the "lord" (of the world: *dominus*) for Satan, and he adds that "circumlocution," *periphrasis* on the basis of etymology, also belongs here, e.g. for "Gospel" (*Euangelium*) "message of salvation" (*salutare nuncium*), not a biblical expression, but a phrase Melanchthon himself uses elsewhere.³⁴ For what the rhetoricians call *catachresis* (improper use of a word) Melanchthon cites a phrase from St. Paul's first letter to the Corinthians (2.14) in Greek (ψυχικὸς ἄνθρωπος), adding: *humano more sapiens, ac iustus* ("natural man, wise and just, as much as it befits a human being"), thus reminding his readers that it is not simply the Bible which is at the back of his mind, but both its Greek and its Latin version.

In the following sections Melanchthon deals with tropes, especially allegories and what he thinks should be classified with them. Again we encounter a good many illustrations from the Bible or the religious language of the Christians; the same is true of the final sections on *schemata*, figures.³⁵ Thus we see that Melanchthon in his first handbook and his early lectures on rhetoric as reflected in the published notes of his pupils enriches the traditional stock of examples and illustrations by passages from the Holy Scriptures, rarely from the Old Testament, mostly from St. Paul's epistles, in his own manual of 1519 primarily for matters of style, in the published lectures of 1521 also for types of arguments.

---

³³ *Ut si quis disputet cur Paulus praecipiat bona opera cum tamen opera non iustificent* (fol. BIVʳ) and *ex ambiguo: ut si disputetur, utrum cum Paulus doceat opera legis non iustificare, velit hoc intellegi tantum de ceremoniis, an de omnibus legis operibus ceremonialibus et moralibus.*

³⁴ Metaphor: fol. CIIIᵛ; *mortificatio* is used only once (2 *Cor.* 4.10), *crux* occurs frequently in the New Testament. Antonomasia: fol. CIVʳ.

³⁵ *Tropi:* CIVʳ⁻ᵛ, *allegoriae:* DIʳ–DIIʳ and *schemata:* DIIʳ–EIIIᵛ, in three sections: DIIʳ–DIIIʳ (*dictiones*), *figurae sententiarum:* DIIIᵛ–IVᵛ, DIVᵛ–EIIIᵛ: *amplificatio*.

The importance of the new elements which Melanchthon thus introduces into the teaching of rhetoric can be fully appreciated only, when one realizes that one year before Melanchthon's work of 1519 Jacob Locher published his *Compendium Rhetorices ex Tulliano thesauro diductum ac concionatum* with no reference to the Bible, while Rudolph Agricola in his *De inventione dialectica* (written before 1485, but not published till 1515) also does not seem to make any use of the Bible nor to be interested in its interpretation.[36] Admittedly, already Johann Ulrich Surgant in his manual (*Manuale Curatorum: predicandi prebens modum*, Basle 1503, often reprinted) exemplifies how the rules and precepts of ancient rhetoric may be applied to the needs and requirements of a Christian preacher, and Jacob Wimpfeling in his (*Rhetorica... pueris utilissima*) once refers to St. Paul's letter to the Hebrews to illustrate a recommended procedure;[37] but Melanchthon is concerned not only with preaching, but with understanding the Holy Scriptures and, therefore, he constantly refers to texts including passages from the Bible, thereby demonstrating how rhetorical categories help to appreciate their meaning. Indeed, right at the beginning of the handbook of 1519 he emphasizes: "Anyone who has dealt with this (i.e. the demonstrative type) carefully and thoroughly, will have a great deal of help for the right method of dealing with literature, that is of interpreting literture, not to mention public issues."[38]

This leads immediately on to the question of how Melanchthon himself interpreted the Holy Scriptures. When we turn to his earliest commentaries and the notes from his first lectures on works of the Bible, we are faced with a large amount of rather heterogeneous material: his *Theologica Institutio*, his editions of the Latin and the Greek text of the

---

[36] Locher (Strasbourg 1518), on him see G. Heidloff, *Untersuchungen zu Leben und Werk des Humanisten Jakob Locher Philomusus (1471–1528)*, Thesis Freiburg 1971 (Münster 1975); I. Guenther in Bietenholz (above, n.9) II 338; on R. Agricola see the comprehensive bibliography in F. Akkerman, A.J. Vanderjagt (eds.), *Rodolphus Agricola Phrisius (1444-1485)* (Leiden: Brill 1988) 314–44; C.G. van Leijenhorst in Bietenholz (above, n.9) I 15–17; he is referred to by Melanchthon in his *De Rhetorica libri tres* e.g. p. 45.

[37] See fol. EII^r (*de fine*) in an edition Hagenau without date, which combines the *elegantiae maiores* (preface dated 1499) with the Rhetorica; on Wimpfeling see B. Könnecker in Bietenholz (above, n.9) III 447–50; D. Mertens in Killy (above, n.13) 12, pp. 341–2. On Surgant see *Allgemeine Deutsche Biographie* 37 (München 1894) 165–6 (A. Bernoulli).

[38] *Quod* (i.e. *genus demonstrativum*) *qui accurate ac diligenter tractaverit, plurimum adiumenti ad literas recte tractandi est habiturus, nedum ad causas communes* (p.12).

epistles to the Romans and to the Galatians with marginal notes, an *Artifitium Epistolae Pauli ad Romanos*, an *Exegesis in Epistolam Pauli pros tous Galatas*, probably all dating from 1520, his *Loci communes*, editions of the two letters to the Corinthians and lecture notes on the epistle to the Romans from 1521, the *Adnotationes...in Epistolas Pauli Ad Romanos Et Corinthios* of 1522 (German version of 1523), *In Evangelium Ioannis Adnotationes* and *Annotationes...in Evangelium Matthaei* of 1523.[39] Clearly they cannot all be presented and discussed here, especially as in several cases, Melanchthon wrote again, later, on the same works, and these later contributions often point to interesting developments and some changes in his approach, especially with regard to the usefulness and the limits of rhetorical interpretation and criticism.

It seems appropriate at this point to remind ourselves of the fact that in 1518 Melanchthon was appointed as professor of Greek in the Faculty of Arts at Wittenberg, and that it was in this position that he delivered his inaugural lecture *De corrigendis adolescentiae studiis*.[40] This lecture

---

[39] For the *Institutio* and the *Artifitium* see Bizer (above, n.30), also for the *Exegesis* (pp. 34–7), the notes in his editions of the Latin and Greek texts of the epistle to the Romans (1520; pp. 20–30) and the lecture notes on the epistle to the Romans (1521; pp. 45–85). Cf. the following editions: *Epistola Pauli ad Romanos D. Erasmo interprete*, Wittenberg 1520 (Latin text); *Pauli Apostoli ad Romanos epistola*, s.l. 1520 (Greek text); *Plena eruditionis epistola...ad Galatas* (Wittenberg 1520) (Latin text); *Plena eruditionis epistola D. Pauli ad Galatas* (Wittenberg 1520) (Greek text); also *Loci communes rerum theologicarum seu hypotyposes theologicae* (Wittenberg 1521) (see Bretschneider (above, n.18) 1, col. 510–12 (introductory letter) and 21, col. 81–230; R. Stupperich (ed.), *Melanchthons Werke in Auswahl*, 7 vols. (Gütersloh: Bertelsmann 1951–75) 2.1, H. Engelland (ed.), *Loci communes von 1521...* (1952) 3–163); further *Pauli Apostoli ad Corinthios prior epistola* (Wittenberg 1521); *Pauli Apostoli ad Corinthios secunda epistola* (Wittenberg 1521); *Annotationes Philippi Melanchthonis in Epistolas Pauli Ad Romanos et Corinthios* (Nürnberg 1522); *Annotationes Philippen Melanchthons Verzaichnung unnd kurtzliche anzaigung des rechtenn und aigentlichen verstands der Epistel die S. Paulus zu den Rhömern geschrybenn hat verdeutscht*, s.l. s.a. (1523); *Annotationes in Evangelium Matthaei* (Wittenberg 1522); *Annotationes Philippi Melanchthonis in Evangelium Matthaei et Ioannis* (Basel 1523) (here used: *Philippi Melanchthonis, Annotationes in Iohannem, castigatiores quam antea invulgatae sunt* (Hagenau 1523) (cf. Bretschneider (above, n.18) 14, col. 1047–220); the commentaries on the two letters to the Corinthians and on Matthew are reprinted in Stupperich (above) IV (ed. P.F. Barton) (1963) 16–84, 85–132 and 134–208.

[40] Cf. Hartfelder (above, n.18) 64–7: *Sermo habitus apud iuventutem Academiae Witenberg. de corrigendis adulescentiae studiis* (Wittenberg 1518) = Bretschneider (above, n.18) 11, col. 15–25 = Stupperich (above, n.39) III, *Humanistische Schriften* (ed. R. Nürnberger) (Gütersloh 1961) 30–42; see also Koehn (above, n.21) col. 1321–2.

seems to me to be important in this context for two reasons: On the one hand Melanchthon emphasizes the need to study Greek (*iungendae Graecae litterae Latinis ut philosophos, theologos, historicos, oratores, poetas lecturus...rem ipsam assequare*); on the other hand he points to the higher aims of such studies insofar as the ancient languages give access to the sources, and thus enable one to understand Christ.[41] Melanchthon adds that he will lecture on Homer and St. Paul's letter to Titus.[42] Clearly, his aim is not simply to train scholars, but Christians, and for this purpose to use all resources made available by the efforts of the humanists.

It is not surprising that a little more than a year after his arrival in Wittenberg and his inaugural lecture as professor of Greek, Melanchthon obtained the degree of bachelor of Divinity, thus becoming a member of the first faculty also; and for the rest of his life, he lectured in two faculties, as professor of Greek and as professor (since 1524) of Theology,[43] a fact one has to remember when one tries to understand his teaching of rhetoric and his interpreting the Bible.

When we now attempt to evaluate Melanchthon's exegetical activities, we have to bear in mind the nature of the material at our disposal: students' notes taken during his lectures and possibly enriched from his manuals of rhetoric or dialectic, but never printed, student's notes published without his consent, and his own editions, commentaries and theological works for the publication of which he himself was responsible.[44]

IV. Melanchthon on St. Paul's Epistles

Melanchthon's *Theologica Institutio in Epistolam Pauli ad Romanos*, published without his consent in 1521, falls into two parts, a doctrinal introduction to the basic concepts (*loci*) of this letter: sin (*peccatum*), law (*lex*) and grace (*gratia*), and a brief summary (*summa*) of the epistle itself and its structure. It is in this latter section that one finds Melanchthon applying rhetorical categories. He determines the type of issue (*status causae*), assigns it to the judicial kind (*genus iudiciale*),

---

[41] Bretschneider (above, n.18) 11, col. 22 = Stupperich (above, n.39) III 38.
[42] For the lecture on St. Paul's letter see above n.21.
[43] See Hartfelder (above, n.18) 71.
[44] See above nn.18, 19, 30, 39; below nn.48, 62.

and registers the presence at least of three essential parts: introduction (*exordium*), statement of facts (*narratio*) and proof (*confirmatio*), adding that they are fittingly put together.[45] In the introduction he registers topics appropriate for this section (i.e. for securing goodwill), next he summarizes briefly the purpose of the statement of facts and the six underlying arguments, identifies two digressions here, stressing their importance for the understanding of the whole, and lists six arguments in the following section of proofs (chapter 4).[46] At the end of that chapter he registers an *amplificatio*, using a traditional rhetorical term, and at the beginning of the following chapter an *exhortatio* (a term not very common in ancient rhetorical theory),[47] before characterizing the next passage as *locus didacticus*. Here a term occurs again which Melanchthon used in his theoretical work for a special kind of the demonstrative genus, later for the new kind which he introduced in addition to the other three.[48] As Melanchthon is at the same time engaged

---

[45] Bretschneider (above, n.18) 21, col. 56 = Bizer (above, n.30) 97.
[46] Bretschneider (above, n.18) 21, col. 57–8 = Bizer (above, n.30) 97–8.
[47] *Exhortatio* is occasionally used by Quintilian in a technical sense for a part or kind of discourse, e.g. 10.1.47 together with *laudes* and *consolationes* in a combination similar to 1*Cor.* 14.3, see also Sen. *epist*. 95.65 (Posidonius) and Mar. Victorin. *rhet*. 1.5 p. 174, 29–38 who emphasizes that some exclude it from rhetoric; however, *exhortatio* occurs in the Vulgate several times, and this may also have influenced Melanchthon.
[48] See above n.28. Melanchthon seems to have been inspired by the Greek διδακτικός which occurs in the New Testament (1*Tim.* 3.2, 2*Tim.* 2.24), the Church Fathers and Philo to introduce *didacticus* which he seems to be the first author to use. However, later in his *Elementa* (above, n.19) he prefers to speak of the διδασκαλικόν *genus* (1536: fol. A8ᵛ–B1ʳ = Hertschneider (above, n.18) 13, col. 421) or the *genus didascalicum* (fol. B3ʳ–B5ʳ = 13, col. 423–8), perhaps because not only διδασκαλικός is more common, but even *didascalicus* is not entirely unknown (cf. E. Lommatzsch in *TLL* 5, 1, col. 1015); see also e.g. on Psalm 51 (written in 1551: Bretschneider (above, n.18) 13, col. 1225, see below p. 319). It should be noted that in his *De officiis concionatoris* Melanchthon, in distinguishing *tria genera concionum* names διδακτικόν with ἐπιτρεπτικόν and παραινετικόν and discusses it at length: *De genere didactico*. I am using the text, as it is printed at the end of the *Enarratio Epistolae Pauli Secundae Ad Timotheum, Praelecta Anno 1562. A.D.G. Maiore* (Wittenberg 1564) (fol. 114ᵛ–122ʳ, see esp. 115ʳ and 116ʳ–122ʳ), a version not mentioned by the modern editors P. Drews and F. Cohrs (*Supplementa Melanchthoniana* V 2: *Homiletische Schriften* (Leipzig 1929), text: pp. 5–14, list of earlier editions: pp. XXXI–XL) who assign this work to May/June 1529 (p. LI); the remark in the edition of 1564 (fol. 114ᵛ) *scriptum ante annos 36* seems to be unknown to them, also other pieces printed there, e.g. *Methodus discendi sacras literas* (fol. 110ʳ–114ᵛ), *Praeceptum de studio et exercitio doctrinae* (fol. 144ᵛ–145ʳ), *De tribus partibus officii concionatoris* (fol. 145ʳ–149ʳ) and *De tribus contionum generibus in enarratione dicti Paulini I. Corinth. XIIII* (fol.

both in presenting the theory of rhetoric and in analysing texts, successful crossfertilization yields new insight in the two areas. His comments here show that he is primarily concerned with theological problems; but his attempts to understand texts lead the professor of Greek to develop new rhetorical tools, and their application in turn helps him in achieving his main aim.

On a lower level one notices the same, when one examines the notes which have been preserved from Melanchthon's interpretation of St. Paul's letter to the Galatians.[49] He assigns the letter to his new type of speech, the *genus didacticum*, even though he says that St. Paul accuses the Galatians of defecting from his teaching; but he does so, as he adds, because the apostle here gives the sum of Christianity (*Christianismi summa*[50]). Turning to the letter itself Melanchthon characterizes its parts and their function mostly with traditional terms (e.g. *exordium ab affectu*), sometimes with unusual ones which one would rather find in contemporary treatises on the art of letter-writing (e.g. *salutatio*, also: ἐπιγραφή[51]). Occasionally, his comments seem to be taken directly from the text-book (*optima exordia sunt ab affectibus*[52]). Here, and even more obviously later, he pays special attention to the arguments, explicitly stating what the apostle tries to prove (*demonstrat...*), pointing to or actually naming particular arguments (*nimirum...*) or inferences or explaining the method he is employing.[53] After characterizing the way in which the apostle deals with the case as such (*per obiurgationem*), Melanchthon continues to analyse his procedure, listing the individual

---

162ʳ–165ᵛ), where Melanchthon speaks of a *species* διδασκαλική (fol. 162ᵛ) besides *adhortatio* and *consolatio* (no date given).

[49] Bizer (above, n.30) 34–7. It is very different from Luther's commentary (published Leipzig 1519) for which Melanchthon wrote a preface (Bretschneider (above, n.18) 1, col. 121–4 and 124–5 and for the second edition 1523: col. 638, see also *D. Martin Luthers Werke* 2 (Weimar 1884) 4435 and 618 (epilogus); 442 (second edition)).

[50] Bizer (above, n.30) 34.

[51] See e.g. Erasmus, *De conscribendis epistolis* (*Opera Omnia* (Amsterdam: above, n.15) I 2 205–579, esp. 276–95), but also so elementary a handbook as *Jacobi Wimphelingi Sletstatensis elegantiarum medulla oratoriaque medulla* (Leipzig 1516) fol. eIVᵛ (= *elegantiae maiores* (above, n.37) DVIIIᵛ). *Salutatio* occurs in the Vulgate several times, see esp. 1*Cor.* 16.21; *Col.* 4.18; 2*Thess.* 3.17; ἐπιγραφή is not used elsewhere in the sense required here.

[52] Cf. *Elementorum rhetorices libri duo* (Bretschneider (above, n.18) 13 col. 417–506) fol. C1ᵛ: *Decent et affectus miciores omnis generis ut Magnam mihi voluptatem attulerunt literae tuae*, see also E7ʳ.

arguments, sometimes with their appropriate label (*a signo, ab allegoria*), or whole syllogisms or at least their parts (*confirmatio subiecta; minoris summa*).[54] Indeed, technical terms from the handbooks of logic (see his own *Compendiaria dialectices ratio*, *De dialectica libri Quatuor* and *Erotemata dialectices*[55]) seem to prevail and stress once more that Melanchthon is concerned to understand the text as such, i.e. that he is neither interested merely in attaching labels to particular phenomena nor in applying rules of a theory, but in using all tools available to come to the most adequate appreciation possible of a text and to the most effective means of making its content understandable for others.

Though the *Artificium*, another set of lecture notes, differs in some respect from the *Theologica Institutio*, I have to content myself with a few remarks here.[56] Surprisingly, now Melanchthon assigns St. Paul's letter to the Romans to his new didactic type, the γένος διδακτικόν, while in the *Institutio* he preferred the judicial type, characterizing, however, the section from chapter five onwards as *locus didacticus*, "by which St. Paul teaches what and wherefrom sin, grace and law are."[57] Obviously, Melanchthon is still trying to find his way in applying the new method of rhetorical criticism, and his own genus in particular. Yet one notices that a few features are explained now which were passed over silently in the *Institutio*, e.g. the "piling up" (*coacervatio*) in 1.29 or the "rhetorical consolation and confirmation" (*rhetorica consolatio et confirmatio*) after 5.1 and several argumentations which he analyses in a detailed manner.[58] On the other hand he does not use the term

---

[53] Cf. Bizer (above, n.30) 34–5.

[54] See on *signa* and proofs *a signis* his *Elementa* (above, n.19) fol. K3ʳ–K4ʳ (= Hertschneider (above, n.18) 13, col. 491–2: on *schemata*); *Compendiaria* (below, n.55) col. 750; *Erotemata* (below, n.55) fol. FIʳ–IIIʳ (col. 618–19: on *enthymema*) and fol. RVIIʳ–SIʳ (col. 704–6: *loci rerum*). The other terms are even more common so that further references are superfluous.

[55] *Compendiaria...ratio*, first printed Wittenberg 1520 (= Hertschneider (above, n.18) 20, col. 709–64); *De dialectica libri Quatuor* (Leipzig 1531) (first published with a different title in 1525); *Erotemata...* (Wittenberg 1547), often reprinted, also with additions, e.g. Leipzig 1580 (= Hertschneider (above, n.18) 13, col. 513–752); for details see Keen (above, n.18) 18–19 and 42–6.

[56] Bizer (above, n.30) 20–30.

[57] Bizer (above, n.30) 99; cf. *Artifitium* (p. 24).

[58] Bizer (above, n.30) 21–4; for the *coacervatio* see *Compendiaria* in Hertschneider (above, n.18) 20, col. 747–8 (*sorites*); cf. also *De dialectica...* (above, n.55) fol. H6ʳ–

narratio again for the section 2.1–4.25; and while in the *Theologica Institutio* Melanchthon virtually stops in the middle of chapter 8, the *Artificium* has comments on the whole letter: a *digressiuncula* is noticed in the tenth chapter, the *consolatio* in the eleventh, also an *inversio*, and an *apostrophe*, in the twelfth chapter a *pareneticus locus*, and in the thirteenth a *generalis adhortatio*.[59] At the end Melanchthon explains the final section (*peroratio*) with explicit reference to rhetorical theory: "The concluding part where he first, with the licence granted by rhetorical theory, excuses why he writes with greater freedom and then assembles many points, as people do in a letter."[60] However, it is not in order to justify anything the apostle does in this epistle that Melanchthon employs the categories of rhetoric, but to explain what he says, to make his arguments more easily understandable. As Melanchthon in his rhetorical manual concentrates on the demonstrative genus and its tools of interpretation and expecially the *loci* which serve a speaker or writer to find arguments for his case or subject and a exegete to reduce a discourse to some basic ideas, in interpreting a text he is obviously anxious to use these tools and the *loci* in particular to elucidate its meaning. We should remind ourselves here, that in his early years Melanchthon in addition to the lectures and exegetical works listed above and the *loci communes* also published a short introduction to dialectic in which he stressed the need of the young to get acquainted with the correct forms of arguments, syllogisms etc. (see above n.55).

Though other notes from students attending Melanchthon's lectures on St. Paul's epistle to the Romans have been preserved in manuscript form, some of which show that he also paid a good deal of attention to elementary linguistic matters,[61] lack of time and space forces me to turn to the notes which Martin Luther published without Melanchthon's consent in 1522 on the letters to the Romans and to the Corinthians.[62]

7ʳ and *Erotemata*... (above, n.55) fol. GIʳ–IIIᵛ (Hertschneider (above, n.18) 13, col. 624–6).

[59] *Texte* (n.30) pp. 28–9. On the *inversio* see above p. 10 and n.32, also *Erotemata* (n.55) fol. RVIᵛ–VIIᵛ (= Hertschneider (above, n.18) 13, col. 703–4). On the *consolatio* as part of the *genus demonstrativum* together with *adhortatio in sacris literis* see *Elementa* (above, n.19) fol. D8ᵛ = Hertschneider (above, n.18) 13, col. 448, see also above n.47.

[60] Bizer (above, n.30) 30: *Peroratio qua primum per Rhetoricam licentiam excusat Quod liberius scripserit, Deinde multa congerit ut solent in Epistola*. One should remember that *licentia* as *liberius dicere* is listed by Melanchthon in his *De Rhetorica libri tres* p. 126 (above, n.19) as one of the *figurae sententiarum*.

Melanchthon refused to acknowledge them and, as he expressly said later, tried to suppress them; but they are instructive, as they seem to point to a shift in emphasis (and serve also as an indication of the kind of effect Melanchthon's teaching had).

In the *argumentum* which precedes the explanation of details two points are emphasized, firstly that in this letter St. Paul wants to describe and depict Christ for the whole world and to teach what benefit the world receives through him; for this reason this epistle is characterized as didactic in the *argumentum* of the commentary on the first epistle to the Corinthians (in the same work); and a few years later, Melanchthon in his own *Dispositio orationis in Epistola Pauli ad Romanos* (1529), assigns it to the didactic genre.[63] Secondly, it is stressed here in the *argumentum* that the first eight chapters of the epistle deal "with grace, law and sin, and they do so in the most appropriate order and clearly in the rhetorical manner."[64] Next the *status* is given, i.e. the central theme, also, a little later, the content of the second half including the final section. Thus, we are alerted to look out for traces and indications of the rhetorical method and wonder where and how Melanchthon draws the reader's attention to them.

Actually, there is not very much: a *parenthesis* is registered in 1, 2, an *antithesis* in 1.3; on 1.8 it is said that the introduction (*exordium*) con-

---

[61] Bizer (above, n.30) 45–85.

[62] They were not reprinted in Hertschneider (above, n.18), but the commentaries on the letters to the Corinthians may be found in Stupperich (above, n.39) 4, *Frühe exegetische Schriften* (ed. P.F. Barton) (1963) 16–84 and 85–132, to be supplemented by Melanchthons later commentary of 1551 (see Hertschneider (above, n.18) 15, col. 1053–220). On the letter to the Romans Melanchthon returned more frequently: *Dispositio orationis in Epistola Pauli ad Romanos* (Hagenau 1529) (= Hertschneider (above, n.18), 15, col. 443–92), here used: edition Hagenau 1530; *Commentarii in Epistolam Pauli ad Romanos* (Wittenberg 1532) (= Stupperich (above, n.39) 5, *Römerbrief-Kommentar 1532* (ed. G. Ebeling, R. Schäfer) (1965) 25–371); second edition: *Commentarii in Epistolam Pauli ad Romanos hoc anno MDXL recogniti et locupletati* (Strasbourg 1540) (= Hertschneider (above, n.18) 15, col. 495–796); finally: *Epistolae Pauli scriptae ad Romanos, Enarratio edita a Philippo Melanchthone* (Wittenberg 1556) (= Hertschneider (above, n.18) 15, col. 797–1052).

[63] *Annotationes* 1522: *argumentum* fol. a III^r; *argumentum* (Cor.) fol. MII^r: *epistola...didactica est*; *Dispositio* 1530: fol. 49^v: *genus didacticum* (cf. above, nn. 28 and 48).

[64] *Prior pars epistolae octo capitum Gratiam. Legem. peccatum. tractat. Idque aptissimo ordine et plane Rhetorica methodo, Status causae, iustificari nos fide, quae sententia probatur multis argumentis, Tum lex et peccatum cum gratia conferuntur. ... Posterior pars epistolae praedestinationem et vocationem gentium tractat* (fol. aIII^r).

sists of two elements which arouse benevolence and attention; 1.18 gives occasion to state the case (*summa narrationis, propositio et status huius disputationis*), 1.32 is described as conclusion (*epilogus*) with its content summarized, 2.17 the second proposition is marked, on 3.1 the difficulties are admitted which make one consider the composition of the whole and the intention of the writer.[65] The author adds that here St. Paul meets the objection by means of a rhetorical anticipation of the objection (see also on 3.9).[66] As for the rest digressions, propositions and again anticipations of objections are marked, and sometimes brief summaries of the content are given, but hardly ever other rhetorical devices are identified. Indeed, when one examines these lecture notes, one soon realizes again that here Melanchthon is primarily interested in the subject matter, and whichever tool he uses from the arsenal of rhetoric is employed in a very direct manner to assist the reader in grasping the meaning of the text, whether he gives summaries of the content of sections or elucidates a particular syllogism or a line of argument.

V. Melanchthon's Comments on the Psalms

However, it would be wrong to conclude that Melanchthon gradually moved away from employing categories of rhetoric for the exegesis of biblical texts, as one sees at once when one examines his commentaries on the Psalms, written only towards the end of his life (1553–55), though he had always been interested in them. Soon after starting his activities in Wittenberg as professor of Greek, he was called upon also to teach Hebrew in 1518 and again in 1519, and he continued lecturing on books of the Old Testament, especially after becoming professor of Theology in 1524. It is probably notes from these lectures which formed the basis for the commentary on some psalms, printed without his permission in 1528.[67] But as early as 1519 he wrote an introduction to Luther's commentary on the Psalms in which he emphasized the impor-

---

[65] On vs. 1.2 see fol. aIV^r, on 1.3: fol. aIV^v, on 1.8: fol. BI^r, on 1.18: fol. BII^r, 1.32: fol. BIII^v, 2.17: fol. BIV^v, 3.1: fol. CI^{r-v}.

[66] See fol. CI^{r-v}: *Quid igitur gentibus circumcisos aequet Paulus, huic obiectioni per occupationem rhetoricam respondet*; on 3.9 see CII^r. On the *occupatio* cf. e.g. *Elementa* (above, n.19) fol. KI^v (= Hertschheider (above, n.18) 13, col. 489).

[67] *In Psalmos aliquot Davidicos Phil. Melanchthonis enarrationes doctissimae* (Hagenau 1528); his introduction to Luther's commentary: Hertschneider (above, n.18) 1, col. 70–3; see also *D. Martin Luthers Werke* 2 (above, n.49) 24–5.

tance of the *renatae litterae* for the interpretation of the Holy Scriptures, and it may not be superfluous to quote one or two of his general observations, before we look at his comments in detail.

"Let us bear in mind" he says in his late commentaries, "that the psalms are the wisdom and the voice of God, and that God is the source of eloquence, of speaking in a wise, correct and orderly manner. Therefore, some single basic point should be sought in each of the psalms as in other poems written with learning, and it should be examined how its parts are connected with each other; thus they will be more transparent (easier to understand) and more pleasant, and the matter itself will show that the parts are not heaped together at random. thus as in other learned writings, similarly here, too, we look for the subject matter, the orderly arrangement of the parts, and adapt the psalms, some to this, others to that type of speech, obviously so that you examine more carefully according to the elementary rules (of rhetoric) what the purpose is, what the text wants to achieve, whether to teach something or to try to obtain something."[68] Melanchthon then classifies the psalms, some as belonging to the didactic kind (Psalms 2, 110, 45, 72, also 133 and 83), others as consolations or expressions of gratitude, yet others as requests, some of which may be regarded as belonging to the advisory kind (*genus suasorium*);[69] but he adds that the types may be mixed, "for emotions may be inserted into the teaching or vice versa, and one should not make these distinctions over-carefully."[70] Similar views may be found in the *Postilla*, a collection of occasional remarks of Melanchthon's, pub-

---

[68] Hertschneider (above, n.18) 13, col. 1224–5: *Cogitemus Psalmos sapientiam, et vocem Dei esse, et Deum fontem eloquentiae, sapienter, recte et ordine loqui. Ideo in singulis Psalmis quaeratur unum aliquod principale argumentum, ut in aliis carminibus erudite scriptis, et consideretur, quomodo membra cohaereant, ita magis perspicui et dulciores erunt, et res ipsa ostendet non esse temere coacervata membra. Sicut igitur in aliis eruditis scriptis, ita et hic quaerimus propositionem, seriem partium, et accomodamus Psalmos, alios ad alia genera causarum, videlicet, ut iuxta puerilia praecepta diligentius consideretis, quis sit finis, quid velit efficere scriptum, an doceat aut petat aliquid.*

[69] Hertschneider (above, n.18) 13, col. 1225: *alii sunt consolationes, et gratiarum actiones. Alii petunt remissionem peccatorum, et alias liberationes. Possunt autem consolationes et petitiones referri ad genus suasorium, ut Psalmus 51.* On the *consolationes* as part of the *genus demonstrativum* (together with *adhortationes*) see above n.59.

[70] Hertschneider (above, n. 18) 13, col. 1225: *Sciendum est autem misceri genera: nam doctrinae intexuntur affectus, et affectibus doctrina, et non nimis anxie faciendae sunt hae distributiones.*

lished by Christoph Pezel.[71] There he also emphasizes: "Ignorant are those who think that there is no art of composing, no eloquence, in the books of the prophets: even if translations or commentators at times depart from grammar, yet in the sources there is superb art of speech (*eloquentia*) and attractiveness (*suavitas*). We should not think that the Holy Spirit takes pleasure in barbarous expression."[72] A little later one meets with another remark which I would also like to quote, as it helps to understand and appreciate adequately Melanchthon's comments on the psalms which we shall be examining presently. He says: "The common grammatical form of explanation about the purpose of expositions, i.e. what the intention of an author is, what he wants to say or achieve, adds more light than voluminous commentaries. All wise people say little."[73]

It is in a corresponding manner that one finds Melanchthon commenting upon the psalms, and one should remember that these notes are a work not of his youth, but his mature age. In almost all cases he gives a general characterisation such as consolation, expression of thanks, request etc., names the types to which it seems to belong (advisory or didactic etc.) and gives the main points, as e.g. for Psalm 51 (50): "It is a request for the remission of sins, justification, sanctification, and mitigation of punishment. These are the main points with which emotions are mixed, and amplifications and arguments."[74] After this general introduction Melanchthon explains that the first verse states the substance of the case ("Have mercy upon me") together with a first argument ("according to thy loving kindness"), and draws attention also to the *antith-*

---

[71] Ch. Pezel (ed.), *Postilla Melanchthoniana* I-IV (Heidelberg/Hanau 1594–95) (= Hertschneider (above, n.18) 24 and 25 col. 1–902) esp. II 582–97 (= Hertschneider (above, n.18) 24, col. 735–43). On Ch. Pezel see *Neue Deutsche Biographie* 25 (1887) 575–77.

[72] Hertschneider (above, n.18) 24, col. 735: *Asini sunt, qui cogitant, non esse eloquentiam in libris Propheticis: etiamsi versiones vel interpretes aliquando discedunt a Grammatica: tamen in fontibus est excellens eloquentia et suavitas. Non cogitemus Spiritum Sanctum delectari barbarie.* (= Pezel (above, n.71) II 583).

[73] Hertschneider (above, n.18) 24, col. 735: *Illa Grammatica expositio de fine narrationum, quae sit intentio scriptoris, quid velit docere, vel efficere, plus luminis addit quam magna commentaria...omnes sapientes sunt pauciloqui* (= Pezel (above, n.71) 583–4).

[74] Hertschneider (above, n.18) 13, col. 1225: *Est autem Psalmus Miserere petitio remissionis peccatorum, iustificationis, sanctificationis et mitigationis poenarum. Hae sunt principales propositiones, quibus mixti sunt affectus, et amplificationes et argumenta.*

esis ("kindness, mercy and my transgressions").[75] He paraphrases what the psalmist says, shows that it corresponds to and is consistent with other passages of the Bible to which he refers, points to particular rhetorical figures such as *emphasis* (vs. 5: the two words "sin" and "iniquity") or *epiphonema* (vs. 8: the exclamation "Behold"), and gives a rhetorical explanation of the figurative expression "Purge me with hyssop" (vs. 9: *signum pro signato*).[76] He is not content merely to paraphrase what the psalmist says, he comments on the function of particular verses, adds philological or theological (doctrinal) explanations and tries to clarify the sense and the structure of the whole, at the end listing the central points of the whole.

On might say that this is not a rhetorical commentary, and when one compares what Melanchthon has to say e.g. to elucidate a Ciceronian speech, one will undoubtedly find far more and far more detailed comments there both on the speech as a whole and on particular arguments or expressions and phrases.[77] But when one looks e.g. on Melanchthon's remarks on the second psalm, one sees him not only characterising the poem as a whole ("a prophecy about the coming Messiah"), not only assigning it to the demonstrative type and pointing to the emotions in the *exordium*; he explicitly justifies the poet and his procedure, referring to the rules of rhetoric ("emotions are appropriate for introductions").[78]

---

[75] Hertschneider (above, n.18) 13, col. 1225: *Primus versus statim est propositio... Huic propositioni addit argumentum... Et antithesis consideretur, secundum misericordiam tuam, non propter ulla mea opera vel merita.*

[76] Hertschneider (above, n.18) 13, col. 1226–7: *Haec dicta congruunt ad doctrinam saepe repetitam de gratuita reconciliatione. Consideranda est autem verborum emphasis. Duo vocabula ponit huius mali. Primum nominat iniquitatem, quod significat curvitates, videlicet ἀταξίαν in omnibus viribus. Deinde peccatum expresse nominat.* On vers 8: *Confessionis asservatio est, et tamquam epiphonema, hoc postulas ut fateamur non simulate, nos esse peccatores.* On vers 9: *ubi figurate dictum necesse est interpretari: nominat enim signum pro signato.* On *epiphonema* see *Elementa* (above, n.19) fol. K3ʳ (= Hertschneider (above, n.18) 13, col. 490).

[77] See my "Cicero orator inter Germanos redivivus, II," *Humanistica Lovaniensia* 39 (1990) 157–76, esp. 163–7.

[78] Hertschneider (above, n.18) 13, col. 1019: *Est prophetia de venturo Messia.* Col. 1020: *Hi adfect-us ac motus conveniunt exordiis, ut ex praeceptis vulgaribus notum est* (cf. above, n.52).

VI. Conclusion

There can be no doubt that Melanchthon is primarily concerned to understand himself what the Holy Scriptures have to say and to assist others in understanding and appreciating their teaching and their message; and for this reason his commentaries on the works of the Bible differ from those on pagan writings which he explains primarily for the sake of their form, i.e. as successful application of the rules of rhetoric, but with less concern for their content. When his later exegetical works on parts of the Bible seem to make less use of rhetorical categories than his earlier ones, this, I think, is due partly to the fact that what we have as early evidence are primarily lecture notes taken down by students who may well have written down, what he said in his lectures, but regarded as too elementary to print in his own commentaries, and that in these lectures, as in his first rhetorical manual, he was breaking new ground, which inevitably tempts one to be unusually explicit. On the other hand, one must not be misled, as some scholars have been, to believe that Melanchthon over the years lost confidence in rhetorical criticism,[79] i.e. the usefulness of rhetorical categories for the exegesis of the Holy Scriptures. On the contrary, his comments on the psalms, ignored by most theologians, as they seem less interesting for Melnachthon's theological views and their development, show that he regarded the instruments of rhetorical criticism as useful as ever for the adequate appreciation and understanding of the word of God. And this, clearly, was Melanchthon's primary aim: For this reason he acquired a thorough knowledge of the three ancient languages at an early age, and provided reliable editions of the Greek text, whenever he deemed it necessary. For this reason also, he absorbed what pagan antiquity had developed and provided as tools for the composition and interpretation of texts: the rules of rhetoric. Convinced that the Word of God was spoken and the Holy Scriptures were written in the most perfect manner possible, he applied these rules to the exegesis of the Bible, and he reproduced these rules with illustrations from the Bible to demonstrate that such an application was possible, and not only possible, but desirable and helpful.

The particular blending of Melanchthon's religious education and his theological aims with his humanistic training enabled him to develop

---

[79] Bizer (above, n.30) 17, see my paper "Paulus und die antike Rhetorik" (above, n.18) 25 with n.85.

new methods for the exegesis of biblical texts or, perhaps, to rediscover methods already practised by some fathers of the Church, but later forgotten or ignored. As Melanchthon applied them to pagan texts also in his lectures and in numerous commentaries for several decades, a large number of pupils became acquainted with them and used them themselves as teachers and preachers. Thus Melanchthon succeeded in changing fundamentally both the approach to and the interpretation of biblical as well as literary texts in the sixteenth century, at least in Germany.

19

"A Kind of Warmth": Some Reflections on the Concept of "Grace" in the Neoplatonic Tradition

John Dillon

If there were one thing, one might imagine, that would distinguish the theological position of Platonism from that of Christianity, it would be the doctrine of divine grace. Unlike the Judaeo-Christian God, after all, entities like the One or Intellect, even if they are regularly referred to as "god," cannot be credited (or debited) with any degree of personal interest or involvement with creatures such as ourselves, such as would normally be considered a prerequisite to any concept of divine grace.[1]

---

[1] Not surprisingly, I can find no discussion of the topic of the concept of "grace" in Neoplatonic philosophy, but there are many useful discussions of the religious and mystical aspect of his philosophy, among which may be mentioned René Arnou, *Le Désir de Dieu dans la philosophie de Plotin* (Rome: Presses de l'Université Gregorienne 1967²); two essays of Vicenzo Cilento, "Mistica e Dialettica" and "Esperienze religiose," *Saggi su Plotino* (Milan: U. Mursia 1973) 135–57, 159–79; and John Rist's chapter on "Prayer" (ch. 15) in his *Plotinus, The Road to Reality* (Cambridge: Cambridge University Press 1967). On the topic of this essay, I quote some pertinent lines from the introductory essay by Fr. Paul Henry to Stephen MacKenna's translation of the *Enneads* (p. xxxvii of the Faber ed., p. xlvii of the Penguin): "Finally, salvation is not to be achieved. It is achieved. For its realization it is enough that the individual should

When St. Augustine, for example, adverts in the *Confessions* (VII 20–1) to what he found wanting in "the books of the Platonists," it is very much this on which he dwells:

> What shall wretched man do? Who shall deliver him from the body of this death,[2] but only thy grace, through Jesus Christ our Lord, whom thou has begotten co-eternal to thyself, and possessedst in the beginning of thy ways: in whom the prince of this world found nothing worthy of death, but yet he killed him; whereby the bond was cancelled, which stood against me.[3] None of all this do these (Platonic) writings contain. Those pages can show nothing of this face of pity, those tears of confession, that sacrifice of thine, a troubled spirit, a broken and contrite heart,[4] the salvation of thy people, the Spouse, the city, the deposit (*arra*) put down by the Holy Spirit, the cup of our redemption. No man sings there, "Shall not my soul wait upon God, seeing from him cometh my salvation? For he is my God, my salvation and my defence; I shall no more be moved" (Ps. 62:1–2). No man in those books hears him calling: "Come unto me all ye that labour!" Yes, they scorn to learn of him, because "he is gentle and lowly in heart." "For these things has thou hid from the wise and prudent, and hast revealed them unto babes."[5] (VII 21, trans. Watts, lightly emended).

If one divests the basic contents of this tirade from its scriptural ornamentation, one gathers that what Augustine finds lacking in the treatises of Plotinus and Porphyry is any sense of the total helplessness of man to attain moral excellence (never mind *divinity*) by his own unaided efforts, and his utter dependence on the "grace" (*gratia, charis*) emanating from God, which may be dispensed (or withheld) in mysterious ways, and for mysterious reasons. Earlier, in ch. 20, he berates himself for, when still under the influence of the *libri Platonici*, "prattling as if he were an expert" (*garriebam plane quasi peritus*), and thinking that he

---

become conscious of what he is already in his inmost nature, where Intellect which is beyond the virtues identifies itself with true being and with the idea which one forms of the self, of the world, and of God. The anchoritism of the soul and of God excludes at once all sacramentalism and all true history of becoming. The latent actuality of salvation and tne cold transcendence of God make it impossible, in terms of Plotinian Socraticism, to conceive of any genuine doctrine of grace." While disapproving of the tone of these remarks, and of the assumptions behind them, I do not dispute their accuracy.

[2] Cf. Rom. 7:21–5, a passage to which he has just been alluding.

[3] This cryptic remark is an allusion to Col. 2:14, where St. Paul talks of God "setting aside the bond which stood against us with its legal demands, nailing it to the cross."

[4] Cf. Psalm 51, *passim*.

[5] A melange derived from Matt. 11:25–9.

had the key to the attainment of the goal of likeness to God. In other words, what the Platonists and their partisans are accused of is spiritual pride, that confidence in the power of one's own reason, and in the constant, unprejudiced backing for that available from the supreme principle, and from the gods in general, that, within the Christian tradition, appealed to men like Pelagius, Caelestius and Julian of Eclanum — and indeed earlier, to Origen.[6]

We have here, it would seem, a very basic ground of dispute. The Platonist tradition stands accused of leaving no place in its theology for a God who can exercise compassion on a personal basis for his miserable creatures, pardoning them their delinquencies, and lifting them up when they fall, as they always must. The Platonist God, whether the One itself or the second hypostasis, Intellect (Plotinus is prepared to give the title of ὁ θεός to either),[7] does not play favourites. He (or It) cannot be thought of as taking any *personal* interest in the question of whether any specific human soul attains likeness to Him or not.

Not, of course, that a degree of good will may not be postulated on the part of the first principle. For Platonists, the basic text on this question is perhaps that famous passage of the *Timaeus,* 29DE:

> Let us now state the reason that he who constructed it constructed the realm of becoming and this universe. *He was good,* and in him that is good no begrudgery ever arises concerning anything; and being free from this, he desired that all should be as far as possible like to himself.[8]

Even if the Demiurge is to be regarded as a mythical figure, the general attitude presupposed in the divinity generally was accepted by all

---

[6] We see Origen wrestling with this problem in a most interesting way in Book III ch. 1 of the *De Principiis,* where he deals with such troublesome passages as the hardening of Pharaoh's heart (Exod. 4:21; 7:3); Jesus' hard saying about parables in Matt. 13:10; and Paul's remarks in Rom. 9:14–18 (all of which would later strengthen Augustine in his convictions), and tries to explain them away from a standpoint compatible with a Platonist view of God's goodness and impassibility. For a later statement of the Origenist position on divine grace, see Maximus Confessor, *Ambigua,* 152b (PG 91 1144), where he states that "God has granted to all equally the natural power of attaining salvation."

[7] E.g. *Enn.* I 1, 8, 9; II 3, 18, 10; II 9, 6, 39, etc. (the One); III 5, 8, 18; IV 3, 11, 11; V 8, 5, 20 etc. (Nous). Cf. J.M. Rist, "Theos and the One in some Texts of Plotinus," *Mediaeval Studies* 24 (1962) 169–80.

[8] Λέγωμεν δὴ δι' ἥν τινα αἰτίαν γένεσιν καὶ τὸ πᾶν τόδε ὁ ξυνιστὰς ξυνέστησεν. ἀγαθὸς ἦν, ἀγαθῷ δὲ οὐδεὶς περὶ οὐδενὸς οὐδέποτε ἐγγίγνεται φθόνος· τούτου δ' ἐκτὸς ὢν πάντα ὅ τι μάλιστα γενέσθαι ἐβουλήθη παραπλήσια ἑαυτῷ.

Platonists.[9] Even the Good of the *Republic* may be regarded as exercising a beneficent, if not precisely *benevolent*, influence upon, primarily, the realm of forms, but, secondarily, the realm of physical objects. The comparison with the sun, both in the Sun Simile itself (*Rep.* VI 509B), and in the Allegory of the Cave (esp. VII 516B), is particularly suggestive. We have in addition various remarks in the course of the myth of the *Phaedrus* which seemed to later Platonists to portray a caring and benevolent God, in particular 246E, where the "great leader" Zeus is described as "ordering all things and caring for them" (διακοσμῶν πάντα καὶ ἐπιμελούμενος). It was his benevolent influence that was later seen at work in the stimulation of the soul, and the re-growing of its wings, e.g. 252C-E, and 255B, where the lover is described as "god-possessed" (ἔνθεος).

There is also the notable passage in *Laws* X, 903B–905B, which is an extended statement of Plato's view of the nature of God's providential care, but there the individual is warned that he cannot expect that everything will be ordained to suit his convenience, but rather what is best for the whole, which may very well involve his (at least temporary) detriment. It is here that Plato gets closest to propounding something like a Stoic doctrine of providence — or rather, such a passage as this may have provided inspiration to Zeno and his successors.

At any rate, such is the heritage which a Platonist such as Plotinus would be conscious of. Is there anything here that would allow of anything resembling a doctrine of "grace"?

Let me make clear at the outset of this investigation that I do not wish to conduct it in the spirit that all too many of such comparisons between Platonism and Christianity have been conducted in the past — that is, on the basis of a patronizing assumption that the "pagan"[10] philosophers

---

[9] Some even of those who accepted a non-literal interpretation of the *Timaeus*, such a Numenius, retained the Demiurge as a secondary, creator god, subordinate to the Good, but in that case both exercise providential care over the world, though in different ways.

[10] I dislike, by the way, the term "pagan." It should be banished henceforth from civilized discourse. It is a derogatory term, meaning something like "country bumpkin," which took whatever justification it ever had from the circumstance that the countryside remained loyal to the old beliefs longer than the city — Christianity being predominantly an urban phenomenon — and it never had any suitability to the representatives of the Greek philosophical schools, who were in general quintessentially urban and urbane figures. I would therefore propose the term "Hellenic" as the opposite to Christian. The present arrangement is rather as if Platonists were to continue to

had not attained, in one respect or another, to the full light of wisdom or truth that was vouchsafed to their Christian counterparts. This is relevant to discussions of such issues as the doctrine of the Trinity, the development of the concept of Will, and the present topic of "grace." I do not happen to believe that a doctrine of grace in the Augustinian sense is a respectable philosophical or theological concept at all, and I should be sorry to think that Plotinus had developed it, but I am prepared to consider whether some rational analogue to it might appear anywhere in his writings.

With that much off my chest, then, let us proceed. The first passage I would like to turn to is one from the latter part (chs. 15–42) of his great treatise, *How the multitude of the Forms came into being, and on the Good* (VI 7 [38]), where he has turned to a consideration of the ascent from the realm of Intellect to the Good (or One). There is much talk here of the "radiance" shed by the Good on Intellect, and of the "love" of Intellect for the Good (cf. esp. chs. 34-6), but in ch. 22, Plotinus employs some particularly interesting turns of phrase, which may be relevant to our enquiry (ll. 1–20):

> When anyone, therefore, sees this light (sc. from the Good), then truly he is also moved to the Forms, and longs for the light which plays upon them and delights in it, just as with bodies here below our desire is not for the underlying material things but for the beauty imaged upon them. For each is what it is by itself; but it becomes desirable when the Good colours it, giving a kind of grace (χάριτας)[11] to them and passionate love to the desirers. Then the soul, receiving into itself an "outflow" (ἀπορροή, *Phaedr.* 251b2) from thence, is moved and dances like a bacchant and is all stung with longing and becomes love. Before this it is not moved even towards Intellect, for all its beauty; the beauty of Intellect is inactive till it catches a light from the Good, and the soul by itself "falls flat on its back" (*Phaedr.* 254b8) and is completely inactive and, though Intellect is present, is unenthusiastic about it. *But when a kind of "warmth"* (ὥσπερ θερμασία, cf. ἐθερμάνθη, 251b2) *from thence comes upon it,* it gains strength and wakes and is truly "winged"; and though it is moved with passion for that which lies close by it, yet all the same it rises higher, to something greater which it seems to remember. And as long as there is anything higher than that which is present to it, it naturally goes on upwards, *lifted by the giver of its love* (αἰρομένη ὑπὸ τοῦ δόντος τὸν ἔρωτα). (trans. Armstrong).

refer to Christians as "atheists" or "barbarians," after the manner of Proclus or Damascius.

[11] Not, of course, in the sense relevant to this enquiry.

This passage is plainly shot through with reminiscences of the *Phaedrus* myth, but these are subjected to an interesting transformation.[12] In the myth, the soul is stimulated by the sight of the beloved to a reminiscence of the vision of the forms. Here, the soul contemplating the world of forms is inflamed to love by the benign influence emanating from the Good. This influence, however, though described here in rather personal terms, is by no means personal, in the sense of arbitrary, in its operation, and herein lies the difference with the grace dispensed by Augustine's deity. The "light" or "warmth" streams down upon all alike, and its influence is limited, not by any exercise of will on the part of the One, but simply by the limits of receptivity (ἐπιτηδειότης πρὸς ὑποδοχήν) of the recipient.[13]

Another important passage in this connection is the slightly earlier V 5 [32], 12, where once again the subject is the illumination of Intellect by the One. Once again, it merits quotation at some length:

> And we must consider that men have forgotten that which from the beginning until now they want and long for. For all things reach out to that and long for it by necessity of nature, as if divining by instinct that they cannot exist without it. The grasp of the beautiful and the wonder and the waking of love for it come to those who, in a way, already know it and are awake to it. But the Good, since it was there long before *to serve as an object for our innate desire*,[14] is present even to those asleep and does not astonish those who at any time see it, because it is always there and there is never recollection of it; but people do not see it, because it is present to them in their sleep. (12, 6–15, trans. Armstrong).

Here again, the emphasis is on *our* longing for the Good, and not its concern to attract us, despite its essential benevolence. A little further on in the chapter, however (33ff.), when contrasting the Good with Beauty, Plotinus remarks that "the Good is gentle and kindly and gracious, and present to anyone when he wishes (καὶ ἔστι δὲ τὸ μὲν ἤπιον καὶ

---

[12] As is well pointed out by Pierre Hadot in his commentary *ad loc.*, *Plotin, Traité 38* (VI,7) (Paris: Cerf 1988) 291–3.

[13] For this important Plotinian, and Neoplatonic, concept, cf. *Enn.* VI 4, 11, 1–9, and 15, 1–19.

[14] ἅτε πάλαι παρὸν εἰς ἔφεσιν σύμφυτον, a troublesome phrase, which I think Armstrong has rather over-translated as "since it was there long before to arouse an innate desire." Certainly, παρὸν εἰς would seem to imply purpose, but not such an active intention as Armstrong seeks to imply. Harder's "welches uns ja seit je beiwohnt als Gegenstand unseres angeborenen Trachtens" seems preferable, even though Armstrong's interpretation would suit my present quest better.

προσηνὲς καὶ ἁβρότερον καί, ὡς ἐθέλει τις, παρὸν αὐτῷ)" — a remarkable sequence of personalising epithets, seeming to imply a postive benevolence. This impression, on the other hand, is countered just below that again by the further statement (41ff.):

> The Good, then, is master also of this derived power (sc. of Beauty), though he[15] does not need the things that have come into being from him, but leaves what has come into being altogether alone, because he needs nothing of it, but is the same as he was before he brought it into being. He would not have cared if it had not come into being; and if anything else could have been derived from him he would not have grudged it existence; but as it is, it is not possible for anything else to come into being; all things have come into being, and there is nothing left.

That is surely laying it on the line in no uncertain terms. When all is said and done, we do not matter one whit to the One, though it (or he) wishes us only the best.

There is another very striking passage, this time from an "early" essay,[16] VI 9 [9], concerning our relation to the One, which states this same position (ch. 8, 35ff.). Plotinus has just been making the point that immaterial entities cannot be distinct from one another spatially, but only in virtue of "otherness" (ἑτερότης), and that is a category which the One transcends, so that it is not "other" than us:

> The One, therefore, since it has no otherness, is always present, and we are present to it when we have no otherness;[17] however,[18] the One does not desire us, so as to be around[19] us, but we desire it, so that we are around it.
> And we are always around it, but do not always look to it. It is like a choral dance: in the order of its singing[20] the choir keeps round its conductor (κορυφαῖος) but may sometimes turn away, so that he is out of their

---

[15] We may note here that Plotinus is now referring to the first principle in the masculine instead of the neuter, something that he quite often does.

[16] In so far as anything by a man who only began writing at around the age of fifty can be regarded as "early."

[17] That is to say, when we are fully in touch with the highest, "undescended" part of our souls.

[18] There is simply a καί here, but I do not feel that it can be rendered merely by "and," as Armstrong does. It is more "and *by the way*."

[19] περί with acc., with the sense of "be concerned with."

[20] Adopting here, with Armstrong, the emendation of Puelma, ἑξῆς ᾄδων, for the ἐξᾴδων of the mss, which has no clear meaning. This emendation conveys the sense of alternately facing one way and then the other in the course of the dance, which is just what is wanted.

sight, but when it turns back to him it sings beautifully and is truly with him. So we too are always around him[21] — and if we were not, we should be totally dissolved and no longer exist — but not always turned to him. But when we do look to him, then we are at our goal and at rest and do not sing out of tune as we truly dance our god-inspired dance around him. (trans. Armstrong)

In this remarkable passage, the imagery of the dance has often been remarked upon, but what concerns me more in the present context is the image of the coryphaeus. Admittedly, it is only an image, but the fact remains that the coryphaeus *is* concerned for his choir. He is not totally self-absorbed. He wants them to succeed. Such a point cannot be used to undermine to any serious extent the overall thrust of Plotinus' view of the One, but it does perhaps indicate that, beneath the surface of Plotinus' thought, there lurks the tendency to postulate some degree of personal interest on the part of the One in its creation (as indeed may be observed in the passage quoted above from V 5, 12).

This would after all not be strange. It is very difficult, if one is as passionately religious a philosopher as Plotinus undoubtedly was, to maintain with full rigour the impersonal detachment of a first principle which is, after all, a force for good and for order in the universe. This does not, however, amount to a doctrine of grace in what I would regard as the *pernicious* sense of an arbitrary (or, as it may more politely be put, an *infinitely mysterious*) playing of favourites by God among his creatures. There is no place for that in the Neoplatonist, nor yet in the Christian Platonist, tradition.[22]

Plotinus, of course, does not represent the totality of the Neoplatonic tradition. Indeed, later Platonists, looking back, as does Damascius in a

---

[21] That is to say, the One, referred to here once again in the masculine (αὐτόν).

[22] As defended eloquently, for example, by A.H. Armstrong in his essay "Saint Augustine and Christian Platonism," R.A. Markus (ed.), *Augustine: A Collection of Critical Essays* (New York: Doubleday 1972) 19–24. To quote him: "The belief that the divine powers which rule the universe are perfectly good is the fundamental tenet of the religion of Plato and his successors. And being good for Plato and the Platonists means doing good, and doing it with perfect wisdom and fairness. To theists of this sort, and to many Christian Platonists who have been led on by the revelation in Jesus Christ from their Platonic belief that God is good to believe that he is Love, and who understand this as meaning more, not less, goodness than Plato or any philosopher was able to conceive, the doctrine of Augustine is intolerable, and no appeal to mystery can justify it" (p. 20). Armstrong is plainly speaking for himself here, and he certainly speaks for me.

famous passage of his *Phaedo* commentary,[23] distinguished between the "philosophic tradition" in Neoplatonism, represented by Plotinus and Porphyry, and the "hieratic," represented by Iamblichus, Syrianus and Proclus.[24] In this latter, "hieratic" tradition, one may expect to see a far greater degree of conventional piety expressed than one will find in Plotinus, but what one will not find, I think, is anything approaching the Christian concept of divine grace, with its concomitant sense of man's nothingness, or at least of helplessness to attain perfection by his own efforts.

A good example of later Neoplatonic piety, I think, is provided by Iamblichus' doctrine of prayer, as set out both in Book V of the *De Mysteriis* (ch. 26: 237–40), and in Proclus' *Timaeus Commentary* (*In Tim.* I 207,23–209,1 Diehl).[25] Iamblichus distinguishes three types or levels of prayer, in ascending order of perfection. The first is given the technical denomination "conductive" (*synagôgon*), leading to contact (*synaphê*) with and recognition (*gnôrisis*) of the divine; the second is termed "complexive" (*syndetikon*), linking us as it does to the divine by a "union of likemindedness" (*koinônia homonoêtikê*), "which calls forth gifts sent by the gods even before we express our requests, and performs all actions before we even think of them"; and the third and highest is "ineffable union" (*arrhêtos henôsis*), "which places all power (*to pan kyros*) in the hands of the gods, and provides that our souls rest completely in them." This highest level of prayer unites the One in us with the One of the divine realm, and really has the effect of divinizing the worshipper.

In all this passage, and in the similar passage in Proclus, there is a pervasive spirit of reverence for the divine, but nevertheless at every stage it is man who takes the initiative (even the placing of *to pan kyros* with the gods at the third level is not really an abdication of man's initiative; every step of the process is still initiated by the worshipper), and once the correct initiative (in Iamblichus' case, theurgic) has been taken, the gods neither wish to, nor indeed *can,* withhold their benefits. Certainly divine "grace" pours out upon the successful theurgist in the

---

[23] *In Phaed.* I 172, p. 123, 3–6 Norvin.
[24] Damascius, of course, like Plato before him (as he asserts), sees himself as combining the best of both tendencies.
[25] I have set this out in Appendix A of my *Iamblichi Chalcidensis Fragmenta* (Leiden: Brill 1973) 407–11.

De Mysteriis,[26] but there is no suggestion that the gods can do other than respond favourably to correctly formulated supplications.

It is here that the late antique theurgist is true to the Hellenic theological tradition in general in a way which the Christian theologian — or at least a theologian in the tradition of St. Augustine — is not. Iamblichus did not agree with Plotinus and Porphyry that one could attain to union with the divine by theoretical (that is, rational) activity alone,[27] but he did feel that at all events it was man, and not God, who was in control of the situation, to the extent that, if utterances and acts were correctly performed, with a properly pious intention, divine beneficence must ensue. That seems to me to remain a very basic distinction between the Hellenic and Christian traditions, and it is not an area, I must say, in which I would find the Hellenic tradition wanting.

---

[26] Another good passage on this topic is *De Myst.* I 15, where Iamblichus, while hotly denying the accusation by Porphyry that theurgists seek to impose constraint (*anankai*) upon the gods, recognises that, if one presses the right buttons, so to speak, the gods cannot do otherwise than respond. They are not constrained, however, because, being good, they are entirely pleased to respond.

[27] Cf. *De Myst.* II 11: 96–7: "It is not thought (*ennoia*) that links the theurgist to the gods: otherwise, what would prevent the theoretical philosopher from enjoying theurgic union with them? But the case is not so. Theurgic union is attained only by the perfective operation of ineffable acts correctly performed, acts which are beyond all understanding; and by the power of the unutterable symbols which are intelligible only to the gods." This may be to some extent a manifesto of irrationalism, as has been frequently alleged (e.g. by E.R. Dodds in his edition of Proclus' *Elements of Theology* (Oxford: Clarendon Press 1933) xx), but it is not really a sign of failure of nerve. The initiative remains with man.

20

Ausonius at Prayer

R.P.H. Green

At first sight the poet Ausonius may seem out of place in a volume to honour a distinguished scholar of ancient philosophy. "From first to last his verse is barren of ideas; not a gleam of insight or of broad human sympathy, no passion, no revolt: his attitude towards life is a mechanical and complacent acceptance of things as they are."[1] This editor's criticism is an anachronistic one — in the next sentence he compares Ausonius with Matthew Arnold — but there is some truth in what he says.[2] In the context of philosophy, certainly, there seems to be very little to say about Ausonius: a few references — not always apposite — to the big names, a flirtation with some popular ideas, especially Pythagorean ones,[3] and some gentle ridicule of the ways of logicians; but no sign of intelligent or informed interest. He had read the Latin

---

[1] H.G. Evelyn White, *Ausonius*, Loeb (London: Heinemann 1968) xxvi.
[2] See the comments by Ausonius' latest editor, in R.P.H. Green (ed.), *The Works of Ausonius* (Oxford: Clarendon Press 1991) xviii.
[3] See *Eclogues* 19–21 Green, where the oldest forms of the title contain references to Pythagoras.

classics thoroughly,[4] but what if anything he learnt of philosophical ideas from them was quite superficial.

The area of religion, especially Christianity, is more rewarding. Again there is a clear tendency in modern criticism to disparage him, and one which, it must be said, has some justification given that he wrote in an age of vehement controversy. In the nineteenth century he was often considered an undoubted pagan; the twentieth has acknowledged his Christianity, but grudgingly. Many have adopted the term "semi-Christianity," to convey not only the undeniable fact that some works of a religious nature lack any sign of Christianity but also a perceived lukewarmness in the works which do contain clear Christian material. There is in fact evidence that his Christianity went quite deep: there are some surely unpremeditated or even unconscious references which may be significant because of their very inconspicuousness and triviality.[5] In a poem on the days of the week he begins with Sunday, not Saturday; in a letter written in mid-December he surprisingly ignores the *Saturnalia*; in the *Technopaignion* of all places he echoes a slogan of St. Paul, and in the last poem of the *Ephemeris* he takes a demonstrably Christian attitude to the question of guilt in dreams. In such an inquiry such straws in the wind may be as important as a deliberate flying of the flag. But there is also some explicitly, one might say exuberantly, Christian work, in the *Versus Paschales* and the prayer best known simply as *Oratio*.[6] The first of these has recently been presented as the work of a worldly and opportunistic Christian, but there are strong objections to this reading of it.[7] The other prayer has also received scholarly attention, notably by Langlois,[8] who has shown how frequently it refers to the Bible and other Christian literature; yet in spite of its bulk and prominence this work seems not to have had a great impact on general ideas of Ausonius' Christianity. Its evidence, however, cannot be evaded; one late manuscript, it is true, ascribes it to Paulinus of Nola, but this solitary attribu-

---

[4] Green (above, n.2) xx–xxii; as for his reading of Greek, see R.P.H. Green, "Greek in Late Roman Gaul: the Evidence of Ausonius," E.M. Craik (ed.), *Owls to Athens: Essays on Classical Subjects presented to Sir Kenneth Dover* (Oxford: Clarendon Press 1990) 311–19.

[5] R.P.H. Green, "The Christianity of Ausonius," *SP* XXVIII (1993) 39–48.

[6] For the spurious prayer in rhopalic verses, see Green (above, n.2) 668–9.

[7] Green (above, n.2) 269–70.

[8] P. Langlois, "Les poèmes chrétiens et le christianisme d'Ausone," *RPh* 43 (1969) 39–58.

tion was perhaps occasioned by the same feeling of surprise as seems to have afflicted modern critics when faced by his strong statements of belief. In fact there could hardly be better proof of its authenticity, since in V, the oldest and in many ways the best manuscript, it is part of a sequence of poems, the *Ephemeris*, which would not make sense without a prayer at this point, since poem two is an introduction to a prayer and poem four refers back to one. It is true that one family of manuscripts includes the *Oratio* but has no *Ephemeris*; however the poem's title, *Precatio matutina*, seems to refer to the function that it has in the *Ephemeris* (where Ausonius turns to prayer immediately after rising and washing) and so confirms its true context.

The *Ephemeris* (glossed as *totius diei negotium*) is an appealing description of Ausonius' daily routine, consisting of seven or eight poems (some truncated in transmission) but certainly longer in its original form. (Its reduced size is not unusual for Ausonius; it seems that both chance and design have mangled Ausonius' works — a sort of modularisation for a less patient age — so that not many long ones remain in their pristine form: minimal harm has befallen the *Moselle* and *Gratiarum Actio*, but the *Fasti*, *Caesares*, and *Bissula* are shadows of their former selves). In the extant version, the *Ephemeris* begins with two slight but elegant poems of about twenty lines; they are immediately followed by the *Oratio* (85 lines), and then there are three short poems about the preparation of lunch, a poem addressing his stenographer, and an unfortunately headless poem about dreams, all of them less than half the length of the *Oratio*. His prayer dominates the sequence as it stands, and was surely designed by its author to do so, although the description of the lunch might have run it fairly close in length. This is a frustrating loss — one would like to know who attended, what they ate, and what they talked about — but to have lost the *oratio Ausonii* would have been worse than losing the *cena Ausonii*, for whereas Ausonius' gastronomic tastes are fairly well known, his relations with Christianity would be much more obscure without this evidence.

It is significant not only that the *Oratio* has such a dominant role, but that it is found in this context at all. Prayer is clearly presented as part of Ausonius' personal life, as he wished it to be recorded and remembered. Those who are dubious about his devotion to the faith are driven to put more weight on the words at the beginning of the poem that followed it: *satis precum datum deo, quamvis satis numquam reis fiat precatu numinis* (sometimes, indeed on the first four only) than on the prayer itself. But even the most fervent must end a season of prayer sometime, and if there is a hint of irony in the way Ausonius puts it then it is no more significant than the apparent diminishing of his masterpiece the *Moselle* by references to Bordeaux and the Garonne. Of course, one should not see in this poem the *ipsissima verba* of Ausonius at prayer, nor is it likely to be a prayer which he composed for his own use. The poem before it, where he says that by naming the Trinity he is beginning to pray, and refers to his personal meditation, gives a better idea of the actual process of prayer. The poem is stylized to a high degree, but not to be disregarded on that account.

All the poems in the sequence are carefully written, sometimes from a generic template — there is a Horatian ode, an epigram after Posidippus — and sometimes not, but the *Oratio* is particularly elaborate. The invocation (which is, strictly speaking, a single carefully constructed sentence) occupies some 30 lines. The remainder of the poem, which is for the most part devoted to petition, is carefully structured by anaphora of the pivotal word *da* and other devices, and continues to make full use of the stylistic resources of Latin as realised in epic and elsewhere. The whole poem shows great verbal elaboration and some highly appropriate neologisms, and a thoughtful blend of classical and Christian vocabulary and ideas. It would of course be dangerous to infer the strength of Ausonius' commitment to Christianity from the fact that he chose to devote such care and presumably time to the work. He was not only a *rhetor* but a great stylist with a versatile talent for writing in various registers, and there is scarcely a poem — except where he chooses the path of *diligens neglegentia* — that does not have remarkable elements of structural or verbal elaboration. Attention will here be drawn to two other features, which may offer better evidence of commitment and insight, if not passion and intellect, than anything in the poem mentioned so far. In terms of doctrine the poem has a weight and richness which complements its verbal elaboration, especially in its majestic invocation of the Father and the Son. There is also a notable range and variety of material in the petitions, especially in the last third of the poem. What follows is not a search for evidence of the poet's sincerity, but an attempt to point out the poem's complexity and variety: for Ausonius may be dressing himself up in his Sunday best, as it were, or giving us details in which we would be better advised to admire the "reality effect" than to essay an assessment of "realism."[9] But in any case the detail deployed is of great interest. This contribution will conclude by arguing briefly that with this personal and literary prayer of Ausonius an old tradition takes a new turn.

I.

Describing the opening invocation is about as easy as describing the ornate façade of a Gothic cathedral; the overall structure is complex though rigorously articulated, and there is a wealth of detail. The prayer begins with an appeal to the Father (*Omnipotens*), and then turns to the Son before stressing their joint activity in creation and salvation history. The theological material is both biblical (especially Johannine) and credal, but there is much that, though orthodox and generally easy to parallel in mainstream Western Christian writing, cannot be so categorised and is expressed in the poet's own way (e.g. line 16: *irrequies, cuncta ipse movens, vegetator inertum*). Stylistically speaking, Ausonius' procedure is to build up short phrases, often linked by means of antithesis, but occasionally to spend two or three lines developing a point in a more or less pictorial way: so the eternity of the Son (9-12), the subordination of heaven, earth, and hell to Him (13-15), the adoption of the Gentiles (17-19), resurrection (24-6), and later the Holy Spirit (46-8), who is not mentioned in the invocation itself.

The first of these short expansions is designed to contradict the Arian doctrine of the subordination of the Son.[10] The Nicene creed of 325 anathematized the statement that ἦν ποτε οὐκ ἦν "there was a time when Christ was not," and had been recently reaffirmed (assuming that it is right to date the poem to the 380s) by the Council of Constantinople (381). The poet alludes to the anathema in the words *generatus in illo tempore quo tempus nondum fuit*, and goes on to emphasize that Christ took part in the creation of the world (less controversial), and that the

---

[9] As urged by S. Georgia Nugent (following Barthes) in "Ausonius' "Late Antique" Poetics and "Post-modern" Literary Theory," A.J. Boyle (ed.), *The Imperial Muse: Flavian Epicist to Claudian* (Bendigo, Victoria 1990) 245.

[10] Lines 8-16, which contain the most obvious anti-Arian material, are missing in one family of manuscripts, with no detriment to the syntax; for the relevance of this to the transmission see Green (above, n.2) 252.

Word was God: *ipse dei verbum, verbum deus*, making clear how he understood this crucial and much debated passage.[11] The phrases *quo numine viso et patrem vidisse datum* (20/1) and *contagia nostra qui tulit et diri passus ludibria leti* (21/2) may also have a polemical purpose: they were certainly used in that way in the course of the controversy, but Ausonius may have been unaware, or only dimly aware, of this. The end of the prayer is clearly and uncompromisingly Nicene: *filius ex vero verus, de lumine lumen* (82). Though often expressed imaginatively and in a way that is not blatantly controversial, Ausonius' allegiance is clear. It may well have been influenced by recent events, but it should not be assumed that after Theodosius had put an end to the controversy Ausonius had followed the winning side simply for the sake of safety or respectability — especially if, as is likely, he had by now lost his influence at court.

Another major theme of the poem is salvation — particularly clear in its central section — and here it is the petitions for sinlessness and for personal resurrection that are most conspicuous. Christ, as *salutifer*, has opened up the way to heaven (23), and Ausonius seeks to follow it (37). The theme of sin, already mentioned in 21 (*contagia nostra*) is very prominent, as is the insistence on the repudiation of pagan practices. In a series of sentences (with notable anaphora of *si*) that recall the tone of bargaining typical of Roman prayer Ausonius claims that he does not worship stones or consult entrails (44; 50/1). This theme has been anticipated in the poem immediately before the *Oratio*, where (following Stoic ideas of prayer) Ausonius emphasised simplicity of worship: *pateatque fac sacrarium nullo paratu extrinsecus; pia verba, vota innoxia rei divinae copia est*. True worship is internal (cf. *Gratiarum Actio* 80), or at least is not dependent on external aids of the (pagan) kind that he instances. But there is more to sinlessness than that: Ausonius presents a vivid impression of the difficulty of the Christian life. The prominence which he gives to the serpentine form of the devil does not detract from the seriousness of all this: indeed it may be argued that in the opening words of this second section *(da pater invictam contra omnia crimina mentem, vipereumque nefas nocituri averte veneni)* he is paraphrasing the Lord's Prayer — *et ne nos inducas in tentationem, sed libera nos a malo*. As well as confessing his sin, and

---

[11] John 1:2, of which the heretical punctuation was *In principio erat verbum, et verbum erat apud deum, et deus erat. Verbum hoc erat in principio apud deum.*

underlining the importance of prayer and an active approach to sanctity of life, he stresses the need for repentance, vividly articulated in a series of five cola ending with an adaptation of Vergil *Aeneid* 6.743 *patiturque suos mens saucia manes.*[12] A further point, that holiness of life is not to be achieved by faith alone, strongly asserted in 52/3 (*et si opto magis quam fido bonus purusque probari*) may be surprising to modern ears attuned to antitheses between *fides* and *opera*, *gratia* and *merita*, but before the development of these points in the Pelagian controversy this may not be theologically significant. Ausonius' wish is that by strenuous action and God's grace he may become pure and sinless, ready for the Last Judgement if it should precede his death (74–8, quoted overleaf).

The Christian's resurrection is another prominent theme. Already when speaking of Christ's work Ausonius has emphasised that resurrection is of the whole body. He later prays that after escaping the "bonds of the sick body" (but not of any body) he may be taken up on high *puri qua lactea caeli semita ventosae superat vaga nubila lunae* (40–2), as Elijah and Enoch were. He seems at pains to stress the physical reality of these visits to heaven: Elijah remained *integer* and went *quadriiugo curru* (perhaps in contrast to the *simulatio quadriiugorum* in the account of this by the earlier Christian poet Juvencus, 2.546), and Enoch *solido cum corpore*. (Lines 33–5 give further evidence of a feeling of continuity with Old Testament figures).

It is also remarkable that he seeks to localise the destination of Christians in the Milky Way, distinguishing this from the moon or the region around it. Christian thinking, unlike that of Stoics, neo-Platonists and Pythagoreans, seems not to have attempted, or to have purposely avoided, such precision, but Ausonius opts clearly for the Pythagorean belief, and does so presumably because it is closer to the common Christian notion that the righteous were received among the stars. It is not clear whether he is speculating *suo Marte*, or following a Christian source: the former is not unlikely. Although he does not make this explicit, he may be placing Hell in or near the moon, using a source like that of Macrobius' commentary on the *Somnium Scipionis* 1.12.3: *hinc et Pythagoras putat a lacteo circulo deorsum incipere Ditis imperium, quia animae inde lapsae videntur iam a superis recessisse.*

---

[12] Interpreted, surely, as in Servius on *Aeneid* 6.743 where *manes* is explained as *supplicia quae sunt ad manes*.

The third main section of the poem contains Ausonius' more detailed petitions, which presumably constitute the *libamina vitae intemerata* (45/6) that he earlier claimed to be his offering. If the earlier comparison with a cathedral has any validity, these are the mosaic pavement, or indeed the stones on the path to heaven. They seem a very mixed bag, and the passage needs to be quoted in full.

>   nil metuam cupiamque nihil; satis hoc rear esse,
>   quod satis est. nil turpe velim nec causa pudoris   60
>   sim mihi. non faciam cuiquam, quae tempore eodem
>   nolim facta mihi. nec vero crimine laedar
>   nec maculer dubio; paulum distare videtur
>   suspectus vereque reus. male posse facultas
>   nulla sit et bene posse adsit tranquilla potestas.   65
>   sim tenui victu atque habitu, sim carus amicis
>   et semper genitor sine vulnere nominis huius.
>   non animo doleam, non corpore; cuncta quietis
>   fungantur membra officiis; nec saucius ullis
>   partibus amissum quicquam desideret usus.   70
>   pace fruar, securus agam, miracula terrae
>   nulla putem. suprema diei cum venerit hora
>   nec timeat mortem bene conscia vita nec optet.
>   purus ab occultis cum te indulgente videbor,
>   omnia despiciam, fuerit cum sola voluptas   75
>   iudicium sperare tuum; quod dum sua differt
>   tempora cunctaturque dies, procul exige saevum
>   insidiatorem blandis erroribus anguem.

Firstly a prayer for contentment, derived from Stoic ethical doctrine, which is no surprise to the reader of classical Latin poetry or of Ausonius, who often strikes such a note. The next prayer, that he may have no evil wishes, seems to have a Socratic pedigree: but the idea may be to avoid disgrace, if the the closeness of *pudor* is allowed to colour *turpe*. Then (61–2), we come across the "Golden Rule", in its negative form: this is found in some early Western versions of *Acts* 15.29[13] and the *Didache* (1.2), but it cannot be determined whether Ausonius knew these. Lines 62–4 have an almost legal flavour; he is aware of the damage that even a false accusation can bring. "May I have no chance to do evil," he goes on, "and quiet possibilities of doing good" — a rather strange pair of requests to which close parallels have not been forthcom-

---

[13] See J. Wordsworth and H.I. White (eds.), *Novum Testamentum Latine* (Oxford: Clarendon Press 1905).

ing in earlier or contemporary literature. Is this a reaction to the great potential for both which he must recently have had as praetorian prefect? This would fit in with the impression of "the small man" which the *Ephemeris* gives in other places, including the following line (66). Prayers to be dear to his friends (that is, to have good friends) and to suffer no loss of children — he had already lost two at an early age — are not surprising; likewise the prayer that he may be spared mental and physical pain. The note of *tranquilla* (65) and *quietis* (68) continues in 71–2, where *miracula* means not "miracles" but "terrifying occurrences." Lines 72 and 73 are a combination of Tibullus and Martial, writers with whom Ausonius spiritually aligns himself elsewhere; but a strongly theological note enters in the rather difficult last sentence, as Ausonius looks forward, through God's grace, to a time when he is "pure from secret sins" and can "look down on everything" (presumably, "despise all things"), intent on God's judgement; while this is delayed, may he be immune from the blandishing wiles of the Devil. A final prayer of seven lines repeats the request for Christ to pass on these petitions, "trembling with guilt," to the Father.

Such is Ausonius' prayer: theologically informed, carefully written, giving an impression of deeply felt personal need. It is both personal and literary. The foregoing analysis shows that Fontaine was too hasty to dismiss it as a mixture of commonplace neo-Platonic theology and typically Epicurean petitions.[14] Christian Latin literature before Ausonius contains nothing to compare with it, excluding perhaps the liturgy, where developments are hard to date with the requisite accuracy. It is very likely that it was Ausonius who was responsible for the first step in this direction: not only was he steeped in classical literature, but he clearly had the breadth of vision to combine it with sacred writing, and probably fewer scruples than many of his Christian contemporaries. It may seem a small thing to combine classical form and Christian content in this way, but it is noticeable that the first known Christian poet of any consequence, Juvencus, made no such attempt to use what since Norden we call the *Du-Stil*;[15] his version of the Lord's Prayer (1.590–600) is written in the same rather artless and cumbersome style as the

---

[14] J. Fontaine, *Naissance de la poésie dans l'Occident Chrétien* (Paris: Études augustiniennes 1981) 106–8.

[15] E. Norden, *Agnostos Theos: Untersuchungen zur Formengeschichte religiöser Rede* (Stuttgart: Teubner 1956; photo mech. repr. of 1913 edition).

rest of his gospel naratives. Proba, the centonist, evidently did not take up the challenge.

II

On the penultimate page of his edition of Ausonius, hidden among the *addenda* and *corrigenda*, the Austrian editor Karl Schenkl[16] made the suggestion that Ausonius imitated Tiberianus, who also wrote a prayer in verse.[17] There has been no agreement among scholars on this point: there does seem to be some formal similarity between Tiberianus' third line *nec numero quisquam poterit pensare nec aevo* and Ausonius' fifth *(cuius formamque modumque) nec mens complecti poterit nec lingua profari*, but certainty as to whether Ausonius used him, in this as in other poems, is impossible. Tiberianus, usually dated to the early fourth century, was an important figure, even if he did not, as Cameron argues,[18] write the *Pervigilium Veneris*, and his work may well have been known to Ausonius, as it was to Augustine. It must be pointed out, however, that in spirit the compositions are very far apart, and the lines just quoted show them at their closest. The neo-Platonist Tiberianus is speculative, Ausonius is dogmatic and clear-cut; to Tiberianus all is uncertain, whereas to Ausonius little is not revealed; Tiberianus admits a plurality of gods, Ausonius excludes all but the Trinity; and Tiberianus' prayer is to know the secret causes of the universe, while Ausonius seeks personal salvation. Indeed, the Christian Ausonius departs drastically from a long tradition in which prayer was part and parcel of philosophical enquiry, which may be seen in Plato and Plotinus, Augustine and Avicenna;[19] the poetic tradition stretches back at least to Cleanthes and forward to Boethius' famous *metrum* (*O qui perpetua...*) and the imaginatively philosophical hymns of Marullus in the *quattrocento*.

Ausonius is not a man of this kind, seeking with the aid of unaided and undaunted reason to penetrate the secrets of the universe, but rather a

---

[16] K. Schenkl (ed.), *D. Magni Ausonii Opuscula*, MGH *Auct. Antiq.* V/2 (Berlin: Weidmann 1883) 303.

[17] For Tiberianus' prayer, with commentary, see E. Courtney (ed.), *The Fragmentary Latin Poets* (Oxford: Clarendon Press 1993) 431–7 and S. Mattiacci, *I Carmi e i frammenti di Tiberiano* (Florence: Olschki 1990) 157–99.

[18] A. Cameron, "The Pervigilium Veneris," *La Poesia Tardoantica: tra retorica, teologia e politica* (Messina: Messina Centro di studi umanistici 1984) 220–4.

[19] The tradition is neatly surveyed by R. Walzer, *Greek into Arabic*: *Essays on Islamic Philosophy* (Oxford: Clarendon Press 1962) 248–51.

committed Christian secure in the teachings of the Church and wishing to live an acceptable life within it — and a highly capable writer. Both the personal and the literary aspects of his *Oratio* — though the division is a crude one; one might rather speak of a close inner circle of influence, and an expanding outer one — proved influential. Similar prayers, seeking safety and salvation, were written by his pupil Paulinus of Nola, whose two short prayers to St. Felix (numbers 12 and 13 in standard editions) may be seen as inspired by the master from whose influence he was intent to escape, and by Paulinus of Pella,[20] in fact the grandson of Ausonius, who not only uses a very similar style but also makes some of the same requests.

The other kind, or sphere, of influence is seen in a group of more formal compositions of the late fourth or fifth centuries which take their lead from Ausonius' elegant articulations of praise. The short poem *de Christo* from the pen of Merobaudes, of which the circumstances and historical context are uncertain, is often similar in vocabulary and structure. Formal prayers of the same basic pattern may be found in the prayers of the more prolific poets Prudentius, Victorius, and Sedulius, each of whom develops the form as an expression of his poetic and religious identity, as the poetic predecessors of Ausonius had not done. With them, and also with Paulinus of Nola, who pursues the formal prayer in various ways after his early experiments, the prayer for divine assistance — whether inspiration, enlightenment, or approval — becomes a regular feature of Christian poetry with its fertile and distinctive blend of rhetoric and meditation.

---

[20] P. Courcelle, "Un nouveau poème de Paulin de Pella," *VC* 1 (1954) 101–13.

21

The Philosophy of the Codification of Law in Fifth Century Constantinople and Victorian Edinburgh

Jill Harries

I. Introduction

This contribution is a dialogue in content, but not in form, between two widely different groups of thinkers with a common preoccupation with the codification of law. One, comprising administrators and lawyers based at the imperial court at Constantinople in the early fifth century AD designed and created the first imperially sponsored codification of imperial law, the Theodosian Code.[1] The other consisted of three Scottish experts on the theory and practice of law, the Professor of Roman Law at the University of Edinburgh, Henry Goudy, A.J.G. Mackay, the Sheriff of Fife and Kinross, and R.V. Campbell, Sheriff of Dumfriess and Galloway. These three delivered a set of addresses to the

---

[1] The texts of the Codex Theodosianus, the Gesta Senatus of December 25, 438 and the Novellae, or 'new laws' of Theodosius II, Valentinian III and their successors were edited by Th. Mommsen et al., 2 vols. (Berlin: Weidmann 1905).

Edinburgh Merchant Company, advocating the creation of a Code of Scottish — or even, more ambitiously, British — Law, a scheme they were never destined to see realised in practice, and published the proceedings in July 1893.[2] Although far removed from each other in space, time and social milieu, the ministers of the emperor Theodosius II (408–50) and the Scottish lawyers addressed substantially the same problems within similar conceptual frameworks. The Theodosian group had the advantage of being in a position to realise its aspirations in the production of the Theodosian Code between 429 and 437 and its formal promulgation in 438. In that respect, the Scots were less fortunate. On the other hand, they had a freedom denied to the subjects of an autocracy to formulate their ideas to achieve, in theory, the best possible result, referring not only to legal thinking present in the Scottish tradition, but to codifications of law issued since the time of Theodosius, notably those of Justinian (compiled between 529 and 534), Frederick of Prussia (issued, 1751) and Napoleon (issued, in five parts, between 1804 and 1810). In the light of these precedents, the Scots set standards for their hypothetical code, which the Theodosian compilers, when tested against it, not surprisingly, failed to meet. Thus a comparison between the two is instructive on a number of counts: it allows assessment of the merits and flaws of the Theodosian enterprise, when set against an ideal which was itself formulated in the light of later experience; it serves as a reminder of the all-important contribution of Rome to Scottish law and legal thought; and, more broadly, it asserts the abiding internationalism of the Scottish intellect, of which the honorand of the present volume is so distinguished an ornament.

In what follows, concepts of codification will be considered under two main headings, definition and motivation. A Code may be defined in terms of its contents, arrangement and stated purpose. The motives for compiling a law code at a given time may be legal or non-legal or a mixture of the two and may in turn determine the intellectual coherence of the Code and its long-term viability as a statement of law. As will emerge, the presence of non-legal considerations may have adversely affected the initial concept of the Theodosian Code, the aim of which was to combine intellectual integrity with practical utility.

---

[2] H.Goudy, A.J.G. Mackay and R.V. Campbell, *Addresses on the Codification of Law*, Edinburgh Merchant Company (Edinburgh: Banks and Co. 1893).

II. Definitions

We may begin with Profesor Goudy's definition of a Code, which he considered as not hard to define; "it means simply an exposition, in precise and logical order, of the rules of law (either of the whole law or of any particular department of it), to which the sanction of the legislature is attached...It is in relation to the form rather than the substance of the law that a Code has its peculiar significance; it is the expression of the law, as adjusted by the legislature, in precise language and orderly arrangement."[3] The emphasis on precision, logic, order and arrangement, on language and form, are characteristic of the mentality of the academic lawyer, who was also well represented among the Theodosian Commissioners. But compilers of law-codes to be used in courts should also include people of a more practical bent, such as Sheriff MacKay, to whom the proper definition of a Code was equally obvious; "A Code is a book composed not for literary but for practical purposes, which people read not for amusement but for business, for it contains the rules that regulate the branch of business with which they are concerned. A Code of Law consists of a book or books, the fewer the better, in which the law, a branch of business which concerns everyone, is written in plain language..."[4] Although their emphasis was different, the ideas of Goudy and MacKay were in fact compatible, provided that a balance was maintained between them. They agreed that a law-code should be properly formulated, simple, clear and useful for establishing at least the principles for legal action. They also accepted that a Code would have its limitations; it would reflect the law of its own time and, to be of continued use, would need to be subject to periodic revision, perhaps at intervals of ten or twenty years.[5]

Precedents also helped to influence the definitions of codification offered by the Edinburgh trio. MacKay recalled that no less than six attempts at revision or codification of the law were made in Scotland prior to the Act of Union. James I in 1425 and James III in 1469 appointed Commissions to revise the two texts fundamental to Scottish law, the *Regiam Maiestatem* and the *Quoniam Attachiamenta*, but Mary Stuart adopted a more radical plan. She ordered a comprehensive review of

---

[3] Goudy (above, n.2) 12.
[4] MacKay (above, n.2) 35.
[5] Goudy (above, n.2) 17.

the "lawis" of the Realm and declared her intention of excluding from her "Code" and thus from citation in the courts, all legislation which lacked the authority of a stated minimum of her counsellors; "so that na uther but the said lawis, sychtit, mendit and correctit be her said traisty Counsalairis and Commissaris, or ony sax of them conjunctly, sal be by her privilege imprintit or have any place, faith or authoritie to be allegit and rehersit afore ony of her Jugeis or Justices quhatsomever."[6] This principle, that what is excluded is invalid and what is included is therefore by definition valid both as a theoretical statement and for purposes of citation in court, is central to the concept of a Code, and does not permit different degrees of validity within a Code. This, as we shall see, was one problem which the Theodosian compilers failed to tackle.

A law-code, then, as envisaged by the Edinburgh group, should be clearly organised, precisely formulated, suitable for use in courts and legal transactions and a comprehensive statement of all law on the matters covered by the Code valid for its own time. It should also be revised periodically to reflect legal and social changes and should have the sanction of the legislature. How well did the Theodosisan Code conform to these criteria?

The Theodosian Code as we have it is a collection of imperial laws, constitutions, "based on the power of edicts or imperial constitutions with general application," which had been passed by Constantine the Great (306–37) and his successors down to Theodosius' own day. The restricted time-span did not, however, mean that imperial constitutions issued by emperors prior to Constantine were invalid because they were excluded from the Theodosian Code. In the reign of Diocletian, in the 290s, two imperial officials, Gregorius and Hermogenianus, had made a collection of imperial rescripts from the time of Hadrian onwards and this had been later thereafter sporadically and unsystematically updated by private legal entrepreneurs. Whatever the official status of the Gregorian and Hermogenian Codes in their own time, Theodosius accepted their work as a true "codex" and regarded it as both a precedent and a model for his own undertaking.[7] The precedent, however, was not a parallel in significant respects. While the Diocletianic law-book was

---

[6] Cited by MacKay (above, n.2) 37.
[7] *CTh.* 1.1.5 (March 26, 429), *Ad similitudinem Gregoriani et Hermogeniani codicis cunctas colligi constitutiones decernimus, quas Constantinus inclitus et post eum divi principes nosque tulimus, edictorum viribus aut sacra generalitate subnixas.*

named after its compilers, Theodosius adopted a more "hands-on" approach, investing the full weight of his authority in the Code by insisting that it should be called by his name. One consequence of this was that the legislator went to great lengths to protect the integrity of his text: *constitutionarii* were appointed who were to supervise the production of very limited copies and keep it safe in their offices, free from the dangers of unauthorised tampering with the wording of existing laws or the interpolation of extraneous material.[8] These strict safeguards should have effectively guaranteed the authority of the Code as a statement of laws valid in all transactions and prevented the abuse of forgery which had so worried Theodosius' predecessors, but it left open the problem of how revision was to be undertaken. Provisions were made for the recognition of new legislation by the emperors of both East and West but nothing was done to arrange for the incorporation of relevant parts of the "new laws" (*novellae*) into subsequent "revised versions." One consequence of this was that subjects of the Empire continued to do what they had always done, namely to check with the court over any disputed matter, in case the emperor had decided something "new" since the appearance of the Code in 438. Without such regular revision as that envisaged by the Edinburgh thinkers, the Theodosian Code risked becoming a museum piece before its time.

Although the Diocletianic compilers had provided a limited precedent, the Theodosian officials were aware that they were embarking on uncharted waters. Not surprisingly, there were differences between the organisers of the project about what it was for and how they should proceed, and Theodosius had to make no less than three attempts to define what he was doing between the inception of the Code in 429 and its offical launch in 438. In 429, he set up his "first commission" of top provincial and palace officials and legal advisers to begin the collection of source material, consisting of general laws, extracts from which would form the Code itself. This undertaking was far more ambitious than it was later to appear, because the collection of imperial constitutions from Constantine onwards was not intended to be the "Theodosian Code" at all. Instead, it was to be the part of the first of a grand collection of three codes. The first would contain the constitutions of Constantine and later emperors. The second was to contain, doubtless in abbreviated form, the treatises and responses of the jurists, an idea

---

[8] *Gesta Senatus* 7 (December 25, 438); 8 (constitution dated December 23, 443).

which foreshadowed the Digest of Tribonian and Justinian. The third, and most ambitious, would combine the contents of the "three" imperial codes (i.e. those of Gregorius, Hermogenianus and Theodosius) with the collection of juristic writings to create an overall synthesis of Roman Law, "which should admit of no error or ambiguity and should reveal to us what courses should be followed and what avoided."[9] This last was intended to be the real Code, the superior status of which would be advertised by its bearing the emperor's name. This was to be lost sight of over the next few years, perhaps because the commissioners were too busy with collecting constitutions for the "first" code, but it was definitely abandoned in 438, if it had not been earlier, when Theodosius agreed to attach his name to the "first" Code, the Theodosian Code as we have it now.

However, the abandoned definitive Code is not without significance. It says much for the intellectual courage of Theodosius'advisers that they were able even to contemplate so radical an innovation. Had Theodosius gone the whole way — as even Justinian was not to do —, he would have provided a model of a "true" Code, such as that visualised by the Edinburgh group in 1893, who were to hear a rejection of even Justinian's *Corpus Iuris Civilis* as a "true" law-code: "the *Corpus Iuris Civilis* was not a Code in the complete sense as I have defined it, because the Common Law and the statute law were not fused together in one homogenous body but were consolidated separately and published in separate parts."[10] But if the entertaining of even the idea of a "true" code, which was revolutionary in its time, is evidence of extraordinary intellectual energy, the abandoning of the project must similarly be taken to mark a failure of intellectual nerve. The "passion" of those who first dreamed up the definitive Code was to be prevented by other, less purely intellectual, factors from bearing fruit.

Further disagreements, on the fundamental matter of content, dogged the inception of the Code project in 429. The constitution of March 26 contains material which appears to reflect an unsatisfactory compromise between two schools of thought in the emperor's council of advisers, the consistory, over the question of whether the "first" code should

---

[9] *CTh.* 1.1.5, *Ex his autem tribus codicibus, et per singulos titulos cohaerentibus prudentium tractatibus et responsis, eorundem opera, qui tertium ordinabunt, noster erit alius, qui nullum errorem, nullas patietur ambages, qui nostro nomine nuncupatus sequenda omnibus vitandaque monstrabit.*
[10] Goudy (above, n.2) 24.

contain laws which had been superseded by later enactments, because they would be of interest to legal historians and scholarly people (like the emperor himself). The wording of the constitution conceded that the omission of such superseded laws would be "simpler and fairer" but did not go so far as to admit that the inclusion of such antiquarian survivals would in fact undermine the basic argument for having a Code in the first place — that it ought to contain only valid law. However, it was the group representing the so-called *diligentiores* who prevailed, for the time being. They argued that the new Code, like its predecessors, should be designed for the benefit of academic lawyers, whose profession it was to know about "laws consigned to silence" and "valid only for the transactions of their own time."[11] They could also urge that this academic publication which they had in mind would still be of practical use because of the strict chronological arrangement of the contents. In cases where one constitution contradicted another, the later entry would be the valid one, and legal practitioners and litigants would thus be able to fasten on the latest — and therefore valid — enactment relevant to their case.

This decision, though it was not seriously to affect the outcome, was a warning of trouble to come. By legislating for the creation of a Code, in which some of the contents would be valid and others not, the whole concept and purpose of a code of law for use in the courts was put under threat. The controversy reveals the existence of an "academic" faction, with a traditionalist approach to legal reform, who could not raise their sights from their narrowly scholastic interest in redundant legislation, who were unlikely to be favourable to radical innovation — and who may well have had the emperor on their side. As one of the advocates of codification at Edinburgh was to ask, "is law a practical matter for the benefit of the nation and its affairs, or is it an academic exercise for whetting the legal mind?"[12]

---

[11] *CTh.* 1.1.5, *Sed cum simplicius iustiusque sit praetermissis eis quas posteriores infirmant, explicari solas quas valere conveniet, hunc quidem codicem et priores diligentioribus conpositos cognoscamus, quorum scholasticae intentioni tribuitur nosse etiam illa, quae mandata silentio in desuetudinem abierunt, pro sui tantum temporis negotiis valitura.* See also J. Harries, "*Pius Princeps*: Theodosius II and Fifth-Century Constantinople," P. Magdalino (ed.), *New Constantines: The Rhythm of Imperial Renewal in Byzantium 6th–3rd Centuries* (London: Variorum 1994) 35–44.

[12] R.V. Campbell (above, n.2) 65.

One point, on which all would have agreed, was that the Code would not contain the full texts of constitutions but only what was required to express their legal purport: full-length imperial laws had the dual purpose of conveying the law and the emperor's justification for his new measure, and did so in high-flown rhetorical language calculated to instill awe and respect in the minds of the emperor's subjects. Much of this could be safely omitted.[13] Six years later, in December 435, Theodosius issued a supplementary edict on this matter, setting out in more detail how the Code was to be arranged under headings, as had been originally stipulated, and instructing that the new Commission also set up by the law had the right to make limited changes to the wording, "to remove superfluous verbiage, add necessary words, clarify ambiguities and emend inconsistencies."[14] These powers fell far short of rewriting the laws themselves, or even of rewriting the more flowery rhetorical productions of earlier legal draftsmen in plainer language. In the process of extraction, some grammatical revision would have been necessary in many cases to make the extract read like a coherent whole, and the same process would have generated apparent verbal inconsistencies which would have required resolution. The job of the Second Commission was thus the revision, in a very limited sense, of the texts of the laws, not of the laws themselves. This modest ambition had the advantage that it could be realised in practice in a relatively short time; the Code was to be completed within the next two years. However, the restrictions on the powers of the Commissioners also meant that a chance to simplify and clarify the language of the law in a more radical fashion was lost.

Finally, on February 15, 438, Theodosius issued his first Novella, validating the Code, which had been completed, to a tight schedule, late in 437. The emperor reiterated the emphasis in the earlier constitutions on clarity and brevity, which he used to reinforce a now unambiguous affirmation of the intended usefulness of the Code in day-to-day legal transactions: "it is now transparent what weight is attached to a gift,

---

[13] *CTh.* 1.1.5, *post haec, ut constitutionum ipsa etiam verba, quae ad rem pertinent, reserventur, praetermissis illis, quae ad sanciendae rei non ex ipsa necessitate adiuncta sunt.*

[14] *CTh.* 1.1.6, *et demendi supervacanea verba et adiciendi necessaria et demutandi ambigua et emendandi incongrua tribuimus potestatem.*

what form of action should be brought in the claiming of an inheritance, what terminology should be employed in the framing of a stipulation."[15] He also reaffirmed the importance of the concept of validity of the constitutions contained within the Code by drawing pointed attention to the invalidity of all constitutions excluded from it. With effect from January 1, 439, "no-one is permitted to cite imperial law in court or in day-to-day legal business, nor to draw up the instruments of litigation, except from these selfsame volumes, which have come to be under our name, and are stored in the imperial bureaux."[16] The integrity of the text itself would be carefully protected by the *constitutionarii* fron revision or interpolation.

For reasons of prestige, it would have suited Theodosius to claim as much for this code of imperial legislation as he might have claimed for the original "true" code, the synthesis of Roman law which was envisaged in 429 as being the final outcome and culmination of his programme of legal reform. He thus felt free to assert that the new code contained all his people needed to know about law and legal procedure. However, he exempted from his general rule that extraneous matter was invalid two categories of regulation, namely those kept in the headquarters of the soldiers (and this despite the fact that Book VII is largely devoted to military matters), and rules concerning the public acounts,[17] perhaps due to pressure exerted in the consistory by the masters of the soldiers and the financial *comites*. Thus the purity of the concept of universality claimed for the Code was already severely diluted. But more damaging for Theodosius' claim was the fact that, because his Code was not in truth the synthesis of all Roman Law originally intended in 429, in that it excluded but naturally did not invalidate the writings of the jurists and other relevant texts, it could not serve as a comprehensive statement of Roman Law. Lawyers and litigants seeking clarification of legal matters would still be required to look elsewhere, if they were to be sure of their ground.

The Theodosian Code was a remarkable achievement for its time, and might never have come to exist at all had it not been for the intellectual

---

[15]*NTh.* 1.1.1, *cum liquido pateat, quo pondere donatio deferatur, qua actione petatur hereditas, quibus verbis stipulatio colligatur.*

[16]*NTh.* 3, *nulli post Kal. Ian. concessa licentia ad forum et cotidianas advocationes ius principale deferre vel litis instrumenta conponere, nisi ex his videlicet libris, qui in nostri nominis vocabulum transierunt et sacris habentur in scriniis.*

[17] *NTh.* 1.1.6.

energy displayed by the legal experts at Theodosius' court and the power of the autocrat himself to set it in motion and override opposition.[18] Theodosius was himself the legislator and accountable to no-one. His Commissioners, therefore, were also accountable to him alone and were not required to have their decisions authorised or amended by any outside constitutional body, such as Parliament or a Supreme Court, independent of the imperial executive. This situation had both advantages and dangers. It enabled freedom and speed of action on the part of the Code compilers. However, the existence of the consistory, with its membership representative of various competing interests, permitted the exertion of influence both openly in the consistory and behind the scenes. This lobbying had its effect on Theodosius, whose grasp on the fundamental concepts relevant to codification seems to have been erratic; the consistory appears to have made decisions along the way which introduced compromise over the intended "market" for the Code and inconsistency as to both its purpose and the intended validity and comprehensiveness of its contents. Thus the initial philosophical impetus for the creation of a "true" third code was slowed and finally lost altogether.

III. Motivation

The aim of a law-code in primitive societies was to make the law available to all in writing; later, in more advanced societies with a long history of legal development, the objective became to simplify and clarify the law. The lawyers of both Constantinople and Edinburgh were confronted with an accumulation of statutes (*leges*) and legal decisions based on cases and the opinions or responses of jurists. Roman law went back to its first codification in the Twelve Tables, which had been drawn up in the fifth century BC in order to inform Roman citizens about what the law was, as it was not otherwise accessible in written form; this was still a point of reference in the Theodosian Code.[19] Moreover, a number of Republican statutes were still in force — although the state of their texts may be questionable — and had attracted an impres-

---

[18] Cf. Goudy (above, n.2) 43. "It must be admitted...that it is easier to codify the laws of a country governed by an executive, than a country governed by the intermittent and inconsecutive action and conflict of Parliamentary parties."

[19] *CTh.* 9.42.9.

sive corpus of interpretations and commentaries; the laws of Sulla, the *Leges Corneliae*, and of Augustus had a special status and also were the subjects of extensive commentaries; this was even more the case with the Praetorian Edict, the text of which had been fixed in immutable form by the jurists of the emperor Hadrian. In addition, Roman *iurisperiti* had to keep up their acquaintance with the massive tomes of the "classical" jurists, especially Papinian, Paulus and Ulpian, selections from whom were studied in the law-schools.[20] Most crucially for the conduct of litigation, they had to keep abreast of the constant stream of imperial constitutions flowing from the offices of the *magistri scriniorum* at the imperial court. Such was the Roman experience, unassisted by any form of official codification, to which the problems faced by the Scottish lawyers of 1893 form a remarkable parallel: "We have produced, besides a crowd of minor law writers, three authors of great ability, who are deemed authorities because they are dead[21] ... We have accumulated a multitude of statutes, some so old that their language can be understood only by antiquarian research... We have printed a still greater multitude of decisions of particular cases, often masterly examples of clear statement, occasionally erudite historical essays, but also often difficult and sometimes impossible to reconcile."[22]

There could therefore be little disagreement about the nature of the problem of complexity and inaccessibility, which codification of the law aimed to solve, or that lawyers were expected to benefit. Theodosius recorded his "perplexity" that, in spite of the great rewards offered to lawyers, "so few and scattered individuals have existed who were fully enriched by expertise in the Civil Law";[23] he remarked also on the pale faces of the students of law, who burned the midnight oil but still fell short of the summit of complete knowledge. The same complaint was voiced by the Scots at Edinburgh, in less ornate language: "the result (of the plethora of laws) is that no person — not the most laborious lawyer — can know the whole law, or even a considerable

---

[20] See P. Collinet, *L'Histoire de l'Ecole de Droit de Beyrouth* (Paris: L. Tenin 1925) 219–40.

[21] The three Scottish authorities lived in three different centuries and described the law as it existed in their own day; they therefore contradicted each other. In this they differed of course from the three canonical Severan jurists who were, more or less, contemporary. Both trios, however, achieved classical status subsequently "because they were dead".

[22] MacKay (above, n.2) 41.

portion of it... One would require indeed to live to the age of Methuselah, and to be gifted with an unfailing memory, in order to acquire anything like an accurate knowledge of the Law Reports."[24]

Moreover, the ordinary citizen was also expected to benefit. Theodosius' autocratic mentality inhibited him from expressing the passionate conviction of the Scottish "men of business and lawyers" who declared in a prefatory statement in their pamphlet that "codification of the Law is the concern of the whole community" and that its advocates "plead not their own cause only, but the cause of every citizen", while Goudy argued that "it is a plain defect of our present system that it prevents ordinary citizens from acquiring a moderate acquaintance with their legal rights and duties" and MacKay urged that public support should be enlisted in favour of codification, "as a debt which lawyers owe not only to their profession but to their country."[25] By contrast, Theodosius refrained from indulging in rhetoric about the public good, confining himself to the observation that one of the consequences of the new simplicity and clarity, and of the "light of brevity" shed on the laws, was that jurisconsults could no longer engage in obfuscation, "while their responses are awaited as if emanating from the depths of the innermost shrines."[26] This was in the public interest because, while the jobs of lawyers would be made easier by Theodosius' reform, in the process their powers would be diminished. It may be noted, however, that the emperor failed to make any explicit connection between the right of the citizen to know the law and the rights of citizens in any abstract sense under the law. Here, again, we may perceive the vacuum in the heart of the completed project; a statement of the content of imperial law had superseded further reflection on the nature of law itself.

Such problems as those outlined above may exist for decades or even centuries without being addressed, and the motives for creating a lawcode at one time rather than another are complex. Although both the Theodosian compilers and the Edinburgh group perceived the need for a law-code in similar terms, only the former succeeded in translating their concerns into effective action. There are therefore wider dimensions to

---

[23] *NTh.* 1.1.praef.
[24] Goudy (above, n.2) 18.
[25] Goudy (above, n.2) 18; Mackay (above, n.2) 44.
[26] *NTh.* 1.1.1, *ne iuris peritorum ulterius...velut ab ipsis adytis expectarentur formidanda responsa.*

the question of why a law-code emerges at any particular time — or not at all — which do not depend only on the presence of a problem and a perceived need to do something about it. Other factors also had a part to play, and there were two preconditions for success: one, the absence, for whatever reason, of effective opposition; and, secondly, a positive impetus for action present at that time and not previously.

One reason for Theodosius' ability to put his (or his advisers') vision into effect already mentioned was his power as supreme executive to deal with such opposition as he might have encountered. The Edinburgh group had no such advantage, and were aware that they faced both academic and practical objections from fellow-lawyers, which the Edinburgh campaigners lacked the political muscle to overcome. The objections on matters of principle were threefold: the existence of a Code interfered with the natural development of law; a Code could not be fixed, as it would need constant amendment in response to changing social and legal conditions; and Britain had managed very well without a Code for a long time. These points were countered in turn by the academic speaker, Professor Goudy: first, the law of a particular time could be fixed without interfering with its natural development any more than the compilation of a dictionary impairs the growth of language; secondly, amendents and revision could be provided for; and, thirdly, the do-nothing argument could be dismissed out of hand, as it was trotted out whenever an innovation was under discussion — for example, the introduction of the railway, which had evoked predictably complacent arguments about the perfect adequacy of existing systems of transport by water and road.[27] More significant, however, would have been the active opposition from other lawyers, whose monopoly of legal expertise was threatened, as had been that of the Theodosian jurisconsults in their "innermost shrines": "the opponents of codification love this dim obscurity[28] — this tangled web of statute and case law. They think that legal learning would perish — that law would cease to grow if a consolidatory and codifying statute were to be passed setting forth in plain terms what the law is."[29] Such active, self-interested op-

---

[27] Goudy (above, n.2) 13–17.
[28] Compare the language of Theodosius at *NTh*. 1.1.praef. on the mass of constitutions, *quae velut sub crassa demersae caligine obscuritatis vallo sui notitiam humanis ingeniis interclusit.*
[29] Campbell (above, n.2) 65.

ponents of codification would have relied not so much on the strength or otherwise of their arguments as on effective action (or lack of action) as a pressure-group and on the ever-potent foe of progress, inertia: they could only be countered either by the autocratic powers available to a Theodosius, a Justinian or a Napoleon — or by the creation of a more broadly based movement for the creation of a Code (or Charter, or Bill of Rights). In the Edinburgh of the 1890s, that was not to be.

Turning now to the positive side, from what did the active impetus for the creation of the Theodosian Code derive? By 429, more than 130 years had elapsed since the labours of Gregorius and Hermogenianus. Throughout that period the imperial bureaux struggled to cope with the referrals and appeals passed on to them from all over the Empire by judges and litigants whose respective decisions and fates rested on the emperor's most recent pronouncement relevant to their case. The absence of an independent judiciary resulted in an exclusive concentration on the emperor as supreme judge, unnecessary delays in the completion of cases and extreme inconvenience for emperor and people alike. Not surprisingly, in c. 369, a Danubian eccentric with a penchant for elaborate military inventions, who may himself have been a retired civil servant, urged on the emperor that he take steps to simplify the law and "throw light on the confused and contradictory pronouncements (*sententiae*) of the laws" (*De Rebus Bellicis* 21). This isolated representation had no apparent effect on the emperors of the time, who had more urgent military problems on their mind, but it foreshadowed what was to come. The message was there, but the imperial administration had yet to hear it.

A key development which was to favour ideas relating to codification was a gradual change in the nature of the bureaucracy of the Eastern Empire. Increasingly, as the fourth century progressed, expertise in the law, rather than rhetoric, became a qualification for advancement in the administrative hierarchy. Consequently, the bureaucracy itself became more preoccupied with legal questions and the comparative political and military stability of the East in the early fifth century gave scope for ideas about legal reform to take root. Legal reforms were pursued under Arcadius (395–408) and further evolved in the early decades of Theodosius II. Imperial rescripts were denied universal validity from 398 onwards (*CTh* 1.2.11), as one part of an ongoing initiative to refine and develop the concept of a "general law" (*lex generalis*). In 426, an *oratio,* or imperial statement of law, addressed to the Roman Senate but almost certainly the work of Eastern lawyers, explained and defined "general law" in terms of the wording used (*CJust* 1.14.3), laid down rules on the citation of the classical jurists in court (*CTh* 1.4.3), and provided a mini-code on the tricky legal issue of the Law of Succession. The possibility exists that the quaestor who drafted the *oratio* may have been later one of the moving spirits behind the Theodosian Code.[30] Thus the legal intellects at the court of Theodosius can be characterised as a group determined to redefine and simplify both the law and the legal system. A Theodosian Code was a natural development of their ideas.

While the changing intellectual climate provides sufficient explanation for the timing of the Code project, it had also a not entirely helpful political dimension. Theodosius' personal ambitions in the 420s to exert his power and enhance his prestige may have inspired the inception of the Code project, but ultimately undermined its full realisation. In 425, Theodosius' army and fleet had restored his cousin, the four-year-old Valentinian III to the throne of the West, after a brief interval of usurpation; in 426, his legal staff had asserted their superiority by taking the opportunity to present their views on a number of legal questions in the *oratio* to the Roman Senate of November 426 already discussed. This set a precedent for the deliberate use of the emperor's power as legislator to advertise political supremacy. Three years later, Theodosius instructed his Eastern lawyers to create law-codes which would be valid throughout the Empire, although no Western input seems to have been envisaged or invited. As imperial legislation was in theory collegiate, there was no technical legal obstacle to one emperor passing legislation applicable to the whole Empire. However, Theodosius' planned universal statement of law was not presented in that light, nor was it called after both emperors, as it should have been, if it was to conform with imperial legislative conventions. Theodosius' personal association with "his" Code was further emphasised in 437, when Valentinian married Theodosius' daughter: the proud father-in-law took the opportunity presented by the wedding to "present" the Code to

---

[30] Tony Honore, "Some quaestors of the reign of Theodosius II," J. Harries and I. Wood (eds.) *The Theodosian Code. Studies in the Imperial Law of Late Antiquity* (London: Duckworth 1993) 81–3, suggests that Antiochus, who was to chair the First Commission in 429, was quaestor in the "slot" covering 1 February 425 to 1 June 426, the date of the last law that can be ascribed to whoever was quaestor then, on stylistic grounds. As the next does not emerge in the evidence before March 427, there is scope for Antiochus' activities to extend down to the end of 426, if not later.

Valentinian, who had no option but to accept the gift "with the loyalty of a colleague and the affection of a son."[31]

The fulfilment of Theodosius' political objective, a high-profile demonstration of the superiority of the East over the West, may effectively have removed a strong motive for proceeding further with the more onerous stages of the plan as set out in 429. The emperor now had a Code of imperial law, established for the whole empire, which was in itself an unprecedented intellectual achievement, and he had exploited its value as propaganda to maximum effect. The compilation of a proto-Digest of excerpts from juristic writings, and the "true" third code, which was to follow, were formidable and comparatively dull undertakings, from which little immediate political gain could be expected. Moreover, on the intellectual side, Theodosius may have suffered from the lack of continuity in the personnel who worked on the Code; in the eight years from 429 to 437, a number of those initially involved passed from the scene. The support of an early equivalent of Justinian's Tribonian, who might have seen the whole programe of 429 through to completion, could have provided the necessary continuity and kept the irresolute emperor up to the mark. In the absence of strong political incentives and with the champions of the "true" Code dead or departed, Theodosius lacked the intellectual "passion" to finish what he had begun.

Conclusion

Ideas and ideals are often incompatible with the perceived exigencies of real life. As the two groups surveyed in this paper found, it was easier to define a Code in theory than to create one. The virtues of clarity and simplicity in the law were admirable ideals but hard to achieve; to change the language of the law ran the risk of inadvertently altering its content. Thus it was conceded by both groups that only minor emendations or revisions to remove obscurity or inconsistency in the language could be permitted; a Code, as Goudy observed, had to be about form, not substance. Even Theodosius, who finally took the easy way out, by confining himself to the excerpting of texts from imperial laws, found

---

[31] *Gesta Senatus* 2, *Quam rem aeternus princeps dominus noster Valentinianus devotione socii, affectu filii conprobavit.*

himself in difficulties: a "universal" Code could not permit exclusions, but exclusions there were; and a Code consisting only of imperial constitutions, which were often decisions about existing laws, could not qualify as a complete statement of what the law was.

A partial success for thinkers wishing to see their notions put into practice is better than no success at all. Theodosius brought his first and only Code to fruition because the time was right: his administration was crowded by legal philosophers eager to implement a programme of radical legal reform; his Empire was stable and at peace and his own position was beyond challenge; and his codification of law could be made to serve as an instrument of his personal supremacy. The autocrat had the power to give his legal thinkers scope to bring their ideals into practice, and the quiet and largely nameless reformers of Theodosius' court were to succeed, in part, where the Edinburgh campaigners were to fail.

Had Theodosius shared the intellectual passion of the advisers who put forward the core of the Code project in 429, more might have been achieved. The legal reformers had access to the emperor, because he saw himself as a scholar, a man of letters and a patron of intellectuals. However, when put to the test, Theodosius was to allow the politician in him to prevail over the the philosopher, and short-term considerations of power and prestige are seldom harbingers of durable intellectual achievement. Theodosius left much for Justinian still to do, and neither would achieve the synthesis of all sources of law briefly envisaged by the moving spirits of 429. But too much blame should not be attached to Theodosius for his failure to achieve his ultimate goal: he had to accept and exploit political realities to survive, and it was his misfortune that he was a Roman emperor, not a philosopher-king.

Index of Ancient, Medieval and Renaissance Sources
(excluding biblical references)

AELIAN
VH
  8.1   46

AESCHYLUS
Ag.
  810–11   258
  1116   258
  1507   52

AËTIUS
  1.3.21   77

ALCINOUS
Didasc.
  9.163.21   78
  12   74ff.

ALKAIOS
  fr. 298   98

ALKMAN
  fr. 1   96
  3.1ff.   102

AMMONIUS
In Arist. de interp.
  108.7 CAG 4.5   169
  84–5   175

ANTIGONUS OF CARYSTUS
  160   191

ANTIPHANES
  fr. 2.124   131

ANTIPHON
De Chor.
  23   133–5

APOLLONIUS DYSCOLUS
Pron.
  87.13   228
  141.4   226
Synt.
  141.4   228
  170.3   228

APULEIUS
De deo Soc.
  24–33   39

ARCHILOCHUS
  fr. 36 Bergk   157

AELIUS ARIST.
  2.79–80   48
  48.347   183

ARISTOCLES
  SVF 1.98   73

ARISTOPHANES
Ach.
  532ff.   85
  850   85
Av.
  250f.   85
  917f.   85
  939f.   85
  941f.   86
  1410f.   85
Eq.
  405   86
  406   85
  703   85
  1264–6   85
  1329   85
Nub.
  929   58
  967   85
  1354ff.   85, 86
Pax.
  775f.   85
  796f.   85

Plout.
  1002   85
Thesm.
  161f.   85
Vesp.
  733–4   51
  1480   58

ARISTOTLE
de interp.
  6.17a33–7   170–1, 175
  7.17b12–16   163
  7.17b14   161–76
  7.17b39   170
  7.18a3   170
  8.18a19–21   170
  9.18a28   164
  9.18a33   164
  10.19b36   174
Cat.
  1.1a1–12   173
Int.
  16b1   227
Meta.
  Γ2 1003b24   68
  N1 1087a33   69
  Z7 1032a23   71
Phys.
  1.2   67
Poet.
  1457a18   227
Pol.
  1451a36–b7   91
Rhet.
  2.24   173
SE
  1.165a 16   175
  4.166a 16   173

ARISTOXENUS		10, 1, 2	273, 275
El. harm.		10.3.5–4.6	276
15	222	10.4.6	276
16	222	10.5.7	277, 278
18	222	10.6.8	278
		10.7.9ff.	278ff.
ARIUS DIDYMUS		10.8.11	279ff.
fr. phys. 1a	74–5	10.10.13	287
fr. phys. 1b	75	10.10.16	281, 287
		10.11.17	288–9, 292
ATHENAEUS		10.12.19	293, 295–6
2.56e	131	12	294–5
		13	295–6
AUGUSTINE		13.19.24	271
Acad.		14	291–2
3.9.20	279	14.17.23	270
Conf.		14.18.24	270
6.3	132		
7.20–1	324–5	AUSONIUS	
9.10	275	*Eclog.* (VII)	
Gn. litt.		19–21	219
4.3.7	276	*Oratio* (II:3)	221–8
7.21.28	277		
trin.		BACKYLIDES	
4	265	3	89, 102
6.1.1	264	3.96–8	86
6.10.12	275	5.1	93
7.1.2	264	11	87
7.3.4ff	264, 271	13	88
7.6.12	264	13.224	93
7.7.11	267	16.31	102
8.pr.1.–5,8	264–6	17.129	102
8.6.9	265–7	18.60	102
8.8.12	265, 268	19	102
8.9.13	268		
9	268, 270–1	CALCIDIUS	
9, 6, 9	275	199.2	50
10	261–96		

CICERO
Acad.
2.118   72
2.132   75
Brutus
58.212   126
de dom.
77   124
inv.
2.53.160   289–96
nat. deor.
2.64   59, 64
3.62   65
De op. gen. orat.
4.10   223
orat.
214–15   228
Tusc.
1.57   81
5.25.70   277
Phil.
11.2.18   123
13.24   127

CLAUDIUS PTOLEMAEUS
De iud. fac.
5   132

CLEMENT
strom.
1.17.86   152
6.17.159   152

CLEOMEDES
De circ. mot.
1.10   178–80, 185–90
2.1.76   190
2.1.79   190

CRITIAS
DK88 B18   63–4

DAMASCIUS
In Phaed.
1.172   331
dub.
267=304R   61
292=325R   61

DEMETRIUS
De eloc.
45–6   228

DEMOSTHENES
18.71   15

DIOGENES LAERTIUS
3.72   152
7.43   229, 231
7.55ff.   230ff.
7.57–8   229
7.103   151
9.71   157
9.96   155
9.101ff.   149–50
9.115–16   146

DIONYSIUS OF HALICARNASSUS
Comp.
2.3   229
12.3   223
14.10–13   224
14.19ff.   225
De Thuc.
29   139

Isocr.
13.3–5   223

DIONYSIUS THRAX
Techne
3   222
6   223–4, 228
12   216
18   228

EPICTETUS
1.14.12   52

EUCLID
1.29   179
3.11   179

EUPOLIS
fr. 148kA   85

EURIPIDES
Alc.
4   109
448   109
Ion   105–15 passim
Med.
844–5   53
Or.
1230   52
Rh.
224   109

DIO
59.8.1   127
69.1   128
75.7   129
76.9   129

GAIUS
1.132   125
2.109–11   128
4.37   119

GALEN
Inst. log.
12.2   184
UP
3.8   178

GEMMIUS
3.15   178

HELIODORUS
Aeth.
9.22.4   183

HERMEIAS
in Plat. Phaedr.
65–9   39
66.1–3   54
66.3–15   55
68.4ff.   53

HERO
Dioptra
35   104

HERODOTUS
1.19   108
5.53   108

HESIOD
Theog
35   102
Op.
123   52

PS. HIPPOCRATES
De vet. med.

1.25	256	24.11–13	250
2	250		
2.16–18	257	HOMER	
3	251	*Il.*	
3.23–4	253	1.37	108
3.39–42	252	12.310–28	89
3.45	255	22.506	108
5	252	*Od.*	
5.20	255	4.237	55
7.12–13	255	8.487ff.	99
9ff.	254	10.306	55
9–11ff.	251	14.445	55
9.17ff.	250		
10	254	IAMBLICHUS	
10.31–3	255	*De myst.*	
10.32–3	255	1.15	332
11.6–7	255	2.11	332
12.7–16	250	5.26	331–2
13.19.23	252		
13.28–9	256	IBYKOS	
13.32	253	fr. 151–287	87
14	251		
14.31–5	250	ISIDORE	
14.33–4	253	*ap.* Clement Al.	
14.35–7	253	fr. 6 Volker	48
17.1	256		
19	255	JUVENCUS	
19.18–21	250	1.590–600	227
19.26–8	251, 256	2.546	225
19–20	256		
22–4	256	*Lex de Imp. Vesp.*	
22.1–3	251	22	130
22.47ff.	257		
22.61ff.	257	JULIAN (Imperator)	
22.67	257	*Or.*	
		2.72	226
		4.6	48

JUSTINIAN
Inst.
2.11.1	128
2.12.pr.	128

LIVY
8.23.12	122
48.42.9–13	122

LUCAN
Bell. civ.
2.587	184, 190
10	205

MACROBIUS
In. Somn. Scip.
1.20.9	184
2.7.16	183–4

MARTIANUS CAPELLA
De nup.
6.596	184
6.596–9	180–1

MAXIMUS OF TYRE
8.1	48, 50
8.6	45, 54
8.7	52
8.8	39, 45

MELANCHTHON
Artificium	314–15
De corrig. adolesc.	310–11
In ep. P. ad Gal.	313–14
In ep. P. ad Rom.	311–13
In Psalmos	317–20
De rhet. lib. tres	303–6

Inst. rhet. 306–8

OLYMPIODORUS
In Plat. Alc.
21.1–14	39
21.2–3	47
21.9–14	53

In Plat. Alc.
61c	63

PHerc.
444	221
460	220ff.
1007	223
1073	223ff.
1074	220

PHERECYDES
DK7 A9	65

PHILO
Leg.
2.3–31	127

PHILODEMUS
De poet.
cols. 14.5–11 Mangoni	220
24.24–9	218–19, 223
29.7–18	218

rhet.
4	223

PHILOPONUS
In Ar. Mete.
132	184

In. Ar. phys.
5.7ff.	68
23.31	73

PHILOSTRATUS
de contemp.
21	150

dial.
2.18	150

VA
313.30–1	50

PINDAR
Isth.
1	88
1.init	93, 94
1.15	89
2.init.	93
2.48	94
3.13	88
4	88
4.11f.	96
5.20	94
6	92
6.19	94
7	88, 97
7.37	94
8	88
8.5	93
8.16	94
8.63	88

Nem.
1.19f.	94
1.24	101
1.25	88
2.16	88
3	100, 102
3.1	93
3.14	88
3.19	96
3.26ff.	100
3.40	88
3.76	94
3.80	93
4	102
4.14–16	86
4.33ff.	99, 100
4.36ff.	101
5	90, 102
5.6	88
5.15ff.	98
6.8	88
7.11ff.	102
7.20ff.	98
7.61	94
8.19ff.	101
8.35f.	98
10.20	100
10.37	88
11	88, 97
11.13	96

Olymp.
1	89ff.
1.11ff.	94
1.17	99
1.52f.	98
1.81	89
2	88
2.17	65
2.83	93
3	95
6.init	99
6.84	94
7.93	95
9.35	98
9.83	94
9.97	91
10	100
10.init	93
10.20	88

11.19f.	88	396b3–6	57–66
12	88	396b7	58
13	89	402b1–4	63f.
13.12	88	409b–c	66
Pyth.		426c6	64
1.92	94	*Ion*	
2.52ff.	98, 100	535c1–2	28
2.87	88	535e	28
4	89, 92, 97	*Leg.*	
4.1	94	737e–744d	186
4.184ff.	89	892c	71
4.299	94	903B–905B	326
5	88, 95	*Phaedo*	
5.17f.	88	99a	71
6.46f.	88	*Phaedrus*	
9.103ff.	99, 100	242b8–c3	51
10	94	243e–245c	15
10.12f.	88	245c5–7	13–22
10.27ff.	96	246e	326
10.53f.	99	256e6	22
10.64ff.	94	257a	13
11.41ff.	93, 99	257a3f.	22
		263a	150
PLATO		*Rep.*	
Alc. I		1.335d	151
103a–106	51, 52, 53, 55	3.386b	29
111	150	3.387b	24
124	49–51	3.387d–8b	32
135e1–3	51	3.393c	32
Ap.		3.394a	108
15.10–14	54	3.396a–b	30
28.15ff.	54	3.398b	26
30.17–18	54	3.401d	26
31d1	43–4, 52	3.402c	33
32.19ff.	53	3.403c	24
40a8–c3	46–7	4.443e1	26
Cratylus		5.496c4–5	42
394b	227	6.509B	326

7.516B	326	131a6–7	54
10.603b1	35	*Tht.*	
10.605b1	35	150d–151a	30
10.605c–6b	32	154a	145
10.605c–d	33, 34	*Tim.*	
10.606b7–8	30	29d–e	151, 325–6
10.607d–e	24	50cd	69ff.
10.595b9–10	26	68e	71
10.605c10-d5	26		
10.606b1	28	**PLINY**	
10.606a–b	29	*Nat.*	
Sophist		2.112	184
242cd	67	2.178	178
Symp.		2.183–6	178
177d6–7	51	2.247	184
192e1–3	54	37.108	191
193c3–6	13		
194e4	14	**PLOTINUS**	
195a1–3	14	*Enn.*	
196b4	14	1.1.8	325
197d1–e1	13–14	1.3.4	285
198c1–5	14	1.6.9	281–2
202d13ff.	53–4	2.3.18	325
203c2	49	2.9.6	325
210e–212a	14	3.5.8	325
212b	52–3	4.3.11	325
218d2	52	5.1.4	65
219c	52	5.1.7	66
237a7–9	51	5.3	283–4
248c6f.	15	5.5.5	286
253c7f.	14	5.5.8	286
254a3f.	15	5.5.12	328–9
255d3	14	5.6	283–4
Thg.		5.8.5	325
122e	53	6.4–5	283–4
128d8ff.	53–4	6.4.11	328
129e–130e	50–2, 55	6.4.15	328
130a4ff.	55	6.7.15–42	327–8

6.7.17	286	56.24	59
6.9.8	329–30	59.5	59

PLUTARCH
Crassus
		in Plat. Parm.	
32.5–6	118	830	152

Mor.
		in Plat. Rep.	
574b–c	51	2.269.28ff.	63
580ff.	54	*in Plat. Tim.*	
588e	39	1.207–9	331
		3.262	48

POLLUX

PROTAGORAS
De de.
1.1.23	108	DK80 B4	114

POSIDONIUS

PTOLEMY
almagest
fr. 44 EK	220	1.12	188

PROCLUS
Theol. Plat.

QUINTILLIAN
Inst. orat.
5	61, 62	1.4.19	229

in Plat. Alc
		SAPPHO	
46.1–3	54		
49.9–13	54	fr. 16	98
60–3	51		
60–85	39–40, 46	SENECA	
79.16	52	*Ep.*	
83.17–18	48	65.7	69
83.21–85	54	*Nat.*	
84.13–14	54	1.pr. 14	206
93.13–15	52	1.17.1–10	207

in Plat. Crat.
		1.pr.3–17	207
54.12	62	2.59.2–13	207
54.17	62	3.pr. 2	207
56.24	62	3.6	207
59.5	62	3.18	207

in Plat. Phaed.
		3.27.2	207
54.12–21	60	3.30.8	207
55.16–17	60		

4a.pr.	207	8.192	149
4b.3.3–4	207	8.206	155
4b.3.6	206	8.215	147
4b.5.1	206	8.234	147, 148
4b.13	207	8.239	149
5.1	207	8.242	149
5.9	209	8.275	230
5.18	207	8.280	149
6.1.4–3.4	207	9.68	150
6.5.3	211	9.69	156
6.32.1–12	207	9.110	157
7.1.1–5	207	9.161	155
7.9.3	207	10.263	155
7.25.5	211	11.69ff.	150–2, 155, 157
7.30f.	207	11.229	149
7.30–5	211	11.240	149
7.31–2	210		

P.

1.10–25	149, 154
1.50	158
1.86–7	157–8
1.123	150
1.130ff.	150, 155, 157, 158
1.175	157
1.193	158
1.211	154
1.217	158
1.236	153
3.179	149
3.216	157
3.254	149
3.266	149

SERVIUS
In Virg. Aen.

3.105	183

SEXTUS EMPIRICUS
M.

1.79	217
1.147	149
1.149	155
1.176	232
1.298	157
7.128	157
7.192	158
7.344	158
7.354ff.	154, 158
7.365ff.	150, 154
8.8	147
8.37	155, 156
8.184	149
8.189ff.	153, 149, 155

SHA Hadr.

4.10	129

SIMOMIDES

fr. 516 PMG	91

514	91	*Tab. duodecim*	
517	91	4.2	125
543	98		
		TERTULLIAN	
SIMPLICIUS		*adv. Hermog.*	
In Phys.		1	72
11.2	68	*De anima*	
22.17	74	20.1	204
25.14ff.	68		
43.4–6	69	THEON	
		Expos.	
SOPHOCLES		124.10–12	184
Ajax			
690	109	THEOPHRASTUS	
O.T.		82C FHS&G	161
154	109	84	161ff.
Ph.		87	161
1317	109		
1423	109	THUCYDIDES	
		1.2.6	140
STOBAEUS		1.132.5	135–6
2.9.7	152	2.53.4	137
		3.38.4	142
STRABO		3.38.8	142
Geog.		3.82.3–4	139
2.1.20	182, 191	6.18.6	140
2.5.7	184	6.34.5	140
2.5.34	184	7.69.1	140
2.57	185		
17.1.48	181	*Timaeus Locrus*	
		206.11	73
SUETONIUS			
Gaius		ULPIAN	
15.2	127	*Ref.*	
23.2	127	1.31.1	130
Gram.		*tit.*	
2	217	20.10	128

VARRO
Ant. rer. div.
   15 fr. 206 Cardanus   74, 79
De ling. lat.
   6.1   228
   9.1   219

VICTORINUS
in Eph.
   1.1262ff.   290
expl. in Cic. rhet.
   2.52   290

VIRGIL
Aeneid
   6.743   225

VITRUVIUS
   1.6.9   184

XENOPHON
Ap.
   5–6   46
Cyr.
   8.7.22   55
Mem.
   4.3.12   52
   4.8.1–6   46–7
   4.48   55